Building a National Literature

PETER UWE HOHENDAHL

Building a National Literature

The Case of Germany, 1830–1870

TRANSLATED BY
RENATE BARON FRANCISCONO

Cornell University Press

ITHACA AND LONDON

Copyright © 1989 by Cornell University

A slightly different version of this book was originally published in German
as Peter Uwe Hohendahl, *Literarische Kultur im Zeitalter des Liberalismus,
1830–1870* (Munich: C. H. Beck, 1985), copyright © Beck'sche
Verlagsbuchhandlung, München 1985.

The publisher gratefully acknowledges the assistance of Inter Nationes in
defraying part of the cost of translation.

First published 1989 by Cornell University Press.

International Standard Book Number (cloth) 0-8014-1862-3
International Standard Book Number (paper) 0-8014-9622-5
Library of Congress Catalog Card Number 89-899
Printed in the United States of America
*Librarians: Library of Congress cataloging information
appears on the last page of the book.*

*The paper in this book is acid-free and meets the guidelines for permanence
and durability of the Committee on Production Guidelines
for Book Longevity of the Council on Library Resources.*

Contents

Preface   vii

1. Introduction: The Institution of Literature   1
2. The Public Sphere   44
3. The Critique of the Liberal Public Sphere   75
4. The Institutionalization of Literature and Criticism   104
5. Literary Tradition and the Poetic Canon   140
6. The Literary Canon of the Nachmärz   174
7. The Institutionalization of Literary History   201
8. Education, Schools, and Social Structure   248
9. Culture for the People   271
10. Epilogue: The Road to Industrial Culture   307

Index   353

Preface

This book was originally published in German in 1985, in somewhat different form. It grew out of and referred to a set of interrelated problems that during the 1970s were at the center of critical debate in Germany. Among the key terms were: reception of literature, history of reading, reading public, public sphere, and social history. Literary history as social history (*Sozialgeschichte*) was an objective that inspired many critics with the hope for a new synthesis. My introduction gives a critical account of these debates and at the same time tries to situate my own position within them. My project, however, did not confine itself to the German discussion. Important theoretical impulses for the method of this book came from other sources, among them French structuralist Marxism, American sociological theory (Parsons), reader-response theory, and structuralist literary criticism.

When I began to think about this project some fourteen years ago, most American critics showed little interest in the questions I wanted to raise. At that time the vanguard of American literary criticism was preoccupied with the lively and sometimes bitter debate over the significance of post-structuralism—a debate that focused on the question of reading and meaning, pitting the defenders of hermeneutics against the proponents of deconstruction. Although the meaning of history was very much part of this discussion, literary history was clearly not something on which critics would spend a great deal of energy. There was almost a consensus that literary history, because of its epistemological connections with nineteenth-century historicism, was not worth saving. In the United States literary history had become a practice without a legitimating theory. Thus literary criticism had to draw on European theory to renew interest in historical arguments. It is noteworthy, for instance, that Fredric Jameson, one of the few American critics who consistently emphasized the historical character of literature and therefore fought formalism, turned to the French structuralism of Althusser, Greimas, and Lacan and attempted to fuse it with the Neo-Marxist theory of the Frankfurt School.

A decade ago there was not much concern with such historical issues as the formation of (national) literary canons or the concept of literature as an institution—issues whose significance has been recognized in recent years. As long as literary critics tended to view literary history as a collection of facts organized in diachronical fashion or as a narrative, stringing together authors and works of literature according to an unquestioned teleological principle, they could not bring into the foreground its more intriguing aspects—for example, the understanding of literary history as a construct created and shaped by professional critics who themselves are, of course, functioning within specific literary institutions. In recent years American criticism has paid more attention to these questions. In particular the problem of canon formation has come under closer scrutiny. Feminist theory and black studies have made us more aware of the power relations involved in the formation and shaping of canons. Yet these important new insights were not limited to feminism and black studies. A more political view of literary criticism, encouraged by Critical Theory, began to probe the professional role of the critic. This work has thrown more light on the way we read, define, and generate the body of texts we call "literature." As a result, the gap between American and European criticism has narrowed. Thus the topic of this book, the analysis of the institution of German literature between 1830 and 1870, will look more familiar to the American reader in 1989 than it would have done a decade ago.

This book does not attempt to cover the familiar ground of German literary history once more; it does not, for instance, offer yet another reading of canonical texts. Rather, it tries to analyze those material and ideological structures which determine the canonical status of such texts. In order to do so, I had to deal frequently with unfamiliar authors and texts, unfamiliar at least from the point of view of literary critics. My task was to bring into view and explore the concept of literature which informed the production and reception of individual literary texts. This examination includes their position vis-à-vis the established national canon, their importance for the "German tradition," their role in the educational system, and their participation in specific public discourses. Hence, I had to question most of the terms and concepts that literary critics and literary historians take for granted. In particular, I had to discard the traditional notion of literary studies as an enclosed field of research centered on the concept of the artwork. This notion had to be replaced by an interdisciplinary approach, drawing on a variety of disciplines and discourses, among them political philosophy, aesthetic theory, and social and intellectual history. What had to be avoided was a traditional base/superstructure model that automatically traps the investigation inside worn-out dichotomies (literature/background, text/context). Instead, the interdisciplinary approach aims at a fresh and different conceptual understanding of inter- and contextuality. This method is based on reading, but it is not restricted to the reading of literary texts. In this respect, my research is not too far from the project of the New Historicism, particularly in its disregard for the traditional division between literary and "historical" texts. However, my readings place a stronger emphasis on a more systematic treatment of the institution of literature, although my examination of its intersecting and overlapping elements describes this institution as a configuration rather than a rounded totality.

It is to be expected that readers of the English edition will bring to the text interests different from those of the audience of the German edition. The German text addresses experts of German literature (and culture) who take a professional interest in the evolution of German literature and therefore want a detailed account of the historical material. By contrast, the English-speaking reader, who views German literature from a more distant vantage point, may be more concerned with the general theoretical and methodological questions I raise. Thus in its new context, this book might serve as a "case study" for the analysis of literary institutions. For this reason I eliminated the ninth chapter of the German edition, which deals with the structure and development of the German reading public between 1820 and 1880. In addition, I cut out a number of subchapters and passages that were, I felt, less important for American readers. In my choices I relied on the advice of American colleagues, especially that of David Bathrick, who offered his careful evaluation of the book.

Without outside support this book would probably never have been completed. I am especially grateful to the Deutsche Forschungsgemeinschaft and to the Freie Universität Berlin, which gave me the opportunity as visiting professor in 1976 to test my hypotheses for the first time. I am no less indebted to the Zentrum für interdisziplinäre Forschung at the University of Bielefeld, where I continued my project in the spring and summer of 1981. Finally, I owe thanks to the Guggenheim Foundation for a generous research fellowship (1983–84) that allowed me to complete this book. During the final preparation of the German manuscript I had the unflagging help of Rolf Schütte and Susanne Rohr, especially in checking sources and quotations. I also express my gratitude to Renate Baron Franciscono, who undertook the arduous task of translating the German text into readable English. Last but not least I thank Daniel L. Purdy for his tireless efforts to improve the shape of the manuscript. Parts of the introduction have already appeared in English in *New German Critique* no. 28 (Winter 1983), and part of Chapter 7 in the book *Zum Funktionswandel der Literatur,* edited by Peter Bürger (Frankfurt am Main: Suhrkamp, 1983).

PETER UWE HOHENDAHL

Ithaca, New York

Building a National Literature

. I .

Introduction:
The Institution of Literature

This book is concerned neither with individual literary texts nor with the influence or reception of literary works. By traditional standards, therefore, it falls outside the field of literary studies. From the point of view of both hermeneutics and reception aesthetics, the problems I examine are "extraliterary"; they form the "background" of the "actual" subject matter. The topics and themes dealt with in this book are considered "helpful" to literary scholars in the interpretation of texts but not indispensable for their work, for the decision about how much "background material" to include in a given investigation is customarily left to the individual researcher. Obviously the conventional dichotomy of literary versus extraliterary gives the concept of literature priority; but in addition—and this point is particularly significant for the evaluation of historical studies—it relegates all other subjects without discrimination to supplemental status. What characterizes all such subjects is that they are *not* literature. This strategy is taken so much for granted in traditional literary studies that it is never so much as questioned. Its consequence is to assume that an *ontological* difference exists between literature and everything else (including nonpoetic types of texts).

As long as this dichotomy prevails, the problems I examine here will remain marginal to literary studies, with respect both to their historical importance and to their inclusion in and penetration of contemporary theoretical discourse. The practical result is obvious: projects that do not deal with poetic texts are declared merely ancillary. The conceptual and theoretical results are less obvious but in the long run more significant: the hegemony of one particular concept of literature, whose explication is made to appear the true task of literary criticism, reduces the extraliterary fields (religion, politics, society, economy) to those specific relationships—understood as causal conditions or functional connections—which merely facilitate the interpretation or analysis of the particular text under consideration. Among the fields thus rendered auxiliary are the sociology of author and public, the psychology of reading, and the economics of bookmaking. Traditional literary criticism characteristically considers these auxiliary disciplines an unordered set and leaves unexplored the systematic interrelationship of literary criticism to such major fields as anthropology, linguistics, and history. Within the traditional model—whether its focus is historical or formal—collaboration is judged possible only if the data and results of the adjunct disciplines can be "put to use." The ingrained dichotomy of literature and nonliterature precludes a comprehensive, theoretical framework.

The historical and empirical study of readers has suffered more than any other from this incompatibility. Hermeneutics and reception aesthetics concede such study has a contribution to make but view this contribution as supplemental. Even the more open field of reception aesthetics, which has distanced itself from the hermeneutical model, assumes a fundamental difference between the concept of an implied reader and a historico-empirical reader. Historical reception remains logically subordinate.

The fruitfulness of a scholarly collaboration in which various disciplines exchange results but generally follow divergent theories and methods is limited. More useful would be models that redefine the field of inquiry and hence make clear where collaboration may be possible. A change of paradigms would first and foremost necessitate a scrutiny of the conventional definition of literature, which is largely responsible for our current problems. The traditional concept of literature is derived from the concept of art; in other words, literature consists of texts with aesthetic characteristics (which then need to be explored by literary critics). Furthermore, literary texts are designated *fictional;* that is, they have a specific referent relationship, self-referentiality, which differentiates them from other texts. This "literariness," however, should be considered an open question rather than axiomatic, for as long as literariness is defined dogmatically, literary studies will remain fixated on those conventional characteristics. If, on the other hand, we resolve the dichotomy between literature and nonliterature, we can then restructure the field of inquiry. (This resolution, incidentally, would not mean leveling the distinction between literature and nonliterature.) The result of such a reorganization would be not only that the concept of literature would define what is nonliterary but also that a differentiated concept of the nonliterary would define what qualifies as literary.

The search for a new paradigm has engaged literary scholarship since the 1960s, and by no means only in Germany. This search has manifested itself chiefly in a reexamination of the hermeneutical model, introduced into German studies by Wilhelm Dilthey. The debate involved linguistic and semiotic approaches, as well as reception aesthetics and empirical studies of reception. Similar confrontations have taken place in Marxist theory, especially in the work of Louis Althusser and Pierre Macherey. A variety of premises and motives undoubtedly underlie the concerted attacks on the hermeneutic tradition. Semiotics and empirical literary studies, mainly concerned with putting literary criticism on a scientific basis, have challenged the confusion of the reader with the scholar, whereas reception aesthetics has directed its attack primarily against the essentialist textual interpretation that characterizes the hermeneutic tradition. Yet in the work of Hans-Georg Gadamer's more radical successors, reception aesthetics retains concepts of text and reader which are closer to the hermeneutic tradition than to the scientific ideal of semiotics and empirical theory; hence no consensus has yet been reached on the character of the posthermeneutical model. Reception aesthetics has criticized empirical studies of reception as a reversion to positivism; empirical scholarship, on the other hand, has viewed the proposed models of reception aesthetics as halfway measures. Thus Norbert Groeben maintains that neither Hans Robert Jauss nor Wolfgang Iser has really broken with the hermeneutical model: "Despite the orientation of the concept of the text toward communication theory, reception aesthetics maintains the confusion of reception with interpretation, of the recipient with the interpreter, which I have criticized as 'confounding subject and object.' "[1] Groeben interprets reception aesthetics as an immunizing strategy, which rescues the old paradigm by radicalizing it. And indeed, the vehement polemics conducted by reception aesthetics against empirical models that draw the historical reader into the investigation gives his reproach a certain plausibility.

At the center of recent discussion is the break with traditional concepts of the text and the work. Modernist aesthetics, which treats the work as an open, multivalent, and multifunctional structure, prepared the way for this break. The radicalization of this subversion leads to a further question: What is the role of the recipient in the structuring of textual meaning? Following Russian formalism and the phenomenology of Edmund Husserl and Roman Ingarden, the school of Constance (Jauss, Iser) has drawn attention to the openness of the literary

[1]Norbert Groeben, *Rezeptionsforschung als empirische Literaturwissenschaft*, 2d ed. (Tübingen, 1980), p. 16.

text and has effectively attacked the traditional, essentialist model of interpretation. By taking account of the reader, reception aesthetics abandons the search for a predetermined meaning, but it remains indebted to the dialogic model of the hermeneutic tradition, for the separation of the implied from the external reader perpetuates the familiar dichotomy. By means of this strategy, which is also evident in the work of Hannelore Link,[2] reception aesthetics establishes a defensive position that, in Groeben's words, "accepts empirical investigations with respect to socioliterary and psycholiterary problems, but keeps the interpretation of a work in reserve for hermeneutical 'understanding.'"[3] This division of labor preserves the conventional distinction between intrinsic and extrinsic investigations. In practice, the new formulation of the concept of the work does not alter the priority of the text, which, just as in formalist interpretation, is regarded as the primary object. The reader's achievements in bestowing meaning, insofar as they cannot be demonstrated in the text itself, continue to be disregarded. This criticism is not limited to the phenomenological approach; it is also directed against radical models that bring the interpretive achievements of the reader to the fore. One may thus ask, with Groeben, whether the attempt to include the perspective of communication theory in the hermeneutical model is frustrated by the model's inner theoretical contradictions. But the more important argument, I believe, is that reception aesthetics, like the American reader-response theory of Stanley Fish, is tied to the formulation of problems that belong to the old paradigm and that consequently draw on the old paradigm for their solutions.

Beyond Reception Theory

It would be interesting to examine why this attack on traditional hermeneutics and literary history was mounted in Europe and in the United States at roughly the same time.[4] Such historical questions, however, are largely neglected in the following pages, which focus primarily on the theoretical implications of reception theory. A radical approach to the theory of reception leads to aporias that cannot be resolved within the framework of the received theoretical model. That is to say, if the premises of reception theory are carried to their logical conclu-

[2]Hannelore Link, *Rezeptionsforschung* (Stuttgart, 1976).
[3]Groeben, *Rezeptionsforschung*, p. 48.
[4]For the historical context, see Frank Lentricchia, *After the New Criticism* (Chicago, 1980); Vincent B. Leitch, *Deconstructive Criticism* (New York, 1983); and David Couzens Hoy, *The Critical Circle: Literature, History, and Philosophical Hermeneutics* (Berkeley, Calif., 1978).

sions, questions will arise that demand a new theoretical framework. No matter how the concept of the reader is conceived, it is too restricted to explain literary structures and processes. Reception theory—wherever it has gone beyond a positivistic history of reception—has prevailed over traditional hermeneutics by bringing the status of the literary text into question. But as its critics have objected, this very step has bound it once again to the text. The criticism of traditional hermeneutics has turned out to be merely another stage of hermeneutics. As formalism and literary immanence have been overcome, a new formalism has developed. Iser, for instance, not only distinguishes between the empirical-historical reader and the implicit reader but expressly bans all questions of historical reception from reception aesthetics; Fish, after radically questioning the objective structure of the literary text, ultimately restores it to its original status.[5] Reader-response theory, as Jane P. Tompkins has noted, shares some basic premises with the older formalism and is inconceivable without it.[6] Of course, this argument does not invalidate reception theory. It merely shows that the break with traditional hermeneutics and aesthetics, the impetus behind the new theory, itself belongs to a tradition; it is part of a historically bounded debate.

In its polemics, reception theory overestimates the degree to which its models can be generalized. We are faced today with the task of striking a critical balance so that new questions can be formulated. My point of departure is a summary of the premises and central arguments of reception theory, which I follow with an attempt to present the consequences to which these premises logically lead. This lays the foundation for the third step, a critique of reception theory the goal of which is to arrive at a new model that will not so much exclude the tenets of reception theory as overcome them dialectically. The outlines of this model, which centers in the concept of the institution, have already been sketched in the work of other scholars, although no satisfactory form has yet been found for it. In a fourth step, I discuss the various solutions that have been suggested, focusing not on a critical discussion of individual theoreticians but on an explication of the problems involved. Since the concept of the institution necessarily involves sociological theories, it gives rise to a question the theory of reception has persistently evaded: How does the institution of literature relate to other institutions in the social system? Or, to put it in Marxian terms: What

[5]Wolfgang Iser, *The Act of Reading* (Baltimore, 1978), pp. 27–38, and Stanley Fish, *Is There a Text in This Class? The Authority of Interpretive Communities* (Cambridge, Mass., 1980).

[6]Jane P. Tompkins, "The Reader in History: The Changing Shape of Literary Response," in Tompkins, ed., *Reader-Response Criticism* (Baltimore, 1980), pp. 201–2.

connection can we draw between the institution of literature and the forces and relations of production? Understandably, formalist theory has no ready answers to these questions, yet they do appear on the horizon of reception theory.

Reception Aesthetics

It has repeatedly and correctly been observed that there is no such thing as *a* reception theory. Rather, we have a series of distinct approaches to reception. Nevertheless, we can identify common suppositions that largely determine theoretical strategy insofar as they highlight some arguments and exclude others. The point of departure in the theoretical work of Iser and Jauss as well as Norman Holland and Fish, to name but a few, is the literary text or work, as it is in formalism. But the basis of operation, unquestioned in earlier hermeneutics—the objectivity of the text or, more specifically, the objective "existence" of meaning—is now called in question. The New Criticism and formalism take it for granted that the meaning of a work of art is inherent in the text itself and needs only to be revealed. In reception theory the locus of meaning is shifted, for a new category—the reader—has been introduced. It is not so much the existence of readers which undermines traditional hermeneutics—the concept of the reader is certainly compatible with traditional hermeneutics or with historicism—as the assumption that the reader, as the inevitable addressee of the text, helps determine its meaning or, more radically, actually generates its meaning. This argument robs the text of the stability that traditionally made it the exclusive source of interpretation.

The category of the reader, which appeared at about the same time in the work of Fish, Jauss, and Iser, serves to destabilize and decentralize the literary text. Their aim in introducing this category was to define more precisely the special character of literary texts and the distinctiveness of literary history (in contrast to political history). This approach, familiar to us from the New Criticism, has left its marks on the beginnings of reception aesthetics, especially in Iser's early work;[7] Jauss shows a similar intention when he proposes the category of the reader in order to construct an autonomous history of literature.[8] Like formalism, early reception aesthetics characteristically took for granted the autonomy of the work of art. Only after the approach had been more fully developed did questions arise to undermine this certainty and lead to the assumption that aesthetic literary discourse, not inherently dif-

---

[7]Wolfgang Iser, *Die Appellstruktur der Texte* (Constance, 1970).
[8]Hans Robert Jauss, *Toward an Aesthetic of Reception*, trans. Timothy Bahti (Minneapolis, 1982), pp. 3–45.

ferent from other kinds of discourse, becomes distinctive only through the actions of the participants.

Iser's attempt to define the "literariness" of a text takes the form of differentiating—with the help of speech-act theory—between expository and fictional texts. In his view, literary texts are distinguished by the fact that they have no single interpretation.[9] An interpretation that draws a particular meaning out of a text diminishes it; it confuses the text with the meaning ascribed to it. What characterizes the literary text is that nothing presented in it has independent existence: "A literary text neither illustrates nor creates anything in the described sense; at best it can be defined as the representation of reactions to things." The reader has to reconstruct imaginatively the point of view developed in the text in order to give the work concrete form. According to Iser, the reader thereby takes on the decisive task of decoding the text, not merely to reveal its meaning but to participate in the establishment of its possible meanings. In other words, the meaning of the text cannot be grasped at all without the activity of the reader. The same can be said of expository texts, but the statement gains significance in the case of literary texts because the act of reading generates meaning that goes beyond the structure of the text. What Iser, following Ingarden, calls concretization of a text is an act of creation that brings to completion the production of the text: "Every reading thus becomes an act of attaching the oscillating structure of a text to meanings which as a rule are themselves created in the process of reading."[10]

As soon as the reader is brought into play, one might object, the generation of meaning becomes arbitrary; in other words, the objectivity of the text is disregarded. Iser counters this assertion by trying to show that ambiguity of meaning is inherent in the structure of a literary text, because a text contains blanks that the reader must fill in.[11] Literary texts carry a certain degree of indeterminacy, which is why they have many possible concretizations. Thus every interpretation and meaning has a subjective element, yet the degree of subjectivity is objectively determined (or limited) by the structure of the text. "The reader constantly fills in or eliminates blanks," says Iser. "By eliminating them he utilizes the room available for interpretation and establishes between individual points of view even those relationships which are not formulated."[12] But since freedom of interpretation is not unlimited, we can distinguish between acceptable and unacceptable readings. Iser con-

---

[9]Wolfgang Iser, *The Implied Reader* (Baltimore, 1974); Iser, *The Act of Reading*, esp. pp. 3–19.

[10]Iser, *Appellstruktur*, pp. 11, 13.

[11]Iser, *The Act of Reading*, pp. 163–231.

[12]Iser, *Appellstruktur*, p. 15.

tinued to adhere to this position, in contrast to Fish, who saw in it a residue of objectivism.

Iser's point of departure is the status of the literary text, and his argumentation consequently focuses on problems of synchrony. Jauss's primary concern in his attempt to define the particularity of literary history is to determine historical shifts in the meaning of literary texts; consequently, he emphasizes diachrony. Both theorists agree that texts are not inherently objective but reveal their individuality only in communication with the reader. "The literary work," says Jauss, "is not an independent object that presents the same face to every viewer in every period. It is not a monument that monologically reveals its timeless essence." The unique history of a work, accordingly, lies in the history of its reception, in which its meaning first unfolds. This argument again points to the danger of subjectivity: How can a legitimate reception be distinguished from an illegitimate one? Won't the destabilization of the text make for arbitrariness? The cornerstone of Jauss's theory is not the reader's subjective understanding. Rather, Jauss tries to find a foundation for a reading that "precedes the psychological reaction as well as the subjective understanding of the individual reader."[13] Jauss anchors the individual reading in a theory of literary communication which shifts emphasis to the concept of a horizon of expectation. Every reading is prestructured in several respects: through contemporary conventions of genre and form, through the existence of other works (intertextuality) with which the new work is compared, and through the antithesis of fiction and reality.

The adequacy of Jauss's theory—for instance, of his concept of a horizon of expectation, which has played a role in the debate from time to time—is not the issue here. For our purposes, what is important is that in his analysis of literary communication—the relationship between text and reader—Jauss, unlike Iser, takes into account elements that lie outside the text, namely, literary and social conventions. The category of the reader is not exclusively immanent in the text but includes social and historical aspects. This inclusion changes the constitution of meaning or sense. Whereas for Iser meaning is generated by the structure of the text and the purely phenomenologically conceived act of reading, for Jauss the act of constituting meaning is mediated by intersubjective social and literary conventions. These conventions help stabilize the establishment of meaning. This step allows Jauss to conceive the history of literature as a process of mediation between literary reception and the production it motivates. The meaning that is reconstructed within the horizon of a particular reception raises questions

[13]Jauss, *Toward an Aesthetic of Reception*, pp. 21, 22–23.

that in turn give rise to new literary production. As Jauss puts it, "In the step from a history of the reception of works to an eventful history of literature, the latter manifests itself as a process in which the passive reception is on the part of authors. Put another way, the next work can solve formal and moral problems left behind by the last work, and present new problems in turn."[14] More precisely, this move leads not to the reader but back to the text, to a reconstruction of the questions whose answer the text was intended to be. In any case, the subjectivity involved in producing meaning will be substantially restricted, if not almost eliminated. The activity of reading and writing is controlled by the intersubjectively stabilized formulation of questions that the text seeks to answer. Thus the evolution of literature is no longer conceived as substantialistic but as functional.

Reader-Response Theory

In contrast to Iser and Jauss, who favor a model based on hermeneutic dialogue, Fish did not attempt to limit the consequences of his reader-oriented approach. On the contrary, implications inherent in his theory led him to change his position and finally brought him to a point where he could no longer overlook the aporias of reception aesthetics. For this reason it is important to trace the evolution of Fish's theory. The earliest phase, which proceeded from acts of reading and interpreting, was merely a development from the New Criticism. But by 1970, when he wrote his seminal essay "Literature in the Reader," Fish's understanding of interpretation had changed. Where the New Criticism viewed interpretation as the objective exposition of the text and thus gave the text priority over the reader, Fish came to a Copernican turning point and put the category of the reader first, thereby making the meaning of the text dependent on the act of interpretation. (Henceforth it would be, strictly speaking, inadmissible to speak of *the* meaning of a text.) Not only does Fish believe that meaning is generated by the reader, but he explicitly separates this meaning from the text and transfers it to the reader. The reader becomes the sole source of meaning, because the production of meaning occurs in the mind, not on the page of a book.

Fish emphasizes, however, that the subjectivity of his approach should not be mistaken for arbitrariness, since the category of reader includes stabilizing elements. The concept of the "informed reader," on which Fish relies, contains the assurance that the experience described by the reader will do justice to the text. This concept has three essential

[14]Ibid., p. 174.

parts: (1) linguistic competence, (2) semantic ability, and (3) literary competence. By the last Fish means familiarity with the particular character of the literary discourse, which allows the reader to pick up signals from the text. When the concept of reader is viewed from this more precise angle, it becomes evident how different empirical readers can arrive at the same, or a similar, understanding of a text; but it still has to be explained how readers whose literary competence is undisputed (critics, for instance) can arrive at widely divergent interpretations. This question proves to be decisive for Fish's theory, because the answer he initially gave—that a distinction must be made between reading and interpreting—proved unsatisfactory. This distinction defended reception theory from the accusation of relativism, but it did not provide a model for explaining contradictory interpretations of a text.

Initially, it appears, Fish misjudged the consequences of his approach. As he later admitted, the movement from text to reader led back to the text, just as it did for Iser and Jauss: "In order to argue for a common reading experience, I felt obliged to posit an object in relation to which readers' activities could be declared uniform, and that object was the text . . . ; but this meant that the integrity of the text was as basic to my position as it was to the position of the New Critics." What led Fish out of this dilemma was the realization that the literary text is not simply a given quantity; it is constituted in the act of reading. The special character of literature is defined foremost by the reader: "The conclusion is that while literature is still a category, it is an open category, not definable by fictionality, or by a disregard of propositional truth, or by a predominance of tropes and figures, but simply by what we decide to put into it."[15] The question What is literature? is based on a *decision*, and henceforth that decision is arrived at by a "community of readers," an "interpretive community."

The category of informed reader has been replaced by that of the community of readers—that is, by a potentially *social* category that now includes discussion of habits and conventions. The individual act of reading always proves to have been prestructured by its social as well as its linguistic-literary context. The result of this decisive step is that the grounding of hermeneutics in the reader leads to an intersubjective understanding of literature, not to a feared anarchy of interpretation.

Fish expounded his new theory of the reader in the Ransom Memorial Lectures of 1979. Whereas in 1970 he had systematically distinguished between reading and interpretation so as to claim a subjective basis for reading, in 1979 he proceeded from the assumption that reading and interpretation can be differentiated only analytically; to put the point somewhat differently, that every reading implies an interpretation

[15]Fish, *Is There a Text?* pp. 7, 11.

of the text. Moreover, individual reading already presupposes interpretive activity. Fish believed this shift in emphasis would allow him to solve a problem for which he had previously had no ready answer: How can divergent interpretations occur when the interpreters have been shown to be informed readers? His answer lies in the priority given to interpretation: the objectively determinable elements of a text can be consistently integrated with various interpretive approaches. Individual readings involve prior decisions based on the shared premises of a community of readers. The text thus becomes a function of interpretation. But even if we grant Fish is right in this respect, we must still ask how and in what way a particular meaning takes precedence over other, competing meanings. If the text is no longer the object by which divergent interpretations can be measured, then relativism seems unavoidable. One interpretation seems as good as another, as long as its consistency can be ascertained.

Unlike Iser, Fish is prepared to accept this conclusion—although he does not regard it as the anarchy feared by traditional literary studies. The concept of the informed reader implies that the act of reading is not unmediated but contains binding, transsubjective presuppositions. In 1979 Fish introduced in this connection the concept of the *institution*. The community of readers is, he suggested, more than a group of people devoting themselves to a particular text; it is an institution that determines how readers relate not only to a literary text but also to one another. Fish thus believes that concurring and divergent opinions can be explained if we assume all acts of reading are part of a game with rules (mostly unwritten) which no one who deals with texts can avoid. If we accept this argument, the correctness of an interpretation depends on certain norms and conventions observed by the players. Thus an interpretation is convincing only within the framework of a specific interpretive community held together by shared values and rules. Fish gives a fair description of current conditions in American literary studies when he writes: "Within the literary community there are subcommunities (what will excite the editors of *Diacritics* is likely to distress the editors of *Studies in Philology*), and within any community the boundaries of the acceptable are continually being redrawn."[16] Acceptable reading strategies are thus determined by groups of readers banded together in interpretive communities.

The Aporias of Reception Theory

Fish's conclusion brings reception theory to a point where it sets its own limits: no longer a new method for correcting the mistakes of

[16]Ibid., p. 343.

historicism and the New Criticism, reception theory is rather a reflection on the possibility of interpreting texts. Interpretation for Fish is still "the only game in town."

At first glance it looks as if within the framework of a methodological pluralism, Fish had renounced the claim to truth. This is not the case, however. Although he is apparently unaware of it, he has changed the level of argumentation through his introduction of the concept of the institution. Whereas his earlier essays tried to show that a literary work is constituted by the act of reading not by the text, since 1979 Fish has attempted to show that readings and interpretations are not individual acts but have always been rooted in what he calls the institution of literature. As far as the truth of the theory is concerned, investigation no longer focuses on the act of reading and its subject but on the structure of the institution. Because for Fish the act of reading is largely defined by the conventions of the community of readers, no objective scholarly discourse can take place on this level. Literary criticism, in his view, can argue only within the framework of a practical, rhetorical model, and one interpretation differs from another merely in that it is more plausible to the community of readers: "In a model of persuasion . . . our activities are directly constitutive of those objects [of our intention], and of the terms in which they can be described, and of the standards by which they can be evaluated."[17] Fish rightly draws attention to the fact that this model describes the practice and the history of literary criticism better than does a demonstrative, scientific model. But he seems to overlook the possibility that his discourse may no longer be comprehensible as an opposition between "persuasion" and "demonstration." The suitability of a model is no longer determined by subjective interpretation but by the conditions under which interpretations first arise.

If we follow Fish in assuming that the interpretation of literary texts is made possible by intersubjectively established rules and conventions, we must expand our epistomological interest. We are no longer exclusively concerned with substantiating specific interpretations; we also have to substantiate the norms and conventions that give rise to those interpretations. Since Fish does not consistently distinguish between these levels, he never becomes fully aware of the problem involved. He is content to offer a relatively unsystematic description of these conventions in order to explain why contemporary American critics and scholars take the attitudes they do. The institution of literature is not systematically and historically substantiated for two reasons. First, Fish's description is quite limited, since it is oriented toward academic criticism in the United States—indeed, he equates American criticism with

[17]Ibid., p. 367.

literary criticism in general. One might ask whether his description is valid for other societies as well. Similarly, the patterns Fish describes did not necessarily exist in the nineteenth century, let alone earlier. The lack of systematic analysis, however, is fundamental. Fish defines the institution of literature as the community of readers together with its subcommunities. Nowhere does he try to investigate the relationship of this institution to other institutions. It is possible to explain consensus and dissent within the framework of his theory. His model also accounts for changes: if norms and rules within an interpretive community change, new interpretations will result. (Known texts are reread and reinterpreted.) But how do these changes in norms and rules come about? Fish assumes that the authority of a particular interpreter will cause certain interpretations to prevail until they are replaced by others. But who gives the interpreter authority? And in what does his authority consist? Fish's model is too abstract to answer such questions. His description of the evolution of literature and criticism remains merely formalistic. Changes occur, but their nature is not predictable or explainable. Interpretations are thus like fashions—they come and go for no ascertainable reason. Basically, nothing changes: "Interpretation is the only game in town."

Fish's model reveals in exemplary fashion the limitations of the theory of the reader. Whenever it draws radical conclusions from its premises—namely, that meaning is generated not by the text but by the act of reading—it confronts the institutional presuppositions of reading. Yet it is unable to rid itself of its formalist origins and mediate between the linguistic-literary and the social realms. Jauss was clearly aware of this task and in 1967 went into the matter in detail; it seems significant that even he retreated from it when he developed his theory further. In his diachronic investigations based on the question-answer model, he emphasized the *intrinsic* aspect of literature or developed a typology applicable to various epochs and social formations.[18] I believe this limitation of the dialogic theory of the reader can be overcome only by a functionalist or materialist approach.

The Contribution of Semiotics

Jonathan Culler's theory of semiotics illustrates this point. His model of a literary institution borders to some extent on Fish's, although he makes a sharper distinction between the level of interpretation and that of the institution that regulates and gives legitimacy to individual inter-

---

[18]Hans Robert Jauss, *Aesthetic Experience and Literary Hermeneutics*, trans. Michael Shaw (Minneapolis, 1982), pp. 152–88.

pretations. In his essay "Beyond Interpretation" (1976), Culler advocated a field of literary studies which would systematically deal with the discourse of criticism. Understandably, he accused Fish of adhering too closely to the concept of interpretation despite his break with the New Criticism. (The validity of this objection—it is probably not applicable to Fish's later essays—need not be decided here.) In any case, he identifies a direction for literary studies: they will have to concentrate on the system of rules and conventions on which individual readings are based.

In establishing his model, Culler follows the fundamental distinctions made in Saussurian linguistics, namely, between language and speech (*langue et parole*), signifier and signified, competence and performance. Just as we can speak a language without necessarily being able to explain its grammar, so we can read and explain texts without necessarily knowing the rules of literary discourse. It is enough to be familiar with those rules; that is, to be capable of literary performance. Culler defines literary competence, on the other hand, as "a set of conventions for readings of literary texts" which members of a society share and to which they consciously refer when reading or interpreting a literary text. The semiotic approach assumes that as a form of linguistic expression, a poem has meaning only with respect to a system of linguistic and literary conventions (genres, styles) that the reader has assimilated. This assumption leads to the conclusion that "the conventions of poetry, the logic of symbols, the operations for the production of poetic effects, are not simply the property of readers but the basis of literary forms."[19] As I understand this passage, the rules and conventions Culler mentions function intersubjectively, and it remains an open question whether they are conceived as objective entities or merely as subjective constructs in the mind of the reader. On the whole, Culler seems to favor an objective concept of metalevels, for such a concept would permit a scientific analysis of literature on the model of linguistics.

Comparison with Noam Chomsky's transformational grammar shows, however, that Culler's project must encounter greater difficulties than the linguist's; a competent speaker of a language is familiar with its rules of grammar, but no comparable standard exists for literary competence. At any rate, divergent readings of a single text make the adoption of such a standard problematic. To overcome this difficulty, Culler posits an ideal reader—a construct embodying those characteristics upon which the community of readers has intersubjectively agreed. For Culler, the fact that a dialogue between readers can result in agreement on interpretation speaks in favor of such a construct: "The

[19]Jonathan D. Culler, *Structuralist Poetics: Structuralism, Linguistics and the Study of Literature* (Ithaca, N.Y., 1975), p. 117.

possibility of critical argument depends on shared notions of the acceptable and the unacceptable, a common ground which is nothing other than the procedures of reading."[20] Experienced readers know what to do with a literary text; they know the current rules of interpretation which will yield an acceptable result.

Culler seems to consider the institution of literature as culturally bound; that is, the literary system of a society is based on conventional, mutable suppositions. Yet he investigates the precise nature of this cultural context—its effect on the production and reception of texts— no more than Fish does, because he introduces the concept of the institution on the basis of common sense, without systematic analysis. Culler fluctuates between a structuralist and an interactionist concept. As long as the institution of literature is understood as a set of norms and conventions defining the role of the reader, it remains an interactionist model and necessarily abstract. It does not take into account the fact that readers, like acts of reading and interpreting, are not exclusively predetermined by literary conventions. They are simultaneously conditioned by material interests and ideological positions. Semiotics has not supplied the conceptual instrument necessary for such a view of the institution of literature.

A first step in this direction is the plan for a semiotics of reading developed by Culler in 1980–81, in "Semiotics as a Theory of Reading." He suggests that the effect of literary texts be investigated and that interpretations—especially contradictory ones—be subjected to semiotic analysis. He would study the operations leading to a specific interpretation. In his critical assessment of Jauss's theory, Culler concedes that the ideologies of an epoch—for instance, assumptions concerning the relationship of the sexes, marriage, and other institutions—play a role in the interpretation of a text. Nevertheless, he argues, "it is easier and more plausible to explain these varying responses as the result of different interpretive operations and the application of different conventions than as the product of different beliefs."[21] The analytical dis-

---

[20]Ibid., p. 124.

[21]Jonathan D. Culler, *The Pursuit of Signs: Semiotics, Literature, Deconstruction* (Ithaca, N.Y., 1981), p. 58. In his most recent work, however, Culler no longer assumes that different readings are to be explained primarily in terms of diverging conventions; instead he suggests that cultural and social conditions to a large extent determine the reader's experience. Hypothetically turning the "informed reader" of structuralism into a woman, he argues persuasively that her experience cannot be identical with that of a male reader. The broader implications of this move are obvious, as Culler himself notes: "The analogy with social class is instructive: progressive political writing appeals to the proletariat's experience of oppression, but usually the problem for a political movement is precisely that the members of a class do not have the experience their situation would warrant. The most insidious oppression alienates a group from its own interests as a group and encourages it to identify with the interests of the oppressors, so that the

tinction between interpretive strategies and ideologies is fruitful, but it should not be construed as an antithesis. It is much more important to determine how ideologies help shape hermeneutical strategies. Reading is a less innocent operation than formal semiotics is prepared to admit. Culler rightly points out that a test case for a semiotics of reading would be to explain dissent, but this task is too narrowly defined if it is restricted to the level of operations.

The Sociological Concept of the Institution

We have now reached the point where we can indicate the course literary theory must take in order to overcome the limits of reception theory. It is certainly justified to point out that concentrating on reception is insufficient, that the link between production and reception must be preserved, but it is not overly fruitful. The category of the institution appears more promising, for it embraces both production and reception. However, literary scholarship has made use of the concept in various ways without adequately clarifying its nature. When Harry Levin used it more than a generation ago to describe the social character of literature, he intended to transcend an expressive and mimetic understanding of literature: literature is not something that has to be related to society; it is itself a social factor. Thus Levin concludes when he has shown that a reflection theory of literature cannot be sustained; it is enough for him to establish that literature is as much an institution as is law or the church. Thus, he observes, literature "cherishes a unique phase of human experience and controls a special body of precedents and devices; it tends to incorporate a self-perpetuating discipline, while responding to the main currents of each succeeding period."[22] This formulation—whether one agrees with it or not—is so general that no new insights can be derived from it. Levin's comparison with law and the church is instructive but also confusing. Is he referring to norms or

---

political struggles must first awaken a group to its interest and its 'experience.'" *On Deconstruction: Theory and Criticism after Structuralism* (Ithaca, N.Y., 1982), p. 50. By the same token, Culler's theory of reading (understanding a text) has changed. Whereas in *Structuralist Poetics* he insisted on the importance of identifying the correct reading of a text, in *On Deconstruction* he favors the notion of different readings without privileging one as the *true* reading. Inverting the traditional opposition of true and false, Culler now argues that "understanding is a special case of misunderstanding" (p. 176). Reading as an act of interpretation includes both understanding and misunderstanding. In other words, all interpretations are, as Culler concludes, *partial*. In connection with this shift Culler drops the category of the *institution* as a privileged point of reference because it seems to be open to the deconstructive move.

[22]Harry Levin, "Literature as an Institution" (1946), in Morton Dauwen Zabel, ed., *Literary Opinion in America*, 3d ed. (New York, 1962), 2:664.

to the organization? Culler's and Fish's use of the concept of the institution has similar problems. The term establishes a vague connection between literary and social phenomena, even though the sociological use of the category is not defined.

Three approaches can be distinguished in recent sociological discussion: (1) the interactionist concept of the institution, found in the work of Talcott Parsons and his school; (2) the materialist approach of Antonio Gramsci and Louis Althusser; and (3) the theory of norms of the Frankfurt school.

The Interactionist Concept of the Institution

The concept of the institution plays a decisive role in the work of Talcott Parsons, where it serves as a link connecting the social role and the subsystems that constitute the social system. Parsons defines it as follows: "An *institution* will be said to be a complex of institutionalized role integrates which is of strategic structural significance in the social system in question." Institutions arise when the role expectations that underlie all social interaction become so stabilized that they determine and at the same time legitimize the actions of a subject. This process includes the internalization of standards, norms, and values to which the acting subjects can mutually refer. Thus, says Parsons, "the institutionalization of a set of role-expectations and of the corresponding sanctions is clearly a matter of degree. This degree is a function of two sets of variables; on the one hand those affecting the actual shardeness of the value-orientation patterns, on the other those determining the motivational orientation or commitment to the fulfillment of the relevant expectations."[23] Such institutions stabilize social interaction with-

---

[23]Talcott Parsons, *The Social System*, 5th ed. (Glencoe, Ill., 1964), p. 39. The beginnings of a materialist critique of systems theory are to be found in Hans Sanders, *Institution Literatur und Roman* (Frankfurt, 1981), pp. 39–40, who correctly points out that a socially homogeneous system such as that posited in Parsonian theory does not exist. But if the normative system (system of norms) of a society cannot be comprehended as being homogeneous, then the systems-theoretical approach is not capable of explaining social antagonisms adequately. (The objections of Ralf Dahrendorf to Parsonian theory point in the same direction.) Sanders would like to relate the concept of the institution to a Marxist model and proceed from the connections between the forces of production, relations of production, and class structures, but he does not explicate this desideratum in detail. Above all, the question where to situate and ground the category remains unclarified in this model. Sanders's attempt to distinguish between objective social structure and the development of structures of meaning on the subjective side suggests he would like to treat cultural institutions such as literature as being part of these structures of meaning; that in turn, however, would involve treating literature as part of the superstructure. Yet his earlier assumption—namely, that institutions consist of both a material apparatus and regulating norms—contradicts this desire. Sanders's formulation—"Taken materialistically, it [the concept of institution] is directed at both the relations of econom-

in an existing social system. They contribute decisively to the integration of the acting subjects.

Parsons distinguishes the concept of the institution from material collectives; thus he explicitly differentiates between the collective church and the system of beliefs, which he regards as a religious institution. By its very nature, the institution is for him an "evaluative phenomenon." From the viewpoint of literary studies, this is not all; equally instructive is Parsons's differentiation of three types of institutions—relational, regulative, and cultural. Relational institutions define the realm of reciprocal social role expectations for the acting subjects; regulative institutions determine the legitimacy of interests; and cultural institutions determine the realm of cognitive doctrines (ideologies), the system of expressive symbols (art), and, finally, the realm of individual morality. The classification of institutions according to their position in the system has undeniable advantages: it allows us to localize individual institutions and establish systemic connections, for example, in the relationship between ideologies and expressive symbols. The disadvantage is equally undeniable: Parsons's division is essentially formal and tells us little about how institutions actually function in concrete historical situations. His concept of the institution does not lead to objective material structures but rather to social subsystems, which Parsons understands as orientational and behavioral systems derived from subjective action.

The Materialist Concept of the Institution

The materialist concept of the institution differs in several respects from the interactionist concept. First, it stresses the transsubjective character of institutions; second, when Marxist theory makes use of the concept of the institution, it attempts to mediate it with social structure. The category of the institution was unknown in early Marxist theory. It was introduced, without systematic consistency, by Gramsci and was later developed primarily in the theory of Althusser, though he used the term only occasionally. In British Marxism, the category of the institution has been used primarily by Raymond Williams, who developed it

---

ic determinacy and the specific functions of cultural as opposed to economic and political systems" (p. 42)—hints, to be sure, at the direction a solution could take, but it remains too general and undifferentiated to serve as a solution. It does not say anything more than that cultural institutions such as literature are related to political and economic ones and are grounded in the relations of production. For a materialist theory, such a view is understood. What is necessary, rather, is a specific analytical determination of the mediations between the relations of production, the social formation, and the cultural institution. For such a determination, insight into the antagonistic character of social formations is essential.

in line with Gramsci's idea of hegemony. Whereas the ruling class possesses an apparatus—the state—which allows it to achieve its goals
through coercion and force, in the realm of civil society (that is, the
cultural and political public sphere) hegemony, as Gramsci says, indirectly serves to assure the dominance of the class. As Williams puts it,
hegemony is "a whole body of practices and expectations, over the
whole of living: our senses and assignments of energy, our shaping
perceptions of ourselves and our world. It is a lived system of meanings
and values."[24] But the importance of hegemony in the class struggle is
not sufficiently clear in this definition. Only when the ruling class controls the cultural and political institutions of civil society in addition to
the state apparatus does its position become legitimate and therefore
secure. The class struggle is waged, as Gramsci emphasizes, not only in
the political and economic spheres but equally, and possibly with even
greater intensity, in the cultural sphere.[25]

Gramsci's distinction between the state and civil society reappears in
Althusser's differentiation between the state apparatus and the ideological state apparatus. Althusser's terminology is misleading because it
implies that those phenomena which are subsumed under the concept of
the ideological state apparatus are in fact part of the state. Nonetheless,
the importance of this concept in Althusser's theory is clear. His point
of departure is the notion that in order to maintain conditions conducive to production every class must reproduce its productive means—
its material means and also its manpower. The reproduction of manpower involves more than concern for the physical maintenance of
workers; it extends, as Althusser emphasizes, to instilling and reinforcing habits, attitudes, and convictions that are indispensable for produc

[24]Raymond Williams, *Marxism and Literature* (Oxford, 1977), p. 110. Following
Althusser, Terry Eagleton, *Criticism and Ideology* (London, 1975), employs the concept
of the institution within the framework of his description of the "literary mode of production." Eagleton proceeds from the hypothesis that literary production can be considered a
part of the ideological apparatus, that is, it has the function of reproducing the relations
of production—in a fairly loose way, he uses the concept of the institution—in a fairly loose way,
significantly—to designate material organizations such as bookstores, publishing houses,
and printing businesses, but also to indicate the manner in which literature as a whole is
anchored in society: "But it is not only a question of the ideological use of particular
literary works; it is, more fundamentally, a question of the ideological significance of the
cultural and academic institutionalization as such" (pp. 56–57). In this sense, Eagleton
speaks of the separation and selection of texts from their original social formation and of
their definition as literature, which then assumes its specific and variable function in the
cultural tradition of a society. On the whole, however, the concept of the institution
remains subordinate to the category of the "literary mode of production," which in turn is
seen in connection with both the general ideology and the specific aesthetic ideology of a
given society.
[25]Antonio Gramsci, *Selections from Political Writings*, 2 vols. (New York, 1977,
1978).

tion. This aspect of the reproduction of manpower is taken over by authorities and institutions belonging to the superstructure. Althusser expressly mentions the school and the church; other institutions, such as the press and the theater, can readily be added. The social function of these institutions is to "assure *subjection to the ruling ideology* or control over its 'practice.'"[26] If all members of a society—of the ruling as well as the subordinate classes—share ideologies and the practices connected with them, they can readily be integrated into the productive process; they will function as quasi-responsible members of an accepted social order.

These reflections on the reproduction of the forces and relations of production assume such importance for Althusser because they allow a more consistent definition of the classic Marxist topology of base and superstructure. State and ideology prove to be not only dependent quantities, as they are in traditional Marxist theory, but indispensable aspects of reproduction which in turn affect the base. In Althusser's interpretation of the Marxist-Leninist theory of the state, class struggle is concentrated on state power: the contending classes try to take possession of the state apparatus (which is not identical with the executive power of the state). Alongside the state apparatus, which is normally controlled directly by the ruling class, are those organs of authority which Althusser calls the ideological state apparatus: "The term . . . will be used to signify a certain number of entities which are perceived by the direct observer as distinct, specialized institutions."[27] Althusser mentions school and church, law, the political system, and cultural institutions such as art and literature.

The institutions embraced by this concept are so heterogeneous that one wonders whether they constitute any meaningful structural unit at all. Althusser concedes that most of them are not part of the state, yet he argues that they fall into the realm of the civil community, which Gramsci distinguishes from the state apparatus in the narrow sense. These institutions have two things in common: they belong to what Jürgen Habermas defines as the bourgeois public sphere,[28] and they fulfill the same function. All ideological state apparatuses operate through the medium of ideology, that is, through the consciousness of the subject rather than through material force.

At first glance, Althusser's concept of the ideological state apparatus seems to lead to a reduction of social praxis, for the affirmative purpose

[26]Louis Althusser, "Ideology and Ideological State Apparatuses," in his *Lenin and Philosophy* (New York, 1971), p. 133.
[27]Ibid., p. 143.
[28]See Jürgen Habermas, *Strukturwandel der Öffentlichkeit*, 2d ed. (Neuwied a. Rh., 1965).

of these institutions seems to be fixed from the start. But his theory recognizes that they are relatively autonomous; they do not simply grow out of the conditions of production but are interdependent with them. They therefore have their own history. Nevertheless, Althusser's definition of these institutions remains functional; in the final analysis they reproduce the existing form of society. His theory is not so much incapable of explaining complex social situations (this is formally possible, since the ideological state apparatus is assumed to be relatively autonomous) as it is lacking an instrument for the analysis of social dynamics. It describes the actual function of institutions in advanced capitalist societies but is less exact about conditions that could bring about change.

With good reason, Williams criticized Althusser for limiting Gramsci's concept of hegemony by introducing the category of an ideological state apparatus. The characteristic feature of hegemonic institutions is that they do not contribute directly to class dominance but work according to their own processes and expend their energy on immanent problems, to the point where even internal opposition can lend general stability to the social system. As Williams remarks, "The true condition of hegemony is effective *self-identification* with the hegemonic forms: a specific and internalized 'socialization' which is expected to be positive but which, if that is not possible, will rest on a (resigned) recognition of the inevitable and the necessary."[29] To prevent reduction of the concept of the institution, Williams proposes a distinction between *institutions* and *formations*. By the latter he means scientific, literary, and philosophical tendencies that influence intellectual production. Such formations can be attached to institutions yet are not identical with them. Formations are specialized practices that take place within or on the periphery of institutions.

Clearly, Althusser's and Williams's interpretation of the concept of the institution has little in common with Parsons's theory. Williams regards organizations as institutions, whereas Parsons does not. Williams's viewpoint goes back to Althusser (and to some extent to Gramsci), who equates the institution with the organization. Althusser's notion of schools, for instance, includes what is taught and the method of transmitting it (didactics), as well as formal organization and physical structure (buildings, etc.). For him, institutions are important because they combine ideology and practice, because their formal organization gives them the capacity to transmit their ideology in the form of concrete practice. This synthetic interpretation is plausible for some institutions—for example, religion/the church. In the case of literature

29Williams, *Marxism and Literature*, p. 118.

and art, however, it makes good sense to distinguish between physical and formal organization, on the one hand, and ideological formation, on the other. Nevertheless, if the relationship is totally dissolved and we emphasize either organization or ideology alone, the concept of the institution loses much of its explanatory power. Above all, we lose a sense of how ideologies are adopted in a society—that is, how they become practice. Williams does not make clear, for instance, how formations relate to institutions. How does the social process give rise to formations? If formations are assumed to be (relatively) independent from institutions, how do they become part of everyday life?

Althusser's approach became fruitful for literary theory through the work of Pierre Macherey and Renée Balibar. What Williams merely touched upon, Balibar and her collaborators systematically explored, for example, in their book on the development of a French national language after the revolution of 1789.[30] Macherey and Balibar, however, move away from Althusser's concept of literature in their later works. Macherey in particular rejects the idea of *literature* and prefers instead to talk about concrete literary practices, which can take different forms in different societies and different epochs. Detachment from traditional aesthetics, not complete in Althusser's work, sharpens the eye for institutional aspects. Macherey's early work is especially attuned to Althusser's theory of the ideological state apparatus and accordingly interprets ideology as a system of material social practices. Thus the task of literary studies is no longer to investigate the genesis of literary production or evaluate it aesthetically but to analyze the effect of literary texts in specific historical situations—in particular, within such institutions as schools and universities. As Etienne Balibar and Macherey indicated in their introduction to *Les français fictifs* (1974), Marxist literary theory has to be reformulated so as to address two problems: the character and expression of class positions in literature, and the ideological mode of literature. These two aspects prove to be essentially identical. The ideological mode and the attitude toward different classes are both revealed through their effects. Balibar and Macherey define literature as an ideological form that becomes manifest in the context and through the agency of ideological state apparatuses. The objectivity of literary production they view as inseparable from social practices within a particular ideological state apparatus. Here the term *literary production* refers not to an individual text or work but rather to social praxis—among other things, the common language

[30]Renée Balibar and Dominique Laporte, *Le français national: Politique et pratiques de la langue nationale sous la révolution française* (Paris, 1974).

from which literature takes its material and which in turn it enriches.[31] A materialistic concept of literature focused on social practices has replaced the idealistic concept that stresses the autonomy of a work of art. Concrete social institutions, such as schools, determine the definition of literature. Thus Etienne Balibar and Macherey emphasize that the manner of teaching languages adopted in the schools both creates the basis for literary production and is the result of that production (inasmuch as the production of literature in turn affects linguistic conventions).[32]

What function does literature have as an ideological form? For Etienne Balibar and Macherey—and this distinguishes them from Althusser—the ironing out and apparent resolution of ideological contradictions is in the foreground. Real social contradictions, which are insoluble in concrete historical situations, are thrust aside so that imaginary solutions can be found for them. These circumstances reverse the relationship between reality and literature: instead of mirroring reality, literature—as social practice—creates a fictive semblance of reality. In other words, realism and fictitiousness are concepts constituted through the praxis of literary production. The institution of literature, or the various apparatuses that represent it, is not the sum total of existing literary texts and their authors; rather, it must be understood as the locus where the literary practices of authors, texts, and readers are constituted. Aesthetic autonomy disappears as a concept: the idea of artistic autonomy manifests itself as a special literary effect whose aim is to conceal the ideological character of the literary process.

To repeat the essential points: the subject and object of literature— authors, readers, and texts—are generated by social practices. Individuals become literary subjects (authors, readers) in the context of apparatuses. In this respect, all empirical analysis directly concerned with "reality" confuses levels, because it regards ideological formation as reality. On the other hand, investigations that begin with an implied reader overlook the fact that the text and the implied reader contained within it are not given quantities but rather the results of literary practice and belong in the realm of ideology; for the implicit reader—who is presumed to play a role in the text—is one of the places where the individual functions as the subject.

Etienne Balibar and Macherey shift emphasis to impact (effects). Un-

---

[31]Balibar and Laporte have shown in *Le français national* that the modern French language contains two separate practices: basic French, taught in the elementary schools, and literary French, taught in the high schools.

[32]Etienne Balibar and Pierre Macherey, "Présentation," in Renée Balibar, ed., *Les français fictifs* (Paris, 1974), pp. 7–61.

like empirical studies of reception, their work considers the reader not as primary but rather as the subject constituted by the ideological state apparatus. The literary effect can thus be described on three levels: (1) the creation of the effect under specific social conditions; (2) the reproduction of the dominant ideology; and (3) the effect as determined by dominance. Finally, Balibar and Macherey also include criticism (that is, texts that comment on and evaluate literature) among the effects. These texts, however, are expressly denied the status of metacommentaries. They are treated instead as expressions existing on the same level as the texts they comment on. Literary texts and critical commentaries thus appear as agents whose task it is to reproduce the dominant ideology. This function is analyzed by Renée Balibar in her investigation of the use of literary texts in schools. The language used to interpret literary texts forces the apparently free reader to pose precisely those questions that will project the dominant ideology; this process does not exclude internal differences and divergent approaches to interpretation.

Obviously this theory has no room for the critical function of art. Because they have an aesthetic character, literary texts remain bound to ideology. Thus far, this approach has not been able to demonstrate how a text can be read against the grain, how a reading formation (convention) can be breached. Althusser's concept of ideology restricts the function of literature. Since Etienne Balibar and Macherey accept Althusser's dichotomy between science and ideology yet reject his concept of art (art lies between ideology and science), literature remains for them a part of ideology. It cannot be equated with scientific knowledge and therefore cannot transcend its affirmative function.

The Concept of the Institution in Critical Theory

The traditional Marxist model of base and superstructure is always in danger of being used in a reductionist manner. Even Friedrich Engels's well-known observations that the superstructure is relatively autonomous and that only in the last resort can the economic base achieve dominance cannot solve this difficulty. The danger has led to the increasing rejection of this model in critical theory, although the concept of social mediation has been retained. Both Theodor Adorno and Habermas insist that the cultural sphere is part of the whole social process, but whereas in his *Aesthetic Theory* Adorno sets forth a theory of the work of art, Habermas's studies are more in line with Herbert Marcuse's and Max Horkheimer's move toward a unified theory of culture. This context can serve as a basis for developing the concept of the institution. Let us begin with the category of the public sphere, which is at the center of Habermas's early work and which he defines "as a sphere that mediates between society and the state, in which the public becomes the transmitter of public opinion." On one side is the state apparatus (bureaucracy and a standing army); on the other, civil society with its "permanent relationships, which had developed with the stock exchange and the press in the traffic of commodities and information." The function of the bourgeois public sphere as it was constituted in the eighteenth century was to articulate public opinion, that is, to deliberate on the control of state power: "The principle of control, which the bourgeois public opposed to this [the state]—namely, publicity—was intended to change sovereignty as such, not merely to exchange one basis of legitimacy for another."[33] The public sphere is more than the sum total of citizens who transmit public opinion; it is the locus of those institutions that Althusser calls the ideological state apparatuses—the press, schools, literature, and so forth. But Habermas's emphases differ from Althusser's; he wishes to show that the historical origin of these institutions was the attempt to restrict the power of the absolutist state and that they assumed the functions Althusser generally ascribes to them only in the late nineteenth century, in connection with the development of monopoly capitalism.[34]

Although these approaches diverge, there are interesting parallels in Althusser's and Habermas's assessment and description of cultural institutions. Both authors make a basic distinction between the state and its apparatus on the one side and a realm of ideological argumentation on the other. Literature is one of the institutions in which this argumentation is carried on. Althusser gives no special emphasis to literature, which he sees primarily as an apparatus established by the dominant class for the purpose of assuring its own dominance. For Habermas (like Marcuse and Adorno), however, the relationship between class dominance and literature is more complex and at the same time more historical. In his view, the literary public sphere did not serve the feudal class or the absolutist state. Rather, it was the area in which the rising middle class developed moral and political self-consciousness. Literary discourse, institutionalized as art criticism, prepared the way for the political criticism of absolutism.[35]

Habermas's theory of the public sphere does not include the concept of the institution, but we can easily derive the latter from his theory. The institution of literature proves to be part of the public sphere; as the public sphere changes, so does the structure of literature. The organization of individual works of art does not directly change along with

---

[33] Jürgen Habermas, *Kultur und Kritik* (Frankfurt a. M., 1973), pp. 62, 64, 65.
[34] Habermas, *Strukturwandel der Öffentlichkeit*, esp. pts. 5–7.
[35] See Peter Uwe Hohendahl, *The Institution of Criticism* (Ithaca, N.Y., 1982), pp. 44–82.

changes in the public sphere; rather, the structure of the public sphere determines the conditions of literary production and consumption. One example is the difference between literary conditions in the early eighteenth century and those of the late nineteenth century. In Habermas's judgment, the function of literature during the transition from feudal absolutism to a liberal bourgeois society was to promote the psychological and social self-understanding of the new class; in advanced bourgeois society, however, the literary functions of criticism and entertainment separated, and literature increasingly took the form of a consumer commodity. The marketplace also came to exert more influence on the quality of literary products, and literature thus became a commodity not only in form (by dissemination in the marketplace) but also in content. This example clearly reveals the founding conditions of the institution. Habermas assumes that in the final analysis the conditions of production determine the structure of the public sphere. (The transition in the late nineteenth century from liberal to organized capitalism changed the structure of the public sphere.) The structure of the public sphere in turn determines the form of the institution of literature. Finally, the conditions under which all communication concerning literature takes place affect the structure of individual literary texts. Thus Habermas assumes a complex interaction between base and superstructure, but at the same time he implies that the levels of the superstructure are overdetermined. The institution of literature is therefore a relatively independent part of the public sphere, and its history is not identical with the economic evolution of society.

Literature and the Concept of the Institution

The sociological concept of the institution occasionally takes literature into account, but as a rule only in passing, as one among many cultural institutions. Its usefulness in literary studies depends on a reconciliation of sociological theory and literary theory. The first step is to inquire which concept of the institution in literary studies fits which sociological concept of the institution. Only thereafter can we discuss the fruitfulness of rival approaches.

The Theory of Reception and Semiotics

For both Stanley Fish and Jonathan Culler the institution of literature is basically an immanent category; it designates not so much the framework of conditions for the functioning of institutions as the norms and conventions that govern the reading and interpretation of texts. Since these critics are primarily interested in the literariness of texts—the same is true for the phenomenological approach of Wolfgang Iser—their studies avoid analysis of the relationship between the institution of literature and other institutions. Their theories, however, include suppositions that go beyond literary immanence. Fish's and Culler's category of the institution contains sociological premises of which they are unaware, because they regard them as self-evident. Both theorists posit an interactionist model of the social system similar to the theory developed most fully by Parsons. Its elements include—especially in Culler's semiotic theory—acting subjects, fixed and predictable role relations, and values and patterns of behavior by which subjects are integrated into the social system. In any case, Fish and Culler assume, in the sociological interactionist sense, that actions such as writing and reading are carried out by individual subjects, albeit within the framework of the social system and its subsystems, which define the possible actions in each case. Although Culler insists that individual acts of reading cannot be viewed in isolation but must be seen as institutionally determined, he holds to an underlying concept of the subject. This point is evident when he discusses the possibility of consent and dissent. Readers are able to reach a consensus because they can refer to common norms and conventions; but more important, when they differ in opinion, they can reflect on the reasons for their divergent points of view. In order to be able to communicate and act at all, subjects must depend on certain conventions, but as autonomous subjects they can in rational discourse come to an understanding about the conventionality of reading: "If the distinction between understanding and misunderstanding were irrelevant . . . there would be little point to discussing and arguing about literary works and still less to writing about them."[36] Culler sees beyond those conventions that determine our reading a rational discourse that leads to a consensus about the correctness or incorrectness of interpretations. The supposition that rational discourse is always available places Culler's *Structuralist Poetics* in the tradition of the Enlightenment and thus close to the norm-oriented communication theories of, say, Habermas and Karl Otto Apel.[37]

Unlike Culler, Fish assumes that acting subjects are totally bound to the conventions of their institutions. They cannot break out of these structures. The discourse of literary criticism is for this reason not

[36]Culler, *Structuralist Poetics*, p. 121.
[37]Jürgen Habermas, *The Theory of Communicative Action*, 2 vols., trans. Thomas McCarthy (Boston, 1984, 1987); and Karl Otto Apel, *Transformation der Philosophie*, vol. 2: *Das Apriori der Kommunikationsgemeinschaft* (Frankfurt a. M., 1976).

evidential but persuasive. Fish's subjects are players in a game they cannot quit; if they dislike it, all they can do is change the rules, possibly against the wishes of other players.

Obviously Fish's and Culler's reader theories offer no more than the rudiments of a social theory; nevertheless, we can recognize some basic patterns. The concept of interpretive communities introduced by Fish has an evident prototype in the university, that is, in the community of scholars who carry out research projects according to mutually accepted rules. This model is tacitly carried over to society as a whole, with the result that those aspects of society which are not in accord with the academic community are ignored. Both Fish and Culler link social relations to the model of the face-to-face group, in which one can overcome contradictions and antagonisms arising in the course of discussion. Even though the theory of the reader began around 1970 with a criticism of traditional hermeneutics, Fish came to the conclusion in his essay "Demonstration vs. Persuasion" (1979–81) that the framework of the institution of literature still includes texts, readers, and interpreters. In other words, nothing has changed except that we now know why things are the way they are. Fish's theoretical conventionalism, which deliberately avoids transcendental norms, can only verify what is already known to be true. This is not an insignificant contribution, if he can show that our conventional understanding of reading does not coincide with our practice. Yet his approach has its limitations, for it indicates no direction for that practice. Conventionalism is indifferent to historical processes. No matter how radical his rhetoric may be, therefore, in the final analysis Fish supports the existing belief system, the status quo. The social function of the conventions and norms that mold the reader remains beyond the horizon of his critical analysis.

The Materialistic Model

The limits of the interactionist model of the institution become apparent when we consider the function of the institution. The functional approach has no part in this model, which assumes the institution to be based on individual subjects whose interaction with other subjects brings the institution into being in the first place. Individual subjects create norms and rules, arrive at decisions, reach agreements, or have different opinions concerning literary texts. If we compare this model with the concept of the institution developed by Althusser, we find that function is a problem of central importance for him, because it tells us how the institution of literature operates within a society. For Althusser and Macherey, apparatuses are not constituted by subjects; rather, subjects are constituted by ideological apparatuses. In this respect, institutions such as schools or the law are the decisive mediators between the base and individuals. For Althusser the institution is indisputably primary. Literature can therefore be described, following Macherey and Etienne Balibar, as a system of practices, norms, and rules which regulates the production and consumption of texts. These norms and conventions, however, should not be isolated from the concrete, material organizations that constitute the apparatus transmitting them to society. This is what Bertolt Brecht had in mind when he described the bourgeois theater of the early twentieth century as an apparatus that transmits bourgeois ideology no matter what is produced on the stage.[38] Walter Benjamin argued similarly in his essay "Der Autor als Produzent" (The Author as Producer) that a true change in literature will be effected not by plays and novels but by taking the means of production out of the hands of the bourgeoisie.[39]

But the fusion of apparatus and ideology in Althusser's concept of the institution also has its disadvantages. It fails to distinguish clearly between *apparatus* and *institutionalization*. There is an advantage in not equating institutionalization with the apparatus (organization). Religion, as a system of beliefs, is separate from the organization of the church. For analytical reasons, it would probably be sensible to make a similar distinction between the institutionalization of literature as a system and its apparatus. In the case of the institution of literature it would be more difficult to describe the organization than the institutionalization, because the organization cannot simply be equated with such concrete establishments as the publishing and book trades, the press, and so forth, as is sometimes done. Rather, the organization should be understood as the way in which literature is regulated by society. In a capitalist society this regulation is accomplished through the marketplace. The organization pertains more to conditions of production, whereas institutionalization occurs in the realm of ideological practices, which show the involved subjects how to interpret and use works and various genres.

Individual establishments such as the book trade and libraries can be investigated on the level of the organization; on the level of institutionalization, such channels as criticism, literary history, and aesthetics. We shall assume that a relationship exists between institutionalization and organizations, though it is not necessarily mechanical: in a capitalist society, for example, the predominant transmission of literary works in the marketplace, which in form makes them commodities, also deter-

---

[38]For instance, Bertolt Brecht, "Primat des Apparates," in his *Schriften zum Theater, 1918–1933*, ed. Werner Hecht, vol. 1 (Frankfurt a. M., 1963), pp. 190–92.

[39]Walter Benjamin, "The Author as Producer," in Andrew Arato and Eike Gebhardt, ed., *The Essential Frankfurt School Reader* (New York, 1978), pp. 254–69.

mines the framework within which they are institutionalized, although it does not define every aspect of it. Such factors as literary criticism and literary history also have their own histories. An approach that examines the organization alone and on that basis mechanically draws conclusions about individual texts—as was the case in commodity aesthetics—neglects transmission through institutionalization, just as the reverse approach, which makes conventions and norms the principal point of departure and views them as sole determinants, gives no role to the social apparatus and accordingly slights the category of the institution.

The Model of Critical Theory

Habermas's theory affords a good point of departure for examining the possibilities and limitations of a theory that puts primary emphasis on the *conception of art*, even though he attempts to ground the category of the public sphere (and with it, literature) in the relations of production. This approach might well adopt Peter Bürger's definition of the institution of art as "the notions about art (definitions of function) generally held by a given society (or by particular classes or strata), viewed from the perspective of their social determinacy." This definition equates the institution of art with the dominant conception of art in a class, stratum, or group. Generally accepted ideas determine both the production and the reception of individual works. Thus the institution has genetic as well as logical priority over the individual work of art. Says Bürger, "The differentiation of function is carried out—through the agency of aesthetic norms—on the production side by means of the *artistic material* and on the reception side by establishing *attitudes toward reception*."[40] As the concept of art changes, according to Bürger's theory, so will the production of art and the manner in which works of art are treated.

Bürger's definition comes close to an interactionist concept such as we found in the work of Fish and Culler: the category of the institution is linked to nonmaterial ideas, not to the concept of the apparatus. But there are also clear differences. Bürger moves from the start on a higher plane of abstraction: the institution is constituted not by norms and conventions but by *general ideas about the function* of art or literature. As a result, conventions are not merely brute facts but are derived from a general determination of function. The classic example of such a generalized idea is the category of aesthetic autonomy, which according to Bürger has regulated the production and reception of art since the

[40]Peter Bürger, *Vermittlung-Rezeption-Funktion* (Frankfurt a. M., 1979), p. 176.

late eighteenth century. The concept of autonomy (on the level of the institution, not of the individual work) implies that art has been freed from the realities of social life; a realm has been created for it in which purposive, rational thinking is not applicable. Whether this assumption is historically accurate, whether literary production was really defined in the nineteenth century exclusively or chiefly by the category of autonomy, is not the issue here. More important for the basic argument is the notion that there exists a *hegemonic category* that determines the outlook of subjects who participate in literature. If one assumes with Bürger that the aesthetics of artistic autonomy predominated between the end of the eighteenth century and the advent of dadaism in Germany, it follows that divergent or rival points of view had to contend with the aesthetic of autonomy. In other words, the specific qualities of this aesthetic are understandable only against the background of the hegemonic point of view.

The advantage of a functional conception of the institution of literature over an interactionist one is apparent: the theory does not stop with groups and "reader communities" but is oriented toward a concept of function within society as a whole. Society is the source of the norms and conventions that mold literary production and reception. This approach is not focused on the individual subject; rather, it assumes that individual subjects share general opinions that go beyond those of the collective class or group. Moreover, a functional model makes it possible to find for historical processes explanations that go beyond mere description.

This last point needs further clarification. Bürger's model can explain historical processes only by making additional assumptions about the course of social processes. This is true especially for the relationship between the institution of art and the social formation. Such a relationship can be established on the level of acting, collective subjects—as in the relationship between the rising middle classes and the aesthetics of autonomy. It can also be established on the level of conditions of production—say, between the creation of commodity markets (capitalism) and the liberation of the institution of art. It may further be assumed that the institution of art has a dynamics of its own and does not depend on an external impetus.

Bürger makes use of all these kinds of explanations, but for reasons to be discussed, he favors the hypothesis that the institution has its own dynamics. Thus he assumes in his *Theory of the Avant-Garde* that in keeping with its own logic, the aesthetics of autonomy transcends itself in its last phase and in surrealism reaches a stage of self-criticism: "The totality of the developmental process of art becomes clear only in the stage of self-criticism. Only after art has in fact wholly detached itself from everything that is the praxis of life can two things be seen to make up the principle of development of art in bourgeois society: the progressive detachment of art from real life contexts, and the correlative crystallization of a distinctive sphere of experience, i.e., the aesthetic."[41] Here Bürger expressly rejects the establishment of a direct connection between the social formation and the category of the institution of art, calling instead for an investigation of the development of components of the social system, each of which has its own logic and consequently follows a separate temporal path. By thus reformulating the problem, Bürger avoids the question of how the institution of art relates to the social structure (through what channels it is transmitted) and specifically how the evolution of the institution of art relates to the evolution of the social system.

In a later reflection on the problem of institutionalization (1979), Bürger was more cautious about assuming a consistent autonomous dynamics of art and accordingly stressed causal determination.[42] In attempting to explain the difference between the institutionalization of art in a courtly, feudal society and in a bourgeois society, he now resorted to the concept of class (nobility/bourgeoisie) but also considered production conditions (the capitalistic, commodity-producing, market commercialization of literature). This shifting of the relational framework—to which can be added a third strategy involving concepts of modernization and rationalization—points to the difficulties with which a functional theory has to contend.

In the first formulation of his theory Bürger defined the institution of art as the "productive and distributive apparatus and also . . . the ideas about art that prevail at a given time."[43] Later he expressly excluded the apparatus as a purely empirical element. The result was the equation of the institution of art with notions of artistic function. Ideas about the purpose of art (including those which assert that art has no purpose) are undoubtedly an important aspect of the institution, but they should not be confused with it. Although the self-understanding of a class will determine the content of aesthetic norms and conventions, it should not be construed as the institution itself. As Bürger rightly stressed in 1974, the institution includes the apparatus. The exclusion of the apparatus—and with it, social practices—intensifies the problem of sociological grounding that Bürger's theory tries to address. This is the point at which the hidden idealism of the functional approach be-

[41]Peter Bürger, *Theory of the Avant-Garde*, trans. Michael Shaw (Minneapolis, 1984), pp. 23–24.
[42]Peter Bürger, "Institution Kunst als literatursoziologische Kategorie," in his *Vermittlung-Rezeption-Funktion*, pp. 173–99.
[43]Bürger, *Theory of the Avant-Garde*, p. 22.

comes apparent. Bürger rightly resists the equation of institutionalization with empirical factors, because the functional point of view cannot
be grasped by this means, but he wrongly treats the apparatus as a
merely empirical factor. The idealism of Bürger's theory is rooted in a
fear of arguing reductively. Bürger tries to solve the problem of grounding by introducing the concept of the norm: the norm mediates between
the individual work, the institution of art, and the social system. This
suggested solution to the problem resembles the interactionist model
insofar as it establishes (albeit tacitly) a relationship between the social
and the aesthetic realms through the concept of the subject. Norms are
transmitted through the consciousness of socialized subjects: as moral
norms they concern (regulate) society; as aesthetic norms they are put
to use in the realm of art. If aesthetic norms are derived from social
norms, the relationship between the institution of art and society can be
described as the application of familiar norms to a special realm. Bürger
makes use of this strategy in his description of the institutionalization of
art in the seventeenth century: "In courtly, feudal society, aesthetic
norms either go directly back to social norms (the *bienséances* and rules
of class privilege come to mind) or they indirectly serve the interests of
society (this could be demonstrated by the dramatic unities). Aesthetic
norms mediate the content of individual works and the prevailing social
norms and assure their relative conformity."[44] In contrast, Bürger
thinks, social norms in a bourgeois society can no longer be directly
translated into aesthetic norms because the content of the work of art is
severed from the social sphere through the aesthetics of autonomy.
Nevertheless, aesthetic and social norms are still brought into relationship, albeit through several channels—for example, when the social
norms in the content of a work of art are made problematic in order to
humanize the author and his or her readers.

If we redefine the concept of the institution in such a way as to
emphasize its intangible character (views of art and their social function), we imply a different concept of the subject. An orientation toward norm theory leads either to a collective subject (a class or group)
representing the institution or to an individual subject (the public conceived as a set of subjects). In either case we lose the priority of the
institution. This is the key difference from Althusser's concept of the
institution, which takes the apparatus as its point of departure and
conceives of what the norm-theoretical model calls the institution as the
ideology of the apparatus.

Theories focusing on social and literary norms and those centering on
the concept of the apparatus are equally burdened by certain problems.

[44]Bürger, *Vermittlung-Rezeption-Funktion*, p. 190.

Although Althusser's approach is capable of showing how the institution of literature functions in society, his analysis remains generalized and undifferentiated with respect to other cultural institutions. It does not take sufficiently into account the specificity of literary practices, which is given exact articulation by semiotic and norm-theoretical approaches (Culler and Bürger, respectively). The functional norm-theoretical model is decidedly better equipped to deal with these questions, but it also has the problem that either it treats norms as autonomous—attributing a unique history to them from which the history of the institution is then derived—or else it has to search for mediating agencies that will give norms and values a social basis. This attempt to find a solution can easily lead back to an interactionist approach: if we derive norms from the groups that carry them, we particularize the concept of the institution, thereby significantly weakening the value of the category for the description of literary structures and processes. This result is a return to the community of readers of conventional literary theory. A theory that is unable to explain the institution of literature as a general social phenomenon (functioning on the level of society as a whole) has limited value or at least offers no model for the reconstruction of the history of literature.

Toward a Theory of the Institution

What, then, are the requirements for an adequate theory of the institution? First, one would expect the institution of literature to be a category distinct from the form and content of individual works. It is directly concerned neither with the analysis of texts nor with their genesis and dissemination, but rather with the conditions under which writing and reading occur. This distinction is independently emphasized by Culler and Bürger. Moreover, one would expect a theory of the institution to deal systematically with these basic conditions. When we speak of conventions and norms, we are concerned not with individual traits but with a system. Third, one would expect the specific character of the institution in relation to other cultural and social institutions (that is, its particular significance and function within society) to be clarified. Finally, one would expect historical specificity to be taken into consideration, for example, the differences between various historical epochs and social formations, and the evolution of the institution of literature itself.

No theory to date has done justice to all these requirements. Conventional literary theory is obviously unsatisfactory, both as a system and historically. A semiotic model such as Culler's is an improvement over

Fish's approach, but it fails to take sufficient account of the status of literature in society as a whole. A materialist approach, which takes function as its point of departure, has the most to offer. One could build on the investigations of critical theory, especially those of Benjamin, but Althusser and his school should also be taken into account. We know that Benjamin sought to explain the changes that took place in the history of art and literature at the end of the nineteenth century as a fundamental shift in function and grounding.[45] Using reproduction as his point of departure, Benjamin argued that the status of art changed when it became technically possible to reproduce it. During the late nineteenth century this innovation changed the basis, existence, and reception of works of art: a political basis replaced the cultic basis; mass reproduction replaced uniqueness; and individual reception, with its absorption in the object, gave way to a collective, dispersed reception. What matters in the strategy of this approach is not its problematic periodization and its disputable reasoning that the structural change in the institution was brought about by a new method of reproduction, but rather its concept of a model in which changes in artistic form and content are related to a change in function. Even if Benjamin's explanation of literary evolution is not accepted, his model can still be fruitful for the theory of the institution.

Bürger agrees with Adorno's and Habermas's criticism of Benjamin but accepts the distinction (contrary to Adorno) between the general function of art—for which he employs the concept of the institution—and its individual use. His theory, which is obviously influenced by Marx's early ideology-critical concept of art, criticizes Benjamin's lack of insight into the function of art in bourgeois society. It underscores the emancipation from religious ritual which has taken place since the Renaissance. Whereas Benjamin assumes that the change in function occurred behind the backs, so to speak, of producers and recipients, Bürger brings the importance of consciousness and the intention of the artist to the fore: "Here, the loss of aura [i.e., uniqueness] is not traced to a change in reproduction techniques but to an intent on the part of the makers of art."[46] The weight of the argument has thus shifted toward the superstructure, toward norms and ideology. Bürger is convinced that the change in function cannot be explained by contradictions between productive forces and the conditions of production. Instead, he tries to shift explanation for the functional change to the level of the institution, describing the change as a differentiation within liter-

---

[45] Walter Benjamin, "The Work of Art in the Age of Mechanical Reproduction," in his *Illuminations*, trans. Harry Zohn (New York, 1969), pp. 217–51.

[46] Bürger, *Theory of the Avant-Garde*, p. 29.

ary production (the differentiation of art as a subsystem). Bernard Zimmermann has rightly objected that this shift in focus does not automatically solve the problem posed by Benjamin: "Instead of looking for periodization only in the realm of the institution of art, a multiperspectival historical methodology would have to clarify in which way change in the institution of art changes the conditions of artistic formation, and in which form artistic production reflects and provokes change in the institution of art."[47] This justified criticism of Benjamin's periodization should not lead us to restrict functional change to the differentiation of art as a subsystem without posing a further question: What purpose does this isolation of a subsystem serve within the framework of the system as a whole? On a metalevel, the question would thus be what function is served by a function.

Benjamin's theory tries to explain the evolution of art and literature by examining the changes in their social use. The question of their status—however one chooses to evaluate Benjamin's answer—throws light on social practices and the perceptions and forms in which such practices are organized. The institution of literature is thus a structure with interdependent elements. It must be assumed, moreover, that these elements are *variably coordinated*: relationships, for instance, can be stronger or weaker. If we were to single out one component as decisive in the hierarchy, we would reduce the institution in either an idealistically abstract or a materialistically mechanical fashion. The historicity of the concept of the institution cannot be understood merely as an external factor (along the lines "we have to bear in mind that literature was institutionalized differently in the eighteenth century than in the twentieth"). Rather, the historicity of the category tells us that its origins lie in the historical process and that its existence is inconceivable outside history. In this respect it is not unproblematic to assume that the category has content in every period. It is no accident that discussion of the concept of the institution has revolved around modern (eighteenth- to twentieth-century) literature. The institution becomes visible, as it were, only in connection with the aesthetics of autonomy. It is legitimate, I believe, to ask whether the concept can be meaningfully applied to medieval circumstances. It is not even necessary to assume, as Benjamin and Bürger do, that art was largely cultic in the Middle Ages and therefore part of ritual in order to ask whether and to what extent the institutions of religion and art were separate in this period.

Finally, a few questions may be raised concerning the internal structure of the concept of the institution. Both Culler's semiotic model and

---

[47]Bernhard Zimmermann, *Literaturrezeption im historischen Prozess* (Munich, 1977), p. 62.

Bürger's norm theory proceed from the hypothesis that the institution of literature is a unity that subsumes all texts and readings. Apart from the possibility of distinguishing analytically between organization (apparatus) and institutionalization, the question arises whether and how much the institution is divided into subinstitutions, each of which has its own dynamics. Furthermore, how do collective bodies—social classes and groups—relate to the institution of literature? Must we assume that the institution is always controlled by one class, or do competing classes develop their own respective institutions?

A sociohistorical derivation of the institution of literature from social strata (classes or groups) may favor the latter hypothesis. It might be possible, for example, to assume a separate, class-linked institution for the literature of the working class which developed over the course of the nineteenth century. But as this very example shows, the assumption would be meaningless. Although proletarian literature differs in form and content from middle-class literature and is certainly directed at a different public, its genres and conventions undoubtedly share a concept of literature which includes that of the bourgeoisie. On the level of the institution, however, the relationship between middle-class and proletarian literature can be described as a rivalry: the new class included literary means in its struggle for recognition and equality, whereas the bourgeoisie underscored its hegemony by suppressing and denouncing opposing concepts and practices. Similarly, the institutionalization of the early eighteenth century can be understood as a rivalry between courtly and "middle-class" conceptions which continued until a new concept became entrenched about 1770 and thereafter dominated. It is thus more fruitful to postulate the existence of contradictory tendencies *within* an institution of literature comprising the entire social sphere.

The institution of literature cannot be identified with one class, but it can be dominated by one class. This is what Althusser says when he speaks of an ideological apparatus whose function is to guarantee reproduction of the conditions of production. For Althusser, one class normally controls cultural institutions; from a historical point of view it is the turning points, when control shifts from one class to another, which are of greatest importance. These turning points, however, do not necessarily correspond to the junctures in political and economic history. The eighteenth-century change of German literature into a middle-class literature (*Verbürgerlichung*) does not correspond to a similar process in the conditions of production and certainly not to the attainment of political dominance by the bourgeoisie. It is consequently better not to separate the concept of the institution into strata, as Bürger proposes for French seventeenth-century literature. In the conflict between classes, where cultural antagonisms play a large role, the important thing is to hold those positions that are strategically decisive. Whoever makes the decisions about what is written, printed, and read to a great extent controls the consciousness of the public. Literary censorship is one of the obvious instruments of domination.

The systematic analysis of class struggle in the institution of literature has to go beyond descriptions of individual phenomena, of course. In this context the differentiation of the institution becomes an important issue. To what degree are *subinstitutions* created which could become effective controlling factors? Since the eighteenth century, literary criticism has functioned as such a factor—an institution within an institution. Because it has been assigned, within the framework of the public sphere, the task of both creating rules for the evaluation of literary texts and putting those rules to use, it commands a central strategic position. The critic's standing in the literary public sphere shows that art criticism involves more than the mere expression of private opinion, even though the critic is a private individual. He or she is backed by the authority of the institution and of the class that occupies it.

In the nineteenth century, literary history became a factor in addition to the institution of criticism. Again we are dealing with more than the mere production of a certain type of text. The rapid rise of literary history in the early nineteenth century becomes explicable only when we investigate its function. Beyond the purported task of describing the evolution of a national literature, its purpose was to secure *literary tradition*. Of strategic importance were the selection of important authors and the analysis of filiation. The canonization of the literature of the past was separated from literary criticism and developed into an independent institution. This new subinstitution created an apparatus for itself within the university, which, incidentally, tied it more closely to the state apparatus than to literary criticism because in Germany the university is controlled by the state. Through the appointment of professors, for example, the state could indirectly influence the methodology and content of literary history.

Literary norms and conventions are an important element of the institution of literature, and so one must ask in what way they become part of the institution. Put differently, does any authority have jurisdiction over literary theory? Whereas in the eighteenth and early nineteenth centuries literary theory went hand in hand with criticism (if we disregard the general field of aesthetics in the universities), since the end of the nineteenth century academic literary studies have increasingly absorbed theory. At least, the academy dominates professional reflection about what constitutes literariness and what effect literature has on society. Today, not only literary tradition but concepts of the function of literature are transmitted through universities and schools, because the literary intelligentsia was to a great extent educated at the universities.

The example of literary theory also shows that the relationship between a subinstitution and the apparatus that brings it into existence is not automatically fixed and may change. Literary theory appears to lack the apparatus that literary criticism and literary history have at their disposal. In the eighteenth and nineteenth centuries it shared the apparatus of criticism (journals, newspapers); in the twentieth century it made use primarily of the apparatus of literary studies (the university). It is clear from this example, furthermore, that subinstitutions are the channels joining the institution of literature to other institutions— via literary history to the institution of education, via literary criticism to the press. In view of the tasks and functions the educational system performs for society, therefore, literary studies can also be analyzed within the framework of the institution of education. (Presumably Althusser would regard this as the more important aspect for society.) Literary criticism, on the other hand, can be treated as part of the institution of the press. It could be argued that the fate of literary criticism has been determined more strongly by structural changes in the press than by internal changes in literary norms. The place literature and criticism have been given by the press in the layout of newspapers has largely determined discourse in literary criticism since the end of the nineteenth century. That this place is peripheral shows that the institution of criticism in relation to the press has a decidedly lower priority than political and economic issues.

As soon as we recognize that the institution of literature consists of subinstitutions that are relatively autonomous and have histories of their own, we find that other problems arise. For one, we have to consider that evolution within the institution of literature can be uneven. For example, around 1900 the positivistic history of literature was oriented toward a concept of the literary work that did not correspond to the contemporaneous concept of the artwork within the avant-garde. Literary history and literary criticism had divergent norms. It is possible, besides, that different social groups, or classes, occupied subinstitutions through their respective apparatuses. Although it was impossible, for instance, for the nineteenth-century proletariat to exert any influence over literary history, it could participate in the discourse of literary criticism by means of the periodicals and newspapers of working-class parties and unions and articulate its claim to a literature of its own vis-à-vis the middle-class press. The workers could never have dominated the institution of criticism at that time, as the Russian revolutionaries did literary criticism in 1917, but they did acquire a voice and were able to exert an influence on critical debate through important theorists such as Mehring and Lukács.

Institution and Reading Formation

Tony Bennett has recently tried to overcome the limitations of Althusser's theory. Although his critique draws primarily on Etienne Balibar and Macherey, his approach differs not insignificantly from French Marxism and in some respects comes close to the work of Raymond Williams, especially in its emphasis on historical concreteness. His objections to Althusser also apply, more than he realizes, to Althusser's students. In Bennett's opinion, abstract structures such as ideology and literature have to be replaced by the concrete practices by which historic individuals express themselves: "What is needed is not a theory of literature *as such* but a historically concrete analysis of the different relationships which may exist between different forms of fictional writing and the ideologies to which they allude." He rightly objects that a generalized concept of literature is unable to comprehend the multiplicity of historical texts produced in different cultures. Like the predecessors he criticized, Althusser generalized a particular concept of literature, that of the middle class. To escape this danger, Bennett suggests, the concept of literature and literary texts should be defined, in the Marxian sense, as a dialectical relationship between production and consumption: "For the process of the consumption of literary texts is necessarily that of their continuous *re-production*; that is, of their being produced as different objects for consumption." This argument leads Bennett to conclude that reading, or interpreting, involves more than appropriating an established text and casting new light on it: "The way in which the literary text is appropriated is determined not only by the operations of criticism upon it but also, and more radically, by the whole material, institutional, political and ideological context within which those operations are set."[48] This formulation moves in the direction of an institutional determination of literary consumption (whether appropriation, reading, or interpretation).

How can this institutional context be described more specifically? In his *Formalism and Marxism* (1979), Bennett offers a few suggestions, based primarily on the work of Etienne Balibar and Macherey. In his essay "Texts, Readers, Reading Formations" (1983), he tries with the help of linguistic theorems to formulate a theory of reading formation that no longer isolates the process of reading in a positivistic or phe-

---

[48]Tony Bennett, *Formalism and Marxism* (London, 1979), pp. 133, 135.

nomenological manner. The category of reading formation has two salient features. First, it brings the active role of reading and interpreting to the fore. That is, a critic does not discover one or more meanings or tensions in a text; rather, his or her reading imposes this meaning on the text. Second, it refers to the sociological and ideological context of any reading. More radically than Etienne Balibar and Macherey, Bennett destabilizes the literary text. In the framework of a reading formation, interpretation takes priority over the text: "Ultimately, there is no such thing as 'the text.' There is no pure text, no fixed and final form of the text which conceals a hidden truth which has but to be penetrated for criticism to retire, its task completed. There is no once-and-for-all, final truth about the text which criticism is forever in the process of acquiring. The text always and only exists in a variety of historically concrete forms."[49] The criteria for the adequacy of a reading can accordingly be derived only from its ideological and institutional context. In this respect, Bennett is obviously in agreement with Macherey and Etienne Balibar, but his emphasis is different. Like Renée Balibar, he assumes the concept of literature is determined by social institutions (for example, schools) that are directly or indirectly concerned with the production and treatment of texts. Thus the acts of reading and interpreting are also activities determined by social institutions (ideological apparatuses, in Althusser's language) and which in turn determine texts through appropriation and cultural preparation. Thus Bennett distinguishes between a university reading formation—that is, the strategies for treating a literary text practiced in universities—and a popular reading formation, which has to make do without such methodological strategies.

The soundness of this distinction needs to be examined more closely; it certainly cannot be generalized. Bennett's equation of popular reading with untutored reading for the purpose of contrasting it with tutored university reading presents two problems. For one, it is questionable whether there is such a thing as "untutored reading," since all reading ability is culturally acquired. Reading depends on schooling, albeit in various forms. For another, the distinction between tutored and untutored reading obscures the implicit class distinction. Tutored reading is not, as Bennett maintains, necessarily identifiable with middle-class reading, and untutored reading is not restricted to the proletariat. The lower middle class is also largely unschooled in literature—even in the twentieth century.

Although Bennett's classification may be problematic in its particulars, his concept of reading formation is unquestionably fruitful, partic-

---

[49]Ibid., p. 148.

ularly as a needed critique of reception aesthetics, which is restricted to the concept of the implied reader. A Marxian approach, in fact, cannot dispense with the *historical reader*. This category becomes productive, however, only if it simultaneously breaks with a substantialistic concept of the text (or work) and the recipient. Until this is done, the study of reception remains subordinate to the investigation of the text, and the text continues to be the point of orientation telling the literary scholar which interpretation is more appropriate. The reading would then have the same (reduced) status in relation to the text that in Saussure *parole* has in relation to *langue*. But as soon as the act of decoding takes precedence, it becomes necessary to establish a relationship between competing interpretations, which can no longer be measured by the "objectivity" of the text. "It is precisely such a dissolution," writes Bennett, "that I wish to recommend: *not* the dissolution of the 'text itself' into the million and one readings of individual subjects, however, but rather its dissolution into reading relations and, within those, reading formations that concretely and historically structure the interaction between texts and readers."[50] The relationship between reader and text is accordingly presented as the relationship between the culturally activated reader and the culturally activated text.

Bennett has not yet succeeded in explaining, however, exactly how a reading formation relates to a reading subject and to social institutions. Apparently, the concept of reading formation is systemically situated between reader and institution. Reading subjects are characterized by a particular reading formation; if they lack such a formation, they are totally incapable of decoding a text—and thus of finding any meaning in it. On the other hand, a formation is not something one lights upon; rather, it is the result of institutional practices. A reading formation can thus be understood as the product of practices, conventions, and standards imposed on authors, texts, and readers by an ideological apparatus. This definition would allow us to describe the reading formation of the *Gymnasium* or university. But in what context could we describe the popular reading formation? Bennett concedes that for the present he has little of a precise nature to say about this reading formation;[51] yet are we really so poorly informed? In the aftermath of Adorno and Horkheimer's description of the culture industry,[52] procedures were developed for analyzing the relationship between the ideological appa-

---

[50]Tony Bennett, "Texts, Readers, Reading Formations, *Bulletin of the Midwest Modern Language Association* 16 (1983), pt. 1, p. 12.
[51]Ibid., p. 16.
[52]Max Horkheimer and Theodor W. Adorno, *Dialektik der Aufklärung* (Frankfurt a. M., 1969); English translation by John Cumming as *Dialectic of Enlightenment* (New York, 1972).

ratus and models of reception. The concept of popular reading formation is nevertheless too unspecific for concrete historical analysis, for it
describes at least two different situations: on the one hand an older folk
culture, on the other a "mass culture" conditioned by capitalism for
which Horkheimer and Adorno introduced the concept of the culture
industry. Although we are relatively well informed about the older
popular reading formation, we have only the basic outlines of the reading formation of the culture industry. We need to investigate in detail
how they reacted to each other when they came in contact during the
nineteenth century.

. 2 .

The Public Sphere

The Significance of the Public Sphere

The bourgeois revolution of 1848–49 is rightly considered to be one of the decisive turning points in the history of Germany and continental Europe. The outcome of the revolution, which confirmed the predominance of conservative, legitimist power in both Prussia and Austria, created the framework for further change, not least for the unification of Germany. The *kleindeutsch* solution was the result of an alliance between Bismarck's monarchic state and a bourgeoisie bent on economic emancipation, who largely relinquished political power after 1866 and responded to the dualism of freedom and unification by favoring national unity. Within the context of this argument, the literature of the Nachmärz thus inevitably takes on a legitimizing function. The issue in question is whether literature was transformed from one oriented toward the concept of humanity to one formulating the special interests of the middle class. This assessment is no doubt justified for works using the political situation as a literary theme—in political poetry, for instance, which was in fact decisively molded by the political reaction after 1848.[1] Apart from this, however, we should bear in mind that the evident changes in literature cannot be linked solely to the failure of the revolution. The decisive changes in the literary public sphere must instead be viewed in a broader context, one taking into account the economic sphere—that is, the interdependence of economic and politi-

---

[1]See Peter Uwe Hohendahl, "Vom Nachmärz bis zur Reichsgründung," in Walter Hinderer, ed., *Geschichte der politischen Lyrik in Deutschland* (Stuttgart, 1978), pp. 210–31.

cal factors. The Industrial Revolution, which began in Germany in the 1840s but was not in full force until after 1850, had an equally strong, if not stronger, influence on the conditions of literary production and reception. In Germany the institution of literature changed no less between 1850 and 1870 than did society, although the decisive shift to an industrial mass culture still lay in the future. These changes are best understood if instead of just pointing out isolated, influential economic and political factors, we trace their transmission through the public sphere. The publicly grounded institution of literature is subject to indirect pressures exerted by political and economic issues on the public sphere. Traditional literary history, which is oriented toward authors, works, or genres, cannot contribute much to the solution of this problem, since it remains blind to the institutional character of literature and thus can comprehend diachronic processes only as isolated series of events.

The debate concerning the structural change in the public sphere essentially has been defined since 1962 by the theses of Jürgen Habermas.[2] Habermas's theory basically distinguishes three phases in the development of a bourgeois public sphere: (1) the early middle-class public sphere of the Enlightenment, exemplified in the theories of Rousseau and Kant; (2) the liberal capitalist public sphere of the first half of the nineteenth century, primarily marked by the dominance of parliaments as exemplified in English history; and (3) the late-capitalist public sphere that took shape in all Western industrial nations at the end of the nineteenth century and continues to determine their political and cultural life to the present day. The first two phases are not sharply differentiated by Habermas, because he assumes that the classic bourgeois public sphere was constituted in connection with, or occasioned by, capitalism. He sees a significant break between the second and third phase, which essentially coincided with the transition from liberal to organized capitalism. As soon as capitalism, in theory and practice, abandoned the free market and full competition—in other words, as soon as it became monopolistically organized and political in its attempts to intervene in society through the regulation of the state—the structure of the public sphere, according to Habermas, necessarily changed. An essential aspect of the classic public sphere was its strict separation of the areas of commodity trade and social labor from the state. The autonomy of middle-class society emerged as the result of an economic system in which competing interests were able to balance one another and consequently were not politicized. The inevitable conclu-

---

[2]Jürgen Habermas, *Strukturwandel der Offentlichkeit* (Neuwied a. Rh., 1962); the following quotations are from the second edition (Neuwied a. Rh., 1965).

sion is that the transition to organized capitalism in the late nineteenth century had to result in structural changes in the public sphere. In Germany, accordingly, we may assume the turning point was the economic crisis that began in 1873 and brought an end to the legitimacy of liberalism. Habermas thus argues: "But now, contrary to these expectations, incomplete competition and declining prices allowed social power to become concentrated in private hands. The fabric of vertical relationships between the collective unities became partly one of unilateral dependence, partly one of mutual pressure. The processes of concentration and crisis tore away the veil of the exchange of equivalent values [*Äquivalententausch*] from the antagonistic structure of society." Visible class antagonisms and conflicts henceforth changed the relationship between society and the state; the state was increasingly called on to arbitrate an equalization of power. This is the source of Habermas's central thesis: the change in the structure of the public sphere was brought about by a process in which, on the one hand, the state was increasingly drawn into the private social domain, and on the other, special economic and social interests became entrenched in the state: "This dialectic of a progressive nationalization of society and the simultaneous socialization of the state is what gradually destroyed the basis of the middle-class public sphere—the separation of state and society."[3] This thesis can be extended to literature in the following way: literature was affected by structural change in the public sphere inasmuch as it was traditionally associated with the middle-class public sphere of the private domain, namely, as a mutual understanding between citizens in their human relations. Conditions were ripe for state interference in the institution of literature in the form of a general cultural policy. This interference was fundamentally distinguishable from the censorship politics of the semiabsolutist states of the Vormärz, which resisted the constitution of a public sphere. One can speak of a cultural policy only when the state began to exploit the apparatus of literature in order to resolve pressing social or political conflicts on a cultural level. Such a constitutive cultural policy is not ascertainable for advanced capitalistic states before 1870. It went beyond the capacity of state government, which to a large extent regulated the organs of education and thereby exerted an influence on literature, but otherwise had to be content with a politically motivated press policy.

If we accept Habermas's theory, then the epochal change did not occur until about 1870, and the Revolution of 1848 did not leave any profound traces because the development between 1850 and 1870 took place under liberal competition capitalism, even though it deviated in

[3]Ibid., pp. 160, 158.

some respects (for example, in the importance of banks) from the English pattern. Yet changes in both the political and the literary realm were too numerous and too significant to be passed off as merely peripheral occurrences. The problem of structural change must thus be reformulated so that the historical validity of Habermas's model can be tested. The first thing that becomes apparent is that Habermas does not always follow the orthodox line, that the structure of the public sphere changed in connection with the rise of monopoly capitalism. When he discusses Alexis de Tocqueville's and John Stuart Mill's concept of the public sphere, we find that the crisis in the middle-class public sphere does not coincide with the crisis in liberal capitalism. Tocqueville's observations on the structure of American democracy, which led him to a new, skeptical assessment of the public sphere, undoubtedly refer to a competitive capitalist society, not to the phase of organized capitalism. The same can be said of Mill's analyses; they, too, are based on conditions marked by free competition. These examples show that the crisis in the liberal middle-class public sphere became apparent before the outlines of the new structure of advanced capitalism were defined. Habermas's view was perhaps influenced by the peculiarity of German history. Since industrial capitalism became established in Germany only after 1850 and by 1873 had already precipitated a fundamental crisis, the crises in the middle-class public sphere and in liberal capitalism occurred so close in time as to be regarded as identical.

As early as 1973 Wolfgang Jäger pointed out in his critique that Habermas's model of the classic public sphere is not applicable to conditions in England in the nineteenth century because it is too closely based on the situation in continental Europe, especially in Germany.[4] Before we examine this contention, let us consider the significance of English history for the theory of the public sphere. Habermas describes English conditions in the early nineteenth century as the model for the development of a political middle-class public sphere. Parliament had been transformed into an "organ of public opinion." He thus accepts the liberal interpretation of English parliamentarianism which is found in Richard Crossman's introduction to Bagehot's *English Constitution* (1963). Jäger maintains that the true situation does not correspond to this harmonizing picture. Economic interests strongly influenced the structure of public opinion in the epoch between the great electoral reforms of 1832 and 1867. The example of the railway association demonstrates that English capitalism used Parliament (that is, the public sphere) to promote its interests. If one of the constitutive elements of the model of the classic public sphere is that private interests cannot be

---

[4]Wolfgang Jäger, *Öffentlichkeit und Parlamentarismus* (Stuttgart, 1973).

taken into account in public deliberations, then it is in fact questionable whether England can serve as the classic example. One can say, rather, that the crisis in the public sphere, which Habermas relates to the rise of monopoly capitalism, had already begun there before 1850; for social as well as economic conflicts were brought into the public realm. The masses, who still had no right to vote, remained a constant problem, which was solved only after 1867.

Habermas's model is more relevant to early German liberalism than to the English situation. Jäger, however, does not draw the necessary conclusions from this justifiable criticism. The economic basis for Habermas's model is a society of small commodity producers exchanging their wares in a free market. Classic economics describes this market, in which supply and demand are equalized over the long term and the competing owners of commodities are not allowed to gain power over each other. Thus Habermas can conceive of the market as free of political domination: "The produced goods and the producing work forces qualify equally as commodities. Since this condition is satisfied only if every seller produces his own wares—or conversely if every worker possesses the means of production—the second requirement amounts to a sociological one: to the model of a society of small commodity producers."[5] Although Habermas at this point rigorously defines both the economic and the social conditions of the classic public sphere, he ignores the contradiction between these precapitalistic conditions and the competition capitalism of the nineteenth century, in which the majority of workers no longer possessed the means of production. By adopting Max Weber's emphasis on rationalism as the essential characteristic of capitalism and taking as a criterion the sure calculability of relationships, Habermas can extend his early middle-class model into the phase of industrialized capitalism without making the fundamental differences apparent.

In analyzing German developments between 1850 and 1870, Habermas's model of the middle-class public sphere deserves a more precise historical basis than it now has. In particular, the boundary between the early middle-class public sphere and the phase of mature liberalism needs to be more precisely defined. This distinction is basically equivalent to the difference between the liberal theory of the Vormärz and the concept prevailing in the Nachmärz. Since institutionalization of the political public sphere extended in the German states up to 1848 and the constitutional foundation was partly the result of the 1848 revolution, German conditions were different from those in Western Europe. In a primarily agrarian and industrially underdeveloped country such as

---

[5]Habermas, *Strukturwandel*, p. 99.

Germany—which, nevertheless, had an advanced educational system—political theory could continue for the most part to follow the principles of the prerevolutionary Enlightenment (that is, the concepts of Rousseau and Kant) without conflicting with social reality. More precisely, because before 1850 Germany was only a conditionally capitalistic society, in which the dominant middle-class element was made up of professors, jurists, theologians, and officials rather than manufacturers and merchants, a middle-class public sphere based on precapitalistic conditions could endure longer there than in England or France, where Parliament had taken on the function of representing classes. As Lothar Gall has rightly pointed out, early liberal theory in Germany between the time of Wilhelm von Humboldt and Georg Gottfried Gervinus is intentionally not capitalistic.[6] Although it incorporates elements of their doctrine of free trade, these elements are not central to the concept of society. Manchesterism is on the whole, rather, an aspect of Nachmärz liberalism, which formulated and legitimized middle-class interests with much greater clarity. Early liberal theory was in any case only conditionally useful to the commercial middle class, because it presupposed the existence of a society of independent producers. Although it was formulated by intellectuals, the theory remained primarily a petit-bourgeois doctrine tailored to workers and craftspersons. Early liberalism—even its radical democratic and socialistic variations—was based on values that could no longer be realized once capital became concentrated and the majority of workers no longer possessed the means of production. The founders of economic liberalism, such as Adam Smith, were not advocates and theorists of capitalism. Hans Medick rightly cautions us not to consider Smith an advocate of industrial capitalism: "Instead of promulgating unlimited self-interest, he called for restraint . . . and the structuring of social relations according to the standard of universal brotherhood. Nothing would be more inappropriate than to consider Smith a simple utilitarian and describe his conception of mankind as a pure doctrine of 'economic man.' "[7] A society united through fair exchange may have division of labor, but it is built on equality. The thrust of this argument was directed against the absolutist state and feudal privilege; but when those privileges appeared to be based on economic rather than political factors, the theory became narrow-minded. Yet as long as the relationship between the leading social groups—especially landowners, the capital-

---

[6]See Lothar Gall, "Liberalismus und 'bürgerliche Gesellschaft.' Zu Charakter und Entwicklung der liberalen Bewegung in Deutschland," in his *Liberalismus* (Cologne, 1976), pp. 162–86.

[7]Hans Medick, *Naturzustand und Naturgeschichte der bürgerlichen Gesellschaft* (Göttingen, 1973), p. 222.

ist middle class, and the workers—seemed harmonious, liberalism could adhere to the theory of the public sphere, which drew a sharp distinction, on the one hand, between the state and the private domain and, on the other, between the political and economic spheres.

Early German liberalism arose in opposition to the monarchic, bureaucratic institutional state, which it found a constant irritation. The government was often prepared to modernize, but only within the framework of a political system determined by the state itself. Even if the interests of the liberal middle class partly coincided with those of the state, state interference was rejected in principle as guardianship. In his attempt to redefine the concept of political liberalism and to distinguish it from state reform movements on one side and the Manchester theory on the other, Gall discusses the prerequisites for liberal theory: "The point of departure for all sociopolitical concepts of the political Enlightenment and early liberalism, as well as the basis for their vehement criticism of the existing social order and its economic and political system, was the idea of a 'natural,' given social order, harmoniously prestabilized in some mysterious way by the complementary needs and abilities of its members." This theory did not serve the haute bourgeoisie but aimed at a utopian, classless bourgeois society opposed to existing conditions. Gall emphasizes that early German liberalism, even when it was radical, was on the whole far more conservative than is generally assumed. Early liberal theory operated according to a concept of order which still largely had recourse to the old European society. To what degree earlier-held concepts were still at work in early liberalism and were incorporated into the rigorous theory of egalitarian middle-class society has no bearing on this study. Indeed, the idea of a natural order, which Gall also emphasizes, is more symptomatic of classical economies. In any case, German theory was not prepared for the social conflicts that sprang from capitalism. Thus Switzerland more than England was seen as the guiding model.[8] Inasmuch as actual social and economic developments after 1850 did not corroborate this theory, its proponents were faced with a fundamental decision. They could insist on the correctness of the theory and accordingly call social developments into question; they could opportunistically support the tendency toward a class society; or they could reconfirm liberal theory revisionistically.

The role Parliament played also shows how different the continental European variant of political liberalism was from the English version. In form and grounding, Vormärz German parliamentarianism was the result of the political theory of the Enlightenment, not the product of

---

[8]Gall, "Liberalismus," pp. 165, 173.

historical struggles. Far more than in England, the parliaments of the southwest German states were conceived as organs of public opinion. Parliament, Karl Theodor Welcker taught, protects the rights of the people in relation to government.[9] Government and Parliament, the state and the public sphere, must therefore be strictly separated; if Parliament were combined with government, Welcker concluded, the function of parliamentary control would be restricted.

Where the position of early German liberalism was strictly developed, Parliament was considered an organ of the public sphere, not a partner of government. This controversial opinion was primarily held by those who expected the state, above all, to modernize society. They were therefore also antagonistic to the notion of parties tied to interest groups, since the common will, not special interests, was supposed to be the determining factor in the political reasoning (*Räsonnement*) of Parliament. This absolute opposition of state and public sphere left no real room for constitutional monarchy, in which the rights of the crown and of Parliament were held in balance, for if public *Räsonnement* were adopted strictly, monarchy would in the final analysis have to be regarded as a historically, but not a morally, legitimized form of rule. But all pragmatic reflection necessarily leads to a revision of this dogmatic position, as the example of Welcker illustrates, because revolution was not in the interest of moderate liberalism. At the same time, however, we see here the beginning of the dissolution of the classic public sphere, because the participation of the parties in government obliterates the strict separation of state and public sphere. This is precisely the tendency one observes after 1848, namely, in the attempt to protect political emancipation and personal economic interests during the phase of liberalization.

The Importance of the Suffrage Issue

The model of the classic public sphere assumes that every citizen takes part in the process of *Räsonnement*. The citizen body consists of the community of male heads of families—as in Kant, women, children, and dependent persons such as servants and workers are still excluded. This was not a central problem for the chambers of Parliament in the Vormärz, because the political participation of the masses was not an acute issue in the traditional social structure of Germany. The situation

[9]See Lothar Gall, "Das Problem der parlamentarischen Opposition im deutschen Frühliberalismus," in G. A. Ritter, ed., *Deutsche Parteien vor 1918* (Cologne, 1973), pp. 192–207, esp. p. 195.

changed during the 1840s due to social upheaval and the pauperization of a large segment of the lower middle class, as well as to the rise of radical democratic and socialistic movements that broke away from the liberal concept of social order. Pressure developing from below made itself clearly felt during the Revolution of 1848. This pressure was expressed in the debate over suffrage, during which the classic model of the public sphere came under scrutiny. The result was that the liberals cautiously abandoned the logical exposition of their own theory. Contrary to the general assertion of the time that the Frankfurt Parliament of 1848 was chosen in a free, general election, Theodore S. Hamerow rightly concludes that such was not the case. Indirect forms of election that worked to the advantage of the middle levels of society were preferred: "It is a fact that elections for the Frankfurt Parliament were not conducted according to the principle of indirect election, no matter what middle-class politicians might have alleged after the event. For this principle was in direct opposition to practical experience as well as to the political theory of the liberals." In accordance with the stipulations of the Preliminary Parliament (*Vorparlament*), only those who were independent—that is, not in the service of someone else—were allowed to vote. This stipulation was then used by the states as a justification for sharply restricting the number of legal voters, which benefited the landholders. Laborers and journeymen were discouraged by government measures and liberal propaganda from taking part in elections. According to Hamerow's calculations, their participation was generally below 20 percent and sometimes as low as 2 percent.[10]

Under the guidance of moderate liberals such as Friedrich Dahlmann, and contrary to the views of the left, the constitutional committees of the Frankfurt Parliament also supported the opinion of the *Vorparlament* that economic independence was required for suffrage. That this would result in the exclusion of half of all potential voters was more pleasing than not to the middle class. Still, this response was obviously no longer the logical consequence of early liberal theory but a strategy intended to keep social conflicts out of Parliament. In the words of one member of Parliament, Lassaux, it would be like "making the goat the gardener if one allowed the propertyless to decide on the purse of the propertied."[11] Similarly, in the suffrage debate of 1849, the liberals of the center and right supported the position that the introduction of

---

[10]See Theodore S. Hamerow, "Die Wahlen zum Frankfurter Parlament," in Ernst-Wolfgang Böckenförde, ed., *Moderne deutsche Verfassungsgeschichte (1815–1918)* (Cologne, 1972), pp. 217, 229–31.

[11]Quoted in Jacques Droz, "Liberale Anschauungen zur Wahlrechtsfrage und das preussische Dreiklassenwahlrecht," in Böckenförde, *Moderne deutsche Verfassungsgeschichte*, p. 203.

general, equal suffrage without qualification would deliver the state over to the rabble or, in the hands of a clever, unscrupulous politician, could give rise to a new absolutism. Welcker proposed a limited right to vote in the name of freedom, and F. E. Scheller, a member of the Casino party, opposed general suffrage with the argument that it would play into the hands of the conservatives. That this fear was not unfounded, that liberalism could in fact not count on the support of the rural masses, was later demonstrated by the policies of Bismarck and the conservatives. Like Western European liberalism, German liberalism avoided the consequences of its program when social conflicts that had not been foreseen in liberal doctrine arose between the middle class and the masses. Heinrich von Gagern's opposition to the view that the middle class wanted to perpetuate the underprivileged status of the proletariat must be viewed in this light. The category of class antagonism contradicted the fundamental liberal concepts of harmony. Consequently, Gagern resisted the strategy of the left, which tried to intensify opposition to the point of conflict.[12] Since the model of the classic public sphere assigned economic issues exclusively to the private sector, in 1849 the liberals were more prepared to modify the scope of the public sphere than to deal in Parliament with problematic social conflicts as if they were political factors. Gagern wanted it understood that the middle class was prepared to solve social problems; but he insisted that this occur on a societal level—just as afterward socially engaged liberalism repeatedly emphasized that the social question was economic and therefore could not be solved by political means.

The political shift could be justified if suffrage was stricken from the list of basic political rights; that is, if its connection with natural right was severed and it was instead considered a historical right. Thus Rudolf Haym favored a "class" solution, and Friedrich Daniel Bassermann recommended differentiating the right to vote by means of a census as the only way in which a calming influence could be exerted on the workers. On the whole, however, those who advocated and pushed through an equal voting rights statute still predominated in the Frankfurt Parliament. Yet even during the revolutionary years the liberal camp included forces that, because they feared a destabilization of society, deliberately aimed to restrict the principle of a general public sphere by means of a modified right to vote. The contradictions in the liberal model came to light even before the Industrial Revolution began in Germany and, along with them, the first attempts to prevent their consequences. These could be made in good conscience, because the classes were not yet definitively divided, so that the demands of the

[12]Ibid., p. 204.

proletariat remained concealed behind the image of an untamed multi-tude that would jeopardize the recently won freedom of the middle class.

Industrialization and the Public Sphere

What the Revolution of 1848 foreshadowed became a structural real-ity between 1850 and 1870 as a result of industrialization. The change could no longer be reversed, and in the long run it sealed the fate of liberalism. Industrialization—whose technological aspect need not be considered here—gradually led to the separation of the industrial pro-letariat into a distinct class and, even at this point, to a clearer separa-tion between the old middle class and the economic haute bourgeoisie. These societal shifts were clearly reflected in the theory of the public sphere. Liberalism strove for a systematic theoretical reformulation through which the category of a class-bound public sphere would be introduced. At the same time, we find the beginnings of a proletarian theory of the public sphere, although in some respects it was still bound to traditional concepts. We will trace this process of separation, begin-ning with the decisive consequences of industrialization for the trans-formation of public opinion.

According to traditional liberal historiography—to which the Marx-ist historiography of the German Democratic Republic (GDR) also par-tially adheres—after 1849 the German middle class renounced the achievement of political emancipation in the form of a liberal democrat-ic state, in favor of an economic buildup made possible through rapid industrialization. The result was an alliance between the old political elite—for example, the Prussian Junkers—and the middle class, an alliance that forced Germany out of the mainstream of European devel-opment. According to Helmut Böhme, as soon as the middle class saw its most pressing demands fulfilled, it turned away from the revolution and became more conservative: "Thus political conditions in Germany after 1848 were marked by a renewed coalition of old and new forces, which was determined by a division of labor, as it were, between the nobility, the landowners, and the middle class; economic leaders ac-knowledged the aristocracy, landownership, and bureaucracy as the traditional stratum of political leadership, and these in turn allowed entrepreneurs to function and at the same time tried to provide for the rural and professional middle class, which was threatened by industry." For Böhme, industrialization resulted in the sanctioning of conservative political leadership, which diverted middle-class demands for power to the economic realm. Because administrative efforts at reform continued and reactionary measures in domestic policy were combined with liberal economic policy, the middle class could regard national Prussian policy as advantageous to its interests. Thus, Böhme maintains, German liberalism exerted an exclusively economic force: "No really liberal policy resulted from the concentration of middle-class power on industrial progress, natural science, and technology. Rather, the traditional rights of agrarian leadership were preserved, and despite all the entrepreneurial achievements, industrial transformation remained bound to the interests of large-scale agriculture."[13] Böhme concluded from this analysis that the Industrial Revolution never really gave rise to a capitalist order in Germany and that accordingly the people were still denied political self-determination. The feudalization thesis meshes readily with this point of view. The unbroken might of feudal and monarchic powers forced the German bourgeoisie to adjust to the ideology and way of life of the old elite. According to Böhme, liberal politicians, who were thinking principally of the economic interests of their own class, allied themselves with Bismarck and the North German Confederation in order to achieve political freedom through national unity.

In his history of the German empire, Hans-Ulrich Wehler also assumes that the defeat of the middle class in the Revolution of 1848 confirmed the political and social leadership of the landed nobility, and the political impotence of the middle class was sealed by Bismarck's victory in the constitutional conflict of 1866.[14] Wehler considers 1866 the decisive turning point in German history. In the constitutional conflict, liberal parliamentarianism was frustrated by the late-absolutist military state. Wehler regards the confrontation between Bismarck and Parliament as the principal event that established the division of power between the middle class and the old elite for the next sixty years. By presenting the constitutional conflict as a confrontation with fundamental consequences, he makes the conciliation of the liberals following Bismarck's successful foreign policy against Austria seem like a moral collapse that prevented the liberalization of Germany for two generations. "A solution [to the constitutional question] was postponed for almost 60 years. This tactically excellent maneuver represented, therefore, a barely veiled victory for the old regime. The nucleus of the authoritarian state in which the military enjoyed autonomy remained essentially intact."[15] The emphasis here is on the defeat of the middle

[13]Helmut Böhme, *Prolegomena zu einer Sozial- und Wirtschaftsgeschichte Deutschlands im 19. und 20. Jahrhundert*, 4th ed. (Frankfurt a. M., 1972), pp. 43–44, 51–52.
[14]Hans-Ulrich Wehler, *The German Empire, 1871–1918*, trans. Kim Traynor (Dover, N.H., 1985), pp. 21–22.
[15]Ibid., p. 25.

class, but Böhme and Wehler are essentially in agreement: the middle class proved too weak to hold out politically against the bureaucratic state and the nobility; consequently, the Industrial Revolution had no lasting effect on the political system. Missing from this argument is the thrust of democratization, which might have led to a different development. Ralf Dahrendorf gave the most trenchant formulation of this thesis when he wrote that in Germany industrialization swallowed up liberal principle instead of developing it.[16] This position tacitly assumes that capitalistic industrialization necessarily leads to the liberalization and democratization of the political system. It defends capitalistic industrialization, which, if it had been properly utilized, would have led to a modern liberal society. The flawed development is thus attributed to the failure of the German middle class. The historiography of the GDR arrives at a similar conclusion when, in agreement with Marx and Engels, it blames the subsequent catastrophe on the betrayal of the German bourgeoisie.[17] In both positions the historical process is derived from class consciousness.

Unlike the above-mentioned interpretations, Annette Leppert-Fögen and Michael Gugel attempt to show that the ideological changes were the result of the process of capitalization itself.[18] It is not their intention to trace the hindrance of liberalism by conservative forces but rather to understand the connection between the change in liberalism and industrialization. From this perspective, the defeat, or compromise, of the middle class, takes on new significance; it proves to be the inevitable result of middle-class interests. Leppert-Fögen emphasizes the division of the middle class into the bourgeoisie and petite bourgeoisie, the latter in turn becoming more sharply differentiated from the proletarian element after 1850. Because of this process of social differentiation, which brought contrasts and conflicts increasingly to view, middle-class liberalism became obsolete between 1850 and 1870. Put more precisely, over the course of the Industrial Revolution the middle class—that is, the petite bourgeoisie—accepted liberalism as its ideology, whereas the haute bourgeoisie abandoned liberalism and in the sixties the proletariat became independent and cast off liberalism's ideological tutelage. Leppert-Fögen refers to the social goals that brightened the liberal program, but she does not identify them more precisely, putting the empha-

---

[16]Ralf Dahrendorf, *Society and Democracy in Germany* (New York, 1969), pp. 39–40, 51.

[17]See *Geschichte der deutschen Literatur*, vol. 8, pt. 1, ed. Kurt Böttcher (Berlin, GDR, 1975).

[18]Annette Leppert-Fögen, *Die deklassierte Klasse* (Frankfurt a. M., 1974); and Michael Gugel, *Industrieller Aufstieg und bürgerliche Herrschaft* (Cologne, 1975).

sis instead on petit-bourgeois interests that led these groups to desert liberalism (and support Bismarck). As a result, the position taken by the Progressive party in the constitutional conflict remains unexplained. This party by no means only criticized the authoritarian military state; it also represented certain economic and social interests. The weakness of the thesis lies in its lack of historical concreteness; it too hastily describes the liberalism of the Nachmärz as merely petit-bourgeois and thereby loses sight of the process of transformation that became evident in the constitutional conflict. In particular, we should look more closely at the bond between the middle-class intelligentsia, which assumed ideological and strategic leadership in Parliament, and the economic middle class, whose interests were at stake. The prominent role played in the parliaments by the liberal intelligentsia precludes the conclusion that the economic elite was apolitical and unconcerned about the success of its goals. The intelligentsia still largely articulated the demands of the middle class in this epoch, not least in the delicate matter of defining the class's lower limits. It resorted to the arsenal of classic liberal theory in its reaction to the decidedly changed social situation— with the result that it eliminated some of the central premises of continental European liberalism.

The antagonism between a policy of national modernization and one of liberalization became especially acute in Prussia. Even though Prussia's position in foreign affairs was weaker than Austria's after 1850, the northern state controlled the larger economic scene and was generally very successful in instituting economic policy to further its political goals. Böhme in particular has shown how effective Prussian commercial policy was in eliminating Austrian competition and bringing about the *kleindeutsch* Prussian solution. This policy should not, however, be regarded simply as a means of manipulating the German middle class. We must also ask to what degree Prussian economic policy was supported and advanced by capitalist forces because it accorded with their interests. Böhme, too, emphasized that the Austrian initiative under the leadership of Johann B. von Rechberg, who sought to take advantage of the difficulties encountered by the Prussian government during the constitutional conflict, was bound to fail because the liberal opposition, which opposed the budget proposed for the army, was on the whole behind the government on economic issues. Thus Böhme concluded that "the Prussia of 1862, with Bismarck as prime minister, concurred with the material interests of Bismarck's commercial policy, once his consistent pursuit of that policy became clear, and the Landtag was able to bring about the shift to a 'new era' because Bismarck's economic policies were carried out in close accord with the front of free-trade interests forged by Delbrück among agriculture, trade, mobile capital, and the export industry."[19] Bismarck was successful in October 1862 because he resolutely pursued Prussia's economic policy and thereby won over an important segment of the middle class, whose interests were represented by this policy. Both the German Board of Trade (Handelstag) and the Congress of German Economists (Kongress deutscher Volkswirte) supported Prussian economic policy, which aimed at an agreement with France that would open a door to the West and end Austria's predominance.

It is clear that Bismarck exploited the dynamics of rapid industrialization and economic expansion in order to establish a social and political order corresponding, or at least not conflicting, with the interests of the landed nobility. The situation was more complex for the liberals, since the ideas central to their political concept could not be represented in the Prussian government—that is, in one led by Bismarck. In contrast to the early liberals, those of the new era (1858–62) deliberately focused on the practical questions that emerged and avoided the fundamental arguments that had characterized classic liberalism. Thus, in his *Woran uns gelegen ist* (1859), Carl Twesten advocated a temperate policy that would refrain as much as possible from engaging in theoretical disputes and confrontations over constitutional questions. From the start, resolute liberals "faced the facts"; they, too, accepted the basis of the imposed constitution. They were not interested in reviving the issues of 1848. On the other hand, among the concrete issues on which the liberals wished to focus was the relationship of the economy to national policy. Here we see a significant difference in comparison to early liberalism: at the center of discussion was no longer the formerly postulated separation of state and society but rather a cooperative effort to achieve maximal economic expansion. This included the abolition of state controls hindering economic development but also, despite a basic commitment to free trade, the demand that the state act as a regulatory force. The Progressive party was in no sense opposed to the state, as one might conclude from its position in the constitutional conflict. To complete the process of capitalization, it called on the state to create the requisite conditions by setting a national standard in the marketplace. In the Nachmärz, liberalism used its theory and political position as an instrument; its horizon of expectations differed significantly from that of the Vormärz. What now mattered was "the power of the state to support national economic interests in foreign markets," where the German economy often found itself at a disadvantage compared to the representatives of other nations, because it lacked political and military sup-

[19]Helmut Böhme, *Deutschlands Weg zur Grossmacht* (Cologne, 1966), p. 117.

port. Characteristically, the nationalism of the Progressive party was no longer based on national self-determination but on the European constellation of power and Germany's position in it. The wary and timid policy of the conservatives was distasteful to the liberals. Instead of thinking legitimistically, they thought in terms of power politics within the framework of a constitutional solution. There was an "instrumentalization of the liberal desire for reform, aimed at achieving the goals of national and political power." Says Gugel: "Domestic political demands were not primarily concerned with reversing the counterrevolution of the 1850s, with winning back what had been lost in 1849. Nor was the intention somehow to trigger a democratization of society. Rather, the liberal demands gained their true legitimacy through the rationale of expediency and their application to questions of primary national importance, or through proof that they were useful in the development of the national economy."[20] This point of view deviates from the prevailing opinion in that it questions the emancipatory intentions of the liberals, so that the constitutional conflict loses its essential significance.

We shall return to this question, but first let us consider the relationship between state and society as the Progressive party conceived it. In their demands for political co-determination, the liberals no longer relied on basic natural principles but, rather, on the logical development of existing historical conditions. Thus, in a speech delivered at the Prussian Landtag in 1862, Twesten argued that a contradiction was created by the discrepancy between the representation of the landed nobility in the upper chamber of Parliament and its actual power: "All real power in the state, apart from the power of government, depends exclusively on number and wealth. But wealth is no longer solely in the hands of property owners; it is found in a variety of circles, and the predominance given to the landowners in the upper chamber is not in accord with actual circumstances. The upper chamber can thus be described as an anachronism under contemporary Prussian conditions."[21] The state is no longer regarded as a threat to middle-class society but as the guarantor of social order, for it stands above the contending parties as executor of the law. Influenced perhaps by Hegel's philosophy of the state, the liberals do not give equal rank to the various social forces. On the other hand, they give the state a central function in the management of society, thereby clearly diminishing the importance of the public sphere as the final authority of political control. Whereas classic liberalism proceeded from the sovereignty of the citizenry, according to the

[20]Gugel, *Industrieller Aufstieg*, pp. 67, 70.
[21]June 6, 1862; quoted in ibid., p. 80.

liberalism of the sixties, the state was a primary force that not only had to be reckoned with but, even more, deserved to be dignified as an institution in its own right because it integrated the divergent interests of society. The liberals of the new era did not want direct intervention; yet here we find the stage set for an intersection of state and society, both on an ideological and on a practical level.

The Conception of Public Opinion in the Nachmärz

Even before postrevolutionary liberalism was reshaped in the new era and resumed its confrontation with the conservative powers, an attempt had been made after the failure of the revolution to reformulate the goals of political liberalism, particularly in the debate with classic liberal theory. The first part of Ludwig August von Rochau's *Grundsätzen der Realpolitik* (Principles of Political Realism), which initiated the revision of classic German liberalism, appeared in 1853. Rochau regarded this revision as a necessary self-criticism of liberal doctrine which he felt obliged to undertake. During the revolutionary years he had returned from exile in France and had offered his services as a writer to the liberal center while strongly attacking both the right and the left. As the editor of the *Constitutionelle Zeitung*, he was expelled from Berlin once the reactionary forces in Prussia were again firmly in control. Unlike other exiles, however, he remained in touch with the German situation, and with *Grundsätzen* took a decisive part in the political debate. Rochau's book was regarded as an important contribution to this debate. Heinrich von Treitschke, who at the time was still considered a radical liberal, remarked that he "knew of no book that destroyed preconceived illusions with a more cutting logic."[22]

Rochau's plea for a policy oriented toward the realities of power politics rather than abstract principles was above all an attempt to find the key to the defeat of 1849. For this reason, it is reasonable to begin with his discussion of the contending parties in the Frankfurt Parliament and to analyze his conclusions, which are presented as natural political laws, against this background. At bottom, his reaction was no less ideological than the liberalism he had forsworn; yet it included some aspects of reality that classic liberalism had screened out. Rochau's sympathies were undoubtedly not with the conservatives. He did not find it difficult to expose the fundamental contradiction of all conservative ideologies: in order to defend the status quo against liberal

---

[22]Quoted in Hans-Ulrich Wehler's introduction to Ludwig August von Rochau, *Grundsätze der Realpolitik* (Frankfurt a. M., 1972), p. 9.

and democratic theories, conservatives had to develop their own ideas and concepts. Consequently, he ended up in the very camp he was fighting against—idealism. Once the actual circumstances had changed, concepts such as authority could not restore them. Rochau reacted against the use of state power to enforce such authority by once again advancing the classic argument of early liberalism: "With the help of a good police force it may be possible to manipulate the citizenry like puppets, but the right to express criticism, which is the opposite of authority, cannot be taken away from them." At this point Rochau, in the tradition of the Enlightenment, takes it for granted that *Räsonnement* will eventually prevail in bourgeois society, so that in the final analysis human progress will not be impeded. As a liberal he had faith in the enlightened state, which does not rely on authority or material force but is able to make its precepts judicious through reason: "Respect for justice and law and those who serve them, which is indispensable to a state, can today only result from a free and reasonable conviction, from a conviction that in their origin and content, justice and law will answer public need, and that in the administration of justice and law, the authorities will do their duty."[23]

Rochau's limits on the right correspond to his limits on the left with respect to democratic and socialist forces. The Democratic party, which in the Frankfurt Parliament consistently supported liberalism, became entangled, in Rochau's view, in a fundamental contradiction: it believed in "the independent power of ideas and principles," in the efficacy of popular sovereignty, the public sphere, the general will of the people, and majority rule; but it could never muster enough strength to carry out these ideas. For Rochau, this contradiction was manifest in the democrats' application of the principle of the popular vote to further the interests of their party: "The character of the National Assembly, elected by universal suffrage, could be impugned by any party, only not by those calling themselves democrats. With the National Assembly, the Democratic party denied its own principles and itself." This formal construction readily lends itself to the objection that the National Assembly was in fact not the result of a direct, universal vote—that the middle class had the advantage, due to the method of voting—but this does not affect the substance of Rochau's argument. He did not regard himself as an apologist for the bourgeoisie, which in his view did not exist in Germany, but rather as a spokesman for the middle levels of society (*Mittelstand*), the educated and enlightened middle class (*Bürgertum*): "One can point to few improvements in public conditions which have not been brought about with the eager help of the *Mittel-*

---

[23]Rochau, *Grundsätze*, pp. 122–23.

stand." Rochau accused the Democratic party of a lack of realism when it denounced this educated middle class as bourgeois and sought to exclude it from political participation: "Politics cannot with impunity disdain the middle class as if it were an appendage to a doctrine; it cannot dispense with it in an emergency and leave it to its own devices, as it could for instance the peasant class; it cannot extirpate it, as it could perhaps an aristocracy. It has to *come to terms* with it." Rochau uses classic liberal theorems and applies them; however, when he deals with the conservative forces and the state, he reverses the relationship between doctrine and class affiliation. Whereas early liberalism wanted with the help of theory, to develop a free middle-class society, for Rochau liberalism was already the Weltanschauung of the *Mittelstand.* Even the arrival of the proletariat changed little in Rochau's notion of this relationship, because he viewed it as a simple addition to the *Mittelstand*: "Instead of recognizing the proletariat merely as an *addition* to the *Mittelstand*; instead of merely borrowing from the proletariat those strengths in which it was superior to the *Mittelstand*—boldness, courage, and capacity for sacrifice—one thought that with the help of the proletariat the *Mittelstand* could be dispensed with."[24] With surprising candor, Rochau pointed out that only economic, not political, arguments could deflect the middle class from a democratic point of view. But in this he contradicted himself, since he had shortly before maintained that the German middle class, unlike the French, was not an economic class but a status group characterized by its education. As Rochau clearly recognized, the economic interests of the middle class contradicted a radical interpretation of basic liberal principles.

That Rochau was here not only an analytical observer but at the same time was adhering to a position—one, incidentally, which points ahead to the liberalism of the new era—is made clear by his discussion of socialism. Rochau is not opposed to social reforms as long as they are undertaken by the state on a social and economic level. But he protests vehemently against the politicization of the social question to which socialism was committed. For Rochau, proprietary rights remain the clear limits of all social measures, limits that he sees as moral, political, and economic. On the strength of his experiences in France, he speaks out against state intervention in the economy, because he is convinced that in the long run the productive forces created by capitalism will solve the social problem: "Again, the great tool of social reform that German national policy has at its disposal is the freedom of the economic movement. It gives the greatest possible latitude to the spirit of

[24]Ibid., pp. 138, 139, 141, 143.

association."[25] In complete accord with liberal tradition, the public and private spheres are separated; existing social problems, whose presence is not denied, are removed from the political sphere, either by being left to themselves or by being left to the national government—whereby they were nevertheless politicized indirectly. Rochau's indecision, his vacillation between demands for a strong state and an independent economy, illustrates the transitional character of his work.

But Rochau's apology for the *Mittelstand* does not exclude criticism of its political theory; and it is precisely this criticism that made his book important for postrevolutionary liberalism. The moderate liberalism that preceded the revolution perceived constitutional monarchy as the fulfillment of its political demands—control of the state by a parliament in which the public sphere could become established. This construction was derived from contract theory (*Vertragstheorie*). By bringing a historical and political point of view to bear on this abstract theory, Rochau came to a different conclusion in his discussion of the Constitutional party. To him, constitutional monarchy is a historical compromise reflecting the position of the contending parties. In a decisive break with concepts of natural law, Rochau describes the confrontation between the crown and Parliament as a pure power struggle devoid of rational deliberation: "Political power recognizes no boundary other than another power, and between incompatible powers a war of extermination is a necessity that no *Räsonnement* can prevent." The inner fragility of constitutionalism as a political theory is due, according to Rochau, to the impossibility of guaranteeing a balance between monarch and citizens. If a monarch has sufficient strength, he can abolish the government at any time; but if the people are stronger than the monarch, the monarch will essentially be superfluous. Thus Rochau concludes: "Constitutionalism, consequently, has not worked out well in practice in the prevailing German political system, and only deliberate self-deception can hide the fact that there is no foundation for it within the present German power structure."[26] Rochau wrote at a time when the Prussian constitution was on paper but, due to the muzzling of the liberal powers, was not inhibiting the conservative forces in the slightest. What consequences did Rochau draw from this observation? His argument is historical and grants constitutionalism the role of a preparatory force. Its function, however, cannot go beyond this, because in its pursuit of liberal principles it would have to abolish the monarchy. Without saying so directly, Rochau is using the principle of

[25]Ibid., p. 151.
[26]Ibid., pp. 125, 127.

popular sovereignty as a standard of judgment; he points out the inconsistency of constitutional monarchy, yet does not draw the expected
conclusion that liberalism would eventually have to establish itself as a
democracy. For Rochau has precluded this argument by using the historical situation, not the theory, as his point of departure. His response
is thus vague—a partial defense of the constitutionalism of the Gotha
party, which he had previously refuted theoretically. Rochau sees a
chance for the *kleindeutsch*, pro-Prussian point of view once the Prussian state again pursues its own interests. This would lead to a situation
reminiscent of 1848—that is, to liberalization, to an alliance between
the state and liberal theory. This prognosis was to be realized five years
later—in fact, within the framework of the very constitutionalism
whose fragility Rochau had demonstrated.

Rochau recognized the weakness of the German *Mittelstand*, which
in contrast to the French bourgeoisie never became dominant. This
Mittelstand was strong enough to criticize the absolutism of the state
but not strong enough to prevail over it. Nevertheless, Rochau maintained in 1853 that without the *Mittelstand*, politics could not be practiced in Germany. The result was that he arrived at a position whose
inconsistency he evidently did not recognize. On the one hand, as we
shall see, he opposed the idealism of the Liberal party and sought to
secure liberalism by strengthening the middle class economically; on the
other, he realized that because the German middle class was not unified
it lacked political impetus. To resolve this contradiction, Rochau put
his trust in social evolution, which would lead to the triumph of the
moderate middle class. Leadership eventually had to fall to the rational,
enlightened middle class, as opposed to the narrow-minded nobility and
the irrational proletariat. The historical argument is directed particularly against the nobility, which Rochau denied any meaningful function
in society: "The German aristocracy brought ruin upon itself; it per-
ished from its inability to adapt its role to changing historical circumstances." Rochau's political "realism" has little to do with a defense of
the existing order but equally little to do with a plea for the people,
whose ability to rule is even more emphatically questioned: "But it is
idle to appeal to the sovereign will of a people who lack both the ability
and the desire, who perhaps have not yet even become aware of their
own identity."[27]

These demarcations are reflected in Rochau's concept of the public
sphere. From the classic liberal premise that the general will should
manifest itself in the public sphere through rational deliberation,
Rochau drew the conclusion that the public sphere must be either re-

[27]Ibid., pp. 60, 42.

stricted or reduced in its importance for the formation of political will. Above all, a different reasoning is given for the efficacy of public opinion. In Rochau's work it has changed from an emphatic construction to a set of opinions that have to work together if they are to exert influence: "An isolated opinion, an isolated intelligence, an isolated fortune means little or nothing in a state; to matter politically, opinion must become public, intelligence must become common property, and prosperity must become native to at least one class." It is no longer the idea that decides the issue but the sum of existing empirical opinions: "Ideas have only as much power as is given them by the people in whom they reside." This reversal of the classic model, in which the rational idea was primary, results for Rochau in the inability to make a distinction in the public sphere between right and wrong ideas: "Thus, an idea which, whether right or wrong, inspires an entire people or time is the most real of all political powers, a power that only poor judgment would undervalue or go so far as to ridicule."[28] By pragmatically replacing the distinction between right and wrong ideas with the distinction between effective and ineffective ideas, Rochau, perhaps unwittingly, explodes the classic concept of the public sphere, which assumes that practical issues have the force of truth.

The importance of public opinion becomes relative; it must be considered because it expresses the spiritual condition of a people. The logical consequence of this interpretation would be to disallow any normative power to public opinion and to acknowledge it as a mere empirical factor of political life. Characteristically, Rochau hesitates at this point. He is skeptical about attributing a particular power to hope, truth, and right; yet he does not abandon the idea of civic freedom. He resolves this ambiguity through historical relativism: although it is impossible to apply the idea of civic freedom to "underdeveloped" nations, it is equally senseless to attach such feudal concepts as legitimacy to a European nation. Thus for Rochau there is a power beyond public opinion which is responsible for the adoption of ideas—that is, history itself.

There is, however, a second means of guaranteeing the rationality of public opinion: the exclusion of irrational elements. Rochau is thus decidedly against a universal and equal right to vote, for universal suffrage gives the "poorer social strata" a problematic preponderance and hence a dangerous influence on Parliament, the organ of the public sphere. Here Rochau assumes an intrinsic relationship between material means and rationality, on the one hand, and poverty and irrationality, on the other. He thus justifies restricted suffrage (a census) on the

[28]Ibid., p. 45.

grounds that the voices of the masses would debase the will of the people, thereby paving the way for dictatorship. To illustrate his point he cites Bonapartism in France. Rochau's conclusion is that "historical experience speaks *for* a census, and political good sense is at least *not against it.*"[29] The political good sense (*Vernunft*) to which Rochau refers is no longer the *Räsonnement* of the classic public sphere but, rather, a prudent consideration of the real political forces. With this in mind, he advocates moderate participation by the people in the development of the political will, namely, participation that will not imperil the predominance of reason—that is, of the *Mittelstand*.

Rochau characteristically combines the devaluation of the public sphere with a higher valuation of the state, whose existence is no longer derived from natural right, in accordance with contract theory, but treated as a historical factor: "In practice, constitutional policy has not gone in this direction beyond unsuccessful attempts and in theory, has not gone beyond fantastic images, grotesque like Plato's republic or idyllic like Rousseau's social contract, but in any case historically untrue, politically unusable, and even philosophically untenable." He replaces the classic doctrine of contract, which was oriented toward individual rights and popular sovereignty, with a pragmatic foundation that introduces the fundamental concept of power on the model of scientific law: "A study of the forces that create, sustain, and change the state is the point of departure for all political understanding, whose first step leads to the recognition *that the law of strength* exercises a similar rule over the life of the state *as the law of gravity* over the corporeal world."[30] Parallel to the devaluation of public opinion is a devaluation of the importance of law. Rochau emphasizes the priority of the state over the law.

The decisive question, of course, is who controls the state or, in abstract terms, what is the relationship between the state and society? In Rochau, liberalism in fact becomes concrete, since he views social forces as primary; because the state is dependent on these forces, its political form must always reflect real forces. The social force that Rochau hopes will succeed is not the conservative elite but, rather, civic groups that would accede to state power with the help of public opinion. To this extent Rochau does not, as has occasionally been claimed, defend pure power politics, supported by government and an army, but desires civic forces to be articulated in public opinion, which can then be used to influence power politics. This desire unquestionably places Rochau in the liberal tradition—with the reservation, however, that for

29Ibid., pp. 88–89.
30Ibid., pp. 27–28, 25.

him public opinion can exercise lasting influence on policy only when it has a social basis: "A weak, uncertain opinion of the moment has no right to political consideration; but to the extent that it becomes established as a lasting view and is raised to a true conviction, it grows in its importance to the state." We must bear in mind that a policy that does not take public opinion into account is inconceivable for Rochau, for the state cannot in the long run govern in opposition to the people: "A *state policy* that dissociates itself from the national spirit forces into being an opposing national *popular policy*." Rochau's political thinking was determined by the idea of a political balance between the power of the state and social power. Thus his viewpoint in 1853 cannot yet be regarded as an apotheosis of the state, although it represents a fundamental shift—the state and its material power moved increasingly to the center, and the public sphere became an instrument for the formulation of political claims to power. Rochau speaks of the power and greatness of the state, "which is essentially determined by the support of a powerful public spirit."[31] This formulation is directed against the reactionary Prussian government; yet at the same time it concedes that greatness and power in a state are relatively independent values.

The convergence of state and society in Rochau's theory becomes especially acute when he turns to the solution of social problems. The postrevolutionary liberalism of the 1850s existed during a transitional phase in which social problems revealed themselves more distinctly as class conflicts. To be sure, this antagonism was not always admitted openly. It is characteristic that Rochau once again tries to make a claim for the proletariat's usefulness to the *Mittelstand* as a goad, as an instrument that could be put to use or held in check according to the demands of the political situation. The liberals felt threatened principally by conditions in France—that is, by Bonapartism, which in the postrevolutionary atmosphere had taken advantage of democratic forms to create a quasi dictatorship. Between 1850 and 1870, therefore, the question of suffrage was also a question of how the masses could be controlled. This issue played a role in the debates of the National Assembly; in subsequent years it was confronted by both liberals and conservatives. The conservatives could count on the reliability of their rural constituency; the liberals feared the masses' economic dependence on the conservative elite and consequently sought to restrict the conservative elite's influence. In the new era, the positions of the democrats and the constitutionalists moved closer together; even such former liberals of the left as Franz Leo Benedikt Waldeck, Johann Jacoby, Johann Carl Rodbertus, and Hermann Schulze-Delitzsch worked within the bounds

[31]Ibid., pp. 33, 35, 34.

of the imposed constitution and no longer called for a fundamental change in the right to vote. Although the supplemental law concerning the regulation of municipal government (*Novelle zur Städteordnung*) was still the occasion for a fight against the three-class system because it divided voters into social classes, no unified position emerged. The majority of liberals supported some form of restriction, and when the Progressive party was created from a coalition of opposition liberals and democrats, the liberals dropped from consideration the issue of the franchise, calling it an insoluble problem.

During the time of the constitutional conflict, suffrage took on new importance. The government and the landed middle class now stood on opposite sides—at least on certain issues. Since the three-class franchise benefited not only the landed nobility but also the economic middle class, the Conservative party became distrustful. It began to consider the political advantages of an equal vote. As soon as the conservatives took up the cause of general suffrage as a means of mobilizing the rural vote, the liberals—especially the left wing of the party—found themselves in difficulty. They perceived that they had lost their influence over the rural and urban masses. The mass of rural voters was under the influence of the conservatives, and Ferdinand Lassalle and the workers' movement were agitating in the cities. In 1862 in Berlin, Lassalle publicly called for universal suffrage in Prussia in order to create a political base that would push through social demands. The liberals regarded this politicization of the social question a serious threat. The party opposed the political organization of the workers which Lassalle was striving for, especially in a form that would diminish the influence of the liberal intelligentsia. In view of the unresolved constitutional conflict, the liberals advocated the creation of a unified front. Thus in December 1862 they rejected the demand by the leaders of the workers' educational association *Vorwärts* (based in Leipzig) for an equal right to vote. Because of this turn to the three-class franchise, to which the Progressive party, after pressure from the right and the left, was now more favorably disposed, the political connection between the liberals and the proletarian masses was severed. Afterward, the concept of universal political participation, a constitutive element of the classic model of the public sphere, was intentionally restricted so that a parliamentary majority would be assured. The liberals defended a franchise that gave them the support of only 15 percent of the qualified voters (535,000 out of 3.549 million).[32]

Pressure from the right and left resulted during the 1860s in the breakdown of the entire social outlook of the liberals. The claim to

[32] See Gugel, *Industrieller Aufstieg*, p. 30.

universal political representation, which the liberals still upheld, was defended by equating civic society with the *Mittelstand* or, in other words, by attributing a greater political maturity to the propertied classes. As Gugel in particular has stressed, the strategy of the liberals in matters concerning suffrage and the political opposition was already largely determined by fear that they would be outvoted by the proletarian masses. Even if one objects that Gugel underestimates the antagonism between the nobility and the middle class in the 1860s, he convincingly shows that as members of the middle class the liberals in fact felt themselves threatened. Organized socialism was declared to be in fundamental violation of their own image of society, since it no longer recognized the middle-class structure of ownership.[33] Where the recognized material disadvantage of the workers was taken seriously— as in the left wing of the party—an economically oriented cooperative policy was advocated which would in the long run transform the proletariat into a socially integrated petite bourgeoisie. For only when a certain degree of education and well-being became commonplace, the argument ran, could the efficacy of a democratic system of government be counted on.

Civic Freedom and the State
during the Constitutional Conflict

The constitutional conflict between 1862 and 1866 was the phase of Prussian history when confrontation with an authoritarian government forced postrevolutionary liberalism to explain its position. In the context of this book, not all aspects of this conflict are equally important. In the forefront was the issue of civic freedom and of Parliament's position with respect to the state. The events of this conflict will have to be largely omitted here.[34] Although Heinrich August Winkler argues that the constitutional conflict represented the decisive confrontation between the nobility and the middle class, he points out that this opinion, held by the liberals, did not precisely describe the situation, because the Liberal party represented neither the rural nor the urban proletariat.[35] This gap between self-image and political reality largely shaped the strategy of the Progressive party in its struggle with Bismarck. It aimed to secure civic freedom and reformulate the role of

[33]Ibid., p. 172, n. 87, and p. 174.
[34]For the relevant literature, see Ernst Rudolf Huber, *Deutsche Verfassungsgeschichte seit 1789*, vol. 3 (Stuttgart, 1963); Heinrich August Winkler, *Preussischer Liberalismus und deutscher Nationalstaat* (Tübingen, 1964); and Gugel, *Industrieller Aufstieg.*
[35]Winkler, *Preussischer Liberalismus*, pp. 24–27.

Parliament without fundamentally questioning the state and the government. The concept of a constitutional state above political parties made it possible for the liberals to draw a distinction between the existing government and the state, so that a revolutionary situation could be avoided.

The quarrel between Parliament and the crown came to a head in two specific areas: in the issue of the right to contest the budget, which was decisive for the army bill, and in the issue of ministerial accountability, which touched on the general character of the constitutional monarchy. A clash ensued between the government and the Landtag when the lower chamber decided on September 23, 1862, not to appropriate necessary funds for the reorganization of the army. Bismarck, the new prime minister, with the support of the crown, announced to Parliament that the government was determined, if necessary, to govern without an approved budget. He disputed the Landtag's right to appropriate money, insisting that a principle of mutual agreement was in force. As a result of Bismarck's strategy, the military question, which naturally included social and political problems, became a fundamental constitutional issue. This change was readily apparent to the liberals. Thus Heinrich Rudolf von Gneist expressed vehement opposition to a compromise suggested by Bismarck and insisted on the right of the Landtag to attach conditions to the budget appropriation: "We would be surrendering the right to contest the budget and the constitutional right to participate in legislation if we did otherwise. Any compromise would only make a muddled situation more muddled, a contradictory situation more contradictory. But precisely for that reason we can expect the government of the state to act according to the constitution and its oath."[36] Twesten addressed the Landtag in a similar vein on September 16, 1862, when he strongly opposed an attempt to withdraw the consent of Parliament in military matters. At this point it was important to the liberals, as Twesten pointed out, to put the constitution to the test; the radical wing preferred to abolish it rather than reach a compromise that would leave unclarified what rights the Landtag had in the decision-making process. Finally, in October 1862, the *Preussischen Jahrbücher* reported a fundamental constitutional conflict, which involved the question whether the government had to take the nation and its elected representatives into consideration: "In a word, what is important in this conflict is that *the traditions from the period of the absolute state should be forgotten* and that the resignation and self-restraint should be exercised which every free state needs in order to

---

[36]Quoted in Claus-Dieter Krohn and Bernd Peschken, eds., *Der liberale Roman und der preussische Verfassungskonflikt* (Stuttgart, 1976), p. 98.

exist." The *Preussischen Jahrbücher* declared the conflict increasingly "a struggle of the middle class [*Bürgertum*] against the Junkers, who were associated with absolutist tendencies."[37] We should bear in mind, however, that the liberals were not unified on the important question of constitutional rights. Whereas the liberal left that formed around Waldeck, Schulze-Delitzsch, and Jacoby considered the right to determine the budget a political weapon that could be used against the anti-constitutional government, the majority took the position that financial and real considerations justified Parliament's participation in the issue of the military budget. They sought to dissociate themselves entirely from an interpretation of the conflict which could be construed as an abandonment of legality. One can nevertheless agree in principle with Ernst Rudolf Huber when he defines the logic of the conflict, from the liberal-left point of view, as a confrontation between the principles of monarchism and parliamentarianism.[38] Prussian constitutionalism, as Huber emphasizes, was an obscure concept; under certain conditions it could be defined as a parliamentary system. Yet characteristically, the majority in the liberal opposition, despite their readiness to resist, did not decide in favor of this radical interpretation.

The issue of ministerial accountability offered one possibility for directing the constitution toward a parliamentary system. According to the Prussian constitution of 1850, ministers were accountable only to the monarch. Although they had the right to speak and offer opinions in chambers, they were not subject to the disciplinary power of Parliament. The confrontation between Bismarck and the lower chamber on the occasion of a quarrel concerning representative Hans Victor von Unruh led to the drafting of a law dealing with ministerial accountability; ministers could be brought up on charges of bribery, treason, or infringement of the constitution. But the adoption of this draft by the lower chamber changed little in the political situation, because its rejection in the upper chamber and by the crown was a foregone conclusion. It showed, however, how limited liberal intentions were in bringing about reform, since no request was made for parliamentary ministerial accountability; the conflict between government and opposition was transferred, instead, to the sphere of the administration of justice, which was thereby saddled with political responsibility.

This avoidance of power politics characterized the attitude of the liberals in the constitutional conflict, who ultimately proceeded from a harmonious concept of the relationship between state and Parliament

---

[37]Quoted in Jürgen Schlumbohm, ed., *Der Verfassungskonflikt in Preussen, 1862–1866* (Göttingen, 1970), pp. 27, 28.
[38]See Huber, *Deutsche Verfassungsgeschichte*, 3:337.

(the public sphere). If the liberals repeatedly stressed the legal point of view with respect to Bismarck, this was in accordance with liberal tradition, for in liberal theory the grounding of political sovereignty did not follow intrinsically, as it did for the conservatives, but was derived from the constitutional guarantee of universal rights and duties. Thus we should not assume, as Gugel does,[39] that the strategy of the liberals was due only to a lack of political determination; we must also recognize that liberal theory was neither prepared for nor capable of facing conservative power as long as it was unwilling to draw revolutionary conclusions during a conflict. That the liberal opposition was not prepared for such fundamental dissent, which ultimately could not be confined to specific issues, may have been due primarily to the fact that domestic and foreign economic interests were at stake, thus requiring cooperation with the government. The leaders of the Progressive party were largely in agreement with Bismarck's foreign policy against Austria. But from the beginning their sympathies were influenced by economic interests—in particular, by the desire to establish a unified national market.[40] The constitutional conflict was inopportune for the Prussian economy; the chambers of commerce in particular held the position that business must not be harmed by political confrontations. Extension of the constitutional conflict to economic policy, therefore, would have encountered decided opposition from the economic sector. The issue of Kiel harbor made this very clear: when the chambers of commerce of the coastal states vehemently demanded its construction, the liberals refused their support.

The outcome of the constitutional conflict left no doubt that national and economic interests were more important to the middle class than taking an opposition stance, which would have exhausted the possibilities afforded by the constitution. The victory of the Prussian army at Königgrätz and the devastating defeat of the Progressive party in the Landtag elections of July 3, 1866, signaled a general reaction in favor of the government and its policy of strength. Twesten voiced the opinion of the moderate wing when he wrote in his essay "Der preussische Beamtenstaat" (The Prussian Bureaucratic State), which appeared in the *Preussischen Jahrbücher* in 1866, that parliamentary government in Prussia was really nothing more than an appendage of the bureaucratic state.[41] This admission of weakness opened the way for a compromise with the government and at the same time signaled the secession of the

[39]Gugel, *Industrieller Aufstieg*, pp. 118–20.
[40]On this, see Böhme, *Deutschlands Weg zur Grossmacht*, and Gugel, *Industrieller Aufstieg*, pp. 154–56.
[41]*Preussische Jahrbücher* (1866), p. 146; see also Winkler, *Preussischer Liberalismus*, p. 97.

left wing, which sought to maintain the constitutional rights of the Landtag over the government. Bismarck's readiness to ask for indemnity was received positively by the right wing, whereas the Waldeck group insisted on the chamber's right to consent and accordingly rejected the compromise. The right wing perceived the Indemnity Act as a kind of atonement by the government for its illegal actions and thus decided against further opposition. It supported instead a constructive participation in policy making.[42] The adoption of the Indemnity Act (September 3, 1866) by a vote of 230 to 75 finally sealed the fate of the opposition and confirmed the lower chamber's consent to government policy of 1862 to 1866. But Bismarck's request for indemnity also made it clear that he wanted to cooperate with the Landtag and not, as he might have done, use the opportunity to humiliate Parliament. Through the Indemnity Act, Bismarck noticeably separated himself from conservative ideologues, thus assuring himself of middle-class support for his policy. Huber prefers to see the indemnity issue neither as the surrender of the middle class (the classic liberal interpretation) nor as the submission of the crown to liberalism (the conservative interpretation of Carl Schmitt), but rather as an alliance from which both sides profited.[43] More recent works have corroborated this view, although in a different sense than Huber intended; the opposition of the liberals contained an element of compromise from the start, since they never really contested the state's claim to leadership and explicitly sought cooperation on economic issues. They became convinced that demands made in principle had no practical effect and saw the settlement of the conflict as a renewed opportunity to make a contribution in practical political matters.

The constitutional conflict consolidated a tendency already evident in the new era, though not yet clear-cut: the transformation of the political public sphere into an entity that was restricted with respect to the state, even in its goals, and no longer open to the proletarian masses. On the other side, a proletarian counter-public sphere split off during those years. Even if one were skeptical about the thesis of a fundamental liberal struggle for the political emancipation of the people, one could not fail to recognize that the shift in political climate between 1860 and 1866 did not favor emancipatory demands. This counters the thesis that the liberals essentially advocated the same goals and interests in 1866 as in 1860.[44] The reversal of public opinion after the Prussian victory over Austria must be understood as a gauge of these changes. One need only

---

[42]See Huber, *Deutsche Verfassungsgeschichte*, 3:357.
[43]Ibid., p. 368.
[44]Thus, for instance, Gugel, *Industrieller Aufstieg*, p. 140.

compare Rochau's interpretation of 1853 with Hermann Baumgarten's later critique of liberalism in order to measure the degree of change. Baumgarten, who belonged to the moderate right in 1848 (favoring hereditary kingship) and later was close to the Badenese circle around Franz von Roggenbach, in 1866 not only drew practical conclusions from the changed situation but expanded them into fundamental reflections on the importance and function of the middle class which show some not insignificant differences from Rochau's point of view. Rochau still contended that policy making was impossible in Germany without the middle class, whereas Baumgarten was already contesting the necessity of middle-class participation in power.

· 3 ·

The Critique of the
Liberal Public Sphere

The Self-Criticism of Liberalism

Hermann Baumgarten's work *Der deutsche Liberalismus: Eine Selbstkritik* (German Liberalism: A Self-Criticism) was first published in 1866 in the *Preussische Jahrbücher* but in the same year also went on the market as a separate book.[1] Response to Baumgarten's thesis was varied and controversial. Heinrich von Treitschke and Julian Schmidt, speaking for the liberal right, welcomed his critique warmly and called for a new foundation for liberalism.[2] According to Baumgarten, who viewed the development of liberalism in Germany from the perspective of state and national strength, the history of German liberalism was a history of failure. He gave the endeavors of southwest German chamber liberalism (*Kammerliberalismus*) no more than condescending approval, because he did not regard emancipatory strivings and political strategies as identical, as they had been by the prerevolutionary liberals, but rather as antithetical. Although Baumgarten conceded that the southwest German administrations were efficient, "it was utterly impossible for these pseudostates to contribute to the development of a real political life." To the limitations of the small German states Baumgarten preferred the moderate absolutism of Prussia, which at least had the advantage of being effective in power politics. He summarized the position of Vormärz liberalism as follows: "Of course,

---

[1]*Preussische Jahrbücher* 18 (1866):455–515, 575–628. Published separately by the G. Reimer Verlag.

[2]On its effect, see Adolf M. Birke's introduction to the new edition of Hermann Baumgarten's *Der deutsche Liberalismus* (Frankfurt a. M., 1974), pp. 7–21, and the documents, pp. 153–73.

anyone who evaluates these circumstances impartially will recognize the failure of liberal efforts before 1848. Surrounded by many small states that attracted only minor strength to the political stage; pressured by Austrian and Prussian absolutism; opposed by dynasties whose unnatural existence could only be maintained if the nation continued to lack a sound political life; opposed by a nobility inseparably linked to these dynasties, in which liberalism predominated; opposed, finally, by an often meritorious bureaucracy that included the best political strength of the middle class, liberalism could never become a governing power in the state." Having already distanced himself so far from classic liberalism, Baumgarten failed to see that liberals did not regard their theory as a governing power but rather as a public force aimed at bringing government under control. It was essentially on the basis of its theory that the role of opposition was ascribed to early liberalism. By concluding that national unity was the principal objective of liberalism and by extending this conclusion back to the 1848 period, Baumgarten treated the classic emancipatory demands of the liberals as "secondary concerns."[3]

The change is strikingly demonstrated by the difference between Baumgarten's view and that of his teacher Gervinus. Whereas the failure of the revolution induced Gervinus to call even more urgently for democratization of the state, this was precisely what Baumgarten opposed: "German liberalism in our time can, indeed, be said to exhibit this [tendency toward democratization] to the highest degree. The question is only whether it is a laudable and desirable characteristic. I maintain that as long as it operates in this one-sided democratic way under the dominance of monarchic forms of government, it will have to forgo realizing its own ideas; i.e., entering with full power into the life of the state."[4] Renunciation of the critical tradition is Baumgarten's prerequisite for participation in state affairs, because the politician is concerned with positive ideas that have practical application.

This position was the basis for Baumgarten's assessment of the constitutional conflict; he regarded the liberals in Prussia and in the smaller states as a narrow party, but characterized Bismarck as the representative not only of Prussian but of national German interests. With a certain masochistic satisfaction, he showed that on the issue of Schleswig-Holstein public opinion was against Bismarck, but that the public did not prevail. He basically identified with Bismarck's position, equating it with the national view while treating liberalism as the particularism of a small state. Characteristically, he scarcely touched on the

[3]Baumgarten, *Der deutsche Liberalismus*, pp. 40, 47, 48.
[4]Ibid., p. 119.

domestic side of the constitutional conflict, regarding the existing Prussian state as essentially identical with the sought-for national state. His failure to express opinions on the organization of the army and the budget issue shows that, after the Prussian military victory and the defeat of the Progressive party, he based his hopes for national unity on the constitutional realities of 1866 and the Prussian government. Baumgarten's pride in the military victory totally obscured his view of the domestic political conditions with which the new liberalism was allied. He openly favored a realpolitik deriving its right from the force of circumstances: "With legal means we would always have come out short against the tenacious particularism of the Hanoverian or Schleswig-Holstein peasants or the inhabitants of imperial Frankfurt."[5] An alliance with the Prussian state included an alliance with the nobility. In contrast, Baumgarten was skeptical about the emancipatory demands of the middle class. Since he denied the middle class the capacity for political sovereignty on the basis of its origins and education, his interpretation came close to a neofeudalist concept of society.

Political *Räsonnement*, Baumgarten proposed, should once again be restricted to the circle of the initiated: "To assume that every capable savant, lawyer, merchant, or official who is interested in public affairs and diligently reads the papers is capable of taking an active part in politics, that absolutely no special preparation, no special study, is required for this, and that politics can be admirably carried on alongside other professional duties is one of the most destructive errors to which our totally unpolitical style and lack of political experience has led us."[6] This was precisely the early liberal interpretation, in which politics was the concern of all citizens. By drawing a distinction between the citizen and the politician, Baumgarten distanced himself from the classic theory of the public sphere.

In the second volume of his *Grundsätze der Realpolitik* (1869), Rochau came considerably closer to Baumgarten's point of view. He reduced the importance of public opinion even more than he had in the first volume (1853). In 1866 Baumgarten had viewed national unity as the central goal of liberal policy—a goal that could not and should not be questioned. From the perspective of 1869, this idea turned out to be an ideological legitimation of powerful interests. National German unity was an answer not so much to idealistic and emotional needs as to material ones: "The German striving for unity does not stem from the sympathy of souls, as is claimed, but from more or less legitimate self-interest; it is aimed not at the fulfillment of a national emotional need

[5]Ibid., p. 145.
[6]Ibid., p. 44.

but at the safeguarding of this or that common interest. . . . In short, unity for the Germans is at heart purely a matter of business, in which no one wants to lose and from which everyone wants to derive maximum personal benefit—reduction of taxes, easing of the military burden, civil rights, and guaranteed internal order and external peace."[7] This list accurately describes the wishes of the German bourgeoisie in the 1860s, and despite his cynical tone, Rochau stood behind these demands; in fact, they alone made the goal of national unity meaningful for him. In doing so, he shifted the problem of political unity much as Baumgarten did, equating moderate liberalism, with its preference for constitutional monarchy, with particularism and viewing it accordingly as the foe of national unity. His discrimination against small-state liberalism led to a higher estimation of preconstitutional Prussia and the conservative policy of unity advocated by Bismarck.

Rochau criticized the Greater Germany faction in the south because it proceeded from abstract demands rather than from actual political developments. In this respect he regarded the resistance of the democrats to unity without political freedom as an illusion: "This protest would have a certain justification only if entrance into the North German Confederation involved some kind of meaningful sacrifice. But anyone who has some knowledge of prevailing constitutional conditions in the German states and judges them with a modicum of understanding would have to deceive himself in order to conclude that they offer even a single guarantee of popular rights which would not be far outweighed by the mere existence of the new federal order and the Reichstag that is dependent on it." Rochau counted on the "egoism of the state" to guarantee a free constitution in a great power, whereas in a small state the egoism of the prince was paramount and thus worked against the constitution. Eventually, however, Rochau returned to an idealistic interpretation, for he argued that only national unity could guarantee internal freedom; yet he failed to take into account the other possibility—the achievement of national unity without basic rights and civic freedom. Despite his polemic against political idealism—against the German tendency to conduct policy according to theory rather than empirical principles—Rochau remained in the liberal tradition, which he modified and weakened but was unable to dissolve. Whenever Rochau advocated a particular system of government, he chose constitutional monarchy, which accommodated the middle class and at least took into account the masses, since they could no longer be denied. On the other hand, he warned against a form of government that "pro-

[7]August Ludwig von Rochau, *Grundsätze der Realpolitik* (Frankfurt a. M., 1972), p. 231.

claims *number* to be the only principle of public law and public power and accordingly wants state matters left solely to the discretion of the majority."[8] The superior strength of the crowd, in his view, was no guarantee of stability.

This judgment affected Rochau's assessment of public opinion: he restricted its function even more decisively than he had in 1853. Public opinion was supposed to articulate the political views of the middle class as against those of the state; in this lay its unquestionable justification: "The claim of public opinion to recognition in the state system scarcely needs to be argued for. The institutions and procedures of the state must accord with the judgment, the wishes, and the intentions of the educated middle class if the common cause is not to suffer. Moreover, in today's world this middle class has the greatest variety of coercive means for restoring harmony." In contrast, the invasion of the political public sphere by the political masses is explicitly described as a danger: "In most cases . . . the opinion of the multitude proves to be a hindrance to progress, if not indeed a tool for reactionaries."[9] Public opinion, for Rochau, was mainly an effective instrument used by the middle class to force adoption of its legal demands against preconstitutional or semiconstitutional cabinet rule. Thus he believed that public opinion was responsible for the achievement of personal and professional freedom, the standardization of law, and the abolition of local police regulations. On the other hand, in his view, public opinion was no help in solving the real problems of power politics. The effective role of the public sphere was that of a middle-class weapon against the absolutist state.

In rethinking the relationship between politics and morality, which had been central to the concept of the public sphere from the start, Rochau went farther than Baumgarten. He drew a distinction between private morality and the morality of the state: the individual was universally subject to moral law, whereas the state could not be held strictly to moral norms, because its existence was of fundamental importance to society. "By acknowledging self-preservation as the primary moral responsibility of the state," he wrote, "one gains a vantage point in the investigation of the relationship between politics and morality which makes it possible to a degree to grasp the scope of this question."[10] The principle of self-preservation, which Rochau thought justified because society needs a functioning state, permitted the use of force and explained the state's insatiable demand for power. Yet Rochau was not

[8]Ibid., p. 239, 240, 265.
[9]Ibid., pp. 339, 340.
[10]Ibid., p. 215.

prepared in principle to remove the state from the realm of morality and surrender it to its own legal authority; he did grant it a special status, however, which made politics subject to its own rules. Rochau's politician accordingly was no longer a citizen carrying out his duties but a specialist—an expert entrusted with an office, who looked after the interests of the state. Although Rochau was apparently unaware of it, this line of argument deprives public opinion of its legitimacy. When a high value is placed on the self-preservation of the state, the public sphere largely loses its raison d'être as a controlling factor. Prevailing public opinion retains only a secondary function as an instrument of articulation.

Between 1853 and 1869 the significance of the state as part of a system shifted in Rochau's political theory. In its later phase, the state is no longer the effective instrument of social forces but tends to be seen as a power independent of society. In 1869 Rochau gives the state an autonomy he had not given it in 1853. He calls this autonomy a bulwark of middle-class interests against the masses, which he denies the capacity for *Räsonnement* and public spirit. He depicts the crowd as "the stooge of conservative forces or in pursuit of imprudent, selfish objectives. . . . The great multitude demands before anything else the lowest possible taxes, cheap bread, high wages, a direct share of public revenues . . . , positive help from the state against all affliction, guarantees for its physical existence from the community, and more of the same."[11] Characteristically, it is the social demands of the proletariat that he considers unreasonable.

Conservative and Socialist Criticism

The weakness in the logic of the liberal position did not escape observers in the conservative and socialist camps. They saw clearly what liberals did not care to admit: that liberal theory no longer gave legitimacy to general interests, but rather to special interests. Liberals thus found it increasingly difficult to develop a consistent democratic interpretation of the public sphere. In *Die gegenwärtigen Parteien in Staat und Kirche* (Contemporary Parties in State and Church), a series of lectures published posthumously in 1863, the conservative political theoretician Friedrich Julius Stahl treated the problem of liberalism in depth. Stahl mainly emphasized the contradiction in liberal doctrine, whose political postulates, unlike those of conservatism, had a general

[11]Ibid., p. 229.

character but were not meant to be applied universally. He described liberalism as the rule of the middle class:

> It [the liberal party] affirms popular sovereignty, inasmuch as the king reigns not by the grace of God but by the will of the people. . . . Except that when it comes to carrying out the idea of popular sovereignty, . . . to not subordinating one class to the authority of another, even among the people, it abandons the idea; it summons only the middle class to power, only the affluent, the educated—that is, itself. Similarly, the Liberal party maintains the idea of equality against the nobility, against all estates as such. . . . Except that if equality should be adopted, if the poor should be given the same rights it has, it abandons the idea and makes politically determined legal distinctions in favor of the affluent. It wants a census for representation, guarantees for the press, admits only the fashionable to the salon, and does not grant the poor the same respect and courtesy as the rich.

Thus the bourgeois public sphere is not what it claims to be—the place where general interests are debated—but rather an instrument for advancing class interests: "Public opinion is but the will of the middle class."[12]

Citing the example of the French monarchy, Stahl tried to show that principles such as freedom of the press were always restricted to the use of the bourgeoisie. Not that Stahl meant to conclude from this criticism that the public sphere should in fact be enlarged; quite the contrary, as a conservative he wanted once again to make it dependent on feudal estates. Yet with satisfaction he determined—and this is characteristic of the Nachmärz situation—that tensions had increased between the middle and lower classes. It was from this observation that Stahl derived his conservative strategy: to restrain the middle class, especially in its attempt to use Parliament to usurp political rule. Even before the Prussian constitutional conflict began, Stahl accurately characterized the conflict between the crown and Parliament: "The heart of the system, the supreme article of faith of the Constitutional party, has always been the right to reject taxes and budgets. This is the magic wand it covets, and once it is attained, only one touch will be needed to bring the state to a standstill and, since the king will have to concede everything in order to free himself from the spell, to make the parliamentary government well again."[13] Stahl imputed to liberalism nothing less than

---

[12]Friedrich Julius Stahl, *Die gegenwärtigen Parteien in Staat und Kirche* (Berlin, 1863), pp. 73, 77.

[13]Ibid., p. 128.

the intention to deprive the king of power and establish parliamentary rule.

But his critique of liberalism did not lead him, as one might expect, to a revision of the conservative position which would give greater validity to the interests of the masses. The accusation of inconsistency was merely a formal argument; for Stahl was no less afraid of the masses than were the liberals. Popular sovereignty, in his view, plainly represented the revolutionary principle advocated by the Jacobins during the French Revolution. At that time, the foundation of the social order was torn down by the demand for equality, and a demonic underground of violence and brutality was exposed. Like a moderate Girondist, Stahl complained about the absence of law and order: "All this is an eruption of the violence that is the very essence of democracy; it is an eruption of the demonic power of destruction, which lies in wait beneath the God-given foundation of the social order like a volcano, and whenever this foundation is maliciously or carelessly undermined, it unleashes its devastating forces."[14] Stahl's stand on practical political issues was not very different from that of the liberals he denounced, since he too regarded constitutional monarchy as the best contemporary form of government, but only as long as the sovereignty of the monarch was respected. A Bonapartian solution, which brings the monarchy and the masses together so that control can be gained over the middle-class center, was still foreign to Stahl's kind of conservatism, since he consistently maintained the theological legitimacy of the ruler.

Ferdinand Lassalle's polemic against liberalism accorded with Stahl's critique in maintaining that liberal theory was a class ideology that ultimately served specific material interests. His attempt at a radical critique was, however, completely contrary to the intentions of legitimism. Unlike Stahl, who insisted on the priority of theory, as did liberalism, Lassalle, in his 1862 lectures on the constitutional system, was interested precisely in showing that from a political and social standpoint, the constitution was nothing else than a transcription of the power structure embodied in political institutions: "The actual power structure, existing in every society, is that active effective force that lays down all the laws and legal arrangements of the society in such a way that they essentially *could be nothing other than what they indeed are.*"[15] For Lassalle, the text of a constitution was never anything more than a justification of actual conditions. Thus the constitutional conflict was for him—in contrast to what the Progressive party thought—not a legal issue but a question of power disguised as a legal dispute.

[14]Ibid., p. 196.
[15]Ferdinand Lassalle, *Gesammelte Reden und Schriften*, ed. Eduard Bernstein (Berlin, 1919), 2:32.

Not only did Lassalle draw the anger of the conservatives with this interpretation of the constitutional conflict, but the liberals too rejected his resolutely democratic exposition of the parliamentary claim as dangerous and destructive. Lassalle sought to politicize the constitutional struggle by stripping away its legalistic form and bringing the actual power structure to the fore. The pseudoconstitutionalism of the Prussian government, he thought, should be called by its proper name. Thus he suggested not that taxes should be rejected, which in his view would have been ineffectual, but "that sessions should be postponed indefinitely, in fact until the government demonstrates a willingness to discontinue the rejected expenditures." The rejection of parliamentary cooperation would expose the force used by the government. Lassalle was clearly proceeding from the assumption that the government could not govern without Parliament, because it had to have a constitutional form in order to function. In this respect he showed himself trapped by the liberal theory he was fighting against; for he was unaware, first, that the government could dispense with the cover of constitutionalism and, second, that the concrete material interests of the middle class necessarily led it to side with, not against, the government, because these interests could not be realized without the help of the state. Lassalle's hope of forcing a democratic solution to the constitutional conflict by denouncing the Prussian government as the enemy of the constitution was based on the assumption that the pressure of public opinion would force the government to yield—that is, it was based not on an understanding of the material power structure but on a belief in a radicalized public opinion. He thus declared: "There should be interaction between the members of Parliament and public opinion. Make the means we have found a slogan for action."[16] In complete accord with the original liberal interpretation, he understood Parliament as the extended arm of the public sphere—as an organ that would destroy itself if it ceased to fulfill its function as an opposition. Lassalle assumed that the members of Parliament were in fact what the constitution intended them to be: representatives of the people as a whole; and he overlooked the fact that as spokespersons for the middle class, they had to take its particular interests into account and could therefore not break completely with the government.

The Bourgeois and Proletarian Public Spheres

The results of this study so far can be summarized as follows: between 1850 and the founding of the Reich—that is, before the onset of

[16]Ibid., 2:105, 111.

monopoly capitalism—significant changes had already taken place in the structure of the public sphere. These were particularly evident in liberal state and constitutional theory and in the strategy of the Progressive party during the constitutional conflict. It was generally conceded, not only by the conservative and the radical democratic camps but also by such leading liberal theoreticians as Rochau and Baumgarten, that classic liberal theory and its category of the public sphere were no longer applicable. It was far more difficult, of course, to understand the character of this change, because it largely eluded contemporary categories. The zones of conflict had shifted, but with few exceptions no overall view of the changed structure emerged in the political theory of the time. A new point of conflict appeared, first, in the intensified contrast between the middle class and the proletariat (the fourth estate could no longer be regarded as an integral part of bourgeois society) and, further, in the changed relationship between state and society (the dependence of the economy on the state, a prolonged cooperation that cast doubt on the autonomy of the economic system). That the economic problems resulting from rapid industrialization were also political problems was evident to clear-sighted observers of the political scene. For the liberal center, which understood the relationship between political and economic goals, Lassalle's radical democratic solution—a total break with the state, a complete rejection of cooperation—was no longer feasible, because the liberal center counted on the help of the state as much as the government counted on the support of the bourgeoisie in its foreign and economic policies.

The collapse of the classic public sphere is best characterized as a transition to Bonapartism. Such a characterization differentiates more sharply between variants of the postliberal public sphere. Some, though not all, of the qualities singled out by Habermas are applicable to the Bonapartian phase.[17] We are assuming here that classic liberal theory was rooted in precapitalist conditions, that it essentially formulated in heightened form the interests not of the haute bourgeoisie but of the petite bourgeoisie. Certainly the economic bourgeoisie was able to participate in the classic public sphere and largely adopt classic liberal theory, since it guaranteed individual freedom of movement and autonomy in economic affairs—desirable aspects in the early phase of Western European industrialization. The educated German middle class was less involved in economic exploitation of the public sphere, because its closeness to the state (the bureaucracy) led it to support state modernization. But here, too, there was a tendency in the Vormärz to enforce

---

[17]Jürgen Habermas, *Strukturwandel der Öffentlichkeit*, 2d ed. (Neuwied a. Rh., 1965), pp. 157–256.

the basic classic rights by institutionalizing the political public sphere (Parliament) in opposition to the late-absolutist state. In this respect, the bourgeois intelligentsia essentially became the spokespersons for the broader middle class. This common interest in a fully developed public sphere broke down after 1850, although the monarchic institutional state survived. Both the educated *Mittelstand* and the entrepreneurial bourgeoisie turned away from the classic model of the public sphere, which had provided for control over political sovereignty, and reconciled itself to the idea that political sovereignty was in itself a necessity. It was desirable to strengthen the executive in order to safeguard economic interests and provide protection in case of social conflict.

The wishes of the entrepreneurial bourgeoisie are relatively easy to understand, but material interests cannot directly explain the changed viewpoint of the educated middle class. Fear of the destructive force of the fourth estate played an important role in this change. The educated middle class had sought since the Enlightenment to provide cultural as well as political guidance; its aim had been to enlighten the population by introducing libraries, educational associations, and so forth—but only in accordance with liberal theory. The lower classes were to be incorporated into bourgeois society. The cultural public sphere, which was to serve as a transmitter, was no less controlled by the middle class than the political public sphere. In the Vormärz it was an organ for ideas and postulates far exceeding the needs of the middle class (the possibility of radicalization through the intelligentsia); but as an institution—as the Nachmärz was to prove—it was tied to the middle class, in particular to the wishes of the educated middle class. The release of the proletariat from liberal guidance of the bourgeoisie, which occurred during the 1860s, marked a turning point. The appearance of a new class antagonistic to the middle class became a threat even where there was no close tie to the capitalist system or, indeed, even where a skeptical attitude toward Manchesterism prevailed. The mentality of petit-bourgeois crafts- and tradespersons changed as soon as the Industrial Revolution threatened their existence. The direction taken by society after 1850 corresponded so little with the expectations of the petite bourgeoisie that the petite bourgeoisie began to change course and moved increasingly toward counterrevolutionary social theories. This tendency, however, became evident primarily after 1873, as a result of the great depression.[18]

The new structure of the public sphere was the outcome of these

---

[18]See George L. Mosse, *The Crisis of German Ideology* (New York, 1964); and Heinrich August Winkler, *Mittelstand, Demokratie und Nationalsozialismus* (Cologne, 1970).

various tendencies. It was supposed to bridge potential conflicts of interest by creating a new relationship between state and society. The *Bonapartian constellation* can be defined as follows: the political system erected by Bismarck in cooperation with the nationalistic liberals essentially corresponded to the system of government developed in France by Napoleon III, although the French system may have had a more theatrical and exotic effect on contemporaries than its Prusso-German variant. This interpretation of Bismarckian policy, in contradistinction to the feudalization theory, follows that of Hans-Ulrich Wehler, which stresses the relationship between an expansionist foreign policy and internal political necessity.[19] Although Wehler sees no economic imperative in the founding of the German Reich, he does see a relationship between the economic and the political interests of the bourgeoisie, between the interests of industrial workers and Bismarck's policy of German unification. We can define as Bonapartian a solution to the problem of social restructuring which replaces inevitable revolution by a state-decreed "revolution from above." Bismarck's Bonapartism was embodied in a system that checked the demands of the workers and at the same time supported the bourgeoisie's desire for law and order. The years between 1862 and 1879 appear in Wehler's interpretation as preparation for a national interventionist policy in view of a social system that was no longer able to find solutions for its own conflicts and contradictions.

Excursus: Marx's Interpretation of Bonapartism

Hans-Ulrich Wehler refers with good reason to Karl Marx's classic analysis of Bonapartism. In comparing France's two great revolutions, Marx came to the conclusion that the later one (1848) was retrogressive, because it represented only the narrow interests of the various bourgeois factions. Marx described Napoleon III's coup d'état as the consequence of a social logic in which the pressure of the revolutionary proletariat, the loser in the June battles, reacted successively on various bourgeois groups—initially on the democrats and strict republicans, then on the middle-class center (that is, the advocates of constitutional monarchy), and finally on the legitimists, who favored the restoration of the Bourbon dynasty:

> The proletarian party appeared as the appendage of petty-bourgeois democracy. It was betrayed and abandoned by the latter on 16 April, on 15

[19]Hans-Ulrich Wehler, *Bismarck und der Imperialismus* (Cologne, 1969), pp. 454–56; see also Michael Gugel, *Industrieller Aufstieg und bürgerliche Herrschaft* (Cologne, 1975), pp. 241, 246–48.

May, and in the June days. The democratic party, for its part, leant on the shoulders of the bourgeois-republican party. As soon as the bourgeois republicans thought they had found their feet, they shook off this burdensome comrade and relied in turn on the shoulders of the party of Order. The party of Order hunched its shoulders, allowed the bourgois republicans to tumble off, and threw itself onto the shoulders of the armed forces. It believed it was still sitting on those shoulders when it noticed one fine morning that they had changed into bayonets.

Thus, according to Marx, the revolution moved in a "descending path." In the process, the result of the February Revolution—that is, the systematic acceptance of the political public sphere in Parliament—was gradually retracted, in fact by the very bourgeois forces that had supported the political public sphere before 1848. The republicans (who were at the helm between June 24 and December 10, 1848) demanded unrestricted rights for all citizens and advocated universal and equal suffrage without a census, albeit only after they had crushed the proletariat and put Paris under martial law. In this sense, the new constitution guaranteed human and political rights, but always with the proviso that their implementation could be restricted for the sake of public security: "The constitution therefore constantly refers to future *organic* laws which are to implement the above glosses and regulate the enjoyment of these unrestricted liberties in such way that they do not come up against each other or against the public safety. These organic laws were later brought into existence by the friends of order, and all liberties were regulated so as to make sure that the bourgeoisie was not hindered in its enjoyment of them by the equal rights of the other classes." The intentions of the new constitution were contradictory, since it simultaneously safeguarded public opinion and restricted it to purely parliamentary use. As Marx showed, however, the parliamentary system gradually undermined the bourgeois public sphere, until it emerged as a postrevolutionary Bonapartian public sphere whose substance was largely lost. Since the bourgeoisie (landowners as well as industrialists and financiers) no longer found the enjoyment of civil liberties an advantage, it used the formalism of the parliamentary system to cancel basic rights and eventually the constitution itself. The emphasis in Marx's investigation was not at all on Napoleon but on the contradictions in bourgeois society which ultimately made the coup d'état possible:

The *parliamentary party of Order* [the advocate of constitutional monarchy] condemned itself to quiescence by its clamour for tranquillity. It declared the political rule of the bourgeoisie to be incompatible with the bourgeoisie's own safety and existence by destroying with its own hands the whole basis of its own regime, the parliamentary regime, in the struggle against the other classes of society. Similarly, the *extra-parliamentary mass of the bourgeoisie* invited Bonaparte to suppress and annihilate its speaking and writing part, its politicians and intellectuals, its platform and its press, by its own servility towards the President, its vilification of parliament, and its brutal mistreatment of its own press. It hoped that it would then be able to pursue its private affairs with full confidence under the protection of a strong and unrestricted government.

The bourgeoisie was prepared to surrender political rule, to subordinate itself to a dictatorial power, in order to end class antagonisms. Napoleon's victory was a victory of executive power and bureaucracy over Parliament and the bourgeois public sphere. As a result of the coup d'état, a situation was created in which the state apparatus became independent and stood against a divided society as a stabilizing authority. In France this authority was able to find support in the mass of conservative small farmers, for whom Napoleon created an illusion of political representation. At the same time, however, Napoleon saw himself as the effective will of the economic middle class, which wanted to go about its business. The Bonapartian system restricted the political power of the middle class in order to assure its material power: "But by protecting its material power he recreates its political power."[20] Since, however, Napoleon could not disregard the interests of the peasants, which were opposed to those of the middle class, the results were contradictory interventions in the social system.

Marx described the early Bonapartian system as a state apparatus that had to establish a precarious balance between competing social groups, each of which was reassured by the knowledge that its needs were temporarily being met. Since the contradictions in bourgeois society prevented it from creating and sustaining an autonomous public sphere, this role was taken over in the Bonapartian system by the political executive. To be sure, this did not turn society back into a feudal society, as the conservatives would have liked; rather, it gave it a plebiscitic character, which was precisely what the conservative legitimists feared most. It was generally agreed in political discussions of the time that Bonapartism, whether welcomed or rejected, was something new, and that it did not fit into such familiar categories as feudalism or absolutism.[21] The Bonapartian system was not legitimate; this was precisely what its conservative and liberal critics meant when they called it immoral: the system neither grew out of the monarchic tradition nor

[20]Karl Marx, *The Eighteenth Brumaire of Louis Bonaparte*, in his *Political Writings*, ed. David Fernbach (New York, 1973), 2:169, 170, 159, 224, 245.
[21]On this discussion, see H. Gollwitzer, "Der Cäsarismus Napoleons III. im Widerhall der öffentlichen Meinung Deutschlands," *Historische Zeitschrift* 173 (1952):23–75.

was justified by liberal theory and parliamentarianism. Even if Bonaparte sought to restore partial civil liberties after 1860, this was not tantamount to restoring the bourgeois public sphere, the traditional role of which had been exhausted. French Bonapartism represented a transitional form restricted to a time when bourgeois society could not act as a stabilizing element and left this function to the state. During the Third Republic, the French bourgeoisie was able to regain its dominance with the help of the parliamentary system.[22]

Bismarck's System and the Public Sphere

Whether Bismarck's system was a variant of Bonapartism is a controversial question. Wehler and Gugel accept the comparison in principle, but Gall has recently questioned the very category of Bonapartism and its value as a basis for comparison.[23] For Gall, the emphasis in Bismarckian politics was on a balance between the traditional leadership (the nobility) and the middle class. The constitution of the North German Confederation, in Gall's opinion, provided for such a state-guaranteed balance, which differed from the French situation in containing fundamental precapitalistic elements that had already been superseded in France. In this respect, according to Gall, the Bismarckian system was endangered by capitalism. One can argue, together with Wehler, against this interpretation that it underestimates the extent of structural change that occurred after 1850.[24] The Industrial Revolution gave rise to a modern class society that had not yet undergone a successful bourgeois revolution. It was this situation that created the Prusso-German variant of Bonapartism: the latter was the product of a postrevolutionary industrial society forced in the course of modernization to seek a balance; and it found that balance in state power. Thus Wehler regards Bonapartism as the typical form of rule in an early industrial society that has undergone revolution without achieving the goals of civil liberty and parliamentary government. This interpretation is applicable to German conditions, but it does not apply to the situation in France, where a successful revolution, one that overshot the material interests of the bourgeoisie, led to Napoleon's coup d'état.

A comparative typological definition of Bonapartism must take into account these special conditions. The significant point, also emphasized

---

[22]See Gugel, *Industrieller Aufstieg*, p. 258.

[23]See Lothar Gall, "Bismarck und der Bonapartismus," *Historische Zeitschrift* 223 (1976):618–37.

[24]See Hans-Ulrich Wehler, "Kritik und kritische Antikritik," *Historische Zeitschrift* 225 (1977):347–84.

by Marx, is the abdication of the middle class, which restricted its own political sovereignty in order to assure its material dominance. Both in France and in Germany the middle class searched for an agent that could assume political leadership without supporting hostile classes. This was achieved in 1866, during the Prussian constitutional conflict, when the unsuccessful liberal opposition finally came to believe that in Bismarck it had found a guarantor of its particular interests. To be sure, this was not simply a repetition of the French events of 1850, because in Prussia the monarchy and nobility had a stability they no longer had in France after 1789 and 1830. Still, the situations are comparable—first, because the bourgeoisie regarded the pressure of the proletariat as a threat that had to be countered by a strong executive and, second, because the rival social groups canceled each other out politically and demanded a strong state. The differences should not be overlooked: the Prussian state could count on the support of a traditional elite interested in its preservation. But beyond such differences, the Bismarckian structure was similar enough to be considered a variant of Bonapartism.

I believe that the structure of the public sphere already differed significantly from its classic model before the foundation of the German Reich. This can be demonstrated by the example of the press under Bismarck. The primary function of journalism in the Vormärz was to disseminate opinion; in other words, commercial utility was of secondary importance. Even Cotta's *Allgemeine Zeitung*, despite its great influence, remained a subsidized undertaking. This did not prevent the publisher from standing behind the paper and its relatively independent editors. A perpetual battle was waged in the mass media against the intrusion of state censorship, making the tactical use of language a necessity. Before 1848 the fight over the political public sphere was largely a fight for freedom of the press. Liberals, democrats, and socialists united in the struggle against suppression of the truth by censorship. The issue was forced even before the revolution by an excessively harsh Austrian plan to make the strict Austrian censorship laws applicable in all states of the German federation—a plan opposed by the other states, especially Baden and Saxony. The events of the spring of 1848 soon surpassed the bounds of the old constitution. Restrictions on freedom of the press were lifted. In accordance with article 4, paragraph 13, of the constitution, every German was given the right "to express his opinion freely in word, writing, print, and pictorial representation." Paragraph 13 expressly assured that "freedom of the press" could not be restricted through political or any other means.[25] Although real

---

[25]Franz Schneider, *Pressefreiheit und politische Öffentlichkeit* (Neuwied a. Rh., 1966), p. 308.

restrictions still existed after the failure of the revolution, and the conservative government returned to the practice of censorship, the principle of freedom of the press was not revoked. This made the situation in the Nachmärz fundamentally different from that of the 1840s. The political press was recognized as an instrument of public opinion—even by the conservative forces, who no longer wished to deprive themselves of this important tool for the formation of public opinion. The public sphere was regarded as an arena in which different opinions could compete until the strongest gained general acceptance. The conservatives, too, saw the possibilities for influencing public opinion through the press and founded the *Kreuzzeitung* as their organ. By and large, the problem of freedom of the press went unaddressed. Censorship was no longer the real issue; the central question was how to influence the public sphere. As the article "Pressfreiheit" in the *Deutsche Staats-Wörterbuch* observed, freedom of the press was taken for granted: "There is scarcely any difference of opinion among discerning men nowadays about the system on which the state should base its laws concerning the treatment of the press; only freedom of the press serves both the law and the interests of politics."[26]

Bismarck's policy, which differed clearly in this respect from the reactionary measures of Manteuffel's cabinet, aimed to have a positive effect on public opinion by influencing the press. Despite Bismarck's often hostile treatment of the press when he became minister president, he did not underestimate its importance as a political instrument. We need to investigate this policy, because it was an essential aspect of the Bonapartian public sphere. When necessary, Bismarck used the classic means of suppressing public opinion. During the Prussian constitutional conflict, for instance, he made full use of the restrictions permitted by the constitution. Nor did he hesitate to violate the constitution. More characteristic, however, was his attempt to make the press tractable, so that public opinion could be swayed toward the government's point of view. Although such press manipulation had been attempted before Bismarck, under his guidance it was systematically developed. By discreet organizational means, he created an effective instrument that allowed him to intervene in public discussion at any time. If for no other reason, he avoided great bureaucratic expense so that this systematic manipulation would not be too obvious: "He considered it decisive for his work with the press that the influence of the state should remain hidden and that official political control should not be apparent from outside."[27] One of the measures introduced by Bismarck in the 1860s

---

[26]*Deutsches Staats-Wörterbuch* (Stuttgart, 1861), 8:228.
[27]Irene Fischer-Frauendienst, *Bismarcks Pressepolitik* (Münster, 1963), p. 27.

was the establishment of a bureau of information, whose task it was to collect information and distribute it to a specified circle of recipients. This was done with the help of news agencies—especially that of Theodor Wolff, whose English competition was largely eliminated by Bismarck in the interest of Prussian policy. Through his connection with Wolff's agency he exerted influence on the dissemination of news and was consequently in a position to manipulate the reaction of the German press and to produce specific, commensurate effects in the public sphere. These measures were accompanied by the founding of an official news sheet, the *Provinzialkorrespondenz*, which all Prussian newspapers would draw on. Another important institution of Bismarckian press policy was a literary bureau (*Literarisches Büro*), which was added to the Ministry of the Interior in 1862 and whose responsibility it was to issue official publications and supply correspondents for foreign papers. In addition, with Bismarck's entry into the government, a special agency had been provided for press matters, which was directly under the jurisdiction of the minister president and served primarily to support Prussian foreign policy. These different organizations were only loosely interconnected. Although Bismarck occasionally complained about the lack of a concentration of power, he never changed the structure of the apparatus. Concentration of power was not in his interest, since a centralized apparatus could easily become independent, and he preferred to keep the various organizations exclusively as his own tools.

Bismarck's press policy, however, was not limited to the development and use of an internal apparatus. It was even more important for him to penetrate the "free" press and transform it into a government organ. This could be accomplished by exerting personal influence on editors or through financial support. Such relationships, naturally, were established primarily with conservative papers such as the *Allgemeine Preussische Zeitung* and that important organ of foreign policy, the *Norddeutsche Allgemeine Zeitung*, since liberal papers remained closed to the Prussian government during the constitutional conflict. This situation changed only after 1866, when the compromise reached between the liberals and Bismarck was reflected in the mass media as well. Liberal organs such as the *Leipziger Allgemeine Zeitung*, the *Schwäbische Volkszeitung*, and *Grenzboten* offered to cooperate with Bismarck.[28] When such cooperation was not forthcoming, it could be exacted—provided there were no ideological reasons to preclude it—by withholding important news and thereby depriving the paper in ques-

[28]Ibid., p. 56.

tion of its topicality. Bismarck was not afraid to apply this kind of pressure.

Bismarck's highly diversified press policy, the full effect of which was not felt until the 1870s and 1880s, was based on the systematic manipulation of the public sphere. He used the public sphere without respecting its purpose, allowing the press to function only to the extent that it preserved the impression of itself as a free and independent shaper of opinion. It was thus important for him not only to have official organs at his disposal but to have influence over newspapers whose independence was generally accepted in the public sphere. Bismarck's actions were always pragmatic: when public opinion supported his policy, it was welcome; when it opposed him, it could be turned. This made the formation of public opinion essentially subordinate to national aims. It also meant that Bismarck denied the public sphere the quality that made it important to the liberals: the *Räsonnement* that was supposed to give rise to political decisions. As a result, Bismarck not infrequently reacted angrily to hostile opinion in the press or even questioned the press's fundamental critical function. Skepticism of, indeed antipathy against, journalists—an attitude that certainly did not exclude their manipulation—was one of the conspicuous hallmarks of Bismarck's style.[29]

The structure of the Bonapartian public sphere is recognizable in Bismarck's press policy. Whenever possible, the Bismarckian system did not encroach on existing liberal institutions (for example, Parliament, the press), preferring instead to use them; it made no difference to Bismarck whether this action fundamentally contradicted the original function of the institution. A redefinition of the function of the public sphere had clearly occurred, undermining its autonomy with respect to the state, which had been underscored in the classic model. Bismarck was interested in agreement, not in *Räsonnement*; he sought publicity, not deliberation among citizens. For this reason a plebiscitary element was by no means unwelcome to him as long as it could be controlled—as it was, for instance, in the fight against the lower chamber during the constitutional conflict. It is known that Bismarck disputed the right of Parliament to represent the people because it had been voted into power by only a small part of the population.

The Bismarckian system was characterized by a fabricated public sphere that was largely dependent on the government, or at any rate never developed an initiative of its own. It became a sounding board for the journalistic self-promotion of the state. In reality this was merely a

[29]See Heinz Schulze, *Die Presse im Urteil Bismarcks* (Leipzig, 1931), p. 155.

tendency, because Bismarck's apparatus was never strong enough to manipulate public opinion continuously. In the long run, he was unable to suppress the partisan press of the right and left. In the Bonapartian phase of restructuring, his primary aim was still to bring the economically weak press to heel. To this end, Bismarck drew on resources from the Guelph Fund (*Welfen-Fonds*), which only he could control. This meant that the commercial dailies, which had dominated the market since the 1880s, could no longer be influenced. Here, as in the case of the newspapers of the workers' associations, common interests played a greater role.

The Beginnings of a Counter-Public Sphere

The reduction of the classic public sphere through self-curtailment or state-induced erosion to a Bonapartian public sphere, in which state and society already tended to intertwine, presented the question whether and in what form the critical element could be restored. Among German socialists, Lassalle had the clearest perception of this problem. In his "Arbeiterprogramm," a lecture delivered in 1862 to an association of Berlin craftsmen, he declared that "even public opinion, gentlemen—I have already indicated by what means, namely, the newspapers—receives its impressions from the mint of *capital*, and from the hands of the privileged wealthy Bourgeoisie."[30] This critical remark was aimed at the assumption that the lower classes presented a danger to the public sphere because they were uneducated. In opposition to this opinion, Lassalle pointed out that from a historical point of view the public sphere was constituted precisely as a weapon against the state and the privileged classes and therefore could not be directed against the people. One might conclude from this critique of the capitalist public sphere that Lassalle was no longer interested in the institution of the public sphere and thus developed no theory of his own. This conclusion would be precipitate, for it overlooks the fact that in his "Arbeiterprogramm" Lassalle fastened on the normative aspect of the public sphere. He argued that the inherent immorality of the third estate, its self-interest, must be lacking in the fourth estate, because it represents the entire citizenry. In other words, the working class lacks the distinction between private interests and general cultural development; rather, interests and morality coincide in the fourth estate. The

[30]Ferdinand Lassalle, *The Workingman's Programme*, trans. Edward Peters (London, 1884), p. 48.

emancipation of the fourth estate thus would lead not to the dissolution of the public sphere but to its realization as a socialist entity.

In Lassalle, this overcoming of the bourgeois public sphere leads to redefinition of the relationship between state and society. In its extreme reduction to the proverbial "caretaker state" (*Nachtwächterstaat*), the liberal state no longer offers assurance that "the unhindered exercise by himself of his own faculties should be guaranteed to each individual." Lassalle in no way wished to minimize the importance of the state. On the contrary, he demanded of the state apparatus that it "carry on *this development of freedom*, this development of the human race until its freedom is attained."[31] Since Lassalle granted the state a central role in the unfolding of a free society, the idea of supervision, of critical examination, lost its earlier significance. The will of the state was made identical with the will of the working class, which propelled and emancipated itself, as it were, through the activity of the state.

Lassalle's assessment of liberalism and parliamentary government largely accords with Bismarck's; he, too, was convinced of the weakness and uselessness of the bourgeois public sphere. In a February 24, 1864, letter to Huber, he spoke out strongly against parliamentarianism. He consequently sought new, unorthodox ways of accomplishing his democratic goals, not the least of which was negotiating with Bismarck over the possibility of an alliance between the proletariat and the monarchy—bypassing the parties of the middle class. What he had in mind was a radical democracy that would unite with a strong monarchic state, as he had already envisioned it in his "Arbeiterprogramm," albeit without considering the possibility that such a state could be the one currently in existence in Prussia. Gustav Mayer spoke of the Caesarean tendencies that led Lassalle to relentlessly advance his leadership role in the *Arbeiterverein* (Workers' Association).[32] But the real question is whether and to what extent one can speak of a Bonapartian socialism. Lassalle was convinced that the historic alliance between the progressive forces of the middle class and the workers, which the left wing of the Progressive party sought to maintain, was no longer in the workers' interest. The establishment of an autonomous, politically independent labor movement would create a new political power, which would pursue its own interests apart from the nobility and the bourgeoisie, and in the process would be able to align itself with the monarchy.

[31]Ibid., pp. 54, 56.
[32]See Gustav Mayer, *Arbeiterbewegung und Obrigkeitsstaat* (Bonn–Bad Godesberg, 1972), pp. 90, 91.

Lassalle's political agitation against the Progressive party in September 1863 (during an election campaign) could only benefit the weak conservatives and Bismarck, for, as Mayer has rightly shown,[33] there was no possibility of independent political representation for the workers. By arguing that three-class suffrage had been introduced in Prussia illegally and should be revoked, Lassalle sought to urge on Bismarck a plebiscitary election reform that would undermine the political public sphere of the middle class. Thus he, too, unmistakably opposed a rational bourgeois public sphere: "But a bourgeois movement, *that* would be altogether impossible without newspapers, for the philistine customarily lets the papers determine his opinion; he rehashes in the evening over his wine what he has read in the morning over his coffee, and he *cannot* do it any other way. The nature of the working class, however, requires that one be able to emancipate oneself from the dominance of the press. The working class [*Arbeiterstand*] has a profound *class instinct*, which makes it stand firm and independent against anything a wretched press may say." That this description was far from the actual situation is irrelevant to our investigation. It is more important that Lassalle wanted to lead the labor movement away from the bourgeois public sphere and at the same time bring it into alliance with the state. He attacked the liberals, not Bismarck; he attacked their moderation and inconsistency, the consideration they gave to their material interests, which was reflected in the press by the combination of political opinion and advertisement. The capitalist press, Lassalle told his listeners, had lost its progressive force. It gratified him to cite Bismarck's remark that "newspapers are written by people *who have missed their vocation.*"[34]

Strikingly, as soon as Lassalle offered positive solutions, contradictions appeared in his argument. At this point Bonapartian elements become evident. To counter corruption in the middle-class press, Lassalle recommended, first, that securities should be abandoned, because they permitted only capitalists to found newspapers; second, that the stamp duty should be revoked; and, third, that all advertising, which gave a paper its commercial value, should be banned. These radical democratic demands would reconstitute the press as an organ of pure political opinion; they amounted to the restoration of an ideal early bourgeois public sphere. Lassalle's argument here is thoroughly idealistic: "These are all papers that neither receive nor publish advertisements, or ever hope or strive to publish them. Thus they are also papers written by men who devote themselves to this career not for the

[33]Ibid., p. 103.
[34]Lassalle, *Gesammelte Reden und Schriften*, 3:343, 360, 366.

sake of their own enrichment but because they have a *real* interest in intellectual argument."[35] To the question how this new press would be financed in a capitalist society, his answer was the state. He expected the press to be liberated because the state would use newspapers as public heralds and would therefore finance them.

This confidence in the state is astonishing and can only be explained if Lassalle conceived it as a neutral, suprasocietal force. In September 1863 he was hoping for an electoral victory of the Progressive party, but only so that it would demonstrate its incompetence in Parliament. He was thus agitating basically for a Prussian state led by Bismarck. The goal of this strategy was a radical democracy with a monarchy at its head and a strong executive—at any rate, a state that would address and solve standing social problems. Lassalle had already developed this program in his *Open Letter* to the central committee of the National Labor Association of Germany, presented in Leipzig in March 1863, in which for the first time he explicitly named the bourgeoisie, rather than the conservative nobility, as the real adversary. Lassalle expected the state to promote workers' associations; that is, he counted on an interventionist state, by whose dynamism social and cultural progress would be generated. With his dubious arguments equating the state with the mass of the population ("you, the people, make the state!"), Lassalle avoided the obvious question how such a state could have fallen into the hands of the conservatives. According to Lassalle, the workers' associations had to depend on the state if they wanted to free themselves from the capitalist bourgeoisie. This position led him to a Bonapartian solution. In contrast to the liberals of the left, Lassalle realized that social problems could not be solved by purely economic means. In other words, he recognized the limited value of the bourgeois public sphere for the proletarian struggle, but his solution moved in the direction of a controlled plebiscitary public sphere. With the help of a universal franchise, Lassalle sought to establish a state under the control of the proletariat which would intervene on the side of the workers: "When the law making body of Germany owes its existence to the popular vote, then, and only then will you be able to control the Government in the interest of labor."[36]

The alliance between Lassalle and Bismarck, which both regarded as merely a tactic, sheds a revealing light on the direction in which the public sphere was changing: on Bismarck's part, the attempt to modernize the Prussian monarchy and state and disconnect it from the

[35]Ibid., p. 369.
[36]Ferdinand Lassalle, *Open Letter to the National Labor Association of Germany*, trans. John Ehmann and Fred Bader (Cincinnati, 1863), pp. 21–22, 26, 31.

policy of the conservative nobility; on Lassalle's part, the intention to exploit the crisis in the liberal public sphere for the benefit of the proletariat by establishing a dictatorial power.[37]

Was there an alternative beyond a reduced Bonapartian public sphere? Habermas concluded that the socialist alternatives conceived by Marx existed only in theory. Since Habermas drew a connection between the collapse of the classic public sphere and the development of organized capitalism and the interventionist state, the direction of change was already established for him: the postliberal public sphere was essentially determined by the changed economic structure, which fundamentally changed the relationship between state and society. In fact, the socialist movement in the German Reich did not succeed in radically changing the character of the political public sphere. The more it could participate in the Reichstag as an organized political party because of its electoral successes, the more it was integrated into the existing political system, which in theory it opposed.

Would it have been possible to develop a plebeian or proletarian counter-public sphere? During the Revolution of 1848, the left wing gave rise to a democratic, plebeian public sphere composed of radical craftspersons and manufacturers. But even this radical variant was more an offshoot of the early bourgeois public sphere than the beginning of a new proletarian countersphere. Initially, the progressive elements still relied largely on the basic concepts of liberal theory, even if they rejected moderate bourgeois liberalism. The labor movement of the 1850s continued this democratic tradition. It was only in the sixties that the democratic and proletarian lines diverged, and by no means in a straight path. When the limitations of the Enlightenment model, which was based on the notion of a civil society rather than one of class struggle, became evident, the labor movement had to find alternative forms.

Discussion began in the early fifties with Marx's decision to break sharply with the democratic movement. He demanded a clean separation of the proletariat from the petit-bourgeois democracy. In his circulars he insisted that "this situation has to come to an end; the workers have to become independent." Marx distinguished between the petit-bourgeois democratic movement and the haut-bourgeois liberal movement, and tried to show what connections were open to the proletariat and what dangers confronted it. Above all, he feared that the labor movement would become part of a political movement that would be unable to transcend middle-class ideology because of its class status:

[37]For a critical presentation of Lassalle's politics, see Gerd Fesser, *Linksliberalismus und Arbeiterbewegung* (Berlin, 1976), pp. 40–49.

"The petit-bourgeois Democratic party is very powerful in Germany. It not only comprises the great majority of middle-class inhabitants of cities—small industrial merchants and master craftsmen—but also counts the peasants among its followers and the landed proletariat as well, as long as the latter has not yet found support among the independent urban proletariat."[38] This coalition was capable of exhausting all the postulates of the bourgeois public sphere: it could demand equality and justice, and it could strive for the improvement of the existing social order—but it could not do away with it. For this reason, Marx warned against the limitations of the democratic movement. He overestimated the momentum of the German petite bourgeoisie, however, which after 1850 was no longer able to assume political leadership. In the sixties, it was not the democrats but the liberals with whom the labor movement had to contend—not infrequently with the help of democratic ideals. Moreover, the sharp theoretical distinction did not correspond to the diffuseness of the actual situation. Both from an ideological and a class point of view, the early labor movement was so closely tied to the guild movement that a separation was practically impossible. The politically aware and organized workers were mostly journeymen who had been trained in the guild tradition and in the customs of the handicraft fraternities. The goal of forming a counter-public sphere could hardly fail to take account of these experiences.

The decision of these journeymen to call themselves workers was of course an important step: a search for freedom and equality while surrendering class guarantees and privileges. The early workers' fraternities of the revolutionary phase were directed not so much against a repressive class as toward the gaining of an acceptable status in society. They demanded a place in the political and cultural community of citizens. Thus Franz Schwenniger remarked in an 1849 proclamation that in 1848 the workers had stepped forward for the first time as people "who wanted to help themselves, fully conscious of their rights and their power, and by working together had laid the cornerstone of the holy Temple of Humanity, which with its battlements still belongs to the future."[39] Here we can probably speak more of a plebeian democratic public sphere than of a proletarian one: it conformed to the classic public sphere and drew radical conclusions, but it did not yet oppose it in order to create a separate public sphere. Apparently insignificant details, such as the desire to share middle-class forms of social intercourse rather than be addressed with the familiar *du* by masters

---

[38]Quoted in Frolinde Balser, *Social-Demokratie 1848/49–1863* (Stuttgart, 1963), 1:212, 215.
[39]Quoted in ibid., 1:51.

and authorities, show clearly that society was still regarded as a unified structure in which the workers could find their proper place.

The organization of the workers' fraternity, led by Stephan Born, similarly conformed to the prototype of middle-class parties and associations, but it went a step beyond the liberal model in its development of a strictly managed apparatus. Whereas liberalism, even in the Nachmärz, scarcely went beyond being a party of dignitaries, the workers' fraternity immediately created a more solid framework for its political and social work. Its characteristic features included a national central committee and an administrative board. This marks the beginning of a professional party bureaucracy that was lacking in the democratic and liberal movements. Characteristically, the founding of the fraternity went hand in hand with the founding of a newspaper that would represent the organization publicly and at the same time provide for communication within the party. Since under Born's leadership the workers' fraternity did not develop a socialist theory—which earned it a negative assessment by Marx and Engels—no fundamental debate ensued over its relationship to the middle-class emancipatory movements. That the idea of fraternity did not accord with liberal concepts can, however, be concluded from the opposition of such a left-wing liberal as Schulze-Delitzsch, who argued that the fraternity offered no material incentives to the workers. On the other side, the complaints of the conservative social politician Viktor Aimé Huber against the political activity of the workers show that the opposition was thoroughly aware of the potential political strength of the labor movement. Schulze-Delitzsch hoped to transform it into a cooperative movement based on the principles of competition capitalism. Early labor movement leaders, who tried to think not in terms of classes and professions but of people, opposed this goal. In contrast, those workers' associations that had formed out of professional groups and whose demands were primarily economic, such as the cigar workers and book printers, were less inclined to join the workers' fraternities.[40]

Association was supposed to take place on a local level and to assure workers an independent position in society—independent of both the conservative guilds and capital. This was to be accomplished through production and consumer cooperatives that could count on help from the state. Thus, in a petition for the workers' associations, ten million taler were requested for the fraternities. These goals can be called socialist only if the concept is extended and not equated with the theories of Marx and Engels. For the representatives of scientific socialism, who sought precisely to dissociate the Bund der Kommunisten from demo-

[40]See ibid., 1:67–69.

cratic trends, the weakness of the fraternities lay in their very disregard for a revolutionary transformation of society. The speeches to the Bund by its central officials in March and June 1850 were explicitly directed against the Democratic party, which was composed of the upper bourgeoisie, the constitutional petite bourgeoisie, and the republicans:

> The democratic petty bourgeois, far from wanting to transform the whole of society in the interests of the revolutionary proletarians, only aspire to a change in social conditions which will make the existing society as tolerable and comfortable for themselves as possible. They therefore demand above all else a reduction in government spending through a restriction of the bureaucracy and the transference of the major tax burden onto the large landowners and bourgeoisie. They further demand the removal of the pressure exerted by big capital on small capital through the establishment of public credit institutions and the passing of laws against usury, whereby it would be possible for themselves and the peasants to receive advances on favourable terms from the state instead of from capitalists.[41]

This description of petit-bourgeois goals applies only in part to the demands of the fraternities. It is misleading in that it draws too sharp a distinction between the petite bourgeoisie and proletarians, whereas this separation was not yet complete in Germany. In reality, the fraternity of the workers saw no necessity for a fundamental confrontation with existing society; but neither did it limit itself to supporting petit-bourgeois interests. The demand for equal rights—that is, the Jacobin heritage—should not be viewed simply as a façade for petit-bourgeois interests; fraternity offered workers trained in crafts a way of life in which they were protected by solidarity against the fragmentation and reification of capitalism. Through fraternity, workers preserved the democratic core of the early bourgeois public sphere—but also its idealistic premises. By inscribing the ideas of equality and fraternity on their banners, they continued to advocate a harmonious solution to social problems adopted from early socialist ideas and suited to their needs.

Although the democratic movement emphasized the plebeian aspects of the public sphere and thus undoubtedly offered a correction of the liberal-capitalist view, after the failure of the revolution Marx and Engels were determined to go beyond the bounds of the bourgeois public sphere altogether. Support of democratic demands therefore became a tactical matter. As soon as the democratic movement had attained its goal and political momentum was on the verge of being lost, Marx and Engels sought to intensify social conflict by posing further demands,

[41]Karl Marx, *Political Writings*, 1:322–23.

which the petit-bourgeois democrats were forced to oppose because their interests were no longer being served. Radicalization of the democratic movement would expose its contradictions, and a crisis would be inevitable. Since Marx and Engels assumed a clear split between petit-bourgeois and proletarian forces in 1850, they anticipated a confrontation between the radical democrats and the proletariat. The revolutionary overthrow of society, as Marx and Engels envisioned it, aimed at a takeover of executive power—that is, at a centralizing solution, not a federalistic one (as in Switzerland): "The democrats will either work directly towards a federated republic, or at least, if they cannot avoid the one and indivisible republic they will attempt to paralyse the central government by granting the municipalities and provinces the greatest possible autonomy and independence. In opposition to this plan the workers must not only strive for the one and indivisible German republic, but also, within this republic, for the most decisive centralization of power in the hands of the state authority."[42] This demand negated an essential element in the organization of the democratic labor movement.

For Marx, the takeover of the state was the prerequisite for revolution. Thus, the relationship of the proletariat to the state apparatus was a decisive issue for the new proletarian public sphere. The liberal bourgeois public sphere had come into existence by confronting an absolutist state. The Marxian model of a counter-public sphere that would supersede the bourgeois public sphere reckoned with the disappearance of this opposition. In the hands of the proletariat, centralized state power would become the instrument of social revolution. Thus, the public sphere of the revolutionary proletariat had to develop in two phases. Before the revolutionary takeover of the state, it existed as a secret society protected from the penetration of state power; afterward, it became the public sphere of a centralized, tightly controlled party. In the latter, progress would depend no longer on the consent of the citizens but on that of the party, which had a revolutionary task to accomplish.

Marx and Engels' assumption, in their second circular of June 1850, that a revolutionary situation existed proved false. Looking back at the communist process in 1875, Marx spoke of the practical harmlessness of the movement: "After the failure of the Revolution of 1848, the German labor movement existed only in the form of theoretical propaganda—limited, moreover, to a narrow circle—which the Prussian government did not for a moment doubt was practically without

[42]Ibid., 1:328.

danger."[43] The success of the labor movement was not the result of a strategy of revolutionary secrecy but rather of confrontation with the existing liberal bourgeois public sphere. As soon as the labor movement began in the early 1860s to build its organizations on a national scale and broke definitively with the liberal party, a peculiar situation developed: the proletariat turned into a Bonapartian public sphere so that it could continue its political struggle, but at the same time it established a position of solidarity by which it set itself apart from the middle class.[44]

[43]Karl Marx, *Politische Schriften*, ed. Hans-Joachim Lieber (Stuttgart, 1960), 3:534.
[44]Oskar Negt and Alexander Kluge, *Öffentlichkeit und Erfahrung* (Frankfurt a. M., 1972), pp. 341–55.

· 4 ·

The Institutionalization
of Literature and Criticism

Since the appearance of the seminal works of Georg Lukács, literary studies have accepted the failure of the bourgeois Revolution of 1848 as a decisive influence on the evolution of European and German literature. Using as examples the works of such authors as Heine, Keller, and Fontane in Germany and Balzac, Flaubert, and Zola in France, Lukács pointed out the difference between prerevolutionary and postrevolutionary literature.[1] The transition from portrayal to description, or lyricism, indicated to Lukács that literary production after 1848, viewed as a whole, had entered a phase of decadence corresponding to that in ideology and society. The literary superstructure, according to Lukács's scheme of development, exactly followed the economic and social base (a transition to monopoly capitalism). The theoretical weaknesses of his position are obvious. His coupling of literary and historical evolution remains mechanical. It assumes simultaneous development without any real proof. He singled out individual authors and works and treated them as representative. What is truly necessary, however, is to relate the presumed transformation—as well as the presumed correlation to political change—to literary production and reception as a whole. In other words, the transformation should be treated on the level of the institution, not of the work.

The question, accordingly, is whether 1848 represents a break—a decisive turning point—in the *institution of literature*; that is, whether the failure of the bourgeois revolution had a decisive influence not only

---

[1]Georg Lukács, *Deutsche Realisten des 19. Jahrhunderts* (Berlin, 1952), *Balzac und der französische Realismus* (Berlin, 1952), and *Essays über Realismus*, vol. 4 of *Werke* (Neuwied a. Rh., 1971).

on individual writers and their works but on the process of institutionalization. The concern here is with the relationship between the state and the ideological apparatus of literature. Lukács's interpretation, which has been followed by such scholars as Fritz Martini and Friedrich Sengle,[2] puts forward a plausible hypothesis. It is not difficult to show that the defeat of the middle-class forces left its mark on the postrevolutionary institution of literature. Since the end of the eighteenth century the institution of literature had largely been occupied by the middle class, which certainly had not been the case in the political realm. The literary public sphere was the field on which the liberal and democratic opposition could marshal its troops before 1848. Thus the victory of the conservative forces necessarily affected literature as well. It remains to be determined, however, in what way the crisis and the conservative stabilization of the political system affected the institution of literature. My argument here is that the change affected the aesthetic program—that is, the literary norms and conventions—and that this is reflected in the literary criticism of the time. Furthermore, the change was related to the concept of art and its function in society, but it scarcely touched on the material side of the institution. The changes in the apparatus had less to do with the revolution than with industrialization and were accordingly of long duration. Thus one can speak of changes within the institution of literature, but not of its destruction and rebuilding.

In general, the restructuring was carried out as a deliberate confrontation in the critical sphere, and for this reason it can be reconstructed. The loci of these clashes were the subinstitutions of literary criticism and literary history. Discussion revolved around the evaluation of prerevolutionary literature, with its leading authors, such as Heinrich Heine and Ludwig Börne, and their claims and goals respecting society and politics. The heart of the conflict was the relationship between the literary and the political public spheres, which had been so intensified by the radical literature of the Vormärz that in literary criticism and history it dominated the definition of literature. Denunciation of the political pretensions of literature, either as an exaggeration or as a basic failure, resulted in a major upheaval within the institution of literature, which affected the relationship between ideological formation (and its practices) and the political apparatus. Here we must distinguish between the conservative forces, which sought to refeudalize literature, and the liberals—Gustav Freytag and Julian Schmidt, for example— who adapted to changes in the political situation and sought to rescue

---

[2]Fritz Martini, *Deutsche Literatur im bürgerlichen Realismus*, 3d ed. (Stuttgart, 1974); and Friedrich Sengle, *Biedermeierzeit*, vol. 1 (Stuttgart, 1971).

part of their program by abandoning the attempt to carry the possibilities of the liberal model to their logical conclusion. The reconstruction in the institution was not without consequences. It created a logic of its own in the field of aesthetic and poetic theory. Both the discussion of realism and the genre theory of the 1850s must be viewed in connection with the changed function of the institution of literature.

In more recent scholarship, the extent to which the unsuccessful revolution left its mark on the theory of realism has been a controversial issue. On the one hand, realism has been related to the ideology of postrevolutionary liberalism;[3] on the other, some critics have proposed that the basic aspects of the theory of realism are indebted to idealism and are, therefore, not specifically postrevolutionary.[4] The historical locus of ideas and concepts, however, is of secondary importance in our investigation. What matters, rather, is their value within the system; that is, the question of the function of art and literature. The reconstruction of traditions and influences, justified though it may be in a work of intellectual history, can distort our perception of structural change, for it strongly suggests the assumption of linear developments, whereas the real task is to recognize the way in which ideas and concepts are incorporated into systematic contexts.

Our evidence of such change will, therefore, be presented in several steps. First, we will set forth the concept of literature in the Vormärz and the debate with conservative theory. Then, against the background of prerevolutionary institutionalization, we will examine the Nachmärz institution of literature, especially the subinstitution of literary criticism.

Literary Criticism in the Vormärz

The left-Hegelian Robert Prutz, who with his critical and historical works took an active part in literary discussion both before 1848 and after the revolution, exemplifies the turn from a radical prerevolutionary liberalism to the moderate, nationalistic liberalism of the Nachmärz. That Prutz is today virtually forgotten as a critic indicates the extent to which the tradition he represented was submerged, if not extinguished, during the late nineteenth century.[5] His concept of literature and its public function typifies the left-Hegelian position. It was

[3]Especially by Helmuth Widhammer, *Realismus und klassizistische Tradition* (Tübingen, 1972).
[4]Especially Ulf Eisele, *Realismus und Ideologie* (Stuttgart, 1976).
[5]See Ingrid Pepperle's introduction to Robert Eduard Prutz, *Zu Theorie und Geschichte der Literatur* (Berlin, 1981), pp. 9–48.

hardly original, but for this very reason his position after 1848 is instructive. What distinguished Prutz from most contemporary critics was a strongly developed historical consciousness with respect not only to literary texts but also to the functions of literary criticism and literary history. His writing on literary history was accompanied by a process of self-reflection resulting in changes in his critical position that followed from political and social change. In this manner, in *Die deutsche Literatur der Gegenwart* (Contemporary German Literature) (1859), Prutz thematizes the development of historiography since the 1920s and at the same time defines what he considers to be his task. He accordingly views the history of literature within the broader context of historical evolution as a whole; it changes as public problems and requirements change. This historical awareness, however, did not prevent Prutz from accommodating to changes in public opinion. On the contrary, as soon as the correctness of the belief that ideas result in human progress became uncertain, his historical approach allowed him to make a relativistic reassessment of his task and point of view.

Prutz's critical writings of 1848 are clearly in the Hegelian tradition of the philosophy of history. They proceed from the assumption "that philosophy indeed moves the world and that every other force is powerless against the energy of a spiritual, of a moral conviction."[6] Since Prutz viewed literature as an expression both of the spirit of the times and of the intellectual and moral convictions of an epoch, he subjected it to the same requirements as philosophy: literature is result-oriented; it claims to bring about change in social and political conditions. On the other hand, the question posed by Hegel and developed further by Heine—whether art can still make a significant contribution—is not taken up by Prutz, because for him the purpose of art is not primarily to create and perfect beauty but to serve the political progress of humanity. Thus, literature is for Prutz an aspect of human progress in a double sense: it reflects the present position of the intellect, and it is itself a driving force of historical development.

Before 1848 Prutz stressed primarily the effective and determinant aspect of literature; the literary movement was the avant-garde of the political and social movement. Once again the Enlightenment view of literary discussion as a prelude to political discussion determined Prutz's outlook. In 1859, reflecting back on the function of the history of literature during the years of reaction, he wrote: "In the bleak period of the twenties, the heyday of the restoration, it was [literary history] that primarily, if not exclusively, kept alive the patriotic hopes of the nation

[6]Robert Prutz, *Vorlesungen über die deutsche Literatur der Gegenwart* (Leipzig, 1847), p. 329.

and sparked some kind of public life."[7] Whether this judgment was correct is not the question here (it might be noted in passing that a greater contribution to the enlivenment of literary-political discussion was made by Heine's prose). Its significance lies in the connection it draws between literature, criticism, and the public sphere. What Prutz says here about the history of literature applies to literature in general: in his view, it has a preparatory character; it is the first step toward political action—that is, toward political revolution. This activist element, however, cannot be abstracted from the concrete historical situation. Accordingly, Prutz speaks of the historically determined imperfection of the literary production of Young Germany. Its one-sided subjectivity can be understood as a justifiable attack on the restoration, which, indeed, later lost its legitimate purpose. The historicization of literature and aesthetics sometimes allowed Prutz to define concrete tasks for an epoch—tasks that were limited in scope and could be superseded by new ones. This approach became vital for Prutz in the forties, as in his program for political poetry—that is, for radical political verses—and again in his program for popular novels.

Robert Prutz's Vormärz Criticism

The postrevolutionary literary program developed by Prutz in the journal *Deutsches Museum*, which he edited, differed markedly from his prerevolutionary writings. Despite his bias against the radical revolutionary forces, Prutz regarded the failure of the revolution without any doubt as a kind of shipwreck.[8] He again called for a realistic popular literature, but this goal had a different significance: it lacked the activist component—the belief that literature can lead to political change. Instead, the other aspect of his historical approach came to the fore: he now emphasized that literature had to express its own historical situation and hence could no longer be what it was before the revolution.

Prutz's depreciation of the bourgeois revolution as a juvenile, amateurish undertaking anticipated Baumgarten's self-criticism of liberalism (1866). Disappointed by the revolution, Prutz looked back at the Vormärz with the feeling that a lack of political experience had significantly contributed to the failure of the liberal and democratic forces. He now criticized the literary radicalism demanded by him before 1848—

[7]Robert Prutz, *Die deutsche Literatur der Gegenwart*, vol. 1 (Leipzig, 1859), p. 3.

[8]This aspect is emphasized by Hans Joachim Kreutzer in his postscript to the new edition of Robert Prutz, *Geschichte des deutschen Journalismus* (Göttingen, 1971); in contrast, Hüppauf emphasizes continuity in his introduction to Prutz, *Schriften zur Literatur und Politik* (Tübingen, 1973).

the concept that it was up to the writers to form the avant-garde—as abstract subjectivity and idealism insufficiently versed in power politics: "We were still newcomers to the world of politics. We were still talking about the storms of history, as the inlander talks about storms at sea which he has never seen with his own eyes and therefore pictures only as grand and picturesque, without remembering how many people they destroy and that anyone who actually is experiencing a shipwreck would gladly give up all the pictures in the world for a single safe, dry spot." The allegory of the storm, which was so popular in Vormärz poetry, has been reversed here in a characteristic way. The inevitability of events inherent in the image of the storm has lost its compelling character. Prutz has taken back his radical variant of the Hegelian concept of history, according to which political action arises from the spirit. He now wants to eliminate the connection between the literary and political spheres, which the *Hallische Jahrbücher* had supported. His assumption of such an inner relationship had been based on the historico-philosophical premise that literature and politics arise from the same zeitgeist. This unity is precisely what Prutz now questions in citing the discrepancy between the events of the French Revolution and those of the Wars of Liberation and its inadequate expression in literature. Even postrevolutionary France had been under the spell of classicism. These doubts, however, lead Prutz not to an out-and-out criticism of his prerevolutionary approach but rather to a relativizing redefinition of the basic maxims concerning the correlation of art and life: "For literature by and large follows the same route as life, except that it sometimes rushes a bit ahead and at other times lags a bit behind."[9]

Thus Prutz did not abandon hope that the revolution would eventually give rise to a new literature, but he now reversed the relationship between the political and literary public spheres. In his youth he had celebrated literature as the driving force of the revolution; after the revolution he viewed political reform as the basis for a new blossoming of German literature. He argues: "But in literature, too, traces of a new development are even now by no means totally absent; for the most part, of course, they are still weak; indeed, in some cases it is doubtful whether they work for or against literature."[10] Even if Prutz was adhering to his earlier theories in such a sentence, we cannot overlook the fact that their function has changed: literature has been relegated to the superstructure, which has no effective power of its own. Life no longer needs literature, as it were, now that the political revolution has taken place.

[9]Prutz, *Die deutsche Literatur der Gegenwart*, 1:42, 51.
[10]Ibid., p. 53.

Rudolf Haym was more critical when he described this postrevolutionary situation in 1857 in his book on Hegel: "Idealism, alleged to be all-powerful, had proved powerless. We were, and continue to be, surrounded by a feeling of deep disappointment. With no respect for the victorious realities, for the triumphant misery of reactionism, we have also lost faith in once cherished ideals. The world of feeling and perception of the last decade is separated from that of the present as if by a heavily drawn line. . . . The interests and needs of the present have taken command over it." This opinion, which is certainly typical of its time, should not be regarded as approval of the reactionary forces in Prussia. Haym adhered to the concept of progress and political self-liberation, as is demonstrated not least by his liberal critique of Hegel, and directed it against a conservative Prussia, which he also saw embodied in Hegel. His critical remark was aimed rather at the young Hegelian interpretation of Hegel's philosophy of history, namely, the derivation of political revolution from philosophical theory. Thus, Haym believed not in a new philosophical system that would supersede Hegel's but in a new relationship between theory and history: Hegel's philosophy "was not abolished by a system but temporarily set aside by *world progress* and *living history*." Haym has marshaled against idealism the technical discoveries by which "matter seems to have been brought to life."[11] In this way, both the concept of history and the category of progress are given a different meaning. The distinction made between actual history—that is, material change—and intellectual history creates a new situation for the concept of literature, a situation that was also to leave its mark on literary theory.

The Postrevolutionary Literary Debate

The postrevolutionary debate over the function of literature was carried on within the framework of the theory of realism. This intensive discussion, whose real significance was not recognized by scholars until the 1970s, was by no means restricted to the question how reality should be represented. The disputants were only marginally interested in formulating a reflection theory; the larger question concerned the function of literature. This touched on its institutionalization. There is no need to describe the Nachmärz debate in detail again.[12] Our concern is with the question—decisive for the institutionalization of literature—

---

[11]Rudolf Haym, *Hegel und seine Zeit* (Berlin, 1857), pp. 6, 5.
[12]Summarized by Max Bucher, "Voraussetzungen der realistischen Literaturkritik," in *Realismus und Gründerzeit*, vol. 1 (Stuttgart, 1976), pp. 32–47.

whether and to what degree the theory of realism presupposed the autonomy of the work of art and thus also a qualitative difference between art and reality. Moreover, we need to know what significance this theory had after 1848.

It is easy to show that the theoreticians and critics of the Nachmärz were not direct followers of classicism and romanticism. Julian Schmidt had considerable reservations about both Weimar and Jena. His objection to the idealistic detachment of art and philosophy, to the division between art and life, initially continued the criticism of prerevolutionary times: the heightened aesthetic claims of classicism have a reverse side, namely, flight from reality. The Weimar authors were unable to transfer the aesthetic visions crystallized in a work of art to historical reality. They thus left behind an unproductive, resigned sense of longing, which made political action impossible. Hermann Kinder has rightly pointed out that this polemic is reminiscent of Young Germany.[13] These arguments are in the liberal tradition of the Vormärz. Collaboration between Schmidt and Arnold Ruge ceased only when it went beyond criticism of romanticism, about which there was little disagreement, and attempted to define the literary-political position more precisely. As in Heine, whom Schmidt denounced, romanticism is linked to a religious supranaturalism that fundamentally removes art from concrete, politically influenced historical reality. Schmidt's objection to romanticism was directed against the civic untrustworthiness of aestheticism, which fosters art for its own sake and denies it a moral, political function.

The rejection of romanticism was by no means restricted to the *Grenzboten* circle; similar opinions were held by Hermann Marggraff and Rudolf Gottschall. By charging the members of Young Germany—especially Heine—with being dangerously subjective, and therefore romantics, they created a picture of German literary history which ignored the decisive break of the literary avant-garde of the thirties with the romantic concept of literature. This inability to distinguish between romantic and Young German literary theory and practice was not accidental. It resulted from an attempt by early realists to rescue for their own theory important aspects of the classic-romantic model (autonomy) by removing them from the context of the critique of subjectivism. Heine's prose, which exploded the concept of a self-contained, organic work of art and consequently satisfied the avant-garde demand for the politicization of art not only in content but above all in form, was thus totally misunderstood and accordingly criticized as subjectivism. The call for objectivity in art, for impartiality and realism—which sums up

---

[13]Hermann Kinder, *Poesie als Synthese* (Frankfurt a. M., 1973), p. 145.

an important finding in more recent scholarship on realism—by no means excluded the idea of the uniqueness of a work of art. To this extent, despite all the polemics against classical and romantic art theory—which characteristically diminished in the 1860s—there existed a relationship with the aesthetics of Goethe's time which gained acceptance with respect to major theoretical issues. This relationship found expression not least where the theory of realism defended the rights of poetry against the claims of reality. The notion that German realism never developed a consistent theory but sought to restrict the presentation of reality in content as well as in form has become a cliché.[14] Not infrequently this is construed as a failure of German literature, which is said to have been too fainthearted to shed the restrictions of the earlier idealist aesthetics. But the actual historical process was a good deal more complicated. In the final analysis, it was not the polemic against Young Germany and the left-Hegelian avant-garde that brought the realists back to the supposition that art is autonomous.

In the postrevolutionary period the leading critics continued to criticize subjectivism and aestheticism and called for a *national literature*, while at the same time they underscored, under the guise of a new objectivity, the inherent individuality of art. They wanted literature to be closer to praxis, but at the same time they sought to preserve the aesthetic autonomy of a work of art, which precluded practical involvement. An admittedly abstract comparison with the twentieth-century avant-garde will perhaps clarify this contradiction. The literary avant-garde (dadaism, futurism, surrealism) aimed to undermine and destroy the model of aesthetic autonomy as the prevailing form of institutionalization. Aesthetic distance, which became a personal cult in the late nineteenth century, was to be replaced by the praxis of life, but in such a way that this praxis would be changed through literary "acts."[15] This fundamental attack on middle-class art was motivated by the experience of advanced capitalism and its consequences during World War I. Realist theory and its formulation of the praxis of life, in contrast, were part of the 1850s, that is, of the first phase of the German Industrial Revolution. It was in this epoch that the German bourgeoisie for the first time formulated its praxis of life in economic terms. Once the idealistic program of early liberalism had failed, the literary elite ap-

---

[14]This idea is expressed with negative dogmatism by Erich Auerbach in *Mimesis*, 3d ed. (Bern, 1964), pp. 478–81; it is historically differentiated by Georg Jäger in "Der Realismus," in *Realismus und Gründerzeit*, 1:3–31.

[15]On this, see Peter Bürger, *Theory of the Avant-Garde*, trans. Michael Shaw (Minneapolis, 1984), and the discussion in W. Martin Lüdtke, ed., '*Theorie der Avantgarde*': *Antworten auf Peter Bürgers Bestimmung von Kunst und bürgerlicher Gesellschaft* (Frankfurt a. M., 1975).

proved rather than criticized this materialistic bourgeois attitude (Haym and Prutz may again be cited as examples). Thus the demand that art should have a relationship to life, that the work of art should not be created for its own sake, ultimately affirmed the status quo. The concept of life underlying the theory of realism was no longer that of the prerevolutionary period, which had been based on politics; it was an economic concept that found expression in industrial expansion. Whereas the left-Hegelian criticism of subjectivism and aestheticism (romanticism) aimed at bringing about social change, the postrevolutionary demand for a close relationship to life appealed to existing developmental processes in which literature had to participate if it was not to lose its social function.

The question that needs to be answered is: How could theories supporting the notion that art has its own laws (autonomy) be developed when the primary concern of postrevolutionary critics was the integration of art and life? For Freytag and Schmidt, the correct—that is, objective—understanding of reality was crucially connected with the concept of *work*, through which the bourgeois-liberal nation-state would be realized. "Not until the year 1848," Freytag wrote, "which gave the *Volk* a share in the state and brought each individual into a hundredfold new contacts with the mainstream of our cultural life,"[16] could the change to praxis and liberation from Vormärz subjectivism occur. The new synthesis could only be achieved through political, "bourgeois work."[17]

The praxis of life sought by the *Grenzboten* circle can be understood as a synthesis of idea and reality. Schmidt's and Freytag's—and one might add, Prutz's and Gottschall's—theory of realism thus required more than a mere copying of empirical reality, which would embody only raw reality. Imitation becomes objective, they believed, only through poetic heightening—that is, through a treatment of the subject that distinguishes clearly between aesthetic and empirical reality.[18] The poeticization of reality, of which German realism is so often accused, had less to do with narrow-mindedness than with the belief that a still imperfect empirical-historical reality had to be brought to harmonious perfection in the aesthetic sphere. The work of art was to create a totality reaching beyond the empirical elements of reality.[19] Put differ-

---

[16]Gustav Freytag, *Vermischte Aufsätze aus den Jahren 1848 bis 1894*, ed. Ernst Elster (Leipzig, 1901–3), 1:34.

[17]On this, see Hermann Kinder, *Poesie als Synthese* (Frankfurt a. M., 1973), p. 174.

[18]See ibid., pp. 175–91; and Ulf Eisele, *Realismus und Ideologie* (Stuttgart, 1976), pp. 48–50.

[19]See Widhammer, *Realismus und klassizistische Tradition*, pp. 121–23; Kinder, *Poesie als Synthese*, pp. 178–80; Eisele, *Realismus und Ideologie*, pp. 104–6.

ently, the theory of art of the *Grenzboten* circle proceeded from the hope for a better, still unrealized, praxis of life which would be anticipated in art. Art can perceive what is merely incipient in reality.

In the opinion of realist critics, then, the demand for reality and faithful imitation did not contradict an interpretation granting the work of art autonomous status. The artist transformed the material of reality "into a harmonious whole"[20] that obeyed its own structural laws. The transfiguration did not make the world more beautiful, as was sometimes too hastily assumed, but—as Wolfgang Preisendanz has emphasized[21]—it allowed art to remain a medium with an intrinsic value of its own. Preisendanz overlooks the fact, however, that with its restoration, artistic autonomy looked different after 1848 than it had around 1800. More recent discussions rightly stress the issue of function.[22] Despite the setback they suffered after the failure of the revolution, liberal critics held to the opinion that art had a public mission, that it was a medium in which all could share. Hence they demanded popularity. But this political function was to be realized through a concept of art in which the idea of autonomy served to correct rather than to question, as had the avant-garde in the Vormärz. The theoretical model of early realism was less advanced than Heine's, which showed a clearer understanding of the problem of artistic periods and their aesthetic claims. After 1848 the concept of autonomy lost the intrinsically negative aspect it had had in classicism and early romanticism, precisely because realist critics were not content to settle for the opposition of ideal and real but instead demanded their synthesis. This synthesis depended on the historical process. The goal—national humanism—was never in doubt; thus literature was surrendered to it unconditionally.

This surrender can be demonstrated in the reception of English and French realism. Although on the whole Schmidt continued to praise Dickens, he was skeptical of Thackeray and rejected Balzac's novels as depictions of "the meanest earthly reality."[23] The disillusioning representation of social problems, of society in general as a capitalist contradiction that could never again be brought into harmonious balance, was

---

[20]Schmidt, *Literaturgeschichte*, 4th ed. (1858), quoted in Kinder, *Poesie als Synthese*, p. 185.

[21]Wolfgang Preisendanz, "Voraussetzungen des poetischen Realismus in der Erzählkunst des 19. Jahrhunderts," in H. Steffen, ed., *Formkräfte der deutschen Dichtung vom Barock bis zur Gegenwart* (Göttingen, 1963), pp. 187–210, esp. 201.

[22]See Helmut Kreuzer, "Zur Theorie des deutschen Realismus zwischen Märzrevolution und Naturalismus," in Reinhold Grimm and Jost Hermand, eds., *Realismustheorien* (Stuttgart, 1975), pp. 48–67.

[23]On Thackeray see Julian Schmidt's review of *The Newcomes* in *Grenzboten* (1856), 1st sem., 1:405–9; on Balzac, see *Grenzboten* (1850), 2d sem., 1:420–30, quote on p. 429.

no longer acceptable to Schmidt and Freytag or, indeed, to Prutz and Gottschall. Schmidt could only explain the gloom that hung over Western European novels as the consequence of a sophistic morality.[24] In such instances, where literary norms were applied to specific works, it is all too clear that the hoped-for historical development was false history—an illusion the Western European realists were right to oppose.

Structural Change in the Subinstitution of Criticism

In a history of literary criticism that aims to go beyond individual characteristics and ideas, a crucial question is how historic changes in the institutionalization of literature affect the function and task of literary criticism. The history of literary criticism has hitherto been severely limited by the assumption that although norms and value judgments may change, the essence of criticism remains the same. It is not enough, therefore, to set forth norms and aesthetic judgments; we must first clarify the context in which they operate. Only against the background of the institution of literature as it appears in a specific epoch and society can we speak intelligibly and in concrete terms about the character and significance of literary criticism. This does not make it a part of aesthetics (applied aesthetics), however, but rather a subinstitution, which together with other subinstitutions constitutes the institution of literature.

The question may be stated as follows: In what way and to what extent was the institution of criticism changed by the Revolution of 1848? This means criticism as a public establishment, not a body of individual critics. Even if it could be shown that Prutz or Schmidt changed his literary views along with his political views after 1848—as in fact was to be the case—it would not necessarily mean that the institution of criticism changed as well. As I will show, after 1848 criticism changed in conjunction with a change in the concept of the function of literature. This change was not, indeed, fundamental. Rather, it was a modification of the earlier structure, which took into account changes in the public sphere. Such leading journals of the Nachmärz as *Grenzboten*, *Deutsches Museum*, and the *Blätter für literarische Unterhaltung* continued a tradition established in the early nineteenth century by accepting the conventional idea of the function of literary criticism. Despite their divergent political ideologies, they adhered to the model developed during the Enlightenment; they relied on

[24]Widhammer, *Realismus und klassizistische Tradition*, p. 120.

the public function of criticism, but without questioning whether the nineteenth-century public sphere was essentially similar to that of the Enlightenment. It was not by chance that they chose Gotthold Lessing as a model for their work.

This adherence to the liberal model was not unproblematic, because the liberal presuppositions, seldom reflected on or specifically formulated, were in any case only conditionally relevant. To the extent that the structure of the public sphere changed significantly during the Industrial Revolution, the liberal model lost its societal basis. It was symptomatic of this process that an organ such as *Deutsches Museum*, in which Prutz continued to display the rational discourse of liberal criticism (albeit in modified form), now had no more than six hundred subscribers, whereas a highly successful journal such as *Die Gartenlaube* offered no literary criticism. On the whole, it may be assumed that the leading critics and theorists of the Nachmärz overestimated the interest of the general reading public in literary criticism. Their claim to speak for the entire public rather than a small elite—a claim still resolutely upheld by the critics who reviewed realist literature—became increasingly doubtful. A gap existed between the professed popularity of realist literature and the actual size of a literary public formed by the rapid urbanization of the population—a gap that could only have been overcome by a revision of the critical model. Such a revision, however, was rejected by the representatives of realist literary theory. To the same degree that their concept of popularity—which was really intended as a criticism of Young Germany—became obsolete, the liberal model of criticism was in danger of atrophying. That such critics as Prutz, Gottschall, Marggraff, and Schmidt were unaware of this danger was due to the fact that they established their position—albeit in different ways—in opposition to the politicized literary criticism of the Vormärz. Forced by the shock of the failed revolution to confront the revolutionary demands of literary criticism in the Vormärz, they concentrated critical attention on one particular aspect of the liberal model, while the basic requirements of that model, which were recognized by the members of Young Germany and the left Hegelians, remained unquestioned in the background.

Since its genesis in the eighteenth century, the liberal model of literary criticism had been inseparable from the bourgeois public sphere.[25] Indeed, the category of the public sphere itself created the framework for the concept of literary criticism. The establishment of criticism as a

---

[25]On this, see Peter Uwe Hohendahl, *The Institution of Criticism* (Ithaca, N.Y., 1982), pp. 44–82; in addition see Christa Bürger, Peter Bürger, and Jochen Schulte-Sasse, eds., *Aufklärung und literarische Öffentlichkeit* (Frankfurt a. M., 1980).

discourse in which mature readers could discuss the character and value of literary texts according to specific rules was based on the assumption that there existed a free space, the public sphere, in which responsible citizens could assemble, without regard for the state and the forces of tradition, in order to reach an understanding about their praxis of life. This public sphere was distinct from traditional groupings and authorities. The principle of criticism, as it was formulated during the Enlightenment, was directed against such traditional, socially determinant forces as the church and the state. In this sense, the concept of criticism, as Reinhart Koselleck has emphasized,[26] was the crucial instrument in destroying the authority of tradition and replacing it by reason. Literary discussion played a special role here: the agreement reached by debating citizens through the medium of literature prepared the way for political awareness. Thus the literary public sphere was, among other things, the forecourt of the political public sphere. Politicization of literary discussion was not the chief political outcome of Enlightenment criticism; it was indirectly brought about, rather, by morality, to the extent that the requirements for a better praxis of life were the theme of literary debate. Moral questions became political the moment they were shifted from the private to the public sector. The early liberal model, as it was constituted in connection with the public sphere of the Enlightenment, aimed at a moral political change. This occurred, on the one hand, when criticism questioned aesthetic and poetic norms and tested them in accordance with the rules of reason and, on the other, when it repeatedly subjected to debate the intersubjectivity of taste involved in the discussion of individual works. The subjectivity of judgments of taste was justified through anthropological consensus, which is necessarily shared by all participants. The normative character of this criticism, which it had in common with absolutist classicism (of, for example, Nicolas Boileau), was derived either from the general rules of reason, which critical opinion only had to follow in order to arrive at the truth, or from insight into the general binding force of subjective judgments of taste.

We must go a step further, however, and emphasize the seldom-formulated premises of enlightened discourse. In the early liberal model, literary discussion was viewed as a subsector of the public sphere—that is, the same basic premises were valid which were generally pertinent to the formation of public opinion: equality and universal accessibility. The early liberal public sphere denied in principle the appeal to privilege based on social status or traditional authority. Theoretically, therefore, the circle of debaters could not be restricted to

[26]Reinhart Koselleck, *Kritik und Krise* (Freiburg, 1959).

specific groups. In the eighteenth century there was obviously a discrepancy between this claim and the literary public that actually existed. Yet this discrepancy between the ideal and reality did not present an obstacle, because it was taken for granted that in the future the public would include everyone. Although the literary criticism of the Enlightenment was normative, it was in principle neither exclusive nor dogmatic. It could not be dogmatic because each of its basic tenets could be critically examined, and it could not be exclusive because there was no place in public discussion for privileged roles. The critic judged in the name of a collective public composed of private individuals; ideally, his *Räsonnement* reflected the outcome of a public discussion that was carried on, for instance, in journals.

The further development of this model will be outlined here only to the extent that it pertains to the development of literary criticism after 1848. At this point, however, we will bracket the problem of how the classico-romantic category of aesthetic autonomy relates to this model.[27] In 1839 the young Georg Herwegh wrote in his essay "Die neue Literatur": "True criticism is really nothing but the transmission of production to the masses."[28] This sentence epitomizes the radical interpretation that was to mark the forties. Criticism was defined as a mediation between the critic and the reading public; but the latter was no longer exclusively an educated, middle-class public. For the first time, reference was made to the entire *Volk*. To the degree that the concept of literature was democratized, that literature and politics addressed the population as a whole, the program of criticism also changed. The radical authors of the Vormärz fully exploited the possibilities of the liberal model, not infrequently in opposition to Young German criticism, which after all had not called for the democratization of literature until after the July Revolution.[29] As indebted as the democrats and left-Hegelians were to the writers of Young Germany, they were at the same time anxious to distance themselves from the earlier movement. In the circle of the *Hallische Jahrbücher* it was generally agreed that such authors as Heine, Karl Gutzkow, and Heinrich Laube had carried out the required politicization of literary criticism halfheartedly because they were still too close to romanticism. The accusation of subjective caprice, leveled not least against Heine, overplayed the similarities and at times gave an impression of radicalism which was not borne out. The Börne-Heine debate showed how little the radicals knew

[27]On this question, see Christa Bürger, *Der Ursprung der bürgerlichen Institution Kunst im höfischen Weimar* (Frankfurt a. M., 1977).
[28]Georg Herwegh, *Über Literatur und Gesellschaft (1837–1841)*, ed. Agnes Ziegengeist (Berlin, 1971), p. 61.
[29]See Hartmut Steinecke, *Literaturkritik des Jungen Deutschland* (Berlin, 1982).

their own limits; the majority sided with Börne, whose exploitation of literature in the service of political progress was regarded as exemplary.[30] The younger generation looked primarily to Börne, and in fact Börne developed the implications of the liberal model more consistently and logically, playing it off against the concept of aesthetic autonomy. By strongly emphasizing the public character of literary criticism—in his debate with the *Jahrbücher für wissenschaftliche Kritik*, for example, in which he maintained that the work of reviewing should not be carried out in a dialogue between critics and authors but by the public—Börne revived the move toward the concept of the Enlightenment and thereby also rescued the political function of literary debate. In this connection, he introduced the theme of the universality of the public sphere, which had certainly been accepted during the Enlightenment yet could hardly be said to have been realized. "I despise any society that is smaller than that of mankind," he wrote in opposition to the Hegelians. Accordingly, the locus of literary criticism was not erudite professional conversation or the small circle of the literary coterie but newspapers and journals. "So what is missing [in criticism]? Nothing but fresh air. It lacks feeling for the public sphere, which died for want of exercise. . . . The only thing missing is public opinion, a ballot box in which all votes could be collected so that they could be counted."[31] Börne's goal as publisher of the *Dramaturgische Blätter* and *Zeitschwingen* was to reconstitute such a critical public sphere, to wrest it from Metternich's restoration period. He wanted criticism to become a rational discourse in which citizens could clarify their own lives through the medium of literature. The relationship between the literary and political public spheres was deliberately emphasized by him. Criticism—in this he went beyond the concept of the Enlightenment—was the instrument of political enlightenment. Discussion was political, even if it passed itself off as literary because political discourse was restricted or forbidden by censorship. That literature could thus be put in the service of political enlightenment, that a close relationship could be established between the literary text and political debate, posed no problem for Börne.[32] In this respect he was an heir and follower of the Enlightenment, unlike romantic literary critics. In the final analysis his position was a mutual reflection of literary and political discourse. Börne had unbounded faith in the universality of rational discourse, although he defined it as a generally comprehensible

---

[30]See Peter Uwe Hohendahl, "Talent oder Charakter: Die Börne-Heine-Fehde und ihre Nachgeschichte," *Modern Language Notes* 95 (1980):609–26.

[31]Ludwig Börne, *Kritische Schriften*, ed. Edgar Schumacher (Zurich, 1964), pp. 55, 57.

[32]On Börne's literary criticism see Hohendahl, *Literaturkritik und Öffentlichkeit*, pp. 102–27.

and public dialogue rather than a scientific one. He regarded the critic as a *Räsonneur,* whose judgment was formulated in a completely normative manner but was open to dispute because it represented merely one opinion among many.

Börne's literary work became a model because of his tendency to democratize literature, not least by stylistic means that removed *Räsonnement* from the realm of learning and brought it into the street. The Young Germans' program for literary criticism included the demand that German literature be brought out of its classicistic and romantic isolation. They intended to write on a journalistic level.[33] It was no coincidence under these circumstances that the question of discourse became the focal point of interest. Since the goal was to produce an effect on the public sphere, the style of writing necessarily became an issue. Once again Heine and Börne became the models to follow, despite the great difference in their styles. Following their example, Young German critics searched for an idiom that would serve as a guide for a new social praxis. Since public opinion was thought to exert an influence, it was tacitly assumed in the literary discourse of the Young Germans that such a change in social praxis was possible. Once the public sphere was no longer suppressed, once censorship and political surveillance of the intelligentsia was lifted, freedom would be extended to the *Volk* in accordance with the model of liberal criticism. This idealistic hope became the object of liberal self-criticism after 1848; the radical concept of a revolutionary popular public sphere was largely retracted and revoked.

The Young German and left-Hegelian concept of literature drew scarcely any distinction between art and criticism. The traditional distinction lost its meaning in a concept of literature which emphasized the crucial role of criticism. We have to define more exactly, however, what is meant by criticism here. The more its judicial, appraising function was preserved, the more belief in objective aesthetic norms was pushed into the background. Börne had already emphasized that he was least concerned in his reviews with the rules to which a piece conformed. Since he regarded literature as part of the historical process, the notion of timeless norms had no meaning. Literary judgments represented a point of view resulting from a particular perspective in history. The possibility, indeed the necessity, for revision was the product of the historicization of criticism.

In the 1830s and 1840s the concept of criticism was inseparable from historico-philosophical discussion, especially of the Hegelian system. To the extent that Hegel's concept of spirit was anthropologically ana-

[33]See Steinecke, *Literaturkritik des Jungen Deutschland,* pp. 29–33.

lyzed by the Young German writers and even more by the left-Hegelians, the dualism of theory and reality, resolved by Hegel, was revived. Theory itself was not reality; rather, it demanded to be made into reality. The anthropological analysis and disintegration of the Hegelian *Geist* gave rise to the revolutionary demand that thinking had to be translated into action. The historical process, which Hegel regarded as the work of the *Weltgeist,* thus became an affair of the human species, whose task it was to realize humane emancipation by means of action. At the peak of self-awareness attained by humanity in Hegel's philosophy, theory—as criticism—was to become reality. Just as Theodor Echtermeyer contended in 1838 in the *Hallische Jahrbücher* that science should no longer be pursued for its own sake but needed to be related to life, literature too was regarded as an experimental field for new possibilities in human praxis. Criticism assumed the task of translation; it abandoned the aesthetic realm and brought literature into the praxis of life. At the same time, however, the contradictory aspect of this radical criticism was revealed. Criticism could call for and discuss the transition of literature to practical action, but it was still part of that literature. The postulated praxis had to remain intellectual: it was realized in manifestos, reviews, discussions, and polemics that remained in the realm of literature. In the anticipated revolution, this criticism, as theory that had become fact, had to be sublated. The outcome of the literary debate was foreseeable; the question was whether there could be any literary-critical discussion at all after the political revolution.

The radicalization of the concept of criticism, which elevated mediation between author, text, and public to a revolutionary act, exhausted the political implications of the liberal model and at the same time brought the aporias of this model into the open for the first time; because literature and literary criticism were primarily intended as instruments of political change, they were overtaxed. In Gustav Schlesier we read that "an indescribable influence is consequently exerted on German literature by criticism, on our culture by literature, and on our history by culture. The criticism of literature helps set the history of the *Volk* on its feet."[34] Not only did the radicalized liberal model fail because such a transmission could not occur in a literary public sphere restricted to the educated—as Georg Büchner alone realized—but its historical functionalism, which had no place for literariness, seriously narrowed the realm of literature and criticism.

The concept of aesthetic autonomy established in classical and romantic literary theory cannot be seamlessly joined to the historico-

---

[34]Gustav Schlesier, "Ueber den gegenwärtigen Zustand der Kritik in Deutschland," in *Zeitung für die elegante Welt* (January 2, 1834), p. 1.

political criticism of Young Germany and the left-Hegelians. It is debatable whether Young Germany merely suspended the aesthetics of Weimar classicism.[35] Both Young German criticism and the concept of the radical Hegelians (albeit less markedly) were at right angles, as it were, to the aesthetics of autonomy. Within the framework of an activist and revolutionary literary theory, the category of aesthetic autonomy was marginal with respect to strategy and system, however much individual critics may have accommodated themselves to it. The philosophy of action and the concept of autonomy could not be systematically combined, because the former demanded that literature be made practical and the latter precluded the transfer of art to praxis on the basis of a categorical distinction between art and reality. The same applies to literary criticism. Whereas liberal criticism spoke for a collective public sphere, romantic criticism, inasmuch as it proceeded from the inherent autonomy of art, saw its task as the interpretation of works. It remained committed primarily to the work of art, not to the public. Liberal criticism of the 1830s and 1840s distanced itself from this hermeneutical model, since it failed to recognize its own concerns—that is, the enlightenment of public opinion—in the discourse of romantic criticism. Because the romantic theory of literature made critical methodology a fundamental problem for the first time by questioning the equivalence of aesthetic and philosophical-critical discourse assumed by the liberal model, it seemed elitist and reactionary to the radical, praxis-oriented critics of the Vormärz.

Postrevolutionary Literary Criticism

How did literary criticism after 1849 relate to earlier models and programs? Did it continue the liberal model, develop a new one, or return to the classic-romantic model? When disillusioned liberals of the Nachmärz accounted for the consequences of their radical political program, their self-critical reflections necessarily included their concept of literature. In hindsight, the hopes they had placed on literature seemed to them particularly exaggerated. Given the course of the revolution, in which material interests played such a conspicuous role, the ability of literature to transform reality proved a total illusion. The reader will recall the analysis of Robert Prutz, who relentlessly criticized the hopes of the Vormärz. As early as 1850 Julian Schmidt made equally harsh statements in *Grenzboten* about the literature of the Vormärz and its political program: "But it was characteristic of the German revolution that with its lyrical pathos, dreamy demeanor, and turbid,

[35]Thus Udo Köster, *Literarischer Radikalismus* (Frankfurt a. M., 1972), pp. 114–15.

obscure longing, it could compete with the poems of its prophets." Schmidt established a connection between the dilettantism of radical art and revolutionary politics, concluding: "The basic fault was that German art did not know how to cope with the richness of the objective world and became mired in dilettantism. Since this was equally true of German politics, we made no progress there either, and science, which took both its studies and its principles seriously, was the only ground for intellectual development." Schmidt flatly demanded a renunciation of political ideals, a return to concrete and positive factors, and a turn toward tangible, naive, and clearly unreflective art. His polemics were directed primarily against the reflexivity of radical Vormärz literature, which he denounced as the inability to form artistically—he meant by this the combination of poetry and criticism in a work of art. By again attributing a limited purpose to literature and confining it to creating form, Schmidt knowingly and intentionally demolished the Vormärz concept of critical poetry. "German poetry," he wrote in 1851, "did not go beyond intention, primarily because it exceeded its limits. It thought it was expanding its range by proceeding from beauty and seeking to throw light on the forces of genesis and decay that belong to the realm of science. It has become apparent, however, that this mixture was an unwholesome one."[36] Schmidt—more radical in this respect than Prutz—proposed a strict separation between poetry and criticism, between literary praxis and art theory. This undoubtedly political decision was in keeping with the revival of the idea of autonomy in the theory of realism.

This objection to the Vormärz program, that poetry and criticism should be separated, characterized the institution of criticism in the Nachmärz. Its function was restricted. Clearly, mediation between literature and life was no longer of primary importance. Schmidt called for criticism and literary theory to return to their old task of defining and judging works of art. That task was to distinguish between wholesome fare and amateurish works. This is remotely reminiscent of the self-imposed task of the Weimar writers to create a German literature by establishing aesthetic values. But the context is entirely different; for consistent early realists such as Schmidt never really revoked the extra-aesthetic purpose of art, or of criticism. Compared to what it had been in the Vormärz, it was merely modified. The year 1848 did not represent the complete break with prerevolutionary tradition advocated in the polemics of *Grenzboten*. The continuity and resumption of earlier concepts can be demonstrated in the work of critics such as Schmidt and Prutz, who came from the circle of the left-Hegelians. Schmidt in

[36]*Realismus und Gründerzeit*, 2:78, 79, 86.

particular conceived his task as critic and historian largely along the lines of the liberal model.

The critics of the Nachmärz rarely said anything about their perception of themselves; and the question of legitimacy was only occasionally raised. Apparently they felt secure in their position. Consequently we must rely on their implicit attitudes to clarify their theories. The climate surrounding literary discussion undoubtedly changed after 1848, becoming calmer and more moderate. There was no shortage of literary feuds—the one between Lassalle and Schmidt recalls the spectacular feuds of the Vormärz—but generally speaking, critics tried to keep objective and personal matters separate. Confrontations between writers were supposed to be conducted according to certain rules, as the case of Freytag's novel *Soll und Haben* (Debit and Credit) demonstrates. The novel was generally well received. The few negative reviews included one by Marggraff in the *Blätter für literarische Unterhaltung*, which provoked a critical reply in the *Bremer Sonntagsblatt* by F. Pletzer: "Our honored friend Hermann Marggraff in Leipzig has reviewed Freytag's novel at length in the 'Blätter für literarische Unterhaltung.' His criticism, as one might expect from Marggraff . . . , is careful, thorough, and kept within decent bounds; but it is false because he, too, has been unable to separate the person from the subject."[37] This complaint was to be expected in view of the rivalry between *Grenzboten* and the *Blätter für literarische Unterhaltung*: although they were in basic agreement, on minor points there was considerable difference of opinion and mutual irritation. The point of departure in Pletzer's metacriticism is typical: he accuses a critic, whose objectivity was generally unquestioned, of a lack of objectivity. In contrast to the Vormärz, personal attacks were to be excluded from literary discussion.

Marggraff and Pletzer were in agreement on the basic question, namely, the appropriate attitude of critic toward subject. Marggraff, too, insisted on objectivity and impartiality. For this very reason he felt he had to defend himself: "Our friend Pletzer has in this case allowed himself to be drawn beyond the bounds of that fine moderation he otherwise observes and which, like others among our friends, we, too, have repeatedly advocated in this paper. He has leveled an accusation we cannot accept, because it calls into question our critical openness and impartiality." He therefore felt it his duty to reiterate the grounds of his opinion—which Pletzer seems to have misunderstood—and to use the occasion to defend his methods. This made a basically insignificant controversy interesting. Marggraff understood Pletzer's attack as

[37]Pletzer, quoted in Hermann Marggraff, "Die Kritik und 'Soll und Haben,'" in *Blätter für literarische Unterhaltung* (1855), p. 662.

part of the *Grenzboten* strategy for fending off, or neutralizing, negative opinions of *Soll und Haben*. Beyond this, he regarded it as interference with freedom of criticism: "We insist, and have the right to insist, on being granted complete freedom to criticize, the denial of which would sign the death warrant of all criticism." Whether Marggraff was really motivated by the struggle for critical freedom so emphatically defended in this statement need not concern us here. But significantly, he regarded freedom of criticism as a prerequisite for a functioning literary life. Marggraff's tacit assumption is that literature cannot exist without criticism. The critic thus has a public duty. As we might expect, Marggraff proceeds to argue that the *Grenzboten* critics have a very incomplete understanding of that duty and therefore abuse it. He implies that there are commercial reasons for this and feels forced to conclude that on the whole journalistic criticism in Germany does not have the necessary objectivity and impartiality. German criticism does not fare well compared to English criticism: "Even though the English journalist finds himself often enough in the position of condemning this or that literary achievement, of contesting this or that opinion as false or destructive, he would never presume in this fashion to throw suspicion on an entire class whose existence necessarily stems from and is dependent on the strongly expressed need for a book trade, because he knows that the private opinions of others concern him as little as his private opinions concern them, and because his practical common sense tells him that he himself would be the most hurt by it."[38]

Marggraff's protest against the accusation of partisan subjectivity and his claim to an objective basis of opinion points to the liberal model. His ideal critic is one who leads literary discussion and thereby guides the public sphere toward self-understanding. At the same time, it is clear that Marggraff regards this ideal as endangered by the intervention of private commercial interests and a polemical subjectivity that he considers a bad heritage of German journalism. The criticism of commercialism was directed against changes in the literary public sphere (and thus against the institution of literature), whose significance could hardly be perceived in 1855. The accusation of subjectivity—leveled, incidentally, by the majority of postrevolutionary critics—concerned the polemical style of prerevolutionary literary criticism, which left the author personally unprotected. These two questions must be dealt with separately.

Literary polemics have been an intrinsic part of literary criticism since the Enlightenment. Once literary works are imputed to have an effect on the public, that effect itself becomes the object of discussion. If a text

[38]Ibid., pp. 662, 663, 664.

can exert a questionable influence on public opinion, the critic has the obligation to come forward. Thus Lessing took a stand against the French theater and classicism because he believed they had a negative influence on the German stage. German classicism also made use of polemics, albeit with a different intention. Whereas Lessing's attacks were primarily intended to have a moral effect, Goethe and Schiller sought through their polemical utterances to make the concept of aesthetic autonomy prevail over the Enlightenment. It was only in Young Germany and the Vormärz, however, that polemics became a fully developed ingredient of criticism. Heine's attack on Platen, Börne's remarks against Heine in the *Pariser Briefe*, and finally, Heine's memorial to Börne, are examples of personal criticism casting aspersions even on character. With the politicization of literature, the author became such a public figure that even the private sphere, in which his subjectivity was grounded, could become the object of criticism. If the separation between art and life were abolished, as the Young German program called for, criticism would touch even the private life of an author if he exposed himself politically. Heine's memorial to Börne (1840), which contemporaries—even radicals—regarded as defamatory, brings together the specific elements of prerevolutionary criticism: subjectivity, engagement, and literariness. It is at the same time a political and a literary commentary, drawing its authority not from general maxims but from the intentionally displayed subjectivity of its author—that is, Heine's notorious frivolity as a writer, which clearly reflects its historical position. Literary critics of the Nachmärz rejected this form of engagement as subjective and biased. They wanted to put an end to the adulteration of discourse, to the blurring of distinctions between the literary and the political, the public and the private, which characterized the works of Heine and the Young German writers. Criticism should retreat to aesthetic and literary norms and thereby weaken the political component in the liberal model or at least make a clean break between literary and political discourse. The literary and political public spheres were still conceived as parts of a whole, but as separate realms with their own norms and conventions. Before 1848 the literary avant-garde considered itself a political avant-garde and was able to expand the task of the critic until it became virtually all-encompassing; after 1848 the concept of criticism was narrowed again, restricted to the concept of artistic judgment which had been institutionalized by the Enlightenment.

To the degree that postrevolutionary liberalism sought to limit the concept and function of public opinion because its extension to the masses seemed threatening, the concept of the relationship between the literary and political functions of criticism also changed. Postrevolutionary skepticism with regard to the political function of art—that is, the scorn for the illusions of the prerevolutionary avant-garde we have encountered in the work of Prutz and Schmidt—ultimately weakened the relationship between the literary and the political public spheres. Certainly, the literary public sphere was no longer in the forefront of the political public sphere; to remain viable it had to allow citizens to relax after the rigors of work. In fact, the normative, judicial criticism of the Nachmärz lacked the very element that had made eighteenth-century criticism progressive: orientation toward the future. The liberal model had itself become conservative; insistence on a judicial function no longer meant freedom from heteronomous authorities but rather a turn toward authoritarianism. The institution of criticism was protected by "objective" aesthetic norms and generic rules, which were taken for granted in reviews.

To be sure, in the epoch between the bourgeois revolution and the founding of the Reich, these were merely tendencies that were overlaid and thwarted by others. The bond between literature and politics had not yet been severed in public discussion. This is clearly demonstrated by the political orientation of the important literary journals, such as *Grenzboten, Deutsches Museum,* and the *Blätter für literarische Unterhaltung.* These publications still viewed literary discussion as part of a general debate. In *Deutsches Museum,* Prutz characteristically addressed not only literary but also political and social issues. A separation between literary and political journalism became evident after 1848; but we should not forget that such critics as Gutzkow, Schmidt, Freytag, and Prutz still availed themselves of both. They saw no problem in switching from political to literary discourse, because they regarded them formally and methodologically as similar. Although the influential organs of public opinion differed in standing from the comparable journals of the Vormärz, they belonged in structure to the liberal tradition. Unlike the family magazines that began to appear after 1850, they were not mass publications. Their circulation—even the influential *Grenzboten*—was modest. Now as before, propaganda for the popularity of literature primarily reached the educated middle class, not the *Volk.* Gutzkow's attempt to address a broader readership in his *Unterhaltungen am häuslichen Herd* had only moderate success compared to that of later family magazines. His promising, much publicized project failed because of its liberal orientation. To create a truly popular journal he would have had to eliminate politics, as Ernst Keil did in the *Gartenlaube.* This neither Gutzkow, Schmidt, Freytag, nor Prutz were prepared to do; they clung to a liberal concept of the public sphere, even though it was much reduced.

Ultimately, Prutz did not regard the founding of *Deutsches Museum* as a political act. Because so many prerevolutionary publications had failed, a public forum was lacking for literary and political discussion. Although Prutz had repeatedly declared himself in favor of popular literature, he regarded the "educated public" as the true readers of his journal. He thus dissociated himself, on the one side, from scientific journals addressed to specialists and, on the other, from popular enterprises that took the wider public into account. On the whole, he still identified the public with the middle class.[39] This was certainly not a progressive journalistic position. *Deutsches Museum* was only cautiously receptive to changes in the literary market. Prutz avoided purely aesthetic judgments of literature, preferring a literary criticism that would respond to and exert influence on the public, but his orientation was still basically normative. The prospectus of his journal thus insistently announced that it would "take pride in restoring to aesthetic criticism the respect due it because of its strict principles, incorruptible opinions, and dignified and charitable representations."[40] The normative point of view and influence were to be combined: literary criticism was not to ignore the needs of its readers. We would misconstrue the historical significance of this development if we were to take this attitude as evidence that Prutz wanted to abolish a normative art criticism based on aesthetics. Prutz, too, exhibited a more literary and aesthetic point of view in his program of the 1850s than he had in prerevolutionary times. With the recovery of Weimar classicism in the Nachmärz, its aesthetics and literary theory were once again seriously considered in criticism. *Deutsches Museum* typifies the epoch in combining aesthetic traditionalism with a moderately liberal political concept. The journal was marked by a dualism of aesthetic and historico-political criteria, a dualism characterizing German realism in general.[41]

The journals reorganized or founded after 1849 clearly demonstrate that the liberal model had been revived by the institution of criticism, albeit in modified form. The intention was to restore literary discourse, which had become politically "chaotic," to its original condition by eliminating political elements or at least restricting them. A critical analysis of authors and works was sought—one guided, however, by an ideal of objectivity and impartiality based on universally binding aesthetic principles. The preceptorial character of this criticism, no longer oriented toward the idea of the future but rather toward the concept of order, is unmistakable. The critic has quietly become a traditionalist reconditioning the past for use in the present. This brings us to the

[39]See Eva D. Becker, "Das Literaturgespräch zwischen 1848 und 1870 in Robert Prutz' Zeitschrift 'Deutsches Museum,'" in *Publizistik* 12 (1967):16.
[40]Quoted in Becker, "Das Literaturgespräch," p. 22.
[41]On this, see Ulf Eisele, *Realismus und Ideologie* (Stuttgart, 1976), pp. 90–92.

crucial question for our argument: Were there typical, epoch-defining forms of critical response in this period which differed from those of both the Vormärz and the *Gründerjahre*? Can we speak of an epoch of literary criticism between 1850 and the founding of the Reich in the same way we can of an early literary theory and praxis of realism?

Only a qualified answer can be given to this question, since we are not concerned with a theoretical system but with critical essays, reviews, and glosses written by individual critics under very different circumstances. One's generation, education, and sensibility all had their effects on criticism. One cannot overlook, for instance, that the most important critics of the Nachmärz—Prutz, Schmidt, Gutzkow, Gottschall, and Marggraff—played a significant role before 1848 and were more or less strongly marked by the literary discourse of the Vormärz. Nevertheless, their post-1848 criticism shows traits that distinguish it from prerevolutionary criticism. It must be borne in mind that the institution of literary criticism did not conform to a single model. Rarely in practice is a given approach displayed in a pure form; the more usual result is a mixture, compromise, or adaptation. The hidden tension in realist literary theory between an aesthetic and a pragmatic historical approach manifested itself in criticism as an exchange between, or a coexistence of, aesthetic, historical, and moral points of view. In general, the strengthening of the classicistic concept of art was accompanied by a greater regard for aesthetic norms: besides its extraliterary functions, an individual work had to have authority as a work of art. This turn toward normative judgment was not restricted to a particular critic or school. It was a general tendency with a number of manifestations, ranging from a dogmatic display of unquestioned aesthetic rules to a conscious resumption of aesthetic reflection in emulation of classicism. A critique of a particular work is thus not infrequently the occasion for a discussion of general aesthetic and literary problems. Theoretical and critical self-understanding took place largely in the medium of criticism.

Some examples will serve to illustrate this critical process: the reviews of Gutzkow's *Die Ritter vom Geiste* (1851–52) by Schmidt, Karl Rosenkranz, and Carriere, and Freytag's review of Willibald Alexis's novel *Isegrimm*, which appeared in *Grenzboten* in 1854.

The reviews of Gutzkow's novel all share the normative approach mentioned above. The work is judged from a general point of view, whether historical, moral, or aesthetic. Each critic sees it as his task, after adequate preparation, to evaluate the novel; that is, to determine to what degree the work satisfies his own requirements and the norms established for the genre of the novel. As we might expect, this tendency is most evident in the detailed review by the Hegelian Rosenkranz in

Deutsches Museum, which comes close to being a systematic investigation. Despite its thoroughness, the review remains abstract. The positions determining the judgment of the novel were obviously fixed before the reviewer began his presentation. The important question for Rosenkranz is whether Gutzkow was capable of writing a social period novel and what presuppositions figure in such a work. Rosenkranz is accordingly least concerned with the complicated story, which Schmidt and Carriere explore in great detail. At the start of his review Rosenkranz refers briefly to the content of the novel in order to establish its character. His intention is to prevent the book from being labeled political, for this would mark it as a polemic, unsatisfying both ideologically and aesthetically. Having justified the novel's content and view of the world, Rosenkranz turns to its poetic execution. His reservations concern the characters and presentation. The characters are classified by him into ideal types, supposedly embodying the idea of the novel; semi-ideal representational types; and amoral figures, who act out of pure egoism. His judgment of the novel conforms to this classification. Of the ideal characters Rosenkranz writes: "The group of ideal characters is the weakest. They lack depth and step-by-step development. These knights of the spirit are noble, brave, and speak cleverly, but they do not undergo a metamorphosis that would place them at the peak of their time. We appreciate them, but we do not learn from them." The other groups are judged similarly. The standard of measurement is not derived from the object and its presentation but introduced into the review a priori. The treatment of the prince is a clear example: "This description of the prince has great style, but it is imperfect. It is like a beautiful statue that has been made from two others and is therefore disharmonious." Gutzkow's figures fail to amalgamate into harmonious characters; they exhibit unresolved contradictions that make synthesis an impossibility. It is obvious that Rosenkranz regards this Young German trait in Gutzkow as a poetic and aesthetic shortcoming. Yet he does not reflect on the question why a harmonious character should be preferable to a fragmented one and why one creation should be aesthetically more perfect than another. As a reviewer Rosenkranz sticks to basic principles without explicitly justifying his norms. The composition and presentation of the novel are treated in the same way. Rosenkranz is not entirely satisfied with the result, but he is not blind to the advantages of the construction. He praises Gutzkow in the following terms: "In fairness to Gutzkow, one has to grant him a pragmatic unity, which he has been able to preserve despite the many episodes and the many characters. Nothing has been idly dropped. . . . Even the poetic justification, nowadays often handled so frivolously, has been strictly managed." For Rosenkranz, however, this technical mastery is not in itself poetic; nor is the style aesthetically satisfying: "The freshness and virtuosity of Gutzkow's narrative must be acknowledged, no matter how severely it may be criticized. His style is clear, fluent, rounded, diversified, and appropriate to the subject matter."[42] But the critic charges the author with a lack of poetic imagination and spontaneity. His narrative remains too rational, too much a product of reflection. Schmidt and Carriere register the same complaints in their reviews. But these complaints are not in themselves of interest here; they concern us only because of the way they are introduced into the review. Rosenkranz formulates his opinion of *Ritter vom Geiste* as if it were the result of his reading; yet the process of reading is not made apparent. His opinion is never really substantiated, either by quotations that would give an impression of the narrative or by the characterization and analysis of the stylistic means. This apodictic opinion presents the critic as a judge who classifies and assigns a rank by merit. Rosenkranz unmistakably exhibits the beginnings of a rigid dogmatism —a lack of reflection, which, however, is not yet pronounced because the reviewer claims to be equitable and fair.

Such fairness is entirely lacking in the *Grenzboten* review. It is partisan and treats the novel as the work of an ideological and literary adversary who has to be brought down. When Schmidt remarks that Gutzkow makes the reviewer's job easier because he is an intellectual and reflective poet and hence pursues clear, discoverable intentions, he hardly means this as a compliment. The reflective writer contradicts the theory of realism. Schmidt quickly reveals his strategy. From the outset he distinguishes between the relatively fixed rules of the drama, which determine the methodology of the critic, and the relatively open and indeterminate form of the novel, which evades judgment. The critic will, accordingly, refrain from applying fixed norms and judge the novel according to its intentions: "These intentions can be discovered and used as a basis for testing the worth of the performance." Schmidt, however, does not follow his own principles when he maintains, in opposition to the theory of the novel set forth in Gutzkow's preface, that it is impossible for this work to present a totally aesthetic view of life: "We would regard such an overall view as a contradiction of the idea of art, and its execution as possible only if fixed, finite, concrete phenomena were dissolved into indeterminate generalities lacking physiognomy; if the individualities were fragmented according to symbolic points of view and the ideas allowed to perish in imperfect representa-

---

[42]*Deutsches Museum* (1852), 1:721–32; quoted in Alfred Estermann, ed., *Literaturkritik. Eine Textdokumentation zur Geschichte einer literarischen Gattung 1750–1975*, vol. 4, ed. Peter Uwe Hohendahl (Vaduz, 1984), pp. 139, 141, 144.

tives, in bad individualities."[43] Schmidt does not judge *Ritter vom Geiste* exclusively according to Gutzkow's formulated program for a multifaceted social novel but by means of an apodictically introduced concept of mimesis (concreteness versus generality). Although the review pretends to argue on immanent grounds and to determine the worth of the novel on the basis of its inherent assumptions, Schmidt in reality supports his methods by a normative approach that explicitly relies on fundamental aesthetic and poetic principles. His search for details accordingly supplies the evidence from which his judgment must inexorably proceed.

Schmidt's criticism, which is eventually directed against the novel as a whole, fastens on the sketching of characters, the composition of the text, the motivation of the action, and the general ideology of the work. This is not the place to pursue his arguments individually, since it is not the theory of realism but rather the act of criticism that is under discussion here. Like Rosenkranz, Schmidt is unable to reconcile himself to the characterization. He complains that Gutzkow is incapable of lending immediacy to his figures. Instead of rounding out features to lead to a harmonious whole, Gutzkow offers reflection, which is meant to link the particular case to the general. Yet characteristically, Schmidt does not ask whether and to what degree reflection is possible, or necessary, in a social novel. Instead, he apodictically rejects this approach: "Such ideas give no real pleasure. One is neither amused nor inspired by them; and the worth of a novel that moves exclusively along such lines can only be sought in its connection to a specific tendency, in the composition as a whole."[44] Schmidt here uses "one" not merely as a variant on the personal "I." His choice of expression is appropriate, because the critic speaks for the reader by presenting the effect made by the novel. He does not, however, verify the novel's reception empirically. Schmidt is not interested in how contemporary readers understand Gutzkow's characters. His argumentation is basically axiomatic: a reflective depiction of character is artificial, so the reader ("one") gets no pleasure from it.

The fullness of the review (twenty-three pages) is not the result of an attempt to investigate the uniqueness of the text or to reveal its structure. Its length is due, rather, to the numerous examples the reviewer presents in support of his opinion. The alternation between apodictic judgment—occasionally explained on the basis of an aesthetic axiom—and textual examples (plot, characters, motivations) determines the

---

[43]*Grenzboten* (1852), 1st. sem., 2:41–63; quotations are from *Literaturkritik*, vol. 4, ed. Hohendahl, pp. 109–30.

[44]Ibid., 4:111.

rhythm of the review. Thus Schmidt summarizes his objections to Gutzkow's characterization after revealing the failure in motivation by citing a number of examples: "*Characterization* has always been Gutzkow's weak point. His total lack of idealism is shared with recent Frenchmen and Englishmen—i.e., with Balzac and Thackeray—but he also lacks the boldness and sureness of line that at least adds a certain interest to the gloomy pictures of these writers." The objection to Gutzkow's characters is twofold. It is directed first against his content, that is, against his concept of people. His figures are too problematic, too negative, for an advocate of poetic realism. But at the same time it is directed against his form of presentation, namely, the pointillist composition of a figure from separate, contradictory traits that do not form a harmonious whole: "There are no organically articulated individuals, only aggregates of empirically introduced, anecdotal portrait elements and arbitrary thoughts."[45]

As we have seen, Schmidt's critical procedure is axiomatic and normative. He always judges the individual work as an example of already existing principles and points of view. The axioms are not always fully developed, but they are not infrequently mentioned. The critic is aware that his judgment is given authority by a theoretical system, but he does not make this theory the object of his critique; he does not usually reflect on it. The review is presented as a judgment, and there is no desire to hide its character as such. The reader has to be told what to think of the novel. A close look reveals that Schmidt even exaggerates the systematic character of his review; for when it seems necessary to him he introduces points of view not in accord with his initially defined strategy. Schmidt concedes, for example, that Gutzkow is successful in drawing his satiric characters, but he then proceeds to underscore their deficiencies. This is why he introduces the moral purpose of literature without further preparation: "The poetic depiction of even wretched characters must always serve the highest purpose of literature, the ethical refinement and purification of the spirit."[46] But he does not explain how this didactic maxim, derived from the aesthetics of the Enlightenment, can be reconciled with the principle of poetic concretization.

Even more striking is Schmidt's method of political criticism, which abruptly introduces extra-aesthetic viewpoints into the review. He calls the political theme of the novel—a program for a new federation that will affect humanity and political freedom—dilettantish. The literary program and the real political conditions in Prussia to which Gutzkow refers have not been brought into line. It is at those points that

[45]Ibid., 4:121–22.
[46]Ibid., 4:126.

Schmidt's political ideology becomes plain in his judgment of the novel. In his view, the political tendency in *Ritter vom Geiste* contradicts the development of realpolitik. This estimation is based, without explanation, on a pragmatic concept of reality, whose relationship to reflection theory is not made clear. Accordingly, the review closes with a moral-political appeal rather than an aesthetic condemnation of the novel. Fictional reality is casually carried over to historical reality and is criticized as such. In place of the secret alliances described by Gutzkow, Schmidt calls for political parties that will further the liberal program. The battle, Schmidt says, can only "be waged by a determined struggle against the insensibility of egoism, . . . only by devoted work and self-abnegating humility."[47] Thus the end of Schmidt's critique is fundamentally different from its beginning and its proposed method. The critic has had the last word and his opinions have taken precedence over those of the novelist and his work. Schmidt's critique of form and composition proves in the last analysis to be a criticism of the message—that is, of Young German tendencies. This again demonstrates the power of the liberal model, in which the relationship between literature and politics plays an important role. This link is no longer established in the review, however; its aesthetic and political points of view exist side by side, independent of each other.

The third critic, Carriere, is willing to concede to Gutzkow all the capabilities and qualities that Schmidt denies him: the ability to make an aesthetic presentation, a feeling for the national character of the German novel, and a capacity for artistic development, which has led to the heightening of his literary achievement. In other words, Carriere approaches the novel through its author, since he compares the novel with Gutzkow's earlier works and views it as the sum of his previous literary experiences. As the critic emphasizes, this process of maturation has allowed Gutzkow to overcome the viewpoint of the Young Germans: "His Weltanschauung has matured in religious and ethical respects as well, and here again he comes close to the viewpoint of a free humanity achieved by Lessing; his earlier doubts about God and immortality and his youthfully brash disavowal of them have given way to a need for faith." It is this retraction of Young German radicalism that makes the novel acceptable to Carriere. *Ritter vom Geiste* appears to him a novel in the tradition of *Wilhelm Meister*. Yet despite his general approbation, Carriere offers a number of criticisms and objections that concur in part with those of Schmidt and Rosenkranz. Carriere sees himself no less as a judge delivering praise and blame. He says, for example: "On the other hand, I have to fault Gutzkow for occasionally

[47]Ibid., 4:130.

portraying static objects descriptively instead of creating a picture through action and movement, as the art of literature must do in contrast to painting." The appeal to Lessing is unmistakable. Carriere, too, introduces axiomatic aesthetic and critical principles. Yet the general impression is not the same as in Schmidt's critique. Carriere is more conciliatory, more flexible, and less systematic in his application of aesthetic theory. The construction of his review is looser and more journalistic than Schmidt would have allowed. We can conclude from a number of details that the essay was written in parts, each intended for a different issue of the weekly publication in which it appeared. Furthermore, Carriere's "I" is more personal and more individualistic than Schmidt's critical persona. When he writes "I have already indicated how different Gutzkow's thinking is in regard to Christianity from what it was formerly, when he wrote *Wally*,"[48] he is referring to himself as an individual, as a journalist writing these lines at a specific point in time. Carriere's review combines normative, historical, and personal approaches. The normative predominates, but its predominance is modified by a historical perspective. Thus Carriere is also decidedly more open to the new creative principles of Gutzkow's novel than is Schmidt, whose dogmatic concept of realism gets in the way of his structural insight.

The fourth review we will consider, written by Freytag for *Grenzboten*, is of Alexis's novel *Isegrimm* (1854). The Prussian orientation of the author and of his novel found an immediate response in the reviewer, who emphasized its ideological-political affinity at the outset and made it the focal point of his review. Alexis was no literary novice: he was well known to the public through his earlier novels. In the second paragraph of his review, Freytag uses this knowledge to place the novel within Alexis's oeuvre as a whole and to demonstrate the singularity of his fictional world. Not until the third paragraph of his lengthy review does he get to the novel itself, which he introduces by summarizing its content and describing its principal characters. Following his description, Freytag begins his critique by asking to what extent this novel can be considered a work of art. The principle of epic closure in a narrative is the standard by which the novel will be measured critically. Freytag first establishes that it was not Alexis's intention to achieve epic completeness and that this norm would in any case have been difficult to realize, given the disparity of the material. But the author's intention is not the critic's ultimate yardstick. Rather, he calls that intention into question, because it fails to achieve its goal—the

---

[48]*Frankfurter Konversationsblatt* (1852), nos. 105–7; quotations are from *Literaturkritik*, vol. 4, ed. Hohendahl, pp. 132–34, 137, 133.

creation of a larger artistic effect. At this point Freytag gives a clear explanation of the relationship between aesthetic theory and literary praxis: if the correct effect can be achieved in practice, it can deviate as much as desired from existing aesthetic and poetic norms. The critic seems to be abandoning the "old pedantic theory." He does so, however, only within the context of a more comprehensive strategy, which once again underscores the necessity for a normative approach. Thus Freytag writes: "The permanent need of a great many of these rules of composition is not difficult to understand." Accordingly, he says about *Isegrimm*: "We expect the novel to depict an occurrence whose parts are comprehensible because they give the effect of having an inner relationship to a complete whole and which thereby makes possible a certain uniform shading of style, description, and characterization. This inner unity, this connection of incidents in the novel, must have its source in the personalities depicted and the logical compulsion of the underlying circumstances of the novel."[49]

The connection to Christian Friedrich Blanckenburg's theory of the novel is evident, whether it was conscious or not. Inner unity—a trans-historical law of composition—which in the novel is derived from the characters, is the deciding factor for him. Freytag goes one step further as a critic; he not only establishes the existence of such norms but gives them authority through his references to the effect produced. For the reader to receive an impression of structural reality, empirical reality has to be transformed. The bare depiction of reality would confuse the reader, since it cannot provide a view of the whole. Alexis's novel is judged against the background of these explicitly introduced and explained norms: *Isegrimm* violates the laws of the epic because it increasingly subordinates the development of the characters to the political events, which should remain in the background. Freytag then extends his criticism to the characters, which according to him lack the inner harmony that is so vital to epic construction: "His main characters almost all lack clarity of action and do things that, given their personalities, are not believable." The logic of the review follows the logic of normative poetics. After a descriptive and historical introduction, Freytag summarizes the content of the novel. In the fourth, and central, paragraph, he sets forth the aesthetic and poetic basis for his judgment. These norms are subsequently applied to the discussion of the work in hand. The review ends in a consistent manner with a summarizing conclusion: "We can thus not grant the writer's claim that his work,

---

[49]*Grenzboten*, 1st sem., 1:322–28; quotations are from *Literaturkritik*, vol. 4, ed. Hohendahl, pp. 227–29.

with the help of free invention, characterizes a great time."[50] This final opinion, which emphasizes aesthetic failure, is explained again in the concluding paragraphs in order to make the aesthetic and artistic quality of Alexis's novel as clear as possible.

Freytag's review is greatly indebted to the ideal of rationalistic criticism. Both its strategy and its logic are derived from that approach: the critic sees himself as a reasoner for the public. Critical judgment is the logical, inevitable result of a thought process in which great principles—that is, aesthetic principles—are established and applied to individual objects. What is compelling in this process is that the reader can follow the judgment. If the aesthetic premises are correct and the description of the work is appropriate, the conclusion will be the same whoever the critic is. As the implied reader of the text, one reviewer can be replaced by another. In his text he remains abstract. The reader is of course aware that the description of the novel is due to Freytag the individual, but the text of the review gives no evidence of this. Rather, it is assumed that his observations have the same character as the theoretical parts of the text. His sentences present the qualities of the novel (action, characters) as given, referring to them as historical phenomena. Freytag's review is based on the certainty that rational *Räsonnement* can accurately describe and judge the essence of a work of art. This assertion should not be misunderstood, however. Freytag by no means confuses art with reality. The lack of distinction between aesthetic and historical representation is precisely what he finds fault with in the novel. What is characteristic of a reasoned critique is, rather, its claim to be able to reformulate the aesthetic text in such a way that it becomes subordinate to a judgmental logic. It never occurred to Freytag that the development of such a judgment could be problematic, that the very objectivity of a description could be a fiction in which the critic passes off his observations and impressions of the text as facts. This same lack of discernment is found in rationalism and classicism. Characteristically, in his review of *Isegrimm* Freytag follows a classic model aiming more at an aesthetic than a moral-practical judgment. As a critic, Freytag represents "the viewpoint of art against the writer himself,"[51] and the public and its interests are only secondary considerations. The reason is obvious: according to the logic of criticism, the public, as the ideal reader, has to arrive at the same conclusion as the critic.

The four reviews under discussion are not a sufficient basis for an exhaustive discussion of critical discourse in the Nachmärz; they do,

[50]Ibid., 4:230, 232.
[51]Ibid., p. 232.

however, provide a picture of the possibilities and limitations in postrevolutionary literary criticism. The dangers inherent in a normative-rationalist approach were not lost on the critics of the time. Gottschall used the occasion of a review of Gutzkow's *Die Zauberer von Rom* (1858–61) to take issue with Schmidt's methodology. This polemic, the outcome of a harsh critique of Gutzkow's novel which appeared in *Grenzboten*, affords insight into the contemporary consciousness. Gottschall's deliberations are interesting because they go beyond the particular case. He accuses the journal of misusing and misunderstanding the purpose of literary criticism: "The harm 'Grenzboten' does to our literary development is more significant than the good it does in fighting pernicious trends." What is noteworthy here is not only the attempt to set limits on the dogmatic realism of *Grenzboten* but also the intention—no matter how incompletely realized—to define criticism as a public institution and to defend it against Schmidt. Schmidt refers in this context to an "economy of literature," in which the critic is given the role of a proofreader deleting what is harmful. The reviewer is compared to the sparrow who devours harmful grubs but can itself become dangerous if allowed to range too freely over the cornfields and vineyards of literature. Obviously, Gottschall prefers a system of checks and balances in which power is carefully apportioned. The *Grenzboten* critics, for instance, are accused of having misused their judgmental position by running down the public: "Through one-sided, often bitter and biased criticism, they have tried to discourage contemporary production and undermine faith in the authority, worth, and motivating force of a public that constantly allows itself to be impressed by emphatic assertions."[52] This complaint is directed against the overestimation of the principle of realism; yet, at the same time, it unintentionally raises the issue of form: the intimidation of the public through rational discourse. Gottschall's critique concludes that the rational discourse of the liberal model, on which Schmidt and Freytag rely, has become doctrinaire and lost its dialogic character. The public no longer plays the role of an interlocutor in literary criticism. Gottschall probably touched a sensitive nerve here. Changes in the structure of the press—in particular, the appearance of family periodicals, inexpensive serial novels, and pulp fiction—indicate that the literary public was changing, that the educated reader to whom journals such as *Grenzboten* and *Deutsches Museum* were addressed was no longer the norm. A critic such as Gottschall was by no means close to

---

[52]Rudolf Gottschall, "Karl Gutzkow's 'Zauberer von Rom,'" in *Blätter für literarische Unterhaltung* (December 16, 1858), no. 51, pp. 925–33; quotations are from pp. 927, 928.

resolving this dilemma. His suggestion to return to classic aesthetics (Schiller and Goethe) remains entirely within the framework of the bourgeois institution of literary criticism. His self-understanding as a critic does not essentially distinguish him from Marggraff, Prutz, Schmidt, or Rosenkranz. The change he observed in the literary public sphere did not lead him to a fundamental criticism of the institution but rather to a typical late-liberal adaptation of the model. The metaphor of the critic as a pest controller who must himself be controlled is instructive. The object of this literary criticism is literature, not public self-awareness. Gottschall's aesthetic rigorism is as ineffective a solution as Schmidt's moral rigorism. The search for fixed norms, the desire to replace the subjectivity of the Vormärz by objective standards, has to be understood as an attempt to bring the changing literary scene under control. Clear-sighted critics of the Nachmärz noticed that literary conditions were changing, yet they did not grasp the nature of those changes. By and large they held to their traditional role until the founding of the Reich. They trusted in the efficacy of the institution of literary criticism even when they distanced themselves from the dialogic model of early liberalism (*Räsonnement*). Earlier critics saw themselves as opinion-forming publicists, not as hired journalists who had to write what their chief editors demanded. The years between the bourgeois revolution and the founding of the Reich were a transitional phase in literary criticism. The dominant model of liberalism had lost its force, and alternative forms appeared, even though a total change in the paradigm had not yet occurred. The New Criticism—namely, a feuilletonistic criticism—did not dominate the press until after 1870.[53]

[53]On this, see Russell A. Berman, *Between Fontane and Tucholsky: Literary Criticism and the Public Sphere in Imperial Germany* (New York, 1983).

· 5 ·

Literary Tradition and the Poetic Canon

The Concept of Tradition

It has been the traditional task of literary history to make the literature of the past accessible to the present by reconstructing its development. The authors, the works, and the various literatures of earlier epochs are to be presented in such a way that today's reader will understand the relation between past and contemporary literatures. Such an attempt has both the positive function of presenting the literary heritage by describing its historical development and the no less important task of determining through emphasis and selection exactly what that heritage is. The individual historian may not necessarily be aware that the historical presentation of "transmitted" material involves not only description and categorization but selection and hence evaluation; for historiography, however, this is an essential part of the task. In "searching for" and then "tracing" that heritage, it creates through selection and assessment what will later be expounded as tradition. What has been accepted in literary history as literary tradition—with its main stream and tributaries—and now appears as *the* literature, is the result of a process of reduction in which a body of material is sifted and divided into the categories of worthy and unworthy of preservation. This is true even if the historian is unaware of the normative aspect, because his or her own cognitive interests often remain hidden. Besides their obvious historical task, histories of literature fulfill a second function: in reconstructing the past they define a corpus of traditionally accepted literature. Moreover, they determine one's reaction to that literature. The categories of development and affiliation introduced into literary histories determine what position a work or an author will have in the traditional corpus of literature.

This function is, to be sure, carried out not only by literary history. Poetics also makes a contribution; it refers either through norms or through examples, approvingly or critically, to the literature of the past and thereby comments on the binding literary canon. So too does current criticism, which in the process of judging new works often directly or indirectly makes comparisons to works of the past. The history of literature is the most recent of these three institutions, and its contribution to the definition of the obligatory literary canon is unquestionably the most complex. For the development of a historical methodology—that is, the evaluation and categorization of works and texts according to their historical interconnections—represents above all a break with any analysis that concerns itself with specific authors and works and makes claims for their importance. Because the historical approach no longer assumes a fixed, normative point of view but instead raises evolution to a cognitive principle, it seems to resist such an unchanging position. Yet the outcome of this treatment, though more complex, is similar. The concept of development, too, includes the model of an order that distinguishes between what belongs and what does not, that determines what will be the center of attention and what will be relegated to the periphery. Discontinuing the dogmatic way of thinking connected with earlier poetics and the literary criticism that served it does not solve the problem; it merely changes the procedure. In nineteenth-century historicism the problem was solved in a different way. Interest turned primarily to the *process* of transmitting tradition, and the literary tradition was thereby questioned as a whole. Harry Levin has correctly observed that the concept of tradition appeared relatively recently in critical discussion; only at a late date did the idea come to be regarded as having a positive value.[1] European romanticism discovered the past as past and completed the transition from a received heritage to a conscious, reflective confrontation with tradition. In this sense, the concept of a literary tradition, as it is found in Johann Gottfried Herder or A. W. Schlegel, is no longer traditional but distinctly modern.

The Heritage of 1848

Until now the epoch between 1770 and 1830 has been regarded as the peak of German literature, when its most important works were written, works that later became models and acquired canonical status. But the writers of that epoch did not see themselves in this light. Neither

---

[1]Harry Levin, "The Tradition of Tradition," in his *Contexts of Criticism* (Cambridge, Mass., 1957), pp. 55–66.

the Weimar group nor the romantics viewed their work as the climax, to say nothing of the end, of German literature. The notion of a time of flowering followed quickly by decline and fall, which has been set forth since 1840, belongs rather to the complex history of tradition.[2] Goethe believed that German literature would not produce classic works as long as Germany had no cultural center and did not achieve national unity.[3] The Schlegel brothers proceeded from the similar assumption that German literature was at the beginning of its development and that its classical period was yet to come. Not until about 1835, after the death of Goethe and Hegel, was it generally accepted that an important phase in German writing had come to an end and a new age had begun. Heinrich Heine and Georg Gottfried Gervinus are important witnesses to this shift. As much as they differed in their estimation of the past, they agreed that the age of Goethe had ended. Whereas Heine, in *Die romantische Schule*, spoke for a modern, politically engaged literature, Gervinus believed that German literature had basically come to a close with Goethe and Schiller. For him romanticism already had the flavor of a postscript. Gervinus ends the fifth volume of his history of literature (1842) with the following often-quoted lines: "The contest in art is over; now we should aim at that other target which no marksman among us has yet hit, and see whether Apollo will now grant us the fame he did not refuse us before." He recalls Goethe's insistence that he did not want the changes required to produce classic works in Germany; and then he demands precisely those changes in the realm of politics: "We, however, want these changes and tendencies."[4] With this demand that the nation think first of its political future, Gervinus concludes his account of the preceding literary epoch, and in spite of all his criticism he grants it heroic status. Heine arrives at a similar conclusion in his *Romantische Schule*: he makes a distinction between Goethe's epoch, to which he attributes an essentially aesthetic character, and his own. This leads him indirectly, despite his sharp criticism, to establish the former as a high point of German *Geistesgeschichte* (history of ideas). Even when critics later disputed his notion of a high point at about 1800, as Rudolf Gottschall did, Gervinus's judgment still exerted an influence. Gottschall emphasized the value of the new, the modern, in his history of literature by measuring it against the old, the classicists: "But as to the claim that our national German literature is in decline, or

[2]See Reinhold Grimm and Jost Hermand, eds., *Die Klassik-Legende* (Frankfurt a. M., 1971).

[3]Johann Wolfgang von Goethe, "Literarischer Sansculottismus," in *Goethes Werke*, Hamburg ed., vol. 12 (Munich, 1981), pp. 239–44.

[4]Georg Gottfried Gervinus, *Geschichte der deutschen Dichtung*, 4th ed. (Leipzig, 1853), 5:667, 666.

that the intellectual ground was so exhausted by Schiller, Goethe, and the classicists that it will have to lie fallow for a time in order to recover, we find ourselves, without overestimating recent developments, in wholehearted disagreement. Since the time of Schiller and Goethe, popular intercourse and the exchange of ideas has increased extraordinarily."[5] This emphatic defense of the modern also indirectly confirmed the canonical status of Weimar classicism.

Gottschall's position in 1854, which takes for granted the canonization of Weimar classicism, shows that more was at stake than the definition of classicism. The problem had too long been restricted to the relationship between classicism and romanticism. The real concern was the establishment of a national literary order, the determination of an independent national tradition clearly set apart from other national traditions. Only in this light does the question whether Goethe and Schiller were the classical authors who brought German literature to its climax become fully significant. The "classical legend" (*Klassiklegende*) becomes understandable only against the background of a specific historical constellation: growing German nationalism, which resulted in a search for cultural identity. Early liberalism found that identity in German literature and established it historically by introducing the category of a classical age of literature.

The Historical Approach

It is for this reason that we cannot restrict ourselves to the question why the Weimar group, especially Goethe and Schiller, was seen as the high point of German literature; the scope of the question must be enlarged to include an inquiry into how literary tradition was perceived. This task was taken over by literary historiography. Gervinus was one of the first to claim that he was not merely recording his material as a whole but was sifting it and presenting it in such a way that the process of literary change would be seen as a meaningful and inevitable development. Thus he was also the first to establish the schemata according to which the supposed evolution would be described and judged. In the introduction to his *Geschichte der poetischen National-Literatur der Deutschen* (History of Poetic National Literature in Germany) (1835), Gervinus makes clear what he considers the task of literary history and what prospects he sees for carrying it out. Although he is skeptical about the possibility of an exhaustive treatment of the material, he is

[5]Rudolf Gottschall, *Die deutsche Nationalliteratur in der ersten Hälfte des neunzehnten Jahrhunderts*, 2d ed., vol. 1 (Breslau, 1861), p. vii, from the preface to the first edition (1854).

convinced that he has found the correct approach. Gervinus takes for granted that the object of a historical presentation must be a self-contained, well-rounded subject that can be described from beginning to end. For this reason, he contends, the political history of Germany cannot be written in 1835: "No political history accounting for Germany's destiny up to the present can have the right effect, because history, like art, must lead to calm, and we must never be turned away unconsoled from a historical work of art." In contrast, the story of German literature can be told, Gervinus thinks, because it is essentially complete: "It has reached a goal, if there is any truth at all to be learned from history, from which one can successfully glimpse a whole, from which one can receive a calming, indeed an uplifting, impression and derive the greatest instruction." For Gervinus, this goal is inherent in the object itself. He strongly objects to the accusation that he has put his own construction on it. In his view, the course of German literature reached its peak about 1800, and he consequently directed his presentation toward that point: "The goal in the history of our German art of writing to which I refer was reached at the end of the last century; my narrative therefore had to be carried forward to that point." What Gervinus means is the alliance between Goethe and Schiller, not romanticism, which he regards instead as a decline: "Scarcely had calm been achieved after the extraordinary ferment stirred up among our artistic men of genius by the German Homer, when Goethe's classical works were followed by a kind of stasis in taste and language; the French Revolution robbed us of the effects of his most recent labors, Schiller died early, and the glaring collapse of our belles-lettres into decay and triviality might well have been in that first moment even more horrifying than recent political events, which will draw us ever farther from the comfortable consideration of the inner history of our education."[6]

The concept of classicism clearly determined Gervinus's approach, even if he did not yet use the term. Goethe and Schiller represented the peak of German literature, because they created works that could educate literary taste. Although this assessment was not in itself original, indebted as it was to the early history of Goethe and Schiller criticism, Gervinus drew conclusions from it going far beyond the cult of personality. When he characterizes the literature of Weimar as the zenith of German literature, he casts earlier literature in the role of prehistory and later literature in that of posthistory. The seventeenth and early eighteenth centuries were related to the decade between 1790 and 1800; their literature was analyzed and judged with respect to its con-

[6]Quoted in Hans Mayer, ed., *Deutsche Literaturkritik im 19. Jahrhundert* (Frankfurt a. M., 1976), pp. 272, 269.

tribution to the development of "classical" literature. Similarly, modern postclassical literature was measured by the program Schiller had promulgated in *Die Horen*.

Even though Gervinus's account was by no means accepted uncritically by later historians and in fact was sharply criticized after 1848, the questions it posed largely determined late nineteenth-century discussion of the literary tradition. Even historians whose judgment of romanticism differed from Gervinus's, or who considered the possibility that C. M. Wieland and Jean Paul should also be regarded as classical German authors, stayed within the framework of Gervinus's basic scheme. The category of evolution, which governed historicism as a whole, led to the search for a final goal, a point of reference for understanding the course of that evolution. A distinction was consequently made between authors representing the end of a development, those merely preparing the way for it, and those with little or no significance for that presumed evolution.

The categories introduced by Gervinus were taken over in the historical discussion of literary tradition. In 1849, for example, Hermann Hettner tried to explain the inner relationship between Weimar classicism and romanticism as a logical unfolding of poetic idealism.[7] And Julian Schmidt added a preliminary volume to his *Geschichte der deutschen Literatur im neunzehnten Jahrhundert* (History of Nineteenth-Century German Literature) dealing with the time between 1794 and 1806; that is, the period of classicism and early romanticism. Although he did not share Gervinus's opinion that later literature could be regarded only as posthistory, Schmidt adhered to the concept of a German classicism validated by Goethe and Schiller: "Continuity and coherence began in German belles-lettres only when Goethe and Schiller met; they ended when Schiller died . . . and we must call this interval our classical period; i.e., the time when the outstanding intellects of our nation had an inner, essential relationship to each other, when their writings represented the highest expression of German culture, and when form came as close to perfection as the German language allows."[8] The political objections advanced by Schmidt—an engaged liberal—against the aesthetic culture of Weimar by no means precluded that for him, too, classicism, and to a lesser extent romanticism, represented the foundation of German literature on which every nineteenth-century history of literature had to be based. Even Got-

---

[7]Hermann Hettner, "Die romantische Schule in ihrem inneren Zusammenhang mit Goethe und Schiller," in his *Schriften zur Literatur*, ed. Jürgen Jahn (Berlin, 1959), pp. 53–165.

[8]Julian Schmidt, *Weimar und Jena in den Jahren 1794–1806*, 2d ed. (Leipzig, 1855), pp. 1–2.

tschall's almost simultaneously published history of early nineteenth-century literature, which emphasized the importance of modern literature above all and in this respect was a polemic against Schmidt, began with the classical authors and ranked Friedrich Klopstock, Wieland, Herder, and Lessing as preparatory figures. In subsequent chapters it dealt with the "disintegration" of the classical ideal brought about by the epigones of the nineteenth century and the tempering of romanticism in the works of Joseph von Eichendorff, August Platen, and Karl Immermann.

In Hettner's *Geschichte der deutschen Literatur im achtzehnten Jahrhundert* (History of Eighteenth-Century German Literature), completed in 1870, part four bears the title "Das klassische Zeitalter der deutschen Literatur," and once again conceives of this period as the goal and high point toward which German literature proceeds in logical and systematic fashion. The scheme is broad enough to include the late baroque, the early Enlightenment, and the Sturm und Drang. For Hettner, not only Lessing and Klopstock but Friedrich von Hagedorn, Justus Möser, Johann Gottsched, and Jakob Michael Lenz, too, belong to the tradition that eventually gave rise in about 1800 to neohumanism. The methodological turn to positivism which marks the work of Wilhelm Scherer also had relatively little effect on the structure of literary history. He describes the slow rise of literature in the eighteenth century, its gradual consolidation into a cultural identity, and its culmination in the works of Weimar classicism as the fruits of an effort that began at the nadir of the Thirty Years' War.[9] Wilhelm Dilthey, finally, followed the same scheme in his inaugural lecture delivered in Basel in 1867, but with the important difference that he included romanticism in the great tradition beginning with Lessing and ending with Goethe's death.[10] Dilthey, however, tempers the glorification of classicism by approaching Goethe's time from a perspective of historical distance, thus placing the heritage itself more in the foreground than did earlier presentations.

Although in the late eighteenth century and even during the time of early romanticism there was still general uncertainty about the canon of German literature, by about 1850 the tradition had largely been established. Bernd Peschken's supposition that it was the literary historians of the Nachmärz—Dilthey in particular—who compiled the corpus of obligatory authors and works is clearly untenable.[11] Dilthey played a crucial role in determining the German canon, but less by recommend-

---

[9]Wilhelm Scherer, *Geschichte der deutschen Litteratur* (Berlin, 1883).

[10]Wilhelm Dilthey, "Die dichterische und philosophische Bewegung in Deutschland 1770 bis 1800," in his *Gesammelte Schriften*, 2d ed. (Stuttgart, 1957), 5:12–27.

[11]Bernd Peschken, *Versuch einer germanistischen Ideologiekritik* (Stuttgart, 1972), pp. 117–19.

ing new authors than by reevaluating the relationship between the Enlightenment and classicism on one side, and classicism and romanticism on the other. Dilthey's literary essays essentially brought the process of canonization to an end; they offered a general historical synthesis that served as the focal point of Germanic studies for the succeeding generations, even if the particulars of his schema were not always accepted. The young Dilthey's judgment corresponded to a large extent with Hettner's. In a later edition of Hettner's history of literature, the editor notes that "Hettner's basic idea continues to triumph; particularly when compared with the most recent 'syntheses' of today, it safely retains its superior unifying power."[12]

Nonetheless, the changes that took place in the Nachmärz were by no means small and unimportant. Discussion of literary tradition took place in a cultural and political milieu differing significantly from that of prerevolutionary times. In the first phase of canonization—from 1830 to 1848—the validity of classicism, and even more of romanticism, was contested for aesthetic as well as political reasons. After 1850, however, there developed a tendency—which became even stronger in the 1860s—to take the value of past literature for granted and thus to focus attention on historical continuity. If by 1835 feeling had already developed that an important epoch in German literature had come to a close, the new generation of critics and historians held the opinion that Goethe's time was irretrievably past and that controversy over its value was therefore meaningless. Rudolf Haym commented on this change in 1870 in his introduction to *Die romantische Schule*. The fight against romanticism which dominated the 1840s, he writes, had lost its importance: "That time . . . is past. We look back on the struggle of the 1840s as on a dream from which we have awakened. A much more serious and practical struggle has begun, the optimistic, joyful work of making progress on the soil of national pride and independence, won as if by a miracle. Of course, we will continue to talk in our usual way about romanticism, which in fact was nothing more than the ghost of a once justifiable movement."[13] In Haym's opinion, the critical polemic with romanticism, which extended from Heine to the early Hettner, should be replaced by a historical assessment that treats the past objectively. Classicism receives the same treatment. Whereas initially Schmidt still offered the traditional liberal objections to Goethe and Schiller and did not begin to take an affirmative view of them until after 1866,[14] Gottschall, in his *Deutsche Na-*

---

[12]Georg Witkowski in part 4 of Leipzig (1928) edition, p. 326.
[13]Rudolf Haym, *Die romantische Schule* (Berlin, 1870), p. 4.
[14]See Peschken, *Versuch einer germanistischen Ideologiekritik*, pp. 73–116.

tionalliteratur of 1854, accepted the classicists as a matter of course. "The *classicists* created for us an artistic form with a humane spirit modeled on the antique," he wrote in the introduction to the first edition; "the *romantics* destroyed that form in order to free the imagination from existing traditions and to make literature *popular*."[15]

Heinrich Heine

Much as the Nachmärz synthesis in the history of ideas seems to differ from what existed in the 1840s, it was based on the preparatory work of prerevolutionary literary history. Such writers as Schmidt, Haym, and Gottschall naturally appealed to Gervinus's monumental work, whose basic plan continued to point out a direction, even if its details were often not accepted. In addition to Gervinus, however, we find Heine's initially no less important presentation in *Die romantische Schule*, which offers much more than a discussion of German romanticism. It was Heine's declared intention to explain the context of German literature to his French readers in reply to Madame de Staël's book on Germany. Not only was Heine's political criticism of romanticism as a retrogressive, catholicizing movement influential in the liberal and radical camps, but so was his thoroughly ambivalent assessment of Weimar classicism. Heine recognized the historical status of Goethe's and Schiller's achievement in German literature more clearly than did Wolfgang Menzel or even Börne. He put particular stress on the change in aesthetic principles which set the Weimar writers apart from those of the Enlightenment. For Heine, the separation of art and reality—in other words, aesthetic autonomy—had already reached a stage at which its original significance and function were lost. The dictum that an artistic period has come to an end casts a shadow over Goethe. Not only Heine's recognition that Goethe's art was "unfruitful"—that is, that classical aesthetics had a conservative aspect—but his even more radical understanding of the historical process showed him that the principle of aesthetic autonomy, to which classicism owed its greatness, had lost its legitimacy and become a conservative ideology. Heine concluded from this that a new art was needed, one with a relationship between aesthetics and reality different from that in Goethe's work.

In the third book of *Die romantische Schule* Heine refers to an author who was neither a romantic nor a member of Goethe's school. He was "totally isolated in his time," because he was "entirely dedicated to his time and absorbed in it." He means Jean Paul, who was celebrated as a model for the young generation. It is in this connection that Heine writes about the young writers "who are at the same time artists, trib-

---

[15]Gottschall, *Die deutsche Nationalliteratur*, p. xii.

unes, and apostles." His reference to Jean Paul is significant, because it points to an alternative tradition distinct from both retrogressively oriented romanticism and apolitical, aesthetically aloof classicism. Two names mentioned by Heine unquestionably set him apart from classicism: Sterne and Shakespeare, both moderns in the sense of the youthful Friedrich Schlegel. Heine—differing in this respect from Gervinus—does not use his criticism of romanticism as a basis for acknowledging the Weimar writers as the norm. He criticizes Goethe for, among other things, the very quality he elsewhere praises most in Goethe's work: its artistic purity. Heine sees a third line leading from the eighteenth century to the present: a progressive pantheism (which is distinct from Goethe's indifference). Its first crucial embodiment was in Lessing, because as the most important critic of his time, Lessing mediated between the older Protestant tradition and more recent critical philosophy on one side, and the literary revolution of the eighteenth century on the other. In his *Zur Geschichte der Religion und Philosophie in Deutschland* (On the History of Religion and Philosophy in Germany), Heine refers to Lessing as the second cultural hero of the Germans, who carried on the emancipating work begun by Luther and thereby prepared the way for a third emancipator (a term he never applies to Goethe or Schiller): "In the misery of the present time we look up at its consoling statues and they nod a splendid promise. Yes, a third man will come who will complete what Luther began and Lessing carried forward, whom the German fatherland so badly needs—the third emancipator!" It is not only Lessing's formal critical ability that attracts Heine; he also attributes to Lessing an important role as a mediator of content: by discovering Spinoza, he helped to further the intellectual revolution that began with Luther's attack on ecclesiastical tradition. In Heine's opinion, Lessing still represented an essentially deistic point of view, whereas German philosophy developed in the direction of transcendental idealism and the philosophy of nature, both of which eliminated the concept of a personal God. Heine views Schelling's philosophy as a continuation of the Spinozan tradition; and he sees in pantheism, which Schelling was unable to sustain, the high point of the progressive emancipatory tradition. At the end of book three, Heine accordingly ascribes an exceptional revolutionary power to the revival of pantheism—more than to the transcendental idealism of a Kant or a Fichte: "But most terrible of all would be the natural philosopher, who would actively intervene in a German revolution and identify with the work of destruction itself."[16]

Since in both *Die romantische Schule* and *Zur Geschichte der Re-*

---

[16]Heinrich Heine, *Sämtliche Schriften*, ed. Klaus Briegleb, vol. 3 (Munich, 1971), pp. 468, 585, 638–39.

ligion und Philosophie in Deutschland Heine is addressing a non-German public that has little knowledge of German literary and philosophical history, he paints with a broad brush. For this very reason, the main lines of development are clearer than in Gervinus's richly detailed history of literature. Heine is patently selective; he mentions only the most important authors and is concerned above all with historical connections. His primary intention is to throw light on the literary and philosophical tradition. In so doing he takes a position no less clear than Gervinus's. For him, the goal of German intellectual history is a revolution that will recapitulate the achievements of the French revolutions of 1789 and 1830. This anticipated goal governs choice and emphasis in his narrative. Heine distinguishes between several lines of tradition, which partly compete and partly complement one another. Above all, however, he does not view the history of the German mind (*Geist*) as a linear development culminating in a personality or group of personalities. Although, for example, he acknowledges the Weimar constellation as one of the high points of German literature, he cites alternatives, such as Jean Paul, whom he links to the tradition of English humor. Even though Heine strongly attacked the romantic school, his concept of the German tradition was remarkably open and broad. He does not gloss over either the limitations of the German Enlightenment or the dangers of Weimar aestheticism. He makes the reader aware of Schelling's reactionary political affiliations and at the same time underscores the extent to which his natural philosophy was part of a revolutionary tradition. His appreciation of Schiller does not blind him to the problem of moral engagement in art. In this he differs from such patriotic liberals and nationalists as Börne and Menzel or even Gervinus, whose aim was to establish a German tradition. This was more obviously true of Menzel and Börne, who emphatically opposed equating German literature with Goethe, but in more subtle form it was also true of Gervinus and his followers, who tried to establish a continuous line in the history of German literature.

Menzel's nationalistic interpretation of tradition and Börne's democratic interpretation excluded Goethe, because his political quietism was unsuited to the political tasks facing Germany. This decision posed a difficult problem for both critics. Goethe could not be ignored, for his reputation was too well established. His doctrinaire exclusion created a vacuum that needed to be filled. Whereas Börne seized on Jean Paul, playing him off in his commemorative talk of 1825 against the courtier Goethe as the true poet of freedom, Menzel celebrated Schiller as the true national author: "We have no writer who has represented justice and freedom with such fervent enthusiasm and such poetic beauty, but also none who has represented them with a sentiment so pure and uncorrupted, with such triumphant truth that avoids all extremes."[17] The overt glorification of Schiller, addressed as the angel of the future, is directed against contemporary literature, which is said to have no such "ethical delicacy."[18]

Gervinus

Gervinus's approach differs from Menzel's topical criticism in the sharper distinction it makes between the tasks of the present and the literary achievements of the past, and in treating as a unit the work created by Goethe and Schiller between 1794 and 1805. This strategy allowed him to overcome the bipolarity of the history that followed Goethe and Schiller, which was apparent even in the 1850s. Once the mature phases of Goethe and Schiller could be thought of as a single entity by virtue of the bond of friendship between the two writers, one could conceive of a steady development. By minimizing the unmistakable differences between their literary works and emphasizing instead those common factors required for establishing a national classicism, Gervinus created the basis for the later reception of Weimar classicism. In this process, Schiller's greater reputation probably worked to the benefit of Goethe's canonical status before 1848, although in the 1850s this relationship began to change. In any case, the pairing of these two writers was so generally accepted that Jakob Grimm, in his observance of Schiller's hundredth birthday, included Goethe as a matter of course: "Goethe and Schiller stand so close together on the sublime heights they occupy—as they did in life, which bound them closely and indissolubly together—that it would be impossible to consider them apart from each other."[19] More such examples could easily be cited. Only a few critics in the 1860s still pitted one Weimar writer against the other. They focused, instead, on a common heritage they thought worth preserving.

But Gervinus was important not only for having established the concept (if not the name) of German classicism. His monumental history of literature answered the question: How should earlier authors be related to the Weimar Dioscuri? They become more or less important precursors whose task it was to prepare the way for Schiller and Goethe. In the following generations this perspective was so taken for granted that today we still find it difficult to recognize that it is merely one of several possibilities.

Lessing's ideas about the future of German literature—to which

---

[17]Wolfgang Menzel, *Die deutsche Literatur*, 2d ed., pt. 4 (Stuttgart, 1836), p. 125.
[18]Quoted in Norbert Oellers, ed., *Schiller—Zeitgenosse aller Epochen*, pt. 1 (Frankfurt a. M., 1970), p. 245.
[19]Quoted in ibid., p. 441.

Hans Mayer has rightly drawn attention[20]—were not borne out by history. During the Sturm und Drang period, German literature took a different path from that marked out by Lessing. Even Weimar classicism, which through Johann Joachim Winckelmann had explicitly reestablished a connection with Greek art, cannot easily be brought into harmony with Lessing's enlightened humanism. Gervinus cleared the history of German literature of these flaws and contradictions and provided a broad base of support for the point of view that would determine the understanding of the German tradition in the second half of the nineteenth century. How did Gervinus succeed in integrating divergent tendencies and contending forces in such a way as to lead up to the alliance between Goethe and Schiller? In his introduction to volume four, which covers the eighteenth century, he points out a number of conditions that set German literature apart from Western European traditions. While the latter—in particular, the Spanish, English, and French traditions—developed in conjunction with the increasing political power of their nations, the German tradition was left completely to its own resources; it was supported by neither the princely courts nor a national movement. "This is why," Gervinus argues, "it has been so strangely set apart from other literatures by the unbounded, unrestrained character given it by the fresh young life sprouting unhindered from it." Gervinus describes the development of literature in the eighteenth century not merely as a rapid change in style and conventions but as an intellectual revolution that involved the entire nation and changed its character. The leaders of this revolution were Klopstock, who as the representative of sentimentalism brought a popular bourgeois element to literature, and Lessing, "the true conjurer of the spirit of youth," who tried to found a national theater in the bourgeois atmosphere of Hamburg. The next wave of the revolution, overwhelming the previous one, was the Sturm und Drang, which vehemently rejected French classicism. Wieland partially falls victim to this assault, but Gervinus sees Jean Paul's contribution as a continuation of the brilliant work of the 1770s. The Sturm und Drang led to the classical moderation of Goethe and Schiller, whose close bond dominated literary life until Schiller's death. The romantics then took the lead, because Goethe, who had been "exhausted by the drive to create," increasingly withdrew.[21]

The familiar division into four epochs was made by Gervinus; they are conceived as steps in the intellectual revolution, each surmounting the preceding one. To reach its goal, German literature had to climb

---

[20]Hans Mayer, "Lessing, Mitwelt und Nachwelt," in his *Von Lessing bis Thomas Mann* (Pfullingen, 1959), pp. 79–109.

[21]Georg Gottfried Gervinus, *Geschichte der deutschen Dichtung*, 4:6, 8, 10.

these steps. Gervinus establishes the following relationship between the authors he considers most important:

> Lessing represents all aspects of the Reformation, which began, as he himself did, with drama, and which evoked the spirit of antiquity, brought new life to science, and purified religion—all of which Lessing, following hard on Luther's heels, would have done if a general lack of interest in religion and political events had not prevented him. Herder carried this work further, leading us, in the spirit of the seventeenth century, to polyhistory and philosophy. Just as in leaving the free spirit of sixteenth-century popular poetry one suddenly emerges unexpectedly in the learned poetry of the seventeenth century, one is surprised to find Herder, immediately after defending the folk song, developing and recommending the didactic poem. In our own time, Jean Paul stands in the very same contrast to Wieland as the humorous novel does to the epics of chivalry. Only with Goethe and Schiller do we find ourselves on our own feet.

The process described here by Gervinus in analogy with earlier literature is one of emancipation; its obvious aim is a cultural identity for the German nation. This developmental model permits the selection and placement of Germany's most important authors, for their position is determined by their place within the emancipatory process described by Gervinus. Thus he writes: "The course of our poetry can be illustrated entirely through Klopstock and Wieland, Lessing and Herder, Voss and Jean Paul, Schiller and Goethe." Not only does Gervinus admit that his narrative is oriented toward primary figures, but he expressly conceives the other, unnamed writers as minor, subordinate talents who only obscure the developmental picture; the historian's task is to overcome "the confusion of literary chaos" by identifying the main lines.[22]

The following examples demonstrate how Gervinus's depiction of his great individuals succeeds in creating the harmonious overall picture developed in his introduction. Three authors are of particular interest— Lessing, Jean Paul, and Wieland: Lessing, because he stands beside Goethe and Schiller as one of *the* canonical figures of German literature; Jean Paul, because he represents a possible, controversial alternative that was never quite accepted; and Wieland, because he has time and again been excluded from membership in the German canon of writers. His reputation has suffered ever since the time he was attacked by the romantics as an imitator of the French.

In the fourth volume of his history, before turning to a detailed discussion of Lessing's development, Gervinus devotes a chapter of about fifty pages to Wieland. He describes Wieland's literary develop-

[22]Ibid., 4:11–12.

ment with relative neutrality; his narrative is at least free of the moralistic prejudices of the Nationalist party. We are aware that Gervinus is not overly enthusiastic about Wieland's philosophy of the Graces, though he accepts it as an indirect step toward the emancipation of literature from theology. But he does not grant Wieland that true understanding of the spirit of antiquity which Winckelmann had. Gervinus is also clearly not in tune with the moral philosophy expressed in Wieland's poetry. He reserves his real criticism, however, for Wieland's aesthetics: "Wieland is always full of moral intentions, even in those licentious tales; and immediately afterward his writing became still more closely allied to history and philosophy than his very earliest writings had been to religion. The main thing is that his grace was not genuine, his art was not beautiful; it directly offends the spirit of the new principle." Gervinus's judgment wavers between aesthetic rejection and historical recognition. When he views Wieland in the context of the eighteenth century, he concedes that the writer represents an important stage: "In these poems, Wieland moved the times an essential step forward; he became the poet and philosopher of love, as Gleim was of friendship."[23] But the moment he applies the aesthetic standards of classicism to Wieland's writing, he sees it as a failure.

Gervinus treats Wieland and Klopstock as opposites: "Wieland is thus the opposite of Klopstock in all conceivable respects. He is sensual while Klopstock is transcendental, rational while the latter is sensitive; his writing is dominated by history and philosophy, as the latter's is by religion and music; he is didactic, Klopstock is lyrical. His language thus comes as close to prosaic speech as Klopstock's does to the language of music. . . . Klopstock takes poetry seriously, even in life; for Wieland it is an amusing game." The comparison is at the same time one-sided and narrow. German literature reaches a state of perfection only when the two writers come together: "Goethe first had to reconcile them."[24] Since the leading figures are thus presented in the light of their relationship to the classical writers, it follows that lesser talents will be presented as members of schools—Heinse, Mauvillon, Unzer, Nicolai, Alringer, and Meissner are introduced as pupils of Wieland; and Boie, Bürger, Claudius, von Schönborn, Cramer, Hensler, Hölty, and Brückner are credited to Klopstock.

The special status granted Lessing is explained by the fact that Gervinus perceives him as the first synthesis. In his chapter on Lessing, Gervinus attributes to him the same reconciliation of northern and southern elements, of moralism and sensuality, which he attributes to

[23]Ibid., 4:264, 265.
[24]Ibid., 4:269.

Goethe: "In Klopstock we heard the cadence of the Latin ode, the rhythm of Greek hexameter, the force of northern bardic speech; we wandered through the terrors of hell, through the glories of heaven, through the horrors of our ancestors' battles. In Wieland, violence was mitigated by geniality and gentleness; he banned this wildness of nature and mankind. The gods of mild conviviality settled down and led us into a world of sensuous images and fantastic adventures in a smooth language of French pliancy and elegance." Lessing surpassed both these writers because he created from an independent tradition: "He derived his language from our own stock of literature and went back to the natural speech of the people."[25] And when he used antiquity as a source (Aristotle, Homer, Sophocles), it was a pure antiquity—that is, the line of tradition transmitted by Winckelmann. This is why Lessing's obvious dependence on ancient literature, which was, incidentally, no different from Goethe's and Schiller's, seems to Gervinus to demonstrate a special affinity between German and ancient literature, a closeness that no other national literature was privileged to have.

For Gervinus, Lessing's special status in eighteenth-century German literature is not only that of a true German author but also that of a truly revolutionary writer: he "was not content to inch ahead by handling the rudder and sails of our existing culture but earnestly questioned himself to see whether it was even possible to make a swift, profitable run if the old ballast was retained; and after answering this question in the negative, he threw overboard everything that could conceivably be dispensed with." By attributing the role of a radical renovator to Lessing, Gervinus makes later literature even more dependent on his achievement. Lessing created no school because he influenced everyone. We need to be clear about the strategic value of this opinion: by depicting Lessing as a literary revolutionary, Gervinus is able to relate his life and work to Weimar classicism, to perceive him as a necessary link in the chain leading to Goethe and Schiller, without claiming that he was a predecessor in the narrower sense or that the Weimar writers were dependent on him. Lessing's criticism appears, rather, as the general prerequisite for the aesthetics developed by Schiller and Goethe. "We see here the ground on which Goethe, Schiller, and Humboldt later developed their aesthetic theories; at the same time we see Lessing's aesthetic contrast to Klopstock and Wieland expressed at its sharpest."[26] The verdict is plain enough: the main line of art theory runs through Lessing, whereas Klopstock and Wieland are relegated to the periphery as representatives of one-sided principles.

[25]Ibid., 4:290.
[26]Ibid., 4:292, 322.

What is Gervinus's opinion of Jean Paul, to whom Heine refers in his *Romantische Schule* as the antipode of classicism? The author of *Titan* is equally unable to escape the fate of being measured against Goethe. Gervinus compares Jean Paul's life to Goethe's and concludes that Jean Paul's cultural formation shows scarcely any development. According to Gervinus, he was one of those authors who reach their stride early and then repeat themselves in their later work. Gervinus does not consider this lack of inner development a strength: "Anyone who has reached a certain age, who wants to understand rationally what he reads, will soon be disgusted by Jean Paul's way of writing and will quickly be able to reach a verdict without having to read any further." Gervinus contrasts his strong rejection to Jean Paul's enthusiastic, uncritical following and concludes that the historian has to take a middle road: "For the best judge of Jean Paul will be the former adorer who has mastered his feelings, who has responded to the many chords touched by his writings and can recognize his good qualities without being blind to his bad ones." Yet even this middle road, though acknowledged by Gervinus, does not allow the nation "to place him [Jean Paul] in the line of its celebrated poets."[27] In other words, Jean Paul belongs only qualifiedly and conditionally to the canon of great German authors. One need only compare this judgment with Börne's *Denkrede* of 1825 to recognize that an important decision has been made. Börne celebrated the singer of freedom, the humorist of the heart; Gervinus sees Jean Paul as a problematic stage in the journey of the German spirit toward maturity and self-determination. Peter Sprengel has rightly observed that Gervinus's ambivalent characterization, that of a disenchanted Jean Paul admirer, effectively influenced later academic criticism until the time of Dilthey.[28]

Gervinus's concept of the history of German literature aims to show, as we have seen, that its highest point was reached about 1800. But this judgment must not be taken out of context. As a liberal, Gervinus, in contrast to later historians who used his model, was not uncritical of the historical conditions of this flourishing age. He argued that in comparison to the peaks of French and English literature, it lacked a social and political basis; the political awareness of the German writers was not on the same high plane as their aesthetic awareness. Thus Gervinus regards the idea of cosmopolitanism promulgated in Weimar as a sign of weakness—as a historically determined inability to establish a national identity.

This criticism of an idealistic inwardness that does not recognize national duty becomes harsher when Gervinus deals with romanticism. In his history of literature his judgment is not yet as severe as it will be in his later *Geschichte des 19. Jahrhunderts* (1855), where romanticism is denounced as a reactionary movement. In 1842 the historian was still prepared to acknowledge the positive sides of romanticism, in particular, the role played by romantic criticism in the dissemination and development of classical art history concepts: "Undoubtedly the romantics have done much to further the aspirations of Goethe's time, to bring some movement into our sluggish private German life, to destroy its philistine elements, to bring a fresh breeze into the stuffy atmosphere, to call academics out into the open, to break the social monotony, and to replace pedantry and striving for honors with serene elegance." Gervinus also acknowledges the merits of the romantics with respect to the history of literature. Yet on the whole he rejects romanticism, its concept of literature as well as its literary production. He refers to the "nebulous character" of romantic poetry, which is remote from reality: "Its goal—to idealize the real— evaporated into airy nothings. One wanted to hold up to the era, whose prosaic exterior was still in conflict with its poetic impulse, the model of another time, when life itself had a poetic streak. The romantic poetry of the Middle Ages and of foreigners was introduced, but one forgot that what one sought to create new life with was for the most part dead to us; because the echo did not prove loud enough, one was all the more determined to pursue this type of literature, and the means almost became the end."[29]

Gervinus links the romantic movement historically to the Sturm und Drang—especially to Herder—thereby separating it from the Enlightenment. He points out critically its closeness to the religiosity of the Catholic church and openly finds fault with the romantics' negative interpretation of the Reformation. Like Heine, Gervinus suspects that the catholicizing tendencies of the romantics must finally lead to political reaction. He thus calls Friedrich Schlegel "a blind instrument . . . of political reaction,"[30] because his philosophy of history brings him close to Joseph de Maistre and puts him in decided conflict with Schiller's philosophy of freedom, which, as we have seen, served Gervinus as a model.

Gervinus adds politically motivated criticism to his literary criticism. For him, the romantic movement is a late manifestation with decadent qualities. Compared to the older generation, the romantic authors appear weak and feminine, more receptive than creative, and dependent in their literary production. "But if we go to the *personal production* and

[29]Gervinus, *Geschichte der Deutschen Dichtung*, 5:546, 535.
[30]Ibid., 5:554.

accomplishments of these men," Gervinus writes after discussing the translations of the romantics, "we find that the same receptivity that made them superior there makes them insignificant here. Besides these translations, nothing during the entire period of our literature in which romantic trends lasted was as prevalent as the imitations and adaptations of earlier or foreign works, a love of parody, and a clever talent for copying the tones of our youngest German writers." No new impulses could therefore be expected from romanticism, and the following generation had to break with it before German literature could be renewed: "This need has also been felt by our youth. Our writers have been opposed as a group to the quietism of romanticism since the most recent movements in the world of politics. Conviction and action have found a response in them as they had not among our romantic nihilists."[31] However, because Gervinus sees two requirements for a flourishing new age—an immanent development of literature and important external relations—his interest finally turns to those political conditions that could give rise afterward to a new flowering of literature.

Gervinus's concept of the history of German literature contains a number of discordances and contradictions that became apparent only in the course of its reception. His estimation of the Weimar epoch as the high point of German literature was accepted and, as we shall see, so would be his method of integrating different tendencies in order to define a teleological evolution. His presentation of the revolutionary development of German literature in the eighteenth century assured the canonization of Weimar classicism. In his view, however, even Goethe and Schiller deserved a certain amount of criticism, no matter how exemplary their work, because their relationship to social and political realities remained problematic. Hence there is a contradiction in Gervinus between the unconditional literary canonization of classicism, on the one hand, and his politically motivated criticism, on the other. His political argument leads to the demand that Germany attain a national identity in the political realm as well, whereas his literary-aesthetic argument leads to a devaluation of the postclassical literature of the nineteenth century. Both of these lines of argument eventually arrive at the same conclusion: that German literature has essentially come to an end and has thus acquired the status of an inheritance on which the future will have to draw. The idea of progress, which remains binding for Gervinus, is confined to the political realm and no longer includes literature. This separation, however, made Gervinus' model susceptible to conservative use. Once his political criticism of idealism had been eliminated; or to put it more generally, once the political and the liter-

[31]Ibid., 5:577–78, 665.

ary points of view were separated, an affirmative attitude could be developed that celebrated Weimar classicism without regard for historical requirements. When the problem of tradition was restricted to literature, it became a matter of course to soften or to suspend criticism of the romantics. This is precisely the situation we find in the 1860s in the work of Haym and Dilthey, following the gradual dismantling after 1850 of liberal and left-Hegelian criticism of the romantics.

The Problem of Inheritance in the Nachmärz

The differences between the literary histories of the Nachmärz and the approaches of the early Restoration period show not so much in their judgments of the eighteenth century and classicism as in the interpretation of romanticism and recent literature. Even though liberal criticism of classicism at first remained very much alive in such authors as Hettner and Schmidt, and the polemic against romanticism continued in the aftermath of the *Hallische Jahrbücher*, Schiller's and Goethe's worth was no longer questioned. The discussion entered a phase in which not even opposition could change the basic lines of the historical process. In the 1840s, following Heine's and Hegel's criticism, romanticism became a catchword synonymous with political reaction and false mysticism. To the radical men of letters romanticism was the crucial error of German literature. This exclusively polemical usage was opposed by Hettner in 1850 in his study "Die romantische Schule in ihrem inneren Zusammenhange mit Goethe und Schiller" (The Inner Relationship of the Romantic School to Goethe and Schiller). In this essentially Hegelian presentation, the young Hettner tries to show that the qualities ascribed to romanticism did not simply represent an unfortunate revival of the Sturm und Drang, as Gervinus had assumed, but rather stemmed dialectically from classicism. By thus establishing an intellectual and historical relationship between classicism and romanticism, Hettner both prepared the way for a reinterpretation of romanticism—though this was by no means his intention—and built a new bridge from the literature of the past to that of the present; for his criticism of idealism eventually led to a demand for a new poetry whose "forms and materials grow, out of inner necessity, from the heart of the times." This postulate pursues a line of reasoning that had been suppressed in Gervinus's model: if national identity is the prerequisite for a flourishing age of literature, German unification will inevitably lead to a new classicism. Hettner was merely drawing the logical conclusion when he wrote about the revolution then under way: "The coming years will be decisive. If we achieve what we are striving for in our current political battles, we will become a great and free nation, as Germany deserves. Our art and poetry will not fail then to see a brilliant new age, which in content and beauty will outshine the literature of Goethe's and Schiller's time, just as surely as this political future will outshine the disgraceful past."[32] If, on the other hand, political freedom is not achieved, Hettner argues, hope for a new literary classicism will also fade. In that case (we can continue his argument) Weimar humanism will remain the irreplaceable model for Germans.

Hettner's criticism of classic and romantic literature in Germany was impelled by his awareness that the revolution could lift cultural development to a higher level, in the attainment of which the epoch of Weimar and Jena was merely a preliminary stage. The dubious aspects of romanticism—which Hettner, incidentally, does not evaluate much differently from Gervinus—were already inherent in classical aesthetics and the humanism of Weimar. Thus Hettner writes (with Gervinus in mind): "But the romantic school is not merely an incidental appendage, much less an empty aftermath, of the period of flowering just preceding it. No matter how inferior it may be in outcome and significance to Goethe's and Schiller's lofty summit, it is and remains the necessary and complementary opposite of these writers." Hettner's point of departure in his attempt to establish a correlation between the two groups is their view of reality. Both the classic and the romantic theories of art are idealistic; that is, their prerequisite for poetic production is the distinction between reality and the ideal: "They demand complete formal independence of art from nature. Only by suppressing a general truth to nature, they assert, can light and air be brought to art." Both the Weimar and the romantic writers remove themselves from reality, according to Hettner, because they share an incongruity with respect to contemporary social reality: "The basic flaw in all this poetry—Goethe's and Schiller's late work as well as romantic poetry—is that it came into being not because of the times but despite the times." Hettner criticizes this view of reality, which appears in the work of Goethe and Schiller as objective idealism and in that of the romantics as subjective idealism. The romantics especially "are driven by their despair over empirical nature surrounding them to reject nature and reality altogether; rather than seeking to create from it, they use their imagination to struggle against it. They disdain sculpture and objective form on principle; they rock themselves dithyrambically in the elementary emotional life of lyrical, musical inwardness."[33] Hettner tries to use this intellectual and formal principle to reconstruct the course of the romantic

[32]Hettner, *Schriften zur Literatur*, pp. 164, 165.
[33]Ibid., pp. 60, 65, 68, 69.

movement: the first stage was a longing for true art; the second, adoption of the Middle Ages as an ideal poetic realm; the third, a turn toward conservative politics.

Hettner's criticism of classical and romantic literature is linked to a concept of history in which the Revolution of 1848 plays a central role. Yet the onset of political reaction in 1849 robbed that concept of meaning. Utopian belief in a new classical literature surpassing that of Weimar collapsed, thereby reviving the question of tradition and literary inheritance. Evidence of this can be found, for example, in Gottschall's history of literature.

Gottschall's *Die deutsche Nationalliteratur in der ersten Hälfte des neunzehnten Jahrhunderts* (German National Literature in the First Half of the Nineteenth Century) first appeared in 1854, obviously in competition with Schmidt's *Geschichte der deutschen Nationalliteratur im neunzehnten Jahrhundert*. Both build on Gervinus's theories and thus are confronted with the same problem: How does one describe the literature of the nineteenth century if one assumes with Gervinus that German literature has already reached its peak with Goethe and Schiller? Gottschall addresses this question in his introduction: "The main problem, however, is that such an undertaking goes contrary to the widespread opinion, supported by some great authorities, that our national literature has brought forth nothing of significance since Schiller and Goethe and has instead been in constant decline—an opinion that, if it had any basis, would necessarily rob a work such as the present one of all meaning; for it would then merely be the Sisyphusian task of rolling a stone uphill only to have it, by the will of Zeus, roll down again." For Gottschall, the situation itself guarantees that Gervinus's thesis does not present the whole truth; that, on the contrary, romantic and postromantic literature has its own inherent value: "The nineteenth century has entered upon an inheritance from the eighteenth century in all areas of art and learning; but far from squandering it, it has doubled its capital and interest." Gottschall gives legitimacy to postclassical literature because it continues tradition by modifying and transforming classical tradition. He no longer speaks of a new classicism, however; if modern literature has a goal, it is to become popular and to reach new readers. Unlike Hettner, Gottschall is no longer interested in criticizing the classic-romantic period; that epoch is past: "The *classicists* created for us a humane art form on the antique model; the *romantics* destroyed that form in order to free the imagination from tradition and to make literature *popular*. But in the process they lapsed into a chaotic, primitive poetry and became dependent on a medieval heritage that merely appeared to be popular. Their desire to reconcile poetry with contemporary life was revived by the *modern* movement, which formed ties with our classicists in its struggle for artistic perfection."[34] Weimar classicism has become the unmistakable, indispensable basis of the new literature, which one could remember, after the formlessness of romanticism, without totally sacrificing romantic awareness. Thus Gottschall conceives modern literature as a synthesis of classic and romantic elements. This dialectic formula allows him to preserve the idea of progress. To be sure, Gottschall restricts this evolution to literature; he no longer poses the question that concerned Hettner—whether and how literature could be renewed by political revolution.

Postrevolutionary discussion of German literary tradition took as its point of departure the canonical validity of Weimar classicism. In this respect, Schmidt was no different from Gottschall. To underscore the connection between modern literature and the epoch of Weimar and Jena, Schmidt introduced the second edition of his history of literature with a comprehensive presentation of the period between 1794 and 1806. It opens with a terse statement: "That we in Germany had a classical age of literature with a precise beginning and end, the whole world agrees."[35] In 1853 (and in his second edition of 1855) Schmidt followed Gervinus's scheme: up to the time of Goethe and Schiller, German literature was developing; after Schiller's death the classical period came to an end and a decline set in. "Since Schiller's death, our poetic achievements have been of dubious value; but in our literary life, taken as a whole, we have come much further."[36]

Gervinus's concept, to which Schmidt is obviously closer than Gottschall, proves to be a problematic inheritance. If his scheme is followed, the history of nineteenth-century literature can be written only as a postscript to the classical period. But this very point of view, to which Schmidt felt indebted, alters the way one approaches the changes of the time. Because Schmidt, unlike Gottschall, was not prepared to justify those changes on an aesthetic basis, he chose a different route: his concept of literature is so broad that it is no longer restricted to "creative literature" alone. He sees advances in philosophical and scholarly writing which he finds lacking in creative literature. In 1855, in the introduction to the second edition of his history of literature, Schmidt again confronted the problematic relationship between past and present. The result is self-contradictory, because he does not want to give up Gervinus's model yet tries to define standards and goals for the present. On the one hand, he formulates the history of modern literature as the

[34]Gottschall, *Die deutsche Nationalliteratur*, pp. vi, x, xii.
[35]Schmidt, *Weimar und Jena in den Jahren 1794–1806*, p. 1.
[36]Julian Schmidt, *Geschichte*, 1:xii-xiii.; from the preface to the first edition (1853).

aftermath of the classical period and disparages the literature of his own time;[37] on the other, he sees positive tendencies in the present going beyond the late eighteenth century. Schmidt grants his own time a certain measure of sound human understanding which was lacking in the epoch around 1800. To this extent he believes that classical culture had a narrower and more problematic foundation. The contradiction in this concept lies in the fact that Schmidt continues the politically motivated Vormärz criticism of classicism and at least acknowledges the possibility that a new literature might overcome the weaknesses of Weimar; but at the same time he regards classicism, no less than did Gottschall, as the absolute fixed point of German literature—as an irreplaceable heritage, a possession that allows Germany to compare itself with the Western European nations. It is indicative of the transitional character of Schmidt's history of literature, however, that romantic literature is not yet included in this heritage. It appears as a mere episode in German history, one that must be reconstructed in order to demonstrate continuity and to make what follows understandable. Gottschall goes a step farther in this respect, including romanticism in the accepted canon, despite its defects.

Where, then, do the differences between Schmidt and Gottschall lie? They have to do above all with different assessments of contemporary literature. Schmidt, as a representative of programmatic realism, promotes authors such as Freytag and Otto Ludwig, whereas Gottschall, siding with Gutzkow, relates contemporary literature to the postromantic writing of the Vormärz. He thus emphasizes continuity, whereas Schmidt, under the influence of Gervinus, sees mainly ruptures after 1805 and again after 1848. This contrast is touched upon at least indirectly when Gottschall, in the foreword to the second edition of his history of literature, criticizes Schmidt for proceeding too schematically and for inadequately tracing the development of individual authors. Gottschall chooses an aesthetic approach to literature and not a moral one because the study of form makes it possible to link modern literature with tradition; Schmidt, as a moralist, is forced to undervalue the necessary changes in form. Gottschall acknowledges the idealism of classicism in order to include—as a polemic against Schmidt's realism—modern writers in the classical tradition: "The true followers of our classicists are to be found only among our best lyricists, dramatists like Hebbel and Gutzkow, and writers of novels, who are still so anachronistic as to have 'ideas.' "[38]

---

[37]"Belles-lettres, which today are for the most part nothing but a coterie of immature talents" (ibid., p. viii).

[38]Gottschall, *Die deutsche Nationalliteratur*, pp. xxvi-xxvii.

The Integration of Romanticism

After the revolution, when the canonization of Weimar had by and large come to an end, discussion thus came to be concentrated on the problem of posthistory: the assessment of romantic literature and the evaluation of Young Germany. The integration of romanticism with the corpus of German literature took place in the 1850s and especially in the 1860s. This process was essentially completed with the appearance of Haym's *Die romantische Schule* (1870). The canonical base had been enlarged to the extent that the romantic authors were henceforth obligatory and part of the heritage. In academic criticism at least, this opinion was accepted; the canon for secondary school anthologies, in contrast, continued in part to follow the earlier concept, acknowledging the romantics as only marginal figures alongside Lessing, Schiller, and Goethe. The explanatory statement that introduces Haym's fundamental work is noteworthy, because it throws an unexpected light on the changes that took place in the course of a single generation. He expressly disengages himself from the 1840s discussion of romanticism, which was basically hostile to the romantics. The battle against romanticism had lost its significance for Haym, because the problems of the Vormärz had already been "overcome": "This frame of mind is well suited, it would seem, for investigating romanticism from a purely historical point of view, for explaining the origins of the romantic school, and for impartially evaluating its content and worth, its enduring and its ephemeral qualities." One has to ask, however, what is meant here by a historical point of view. Not only does Haym claim that his presentation is more detached than Gervinus's, Hettner's, and Schmidt's could have been, but he gives a higher valuation to romanticism. When he speaks about his predecessors, he immediately plays down their critical attitude, emphasizing instead, as the essential point in evaluating romanticism, its relationship to the eighteenth century. Thus he says about Gervinus: "He shows . . . how everywhere in it only those seeds that were already at hand continued to develop: how Winckelmann and Lessing, Klopstock and Wieland led the way and where the romantics followed; how the latter were supported by the new philology; how the spirit of Schiller's criticism, Goethe's poetry, Herder's receptivity, and Vossen's art of translation hovered over all their activities." There is no way of knowing from this description that Gervinus, and after him Schmidt, considered romanticism a decline. Haym's verdict on Schmidt's contribution to the study of romanticism is accordingly guarded. He grants that Schmidt's attitude is critical, but he faults his representation for not grasping correctly the historical context of romantic literature. Haym thus sees it as his primary task to anchor early romanticism in the literary tradition of the eighteenth century. He offers proof of continuity: "Only a very small part is played in this wonderful story by those younger idealists who took up the imaginative and conceptual world of Goethe's and Schiller's poetry and Kant's and Fichte's philosophy at the turn of the nineteenth century, bringing it to a radical conclusion and transmitting it." Although they do not expressly state it, these sentences reveal a fundamentally different concept of the relationship between classicism and romanticism than we find in Gervinus and Schmidt. Haym has abandoned the focus on classicism and with it the devaluation of romanticism. He understands romanticism—in this he goes a step beyond the early Hettner—as the logical fulfillment of classicism. When Haym speaks of the great epoch of German literature, he includes romanticism. The developmental scheme introduced by Gervinus has thus become the basis for a new interpretation. Now as before, Klopstock, Lessing, and Wieland appear the crucial forerunners; but the true precursors of romanticism are Johann Hamann and Herder. Haym's point of departure for the literary evolution of Germany—for the Sturm und Drang, classicism, and its culmination in romanticism—is not Lessing but Herder. The romantic school, in his judgment, was based on the historicism of Herder, the neohumanism of Schiller and Goethe, and the transcendental philosophy of Kant and Fichte. But this classification is no longer meant pejoratively. Haym argues that the task of romanticism was to synthesize the various tendencies that preceded it:

> But to bring together existing ideal themes and mix them in many different ways; to make completely one's own the noble culture that creative minds have only now achieved, and to defend it and make it prevail against those who have been left behind, against those who are still captives of the darker side of German life; to test the basic concepts of this culture by applying them in a variety of ways, to transmit them through as many channels as possible, to carry over the spirit of poetry into the sciences, into life and customs; in a word, to make the new ideas dominant—this was the work that still remained to be done, that was great and rewarding enough to kindle people's enthusiasm and fill their lives.[39]

Once again an integrating, synthesizing formula is used to justify an epoch: romanticism, for Haym, proves to be a synthesis of Sturm und Drang, classicism, and critical philosophy; and its legitimacy for German tradition lies in its having combined these elements.

[39]Haym, *Die romantische Schule*, pp. 4, 5, 7, 13.

Since Haym deals only cursorily with the prehistory of romanticism, the question how the earlier Enlightenment fits into this development never becomes acute. In Hettner's exhaustive work on the eighteenth century (1864–70), it becomes a test case. The reassessment of romanticism, even under the quise of scholarly "objectivity," raises questions about the developmental scheme introduced by Gervinus and—not the least of them—about the function it assigned to the Enlightenment. Although Hettner's assessment of romanticism is closer to the earlier concept of Gervinus and Schmidt than to Haym's, and he deplores the "one-sided arrogance of the life of the imagination [as] sophistical fantasy, fantasticality," which contrasts unfavorably with the clarity and moderation of classicism, his judgment of the Enlightenment demonstrates a significant shift away from this early concept. Hettner emphasizes not only the achievements of the early and mid-eighteenth century but also the "limits" of the Enlightenment. Now as before, the goal of German literature is Weimar classicism, in which neohumanism, schooled in the antique, and critical philosophy are united in the work of Goethe and Schiller; but Hettner thrusts the Sturm und Drang between the Enlightenment and classicism as a separate epoch, in which presumably "struggles and battles" were played out before perfection could be attained: "That first stage of development, the first audacious but still incredibly unclear flash of a new, heightened, and intensified ideal of life, is the passionate agitation of mind which we are accustomed to calling the Sturm und Drang period." In the aftermath of Rousseau, according to Hettner, the Sturm und Drang developed an expanded view of life that did away with the limits of earlier rationalism. Even though Hettner is not inclined to give unqualified sanction to the literary rebellion of the Sturm und Drang and comments repeatedly on its lack of moderation, his assessment of the development has nevertheless shifted. He draws a sharper distinction than did Gervinus between the rationalism of the Enlightenment and the irrationalism of the Sturm und Drang period. The literary production of Lessing, Christian Gellert, and Moses Mendelssohn is no longer considered to the same extent the foundation on which German classicism was erected. The Sturm und Drang appears, rather, as a necessary transitional phase in which German literature had to undergo fermentation before it could reach its highest stage of development. The concept of classicism is again determined by such notions as maturing and refining, but this definition now reduces the importance of the earlier phases. Only in Kant's critical philosophy is the Enlightenment still considered to have had a direct influence on classicism: "In scholarship, refinement was achieved by Kant. . . . It was the death blow of the frivolous philosophy of emotion, which substituted dreams and fantasies of the heart for investigation and thinking."[40]

What Haym merely outlined and Hettner alluded to with some reservation, Dilthey developed into a cohesive, harmonious concept that redefined the tradition of German literature. In his inaugural lecture of 1867 in Basel, Dilthey draws a complete picture of the development of German literature for the first time, citing essays by individual authors and a succession of discussions on literary history. In earlier epochs, he argues, Germany was part of a common European tradition, but in the middle of the eighteenth century—he cites Lessing—an independent cultural development began which was distinct from the Western European tradition: "From a number of stable historical conditions there arose in Germany in the last third of the previous century an intellectual movement that ran a closed, continuous course—that formed a unified whole—from Lessing to the death of Schleiermacher and Hegel." Dilthey found more to discuss in 1867 than the course and historical context of German literature. The unity that mattered to him was based on a common view of life: "And indeed, the steadily effective strength of this movement lay in the historically determined urge to create a view of life and the world in which the German spirit could find satisfaction." When Dilthey draws attention to the fact that the heyday of German literature, about 1800, differed from those of England and Spain in not being rooted in a political national culture, he is unmistakably returning to one of Gervinus' basic ideas; for the latter had already explained the peculiarity of German classicism as the result of its having been an exclusively cultural movement. Using this argument, Dilthey speaks of the internalized formation of the German *Geist*, the central core of which was personal cultivation, the humanistic ideal of self-realization. For Dilthey, too, German literature unquestionably reached a climax with Schiller and Goethe, but it did not stop there; their legitimate succession was the romantic generation, which built on the achievements of classicism. "With this," Dilthey explains, "I have presented the foundation laid by two generations of poets and scholars for the work of the speculative thinkers which now commenced." At the end of his lecture, Dilthey sketches the romantic movement showing two continuous lines. One leads from Lessing, Kant, and Schiller to Fichte and Friedrich Schlegel; the other from Goethe to Schelling and the romantic nature poets. But more important than this mere suggestion of an affiliation is Dilthey's conclusion, stated in the last paragraph

[40]Hermann Hettner, *Geschichte der deutschen Literatur im 18. Jahrhundert*, 3 vols. (Braunschweig, 1864–70), 3:437, 1–3.

of his address: "What I have traced in its essentials from Lessing to Schleiermacher and Hegel is an intimate nexus of great ideas."[41]

Dilthey is not referring here to just any movement but to a binding tradition in which he includes himself and his listeners. For this reason his evolutionary scheme warrants attention. The inclusion of romanticism in the great tradition of the German *Geist* results in substantial changes in the evaluation of earlier phases. The Enlightenment is especially affected. Gervinus had already relegated it to the role of an essentially preparatory epoch. Dilthey reduces its significance still further—making an exception for Lessing, to whom he attributes a new role. Lessing is regarded as the victor over a one-sided literary culture. Whereas Wieland and Klopstock presumably remained at the level of the Enlightenment, Lessing moved ahead to a new ideal of life. In other words, Dilthey separates Lessing from the Enlightenment, emphasizing the intuitive in contrast to the rational and thereby bringing him closer to the Sturm und Drang and classicism. This feeling for life attains its "consummate poetic expression" in *Nathan*: "In the hero of this play, the idea of the Enlightenment has been transfigured into perfect moral beauty." This ideal, however—and here Dilthey diverges from earlier literary history—is the result of *intuitive perception*, not of rational criticism. The strategic importance of this interpretation can be gauged by comparing it to Dilthey's opinion of Wieland. Dilthey concedes that Wieland has a rich poetic talent, but in the same breath he draws attention to its limitations: "Yet nowhere in all this wealth is there an original answer to the question put to him by his time. He was content to remain at that level of development which the ideal of life had then reached in England and France."[42] This is not simply an echo of the romantics' criticism of Wieland; the thrust of the argument is directed against Wieland's link to the Western European Enlightenment, from which, Dilthey thought, the German *Geist* had begun to disengage itself in about 1770.

Dilthey gives Lessing a national mission that neither Wieland nor Klopstock can fulfill. One has only to compare Dilthey's views with those of Gottschall and Schmidt to recognize the far-reaching importance for the assessment of the literary heritage of his complete integration of romanticism into the German tradition. Gottschall makes the usual distinction between forerunners and perfecters; the pioneers include Klopstock, Wieland, Herder, and to a certain extent Lessing. They are not "in the same rank" as Goethe and Schiller because they are

---

[41]Wilhelm Dilthey, "Die dichterische und philosophische Bewegung in Deutschland 1770 bis 1800," in his *Gesammelte Schriften*, 5:13, 24, 27.
[42]Ibid., 5:17, 16.

only "fragmentary geniuses." Wieland and Klopstock, in particular, do not deserve to be called classicists, in Gottschall's opinion, because "only a few threads carry over [from them] to the present." Yet characteristically, Lessing is excepted from this verdict. Although he is not called a classicist, he is expressly singled out as "the chief carrier of a national importance in criticism and production which has extended even into our own century." Up to this point, Gottschall clearly anticipates Dilthey's concept; yet he sees Lessing above all as a rationalist: "Lessing [was] a man of *intellect*, indeed of such great, clear, and sharp intellect that German literature has no rival to set beside him."[43] Gottschall is aware of the Aristotelian critic and theological deist, but he extends this concept to Lessing's poetic works: his dramas are the product of a creative intellect.

What Dilthey was able only to outline in his inaugural lecture of 1867 he develops in his early essays on Lessing and Novalis. Inasmuch as he relies on the earlier works of Gervinus and Theodor Wilhelm Danzel, he does not deny Lessing's indebtedness to the Enlightenment; yet he claims a special place for him within that movement. Whereas such representatives of the German Enlightenment as Gottsched, Johann Bodmer, Gellert, and Klopstock remained bound to the religious content and theological discussion of their time, Lessing broke out of it and developed a new Weltanschauung on which following generations could build. Lessing appears in these essays as the representative of the Enlightenment who overcame theological rationalism. Dilthey's cautious, not to say negative, estimation of the forces of the German Enlightenment leads him to this judgment: "The dominant fact in the course of our literature is that the Reformation took hold in Germany with an energetic religious awareness surpassing that of any other country; as a result it was uniquely dominated by theological interests, which were perpetuated for a long time by the absence of those other motifs that in England and France were determining influences on the elements and interests of the Enlightenment. This decided the character of everything that was native to our development, from dogmatic compendia and hymns to Haller's religious didactic poem and Klopstock's *Messiade*."[44] Dilthey speaks candidly of the immaturity of German thought, which was not yet equal to the secular tasks and political problems being solved in Western Europe.

Because Dilthey puts the weight so one-sidedly on the religious themes in German literature, the young Lessing appears as the rebel

---

[43]Gottschall, *Die deutsche Nationalliteratur*, pp. 3, 17, 17–18.
[44]Wilhelm Dilthey, "Über Gotthold Ephraim Lessing," in *Preussische Jahrbücher* 19 (1867):117–61, 271–94; quotation from p. 122.

who broke out of this theological context, as the first modern writer who shook off the tradition of theological thinking, argumentation, and feeling. Dilthey denies, in other words, that the early German Enlightenment contributed to the unfolding of the German *Geist*. He recognizes formal achievements in Haller's and Klopstock's work, but no new direction for German literature:

> Whereas the literature of that time—that of Klopstock and his friends included—was all dependent on long-existing, but strongly restrictive, elements in society, princely courts, and universities; whereas even the most independent among them, such as Klopstock and Haller, were merely highly gifted representatives of the religious sensibility that had dominated Germany since Pietism and were accordingly incapable of giving direction to the German spirit, Lessing—who was sustained by his original, energetic north German element and carried along by the public spirit of a burgeoning metropolis and a state struggling to come into existence—gave brilliant expression to a wholesome feeling for life.[45]

Only by detaching himself from the Protestant tradition, Dilthey thought, was Lessing able to become the precursor of German classicism and idealism.

Thus Dilthey retains the familiar developmental scheme that sees Lessing as the precursor of German classicism, but he fleshes it out in a different way. He emphasizes those elements that link Lessing to the next generation: the development of an independent, self-contained aesthetic theory, and the unfolding of a new Weltanschauung. Dilthey puts great value on Lessing's having developed a philosophical world view under the influence of Leibniz and Spinoza, for it brings him into the line that includes Schleiermacher, Schelling, and Hegel—that is, into the great idealistic tradition of the romantic generation. Because Lessing's criticism of theology did not turn materialistic but instead developed philosophically into idealism, Lessing, in Dilthey's eyes, became the central figure of the eighteenth century in Germany.

Philosophical problems were certainly uppermost in the young Dilthey's mind, if for no other reason than his theological background. In 1867 he treated Lessing's aesthetic theory in a relatively cursory manner, but he examined his philosophical and theological themes in detail. Lessing's contributions to art theory in *Laokoon* and the *Hamburgische Dramaturgie* were mentioned only briefly. As a result, Dilthey held that Lessing developed a theory that recognized art as an independent realm; and in this connection he expressly stated that German classicism took over Lessing's conclusions: "The rules for poetry established by Lessing

[45]Ibid., pp. 127–28.

were nothing less than guiding principles, especially for Goethe and Schiller. The way in which both dissolve static phenomena in movement and action in their lyrics and epic creations, sometimes by the most carefully thought out means, follows not only the instinct of genius but the insight and study that guided Lessing in these matters."[46] Dilthey aims to define Lessing's theory of art as a concept of aesthetic autonomy, although he never actually uses the term. This emphasis makes Lessing seem the one representative of the Enlightenment who avoided a moral, didactic understanding of art.[47]

In Dilthey's work of 1867, Lessing becomes the founder of the German movement, who helped express for the first time the new feeling for life on which classicism and romanticism were based; and he accomplished this through literature. Poetry overcame the narrowness of the German Enlightenment: "The prevailing conceptual style of morality influenced by theology was made obsolete by the vivid concept of life in literature." *Nathan* consequently appears as the perfect expression of the new feeling for life. In the ideal of the man who has attained his majority, Lessing had reached a stage, Dilthey believed, that differed only insignificantly from the humanism of Weimar classicism. A pantheistic Weltanschauung pervades both the writings of the mature Lessing and Goethe's work in Weimar. But pantheism, as is also pointed out in the Basel inaugural lecture, is precisely the intellectual element that distinguished the new German humanism from the Western European Enlightenment—the hidden link between the Enlightenment, classicism, and romanticism. Dilthey is also concerned about this continuity when he discusses Lessing. German literature, insofar as it had any claim to originality, began with Lessing and only Lessing, not with Klopstock or Wieland, who were still valued in liberal historiography as forerunners. "What follows from this is that Lessing became the true bearer of the progressive spirit of our literature," whereas Klopstock and Wieland were only the forces that determined his development; their works were short-lived and merely the fertile soil for the further development of that spirit.[48]

In ending his essay with the statement that Lessing "is the immortal leader of the modern German spirit,"[49] Dilthey was expressing an opinion shared by literary historians who had a different assessment of Lessing's position in the Enlightenment. But in his essay on Novalis, which appeared in the *Preussische Jahrbücher* in 1865, he diverged

[46]Ibid., p. 132.
[47]This connection was later considerably broadened by Dilthey when he revised his essay for *Das Erlebnis und die Dichtung*; cf. 14th ed. (Göttingen, 1965), pp. 34–47.
[48]Ibid., pp. 88, 293.
[49]Ibid., p. 123.

emphatically from the prevailing opinion.[50] As Dilthey later rightly noted, his positive assessment of that central figure in early romanticism contradicted both liberal historiography and the historical assessment of, for instance, Haym. Haym was closer to the older liberal view—inimical to romanticism—than Dilthey, who tried "to demonstrate the untenability" of the view that there is "confusion and vagueness, obscurity and contradiction in the romantic writings."[51] Dilthey was interested in saving the romantics—in fact, romanticism itself—and in this he went far beyond the historicism of a writer such as Haym. Whereas Haym believed that romanticism could be judged objectively precisely because it lay entirely in the past, Dilthey implicitly maintained that, like classicism, romanticism was still obligatory for the present. He thus used Novalis's life and work as an example of the relationship between the early romantic generation, born around 1770, and Goethe and Schiller. By emphasizing the close connection between Schiller, Kant, Goethe, and the younger writers in Jena, he tried to show that the liberal criticism of romanticism was a bias founded on false premises. In particular, the accusation of subjectivity and inwardness, as well as of a partiality for the policies of the reactionary forces, was to be blunted by evidence that when the new generation, which built on the abstract idealism of the old and carried it to its ultimate conclusion, radicalized preexisting ideas and programs, there was a certain inevitability to its development.

The close relationship between the religious-theological and poetic-aesthetic elements in Novalis's work exemplifies this process of radicalization. It is precisely in this relationship that Dilthey sees Novalis's modernity. Novalis developed a view of reality in which science, poetry, and religion were combined. The key concept applied by Dilthey to both Novalis and Goethe is that of an aesthetic Weltanschauung: "The epoch that viewed the moral world in aesthetic terms made this right to a free, concrete perception a reality over rigid ethical doctrines, and it thereby began a revolution in our moral thinking which Schleiermacher, Johann Herbart, and Hegel intended to bring to a philosophical conclusion but which is still in full course."[52] Two aspects of this judgment are noteworthy: Dilthey readily includes Hegel in his considerations without going into his fundamental criticism of romanticism, which had shaped the 1830s and 1840s; moreover, he does not regard the aesthetic view of the world as an attitude that has been overcome (this is Haym's point of view) and is no longer relevant in the

[50]Wilhelm Dilthey, "Novalis," *Preussische Jahrbücher* 15 (1865):596–650.
[51]Dilthey, *Das Erlebnis und die Dichtung*, 14th ed., p. 324.
[52]Ibid., p. 228.

present. The scholarly interests of the young Dilthey cannot be characterized as purely historical. In this respect, his essay on Novalis speaks the same language as that on Lessing: its aim is to trace a literary-moral tradition that can serve as a point of orientation for the present.

The antithesis of classicism and romanticism, which had been all but obligatory since Gervinus, plays scarcely any role in this context. Aided by the notion of a literary generation, Dilthey has been able to invalidate the assumption of an opposition, which had largely determined the criticism of the Vormärz. Romantic thinking for Dilthey was a continuation and radicalization of ideas and viewpoints in existence around 1790. He claims Goethe, in particular, for the romantics; he was a point of departure for their literary production. Even though Dilthey does not approve of all the romantic experiments connected with *Wilhelm Meister,* he nevertheless underscores the importance of the romantic Bildungsroman and novels about artists, acclaiming *Heinrich von Ofterdingen* as "the most significant [novel] that this first generation of romantics has produced." This judgment makes Novalis one of the great authors of the German tradition that was headed by Lessing. Dilthey's essay concludes: "The generation in which he lived gave rise to three outstanding poets: him [Novalis], Tieck, and Hölderlin."[53] This judgment establishes the legitimacy of romanticism far more radically than Haym does in his presentation, which proceeded from the assumption that romanticism could be objectively presented because it had been overcome.

[53]Ibid., pp. 233, 240.

. 6 .

The Literary Canon
of the Nachmärz

Rearranging the Pantheon

What effect did the developmental scheme that gained acceptance through Dilthey have on the establishment of a canon? The incipient devaluation of the early Enlightenment and sensibility led to the suppression of two writers who had had a place in the liberal literary history of the Vormärz. Wieland and Klopstock, albeit for different reasons, were no longer credited in the full sense as pioneers of the new German literature. Wieland's position had been problematic since the time of romanticism, when he had been denounced as the epigone of French literature. Still, Gervinus devoted an entire chapter to him and discussed his "school" in detail in the fifth volume of his history of German literature. Schmidt had omitted him from his list of crucial mediators, and Dilthey excluded him altogether from the German movement. Klopstock received similar treatment. Although Gervinus still regarded him as the leader of an important school and Schmidt at least granted him the role of a pioneer (together with Lessing, Winckelmann, and Herder), Dilthey concluded that his religious writings did not reach the requisite degree of maturity for a modern secular culture. Danzel, who died in 1850 at the age of thirty-two, had already begun this devaluation of Wieland and Klopstock. Besides Lessing, to whom his major work is dedicated, Danzel refers primarily to Goethe, from whom the new literary studies were to draw their inspiration. In contrast, his essays on Goethe's time push Wieland into the background and mention Klopstock only marginally.[1] This assessment, as we shall

[1]Theodor Wilhelm Danzel, *Zur Literatur und Philosophie der Goethezeit*, ed. Hans

see, was largely shared by publishers of textbooks. After 1850 Klopstock and Wieland were considered marginal figures in the institution of German literature. Although interest in the young Goethe, which developed later, brought such writers as Hamann and Herder to prominence again, Klopstock and Wieland were apt to be excluded as representatives of an "earlier phase."[2]

The Case of Jean Paul

The case of Jean Paul is more complex. By about 1850 he had already gone through a succession of phases in which he was received in contradictory ways, and to which Nachmärz criticism and historiography responded. The polemical reaction against Jean Paul in the Nachmärz can be explained largely as a criticism of his Biedermeier tendencies.[3] But we should bear in mind that as a cult figure of Young German anticlassical criticism, Jean Paul was included by programmatic realists in their denunciation of romanticism and Young Germany for both literary and political reasons. Jean Paul's style was considered dated after 1848, because programmatic realism demanded more moderation.[4] But just as Schmidt and Freytag's realist program did not go unchallenged, Jean Paul's position remained controversial in the Nachmärz period. If one compares the expenditure for the Schiller celebration of 1859, or even for the 1849 festivities for Goethe, with the commemoration of the centenary of Jean Paul's birth, it becomes obvious that the latter's reputation as a public cult hero had been severely damaged. Karl von Holtei believed this neglect was inevitable because of contemporary concern with other problems: "In truth, it does not suit the tenor of our time, it is not compatible with the direction of our youth, to descend into the deep, substantial well of his wisdom, truth, virtue, and gentleness, hidden behind strange vegetation and thornbushes. In our day there is no longer time for this."[5] This untimeliness was, of course, the very reason that the opponents of programmatic realism supported Jean Paul. If they were inclined to anticlassicism, they praised him as an alternative to Weimar classicism; if they were closer to classicism, as was Gottschall, for instance, they placed him in the temple of German literature beside Goethe and Schiller. One must view

---

Mayer (Stuttgart, 1962), p. 70.

[2]The exception is Hettner's history of literature, which shows a full appreciation of both Klopstock and Wieland. Wieland is characterized as "Lessing's most important partner" (vol. 2 [1864], p. 461); he is credited with having initiated the German novel.

[3]Thus Sprengel, in Peter Sprengel, ed., *Jean Paul im Urteil seiner Kritiker* (Munich, 1980), pp. lxiii–ix.

[4]See Friedrich Sengle, *Biedermeierzeit* (Stuttgart, 1971), 1:307.

[5]Quoted in Sprengel, *Jean Paul im Urteil seiner Kritiker*, p. lxiv.

Schmidt's severe judgment of Jean Paul, as well as Gottschall's and Hettner's appreciation, against this background.

Schmidt's vehement criticism of Jean Paul in 1855 was connected with his fundamental confrontation with romanticism and Young Germany (which he understood as a second romantic generation). He expressly addresses Jean Paul as the father of the Young German style, and in so doing sets the tone of his attack. Schmidt turns the criticism of subjectivity advanced in the *Hallische Jahrbücher* against Jean Paul, measuring his novels against the sureness of form and objectivity found in Goethe's work. Goethe had tried to achieve a harmonious development of his talents in both his life and his work, whereas Jean Paul had no independent existence: everything became literature in his hands; he lived only for his writing. Schmidt classifies Jean Paul with the subjective, reflective writers: "Even though he tended to be sentimental and effusive, in his early life he gave himself over entirely to reflection."[6] Measured against the norms of poetic realism, which Schmidt believes were at least partially realized by Goethe, Jean Paul is a fundamental failure and cannot be regarded as an essential figure in German tradition. He falls, Schmidt contends, between rationalism and romanticism, without achieving a synthesis: "As a contemporary of romanticism he strives for mystery, wonder, the inconceivable; but as a born rationalist he then perceives everything as natural again." The result is a force of imagination that does not extend beyond the fragmentary, which is mired in detail and thus cannot do justice to a person's "real content."

This harsh judgment unmistakably followed Gervinus, who had called Jean Paul immature and characterized him as an author whose creative power was constantly hindered by reflection. Schmidt takes up this thesis: "To feel intensely, the poet has to take a running start; to protect the inspiration of his unhampered will against all opposition he becomes excited, and his heroes become the same. This is what children do, but in Jean Paul childhood goes beyond the limits of decency."[7] Schmidt, however, goes a crucial step beyond Gervinus; although he does not exclude Jean Paul from the history of literature, he expels him from the German tradition. Despite his detailed criticism of *Wilhelm Meister*, Schmidt asserts again at the end of his history of literature that Goethe's work represents the high point of the German novel and that no later novel has surpassed it.[8] Jean Paul, in contrast, is denied the role

---

[6]Julian Schmidt, "Jean Paul im Verhältnis zur gegenwärtigen Romanliteratur (1855)," in Sprengel, *Jean Paul im Urteil seiner Kritiker*, p. 173; this sentence is missing in the second edition (1855) of his history of literature.

[7]Ibid., p. 180.

[8]Julian Schmidt, *Geschichte der deutschen Literatur im neunzehnten Jahrhundert*, 2d ed. (Leipzig, 1855), 1:227.

of model; he appears as the forerunner of a false tendency, from which Schmidt would like to free German literature. Although Gervinus was willing in his comparison of Goethe and Jean Paul to accept Jean Paul's romantically unformed nature as a lesser alternative, programmatic realism is no longer interested in the "most secret moods of the soul."[9]

Classicists and realists were equally opposed to Jean Paul. His public reputation diminished, and in 1913 Hugo von Hofmannsthal was able to speak of the "scant regard for and impending oblivion" of this author in the preceding five decades.[10] He was appreciated and acknowledged as part of the tradition only by those who still had a connection with the Vormärz and by those who resisted realist theory. This is made explicit by Carl Christian Planck, whose more comprehensive study of Jean Paul (1867) takes a position against the classicistic idealization of the German plight and thus joins Börne's and Georg Herwegh's tradition of reverence for Jean Paul.[11] Yet it is characteristic that the two most important histories of literature besides Schmidt's— those of Gottschall and Hettner—avoid such an extreme position and try instead to mediate between the canonization of Weimar classicism and a commitment to Jean Paul.

Gottschall begins his section on Jean Paul as follows: "An influence on the further development of our literature as important as *Schiller's* and *Goethe's* was the third coryphaeus of the German intellect, *Jean Paul Friedrich Richter*, whom only an aesthetic, biased one-sidedness could ban from the circle of our intellectual potentates." He cites the aesthetics of Friedrich Vischer in order to legitimize Jean Paul as a classic humorist whose creative method differs from that of the romantic style. Gottschall is not deciding against the Weimar writers in this argument; rather, he is describing Jean Paul as a necessary *supplement* to Goethe and Schiller, to the authors to whom modern readers turn: "Jean Paul seized every aspect of *modern life*, never depicting it objectively but always hovering over it with a free spirit that drew its independent strength from the depths of his soul and from the ideal of *humanity* forever alive in him." The expressive forms in which Jean Paul excels are the idyl and satire. His achievement lies in having combined idealism and realism, the sublime and the humorous, thereby supplementing the one-sided classical ideal of form. Yet despite this positive assessment, Gottschall remains enough of a classicist to raise significant objections to Jean Paul's novels. Thus his judgment differs

---

[9]Georg Gottfried Gervinus, *Geschichte der Deutschen Dichtung*, 4th ed. (Leipzig, 1853), 5:215.

[10]Quoted in Sprengel, *Jean Paul im Urteil seiner Kritiker*, p. 227.

[11]Karl Christian Planck, *Jean Paul's Dichtung im Lichte unserer nationalen Entwicklung. Ein Stück deutscher Kulturgeschichte* (Berlin, 1867).

less on the whole from Gervinus's and Schmidt's than one might initially expect. With respect to *Hesperus*, Gottschall too writes of an unsatisfying form and insufficient action. Only *Titan* is excepted from this criticism; it is said to be classicistic because it has poetic power and originality, despite a certain capriciousness. When Gottschall praises Jean Paul, he follows Börne's tradition: compared to the aristocratic Goethe, Jean Paul has the look of a popular writer: "He had the makings, as Goethe and Schiller did not, of a German Shakespeare, a poet he was as close to in the originality of his Weltanschauung, in his profound grasp of and insight into life, in his universal humor, glowing imagination, and unbounded richness of image and wit, as he was separated from him by the one great gulf of having found no popular and sustaining art form for this richness and, with all his enthusiasm for the breadth of historical life, no room for expressing it in his creative work."[12]

Hettner's history of literature follows a similar strategy. He places Jean Paul beside Goethe and Schiller and emphasizes their common distinction between the ideal and reality. Jean Paul, however, has a special status: "He was not able to achieve Goethe's and Schiller's free and beautifully harmonious ideal of humanity; he was far behind these giants both in talent and in the moral energy required for unsparing self-education. On the other hand, he was just as safe from the weaknesses and biases of the other stragglers of the Sturm und Drang period; his spirit was too tender and loving to harbor Klinger's harsh contempt for the world, and he had too earnest a disposition and too fresh and immediate a sense of reality for the unstable fantasticality of the romantics." This qualification allows Hettner to appreciate Jean Paul as a true humorist. He, too, views Jean Paul's work against Goethe's novels. He thus compares *Titan* with *Wilhelm Meister*, describes the *Flegeljahre* as a deepening of *Titan*, and again compares these with Goethe's work. Despite his high estimation of Jean Paul's achievement, however, Hettner ultimately concludes that his novels as a whole represent a danger to the German tradition and that they are no longer directly accessible to contemporaries. Nothing speaks more for Hettner's late political resignation than this judgment, which renounces the critical social function of the poet he had emphatically defended in about 1850. In his judgment of the novels Hettner ultimately comes closer to the position of Gervinus and Schmidt, who complained mainly about their formlessness. Thus he, too, observes that "it is inconceivable how destructive an effect Jean Paul had because of this dissolution of artistic form. We still

[12]Rudolph Gottschall, *Die deutsche Nationalliteratur in der ersten Hälfte des neunzehnten Jahrhunderts*, 2d ed. (Breslau, 1861), 1:141, 144, 158, 169.

find this bad influence in Heine and the writers of Young Germany."[13] Hettner's judgment remains dichotomous and self-contradictory. On the one hand, he follows the classic model, depreciating Jean Paul aesthetically; on the other, he adheres to the politicized literary criticism of the Vormärz, underscoring Jean Paul's political importance. But since this form of literary public sphere had been disrupted by the unsuccessful Revolution of 1848, it was unable in the late 1860s to come to Jean Paul's rescue.

The Schiller Celebration of 1859

Monographic histories of reception tend to isolate their subject. Thus continuous lines can be traced in the reception history of Jean Paul as well as, albeit less clearly, in that of both Wieland and Klopstock. Certain groups of readers and critics continued to value these authors, while the literary public as a whole was neglecting them. For the most part, however, the reading public's interest in its literary heritage was focused on Weimar. The Schiller celebration of 1859 afforded contemporaries a special opportunity to articulate their cultural and national identity. This example in particular makes it clear that by reconstructing the history of literature, light is thrown on only one aspect of the process of canonization. Discussions in periodicals, school programs, and public lectures, which were part of the centennial celebration, carried a weight of their own. Popularized material, excluded from scholarly history as a rule because it was considered incongruous, becomes highly significant from the standpoint of canonization. As the Schiller celebration clearly shows, the development and consolidation of a literary canon was more than a literary, aesthetic matter. The public was celebrating a cultural hero in whom it saw itself reflected and whom it could claim as its own.

The Schiller celebration was less a literary than a *cultural and national-political event*. The protest registered by Franz Grillparzer, who did not want to see his appreciation of the poet confused with the political goals of the German liberals, demonstrates this point.[14] The surviving documents of the celebration, published lectures and addresses, present a one-sided picture, because they do not mention the actual ceremonies, processions, and festivities in schools, universities, churches, and synagogues which formed the background for the countless speeches in which the German bourgeoisie—and to some extent the

---

[13]Hermann Hettner, *Geschichte der deutschen Literatur im 18. Jahrhundert*, vol. 3, bk. 3 (Braunschweig, 1870), pp. 393, 411.

[14]See Norbert Oellers, ed., *Schiller—Zeitgenosse aller Epochen*, pt. 1 (Frankfurt a. M., 1970), p. 428.

working class—affirmed that, more than anyone else, Schiller had voiced the longings and aspirations of the German nation; that he could consequently be regarded as their *spiritual leader* on the road to national unity.

The Schiller celebration in Hamburg was rightly described as a national festival, for the three-day-long festivities exceeded the dimensions of the bourgeois public sphere.[15] The great procession through the lighted streets on the third day brought the festivities directly to the people, linking the literary and popular public spheres to an extent hitherto unknown. For the participants, the festival was more than a commemoration; it was a historic act that was to give rise to something new. In Schiller's name, the community of celebrants swore an oath to the cultural and national unity to which it aspired. Any attempt to separate the literary and political aspects of the Schiller celebration is futile, for the festival itself was understood as a political act.

The history of Schiller's reception before 1859 suggests such an identification with the glorified author, but one should not forget that in 1859 only certain elements of that tradition were accepted. The criticism of abstract idealism and political distance expressed by the young Hettner in 1850 finds no place in the speeches delivered at the festival. At most one heard that Schiller was not necessarily the nation's greatest writer—probably a clue that the speaker regarded Goethe as more important. The liberals, who had regained hope in the new era, avoided criticizing classicism. Instead, they sought in 1859 to use the literary tradition culminating in Schiller (and Goethe) to unlock and grasp the political future.

A number of recurrent themes and motifs can be traced in the many, generally not very original, talks. One was Schiller's popularity. Vischer, for example, referred to the modest, trusting life of the German poet, adding that "one has to love him; it is impossible to keep a distance from him."[16] And Carriere, comparing him to Goethe, emphasized that only Schiller took the people seriously and considered them in his work: "And whereas even Shakespeare treated the *Volk* ironically as the unstable, polycephalous masses, and Goethe in *Egmont* merely gave us pleasure through the individual portraits in his folk scenes, Schiller was the first to visualize the *Volk* poetically as an organic and capable entity, as the worthy bearers of its excellent guides." Schiller's proclaimed closeness to the people legitimized the conception of Schiller as the chosen leader of the German nation. In this sense, Carriere observed

---

[15]See *Die hamburger Schillerfeier. Ein deutsches Volksfest* (Hamburg, 1859).
[16]Friedrich Vischer, *Rede zur hundertjährigen Feier der Geburt Schillers* (Zurich, 1859), p. 12.

that "even when his force attained the proportions of formal beauty and artistic perfection, poetry remained a serious mission, a service in a temple, a priesthood."[17] It was precisely the abstract idealism that Hettner and others had criticized which was evoked in 1859 as the reason for Schiller's ideal leadership. Jacob Burckhardt distinguished between aesthetic perfection, which he denied Schiller, and literary effect, concluding that his "individuals, who are really ideals, are depicted with such glowing enthusiasm that they will forever remain the beloved property of the German *Geist*."[18] Vischer was more emphatic about the poet's mission as a leader: "Thus he strides ahead hovering, hovers as he strides ahead of the people, all peoples, *his* people above all, whose power and greatness still lie buried under the ruins of the past, forward toward the lofty goal!" Even though Vischer had earlier spoken expressly of freedom and the beauty of human nature, which all humankind shares, the commemorative celebration was the occasion when Schiller's idealism was pressed into service for national unification. Vischer could thus not totally absolve Schiller of the blame of cosmopolitanism: "When the idea of freedom becomes totally dominant, it easily disguises the fact that above all we simply must have a fatherland, free or not free."[19] Only in *Die Jungfrau von Orleans* did he find that shift toward national patriotism which the liberals believed they saw in 1859. Hence Jakob Grimm, too, believed that he had to defend Schiller against the accusation of political indifference, and he tried to reduce the cosmopolitan and national aspects of Schiller's work to a common denominator: "'Wallenstein' was created for German freedom and so was 'Tell,' whose heroic deed is aptly expressed in stanzas accompanying the copy presented to the Elector Lord Chancellor. The universal human rejoicing inspired by the choruses of the 'Ode to Joy' will never die."[20]

This very aim—to exploit Schiller's dramas for national liberalism—brought the conservatives into the picture. They either pleaded for the strict separation of literature and politics or undertook to prove, like the critic of the *Kreuzzeitung*, that Schiller was anything but a friend of the people, that his proper place was in the Conservative party.[21] In 1859 both liberals and conservatives exploited Schiller's texts for their own purposes. Liberal critics in particular posited their specific inter-

[17]Moriz Carriere, *Lessing, Schiller, Goethe, Jean Paul. Vier Denkreden auf deutsche Dichter* (Giessen, 1862), pp. 46, 47.

[18]Jacob Burckhardt, *Gedächtnisrede auf Schiller*, quoted in Oellers, *Schiller—Zeitgenosse aller Epochen*, pt. 1, p. 418.

[19]Vischer, *Rede zur hundertjährigen Feier der Geburt Schillers*, pp. 20, 16.

[20]Jacob Grimm, *Rede auf Schiller*, quoted in Oellers, *Schiller—Zeitgenosse aller Epochen*, pt. 1, p. 449.

[21]See doc. 53, in Oellers, *Schiller—Zeitgenosse aller Epochen*, pt. 1.

pretive models as absolute, thereby creating an image of Schiller that invited identification with the playwright. If, on the whole, postrevolutionary literary studies tended to safeguard the literary heritage by historicizing it, the Schiller celebration went counter to this tendency, for it was aimed not at the past but at the present and future. Those celebrants who spoke of "our Schiller" were contemporizing him even as they viewed his work historically. Political unity appeared to be the realization of what Schiller had created in his dramas. The conclusion of the description of the Hamburg festival is characteristic. The recorder of the event evokes an image of the procession, the masses of "active, youthfully vigorous men," adding: "And consider that perhaps only a fourth of the unions and corporations were represented; quadruple the number and imagine this army of valiant men adorned with weapons and obedient to one will, one idea, and thus obedient because it is their own will, their own idea!"[22] This observation comforts the writer and lets him imagine the next centennial celebration taking place on the ground of a unified, free Germany.

The commemoration of Schiller's centennial presupposed that his work was an inalienable part of the German literary tradition. In this respect, the ceremonial speeches merely corroborated what was already firmly fixed in the general consciousness. Not surprisingly, 1859 was the year not only of Schiller's celebration but also of Goethe's. In the classic model developed by Ruge and Gervinus, the two names were no longer separable. Any position taken on Schiller presupposed a judgment of Goethe. Grimm offered the clearest statement on the matter when he observed that "Goethe and Schiller stand so close together on the sublime heights they occupy—as they did in life, which bound them closely and indissolubly together—that it would be impossible to consider them apart from each other."[23] The Schiller jubilee was supposed to emphasize not what separated Schiller from Goethe but what they had in common. For this purpose well-established formulas were used. Grimm chose the concepts of idealistic and realistic to describe how they differed; Carriere referred to their friendship, calling the bond a "beautiful moral act." He described the difference between them: "Schiller gave his ideas a lifelike basis in nature and embodied them in viable individual characters, whereas Goethe gave his creations a symbolic significance and rose more and more into the realm of pure thought."[24] Thus the bond between the two authors resulted in a balancing of their points of view and ways of working, which had a sta-

[22]*Die hamburger Schillerfeier*, p. 64.
[23]Quoted in Oellers, *Schiller—Zeitgenosse aller Epochen*, pt. 1, p. 441.
[24]Carriere, *Lessing, Schiller, Goethe, Jean Paul*, pp. 48–49.

bilizing and integrating effect on literary tradition. Even Goethe's advocates, who were convinced of the greater worth of their author, in 1859 avoided attacking the more popular Schiller or even putting too overt an emphasis on their differences. The purpose of this strategy is unmistakable. The bond between Goethe and Schiller, which found literary expression in their exchange of letters, guaranteed the integration of potentially divergent literary and ideological tendencies and brought them into line with liberal demands. That the admiration for classicism did not stop there but was later to be part of the liberal German turn toward conservatism is demonstrated especially by Goethe's reception in the 1860s.

Goethe's Significance

Viktor Hehn's essay "Goethe und das Publikum," published in 1888 in his *Gedanken über Goethe*, strongly affected our view of the history of Goethe's influence in the Nachmärz. Hehn describes 1849 as a low point in Goethe's recognition and fame. Taking the liberal criticism of Goethe in the Vormärz as his point of departure, Hehn charges that Goethe's hundredth birthday was virtually forgotten: "The centennial celebration of 1849 met nowhere with open approval; indeed, those who requested it were hissed. Smaller circles may have solemnly remembered the day, but only quietly, far from the noise of the market, where no procession assembled, no banner was unfurled, and where different business altogether was being transacted."[25] This statement deliberately distorts the historical facts, because in 1849 there was no lack of public celebration taking place in public buildings, or even in marketplaces. It was not only an elite of Goethe admirers who acknowledged the poet in 1849. Hehn suggests a causal relationship between the alleged indifference of the public sphere and the political radicalism of 1848 and 1849. But this equation is not borne out, because Gervinus, on whom the later liberal history of literature was built, was by no means as disdainful of Goethe as Hehn makes him out to be. It was he who, despite his critical remarks, had established Goethe's canonical validity with his history of literature. Discussion, in which Hehn played a crucial role, centered on the question how Goethe's undisputed classicality could be reinterpreted after the failure of the revolution. Goethe's aesthetic and ideological rescue took place against the changed political and ideological background of the postrevolutionary period. Its goal was to give sufficient reason for the status of the Weimar author so that he would remain untouched by the defeat of

[25]Viktor Hehn, *Gedanken über Goethe*, 2d ed. (Berlin, 1888), p. 170.

radical early liberalism. Hehn's posthumously published *Ueber Goethes Hermann und Dorothea*, written in 1851, is one of the most important documents of this reinterpretation.

Hehn dissociates himself from two traditional interpretations that he regards as ahistorical. On the one hand, he defends Goethe against the politically motivated criticism of Börne and the radical camp, which accused the poet of political indifference; on the other, he opposes the early socialists' intention to vindicate Goethe's works because they contain a socialist message. In Hehn's view, both of these tendencies removed Goethe from his epoch and measured him according to concepts not of his time. Hehn—and in this he would be followed by Wilhelm Dilthey—emphatically places Goethe in the context of the eighteenth century, which he understands as prerevolutionary and apolitical. Unlike the French Enlightenment, the German Enlightenment was restricted to religious and aesthetic issues: "All political questions were left unconsidered in this naturalistic-aesthetic emancipation. The struggle was directed against the boundaries limiting free subjectivity: the individual was to make use of the profound enigmas and mysteries of his inner being, his infinite sensations, to break out of the poor schema of finished externalized types." Hehn describes the old German class society as a given, unalterable fact of eighteenth-century life, so that the rising political movement that had gripped Germany since 1770 appears to be something foreign. As a result, Goethe becomes an unpolitical author, exclusively preoccupied with his own problems: "But Goethe himself, and his century, did not feel called upon either to be politically effective or to give poetic expression to a political efficacy that did not exist." In order to explain Goethe's work historically, Hehn is prepared, indeed resolved, to suppress everything that does not fit his picture of an unpolitical Germany. With him, historicization becomes the instrument of both an aesthetic and an ideological legitimation of his subject, for he goes beyond giving historical distance to the literature of the past. He denies that Germans had any political interest at all after the experiences of 1848: "We are a people attached to family, private life, and feelings, and this trait runs through the entire history of Germany."[26] Hehn suggests accordingly that the conditions under which *Hermann und Dorothea* was written were identical to those of his own time, in other words, that the apolitical character of this work not only was determined by its genesis but must also influence the work's later reception. In his hands, Goethe's epic becomes a modern poetic witness in which the reader of 1851 can find pleasure.

[26]Viktor Hehn, *Ueber Goethes Hermann und Dorothea* (Stuttgart, 1893), pp. 37, 44–45, 41.

To be sure, Hehn does not want to protect only Goethe from radical political constructions; he characteristically includes Schiller in his a-political interpretation. Schiller's historical dramas are explicitly described as private, and his letters *Über die ästhetische Erziehung des Menschen* (On the Aesthetic Education of Man), whose subject is the relationship between aesthetics and politics, are read—in opposition to Gervinus—with the intention of showing that "aesthetic education aims only at a beautiful moral rebirth that, if it is ever achieved, will replace a political rebirth." Although this interpretation of Schiller did not gain acceptance in the 1850s, Goethe criticism had a tendency—already incipient in Theodor Wilhelm Danzel—to use the historicization of its subject to create a conservative portrait of a classicist. The classicistic aspects of the literary theory of programmatic realism, even when its adherents regarded themselves as liberals, represented a decided effort to accommodate this tendency. This effort is part of the contradiction demonstrated by Hehn's celebration of *Hermann und Dorothea*: the intent was to historicize Goethe's work but at the same time to define it as exemplary—that is, as timeless. Hehn's interpretation is characteristic of Goethe criticism of the 1850s and 1860s: "The epic and pictorial tendency that the poet had acquired by nature and through Spinoza came to full maturity in the vivid air of Italy. The natural and artistic world of Italy gave him the lucid clarity, consummate form, objective precision, and gentle tranquillity that henceforth marked his works."[27] Goethe's greatness lies in his presumed objectivity, which places him, in the opinion of his admirers, above the politically engaged Schiller.

Whereas the influential *Grenzboten* reported critically on Goethe's centennial celebration, disparaging, in Schmidt's essay "Zu Goethes Jubelfeier," Goethe's "subjective willfulness, his characterless dissolution in a sea of chance sensations, and his revolt against regulation and authority,"[28] *Deutsches Museum*, edited by Robert Prutz, took a more positive attitude. Prutz, as he put it, used Goethe's name for his journal.[29] But Schmidt and the *Grenzboten* circle should not really be counted among Goethe's opponents either. For them, too, the poet's canonical status was already established. Schmidt turned against the romantic and postromantic criticism that especially valued Goethe's irrationalism, praising instead the "self-discipline of a beautiful nature"—that is, Goethe's objectivity—in the name of common sense.

---

[27]Ibid., pp. 40, 25–26.
[28]Quoted in Karl Robert Mandelkow, ed., *Goethe im Urteil seiner Kritiker*, pt. 2 (Munich, 1977), p. 335.
[29]See Helmuth Widhammer, *Realismus und klassizistische Tradition* (Tübingen, 1972), p. 98.

The bias of the *Grenzboten* circle against certain aspects of Goethe's work was closely connected to the outcome of the revolution; every form of subjectivity that could be interpreted as political weakness was rejected.

Whereas programmatic realism extensively incorporated the aesthetics of Goethe's time into its own program,[30] academic literary studies tried to protect the classical heritage by approaching it historically. Danzel, whose essays on Goethe stand apart from the historico-philosophical thinking of the Hegelians, acknowledges, as does Hehn, the aesthetics of classicism. Danzel's essay on Goethe and his fellow art lovers of Weimar represents nothing less than a rescue of Goethe's literary theory.[31] He argues that Goethe's commitment to the art theory of the ancient world had no effect on his concept of literature, because there, in contrast to the visual arts, no compelling model was available, or at least not to Goethe. Thus Danzel was able to present Goethe as the creator of a new concept of literature.

This shift in opinion on Goethe was continued in the 1860s by Hettner, who retracted his old accusation of abstract idealism on the occasion of a lecture on *Iphigenie* delivered at the Berlin Goethe colloquium; henceforth he celebrated that drama as one of the pinnacles of the classical style.[32] At the same colloquium, Berthold Auerbach spoke in similar terms on the objectivity of Goethe's art of narration as exemplified by *Wilhelm Meister*.[33] Herman Grimm, anticipating the cult of classicists in the *Gründerzeit*, already considered himself so far removed from the Goethe period that critical analysis of the classical heritage seemed unnecessary.[34] As Goethe's time receded into the past and people became less familiar with his cultural milieu, there was criticism not of Goethe but rather of the safeguards of philology and biography. Grimm's introduction to his lectures on Goethe of 1874–75 is characteristic of this approach. Goethe has become an event forever shaping the fate of those within cultural reach: "Opinions of his worth will change; in different periods, the German people will seem closer to him or farther away. But he can never be deposed; nor will he disappear

---

[30]Besides the work of Helmuth Widhammer, see on this Hermann Kinder, *Poesie als Synthese* (Frankfurt a. M., 1973), and Ulf Eisele, *Realismus und Ideologie* (Stuttgart, 1976).

[31]Danzel, *Zur Literatur und Philosophie der Goethezeit*, ed. Hans Mayer (Stuttgart, 1962).

[32]Hermann Hettner, "Goethe's Iphigenie in ihrem Verhältnis zur Bildungsgeschichte des Dichters," in his *Kleine Schriften* (Braunschweig, 1884), pp. 425–74.

[33]Berthold Auerbach, *Goethe und die Erzählungskunst* (Stuttgart, 1861); see also Karl Robert Mandelkow, *Goethe im Urteil seiner Kritiker*, pt. 2, p. lxiii.

[34]See his review of Dilthey's *Das Leben Schleiermachers* (1870) in *Grenzboten* 29 (1870), II, 1, pp. 1–3.

on his own, melting away like a glacier of which nothing will remain when the last drop has run off." Goethe has attained a position raising him above the history of literature; together with Homer, Dante, and Shakespeare, he belongs to the timeless Olympians who will forever be above the history of their reception. There can no longer be any doubt about the perfection of the works Goethe created in Italy; the disappointment of his contemporaries with his development must be blamed on their lack of insight. Grimm calls Goethe's problematic friendship with Schiller a "collective concept within German history,"[35] by which he means to establish their great significance for all time.

Herman Grimm's historicization of Goethe is really the *mythicization* of a cult hero whose life, with all its philologically revealed details, assumes the form of a legend. In Grimm's lectures, the critic's position is identical to that of the author under consideration. His introduction frankly concedes, on the other hand, that this affirmation is connected with the change in political circumstances: "We possess a present that far surpasses our desires. Its offerings are no longer, as before, merely something to be hoped for or attained, but something to be held fast, developed, and exploited. In the dawn of this new day, we see past ages in a different light. We no longer search in them for weapons to help us win our freedom. Rather, now that the battle for freedom has been won, we search for that which will strengthen our new position and secure our possession of the goods we have gained." Once national unity was achieved under Bismarck, the liberals' political criticism of Goethe seemed outdated and incongruous. Gervinus and his students had regarded Goethe's political indifference as one of the deficiencies of classicism; Grimm regards the conservative sentiments of his author as the prerequisite for Bismarck's recently founded Reich: "Goethe's labors have helped prepare the ground we sow and reap today. He belongs among the noblest founders of German freedom. For all our victories, without him we would lack the best ideas for exploiting those victories."[36] The depoliticization of Goethe criticism demanded by Hehn after 1848 has here reached its political conclusion: Goethe, and with him Schiller, prepares the way for the second Reich.[37] Even such a moderate liberal as Schmidt showed a similar change in thought after 1866.[38] Following the Prussian victory at Königgrätz, Schmidt, too,

[35]Herman Grimm, *Goethe. Vorlesungen gehalten an der Kgl. Universität zu Berlin* (Berlin, 1877), 1:7, 2:160.

[36]Ibid., 1:8, 9.

[37]This monumentalization is already apparent in 1859 in Grimm's essay "Schiller und Goethe," which, however, still contains a concept of history oriented toward the future which was later lost; Herman Grimm, *Essays* (Hanover, 1859).

[38]See Bernd Peschken, *Versuch einer germanistischen Ideologiekritik* (Stuttgart, 1972), pp. 88–108.

was prepared to forgo political criticism of classicism, because national unity was more important to him than self-determination. In Schmidt's *Geschichte der deutschen Literatur seit Lessings Tod* (History of German Literature since Lessing's Death) (1866), he judged Goethe more positively than he had in 1855. One should not overemphasize this change, however, as Bernd Peschken does, because Schmidt's opinion of Goethe was already ambiguous during the 1850s. The main point is that despite his polemic against Goethe, he never contested the basic canonical validity of Weimar classicism. Since the early 1860s—that is, after the essays of Adolf Schöll—one of the familiar arguments of Goethe criticism had been that classicism prepared the way for German public spirit; that is, that it initiated a political consensus among the Germans.[39] Schmidt had only to change emphasis in order to complete what scholars such as Danzel, Schöll, and Herman Grimm had already begun.

Prussia and the Literary Tradition

The linkage of Weimar classicism with Prusso-German history—since the new Reich fulfilled the aspirations of classicism—brought a factor into play on which Franz Mehring was the first to focus attention. Postrevolutionary literary history began, especially after the 1860s, to draw a connection between Prussian history and the development of German literature. This tendency has a bearing on the function of the canonization of the German tradition. As Mehring showed,[40] the beginnings of the Prussian legend are found in scattered references in Goethe, particularly in a passage in *Dichtung und Wahrheit*, where Goethe attributes a certain degree of importance for German literature to Frederick the Great. Goethe refers to an ambitious young national literature that was challenged by the king's rejection. This situation was reversed, to be sure, after 1850. Henceforth the Prussian king would appear as the direct or indirect patron of German literature.

When Gervinus speaks of "Prussian literature"[41] in the fourth volume of his history of literature, he means writers such as Johann Gleim and his circle, and after him Thomas Abbt, Mendelssohn, Christoph Nicolai, and Lessing; he has in mind literary life in Berlin, not the Potsdam court. He frankly concedes that because of its French orientation, the latter had little to offer to German literature. Gervinus sees the

---

[39]Adolf Schöll, "Goethe als Staatsmann," *Preussische Jahrbücher* 10 (1862):423–70, 585–616.

[40]See Franz Mehring, *Die Lessing-Legende*, in his *Gesammelte Schriften*, vol. 9 (Berlin, 1963), pp. 36–44.

[41]Georg Gottfried Gervinus, *Geschichte der deutschen Dichtung*, 4:188.

court's contribution to German culture in the fields of philosophy, theology, and music. And even then he makes a distinction between the achievements of Prussian citizens and what the Hohenzollern contributed. Still, we find in Gervinus the beginnings of a Prussian orientation in the history of German literature to which later historians could appeal. Gleim's grenadier songs appear beside bardic poetry as the start of a national poetry in Germany. On the other hand, Frederick II's contempt for German literature is defended; his enmity toward the most important authors of his time is explained as the result of his French education. But under no circumstances would Gervinus have considered the culture of the Prussian court a prerequisite for Weimar classicism, or even have established a causal relationship between the Prussian state and Goethe and Schiller. Even the conservative August Friedrich Vilmar, who wanted to reconcile German classicism with Christianity, in his well-received *Geschichte der deutschen Nationalliteratur* avoided grounding Weimar classicism in Prussian history. Only after 1850, owing to the Prusso-Austrian conflict—to the impending decision between a Little German (*kleindeutsch*) solution and a Great German (*grossdeutsch*) solution—did this question become acute for the construction of a literary tradition. The closer the pro-Prussian, *kleindeutsch* solution came to becoming reality, and the more unification came to be seen as the fulfillment of the cultural and political hopes of the German people, the more pressing became the question how earlier Prussian history had contributed to the development of the now secure literary canon. Prussian victory over Austria in the summer of 1866, which decided the issue in favor of the *kleindeutsch* solution, provoked an immediate revision of opinion, not least among the liberals who had opposed the Prussian state between 1862 and 1866. Schmidt's preface to the second volume of the new edition of his history of literature, dated September 7, 1866, is a striking document of this revision. In reference to the Prusso-Austrian war, he says that "anyone who has read my work carefully will recognize the thread running through it: particularism has destroyed the boldest and proudest flights of our spirit. To have seen the day when Germany, led by a strong arm, finally threw off these crippling shackles must be one of the great joys of life."[42] Prussian victory is frankly equated here with German victory; the *kleindeutsch* solution is taken as the natural one. It is worth noting that Schmidt immediately draws conclusions for the history of literature from this change: in 1866 the polemical approach to classicism which characterized his early works seems antiquated to him.

[42]Julian Schmidt, *Geschichte der deutschen Literatur seit Lessing's Tod*, 5th ed. (Leipzig, 1866), vol. 2, preface.

This revision is evident in the first volume of Schmidt's history of literature. He depicts both classicism and romanticism with greater understanding than he had in 1855. Although Schmidt remains true to his earlier position when interpreting individual works—*Wilhelm Meister*, for example—his overall judgment is closer to the affirmation of someone like Herman Grimm. Volume three, which appeared in 1867 and covered the period from 1814 to the present, shows a considerable change in point of view, approaching the national-conservative interpretation of German tradition.

What Schmidt began was consciously and systematically developed by the young Dilthey. Although it is an exaggeration to maintain that Dilthey initiated a "total change in literary historiography," he drew conclusions from the traditional liberal model of classicism which were unmistakably foreign to Gervinus and his students, indeed even to Danzel. As long as Dilthey regarded German idealism as the driving force of Prussian history, as in his early essay on Schleiermacher, he remained part of the liberal tradition, which during the constitutional conflict tried once again to realize the idea of a constitutional state opposed to Bismarck's government. The turning point came in 1866, when in the course of his critical analysis of recent literary history Dilthey reversed the relationship, declaring Prussian tradition—that is, the combination of Enlightenment and absolutism—to be the foundation of the German literary tradition. One must clearly distinguish here between his idealistic approach of the early 1860s and his "realistic" revision of about 1866. It is not enough to say that in his essays on Goethe, Novalis, Hölderlin, and Lessing, Dilthey was trying to carry out a program of instruction,[43] for this intention was equally shared by the liberals, who by no means denied the literary and aesthetic supremacy of classicism. His conservative turn lay in his assumption that these authors had a message that brought them into line with the impending Little German solution. Dilthey explicitly formulated this idealistic and Prussian synthesis in a later addition to his essay on Lessing, first published in 1867: "Thus two great intellectual forces of this German period of enlightenment have come together here, the exalted concept of honor held by Frederick the Great's army and the noble humanity that is the most beautiful product of our literature of that time."[44] Dilthey sees the conflicts in eighteenth-century German drama as a reflection of tension between a humanistic culture and "Prussian power." Lessing's comedies, especially *Minna von Barnhelm*, are ac-

[43]Thus Peschken, *Versuch einer germanistischen Ideologiekritik*, pp. 126, 128.
[44]Wilhelm Dilthey, *Das Erlebnis und die Dichtung: Lessing, Goethe, Novalis, Hölderlin*, 9th ed. (Leipzig, 1924), p. 55.

cordingly interpreted as the resolution of this tension. In Dilthey's view, Lessing achieved a synthesis that anticipated *Tasso* and *Faust*.

Dilthey was not the only one to hold this opinion. In his history of literature, Hettner also tried to prove that the Prussian tradition was important for the development of German literature, if not directly through the person of the king, then at least indirectly. He examined in detail the influence of the Western European and German Enlightenment on the young Frederick II, and then he tried to show that the Prussia shaped by the Enlightenment shared the same spirit as German literature. Hettner did not, however, succeed in disguising the flaws in this concept. After describing the philosophical aspirations of the crown prince, he cannot conceal the fact that the young king did not adhere to his program in the first Silesian war. This contradiction is revealed in the following statement: "Frederick redeemed his word as sincerely" as ambition, the impressions made on him since his youth, and the peculiarities of the Prussian military state allowed. As one might expect, his justification of the Prussian state relies on Kant's treatise on the Enlightenment, which attested to the Prussian king's fundamental contribution to that movement. Hettner remarks that "the philosophical king brought to realization the spirit of the rationalist law of nature, which derives the creation of the state from a contract between citizen and sovereign and thus puts the legitimacy and regulation of the government solely and exclusively under the protection of the law and universal freedom." As a consequence, the Seven Years' War is characterized boldly as a "fight for freedom and enlightenment against the dark powers of clerical and despotic oppression." Through this forced progressive interpretation of Prussia, which is oriented toward constitutional reform and especially the land law of 1794, Hettner seeks to save Prussia for the further development of the German intellect. He cites *Dichtung und Wahrheit* in order to clarify the significance of the Seven Years' War. Far from explaining the war in relation to the European politics of alliance, Hettner emphasizes only its cultural aspect, that is, its allegedly stimulating influence on contemporary writers. In extolling its cultural significance, Hettner goes so far as to draw a comparison with Greek history: as the wars with Persia opened the Periclean age, so the Seven Years' War initiated the golden age of German literature. By distinguishing between Prussian enlightenment and the plight of the small German states, Hettner brings Prussian history into the tradition of an emerging national German literature. In his view, German culture became national in scope because of the policies of Frederick II. Yet he is still close enough to the liberal tradition to recognize the limitations of absolutism: "Everything for the people, nothing by the people. This motto of enlightened despotism is enough to show that even under this new form of government, the *Volk* and the administration are separated by a wide, impassable gulf, just as they were under the cruelest princely domination."[45] Hettner maintains—and this makes him old fashioned in 1870—that the historical process has to legitimize itself as the course of human emancipation. Thus in the introduction to his second volume, he again separates the violence of the aging Prussian king from the real task of German history. The latter leads, on the one hand, to Kant and, on the other, to the literary bond between Goethe and Schiller.

The Literary Canon in Education

Until 1870 the history of literature played a leading role in the establishment of literary tradition: historians and critics debated over which authors were to be regarded as classic, how German literary history had developed, and where its climaxes occurred. The available histories of literature, however, were not binding on institutions of learning. They tell us nothing about what was taught at universities or how educational programs were developed in schools, particularly in *Gymnasien*, or secondary schools. Discussion among educators over the canon of reading matter was in fact largely independent; in any case it has a history of its own in the continuing discussion of the tasks and goals of the educational system. One must remember that the teaching of German in the *Gymnasium* was subordinate to that of classical studies (Greek and Latin). Before 1840 literature was taught primarily by the rhetorical method. Assigned texts were used for rhetorical analysis. It was not until the 1840s, with the encouragement of educators such as Robert Hiecke, that it began to be recognized that the teaching of literature could contribute to the development of national literary awareness.[46]

The first attempts to teach literature of Friedrich Niethammer at the beginning of the nineteenth century made no headway against the new humanism of Friedrich Thiersch. It was Hiecke, in his fundamental work of 1842, *Der deutsche Unterricht auf deutschen Gymnasien* (German Instruction in German Secondary Schools), who presented a reading program for German studies conceived as a national program of education. His ideas largely coincided with those of the liberal literary historians. Returning to Herder's position, Hiecke insisted that *Gymnasium* education should include a systematic consideration of German

[45]Hermann Hettner, *Geschichte der deutschen Literatur im 18. Jahrhundert*, pt. 2, "Das Zeitalter Friedrich des Grossen" (Braunschweig, 1864), pp. 25, 29, 33, 159, 161, 105.

[46]The fundamental work is Georg Jäger, *Schule und literarische Kultur*, vol. 1 (Stuttgart, 1981).

literature. His immediate concern was to put instruction in German literature on an equal footing with that of Greek and Latin literature. Hiecke justified this extension of the canon by maintaining that drills in the ancient texts was meaningful only from the standpoint of native literature. His task, however, was different from the literary historian's, because he had to find a selection of readings which was suitable for the schools and took into consideration the intellectual maturity of various age groups. For this reason, his program does not yet expose the lower and middle *Gymnasium* classes to the grand tradition.[47] On the lower and middle levels of instruction in German, biblical stories, fairy tales, travel accounts, and the like are used to prepare the student for the reception of literature in the narrower sense. That task begins in the *Sekunda* (the sixth and seventh years of secondary school), where Herder's *Cid*, the *Nibelungenlied*, patriotic lyric poetry by Ewald von Kleist and Karl Wilhelm Ramler, and some of Klopstock's odes are read. In addition, Hiecke recommended selected dramas by Goethe and Schiller, such as *Götz von Berlichingen* or *Wilhelm Tell* and possibly *Wallenstein*. Only in the *Prima* (the eighth and ninth years) was the strict classical canon of German literature to be studied. Some of the decisions made by Hiecke in his program had considerable influence on subsequent debate. He wanted not merely to educate students but to create a profound intellectual relationship between them and their nation, and he chose his texts accordingly.

Hiecke's selection corresponds largely to the authors emphasized in literary history. It centers on Lessing, Schiller, and Goethe, who give clear expression to the "national spirit." Their works are to be more highly valued than those of others because, in Hiecke's view, they afford a greater understanding of the development of the German *Geist* and a better grasp of its ultimate goal. Characteristically, neither Klopstock nor Herder have comparable standing in this respect. Like Wieland, they qualify as precursors, who must be considered, of course, but who are not the main focus. Hiecke at least refers to Klopstock and Herder by name, but he no longer recommends Wieland.[48] Jean Paul is considered marginally, and the romantic generation is mentioned, though not without bias. To study the German character, students should read something by Ludwig Tieck and above all be familiar with Ludwig Uhland's works. At this point it becomes eminently clear that Hiecke's choice of works to be studied is not governed exclusively by a literary point of view but by a national-political one as well. He wishes

---

[47]Robert Heinrich Hiecke, *Der deutsche Unterricht auf deutschen Gymnasien* (Leipzig, 1842), pp. 89–91.
[48]Ibid., p. 106.

to reshape the concept of humanistic literature, which was linked to antiquity, by giving it a basis in the national German tradition.

Hiecke's program was by no means generally accepted in the 1840s. It was strongly criticized by Christian educators such as F. J. Günther and H. Hülsmann. From a Christian point of view, Günther would sanction only Klopstock, whereas Hülsmann was at least willing to acknowledge Lessing and, to a certain extent, Goethe and Schiller.[49] Christian objections to the "pagan" classicists of Weimar—to neo-humanism in general—also helped shape the literary pedagogy of the 1850s. The Stiehl regulations on elementary education were the clearest expression of this attitude. On the whole, however, religious objections to Weimar classicism played a minor role after 1850.

The issues addressed by Hiecke were raised again by Rudolf von Raumer in his section on German studies in the second edition of Karl von Raumer's *Geschichte der Pädagogik*, even though he advocated an entirely different didactic theory. Although Raumer rejected the analytical method of literary instruction and argued for an affirmative, unreflective assimilation, he continued to agree for the most part with Hiecke's literary canon. The number of authors and works included in the permanent heritage, and thus made recommended reading, has in fact become even smaller. Raumer's selection includes: "By Goethe: *Götz von Berlichingen, Iphigenie, Hermann und Dorothea*. By Schiller: *Wallenstein, Wilhelm Tell, Jungfrau von Orleans*. By Lessing: *Minna von Barnhelm*. In addition, some of Shakespeare's plays (perhaps *Julius Caesar* and *Macbeth*, but not Schiller's), Herder's *Cid*, and a play by Calderon." There is a conspicuous preference for the classicistic phase of Goethe's and Schiller's work and a total neglect of their early and late works. In Lessing's case, surprisingly, not even *Nathan der Weise* is included. Authors such as Klopstock, Wieland, and Jean Paul are not mentioned. Both the romantics and more recent literature—Heine, for instance—are omitted. Raumer's reduction of the canon to Lessing, Herder, Schiller, and Goethe is an isolated phenomenon, however, and he was not followed with such strictness by educators and writers of textbooks in the 1850s and 1860s. Classicality, on the other hand, became the crucial criterion for selection. Raumer, in fact, demanded a form of learning by students which precisely repressed reflection. "The task of the school with respect to recent German literature," he writes in opposition to Hiecke, "accordingly will be far more to transmit than to enlighten." What Raumer meant by this is clear from his suggestion that lyric poetry should be left primarily to classes in singing; it would

[49]See Hans-Georg Herrlitz, *Der Lektüre-Kanon des Deutsch-Unterrichts im Gymnasium* (Heidelberg, 1964), pp. 105–7.

thus be learned and assimilated through "singing and recitation." For didactic reasons Raumer opposes the expository method: explanations presumably remain subordinate to the direct impression made by a great work. Though justifiable in part, this argument has one (perhaps unintentional) side effect: German instruction as envisioned in Raumer's pedagogy dogmatically defines tradition. It tacitly assumes that the reception of masterpieces is an affirmative one, because appropriate selection by an experienced educator has already eliminated those texts that could "confuse" the student's education. Raumer is aware that educators and teachers interfere in the process of a developing literary tradition, and he therefore asks himself, "Who then should decide what is superior and what is not?" His conclusion is that "no matter how uncertain the judgment may be in individual cases, this question can still be answered. The decision depends on *lasting* recognition by the best among the *Volk*."[50] He expounds this viewpoint of historical efficacy in such a way that, in the final analysis, the decision falls to public opinion. The schools merely follow prevailing opinion in their selection. It thus follows that Raumer's selection ultimately reflects the conclusions arrived at in the course of literary historical discussion.

Despite some disagreement, Ernst Laas basically still follows Raumer in the 1870s. He extends the canon somewhat, allowing the poems of Uhland, Hoffmann von Fallersleben, Adalbert von Chamisso, and Heine, for example, to be read in the lower classes. But he, too, concentrates his selection for the upper level on Goethe, Schiller, and Lessing. In addition, he suggests as reading material for the upper *Secunda* Walter von der Vogelweide, Herder (*Der Cid*), and Shakespeare. Unlike Raumer, he again gives a more prominent place to literary history. The history of German literature, beginning with the poetry of the Germanic tribes and ending with the sixteenth century, is to be briefly covered in the *Secunda*, so that German instruction in the *Prima* can concentrate on the period between 1500 and 1800. As in Gervinus, Laas's introduction to recent literature ends with 1815. After that, Germany had a political task to fulfill: just as a classic national literature had to be created in the eighteenth century, so a national *state* had to be built in the nineteenth.[51] In Laas, the history of literature, which Raumer wanted to exclude from *Gymnasium* instruction, has become a solid part of the reading program. But with him, too, the notion that students must be guided toward the apogee of German literature in the late eighteenth

[50]In Karl von Raumer, *Geschichte der Pädagogik*, pt. 3, 6th ed. (Gütersloh, 1897), pp. 229, 225, 232.
[51]Ernst Laas, *Der Deutsch-Unterricht auf höheren Lehranstalten* (Berlin, 1886), pp. 268–97, esp. 295.

century is always in the background. Literary history is a preparation for masterpieces. This tendency was legitimized by the Austrian government in 1849 in an organizational plan calling for the reading of Middle High German texts in the *Obergymnasium* along with a cursory treatment of the history of literature. Recent German literature, from Herder to the present, was delegated to the third class (fifteen- and sixteen-year-olds), while the fourth and last class was to grapple with the masterpieces of Greek, Roman, and German literature.[52] In Prussia, in contrast, literary history gradually replaced rhetoric in the 1820s and 1830s, until Hiecke raised objections to this equation of literary instruction and literary history. Georg Jäger has rightly pointed out that the combination of literary history and selected readings had already formed the nucleus of German instruction in the Vormärz.[53] We might add that this linkage is the very reason that the problem of constructing a canon became a fundamental issue.

The Literary Canon about 1870

If one attempts to reconstruct the literary tradition as it appeared to the educated literary public in about 1870, no uniform picture emerges. With a few exceptions, however, it was generally agreed that the unified German Reich under Bismarck had a literary heritage that could be drawn on collectively. Guiding principles for the legitimation of the new Reich were discovered more in the history of literature than in the history of politics, where Prussians, Saxons, Holsteiners, and Württembergers could hardly be said to have a common fund of experience. The fragmentation of Germany was overcome earlier in the literary than in the political sphere. In the former, a significant change did in fact occur around 1870: the concept of national literature no longer had to serve as a blueprint for a national political history; the political unity that had been achieved henceforth exerted its influence on the history of literature. The literary heritage now became the property of the newly formed nation. No matter how the literary tradition was defined by critics, historians, educators, and journalists—no matter which authors were included or excluded—the educated had agreed by about 1870 that, like their European neighbors, the Germans possessed a corpus of classic authors and works which gave them legitimacy as a "civilized people" (*Kulturvolk*). Despite the many changes and shifts occurring after 1870 (Hölderlin and Kleist were more highly regarded, and

[52]See Adolf Matthias, *Geschichte des deutschen Unterrichts* (Munich, 1907), p. 394.
[53]Georg Jäger, "Der Deutschunterricht auf Gymnasien 1780 bis 1850," in *Deutsche Vierteljahrsschrift für Literaturwissenschaft und Geistesgeschichte* 47 (1973):145.

Büchner was discovered), the process of establishing this canon was essentially complete. The outlines of what was regarded as the true tradition were set. Goethe scholarship no longer had to justify itself after 1870, and for this reason alone it had a different mode of articulation. In 1872 Goethe's greatness and importance were so taken for granted by David Friedrich Strauss that it was inconceivable for Strauss to criticize the "primeval rock that dominates our horizon." In his affirmation of the new belief, Strauss expected educated Germans to identify with Goethe: "His works in themselves constitute a library so rich, so full of the most wholesome and strengthening nourishment for the spirit, that one could reasonably dispense with all other books."[54] What matters here is not Goethe's distinguished position but rather the assurance that the works of this canonical classicist suffice to give intellectual fulfillment to the educated reader. A remark in Nietzsche's posthumous papers shows clearly what was involved: "'Culture' tried to settle down on the foundation laid by Schiller and Goethe as if on a couch." The establishment of a literary heritage did in fact give rise to the claim that Germany was a cultivated nation, a claim Nietzsche disputed: "There is *no German culture* because there is not yet a *German* style of art. Incredible amount of work by Schiller [and] Goethe to achieve a German style. Cosmopolitan tendency necessary."[55] The first of his *Unzeitgemässe Betrachtungen* (Untimely Meditations) demonstrates by the example of Strauss what canonization had led to: the erection of a wax museum in which the classicists retain no more than a semblance of life. They have become counters in the game of learned commentary and sophisticated tea-table conversation. In Nietzsche's view, the greatly admired classicists have become harmless, the property of a public who fancied that in the war of 1870 it had triumphed over French culture.

Herman Grimm's lectures on Goethe, delivered in 1874 and 1875, illustrate the attitude to which Nietzsche objected. Grimm assures his audience that Goethe's place is beside Homer, Dante, and Shakespeare, and that neighboring modern nations have no one comparable to him. When Grimm compares Goethe to Voltaire, the verdict, as might be expected after 1870, is not in favor of the French writer. Grimm puts the literary tradition frankly at the service of politics. As he openly says, the founding of the Reich changed the relationship between Germany and its heritage: "Before Germany became unified and free and stood politically on its own feet, the goal of our historical work was to sub-

---

[54]David Friedrich Strauss, *Der alte und der neue Glaube. Ein Bekenntniss* (Leipzig, 1872), p. 303.
[55]Quoted in Mandelkow, *Goethe im Urteil seiner Kritiker*, pt. 3 (Munich, 1979), p. 21.

merge ourselves in the past, from which, as secret advocates of a process that could not openly be called by its true name, we dared to derive a better present for ourselves. All historical works bore the secret motto: things cannot possibly remain as they are in Germany." In 1874, in contrast, gifts no longer had to be won but instead could be "held fast, developed, and exploited."[56] Grimm, like most of his contemporaries, was so preoccupied with this reversal that he was unaware of the consequences of such a redefinition of what tradition had to accomplish. What was the significance of retaining a more or less fixed concept of canonical authors and works once the ostensible goal of history had been achieved? What task fell to the classic writers? What would happen if the process described by Grimm continued; if the new Reich changed historically?

The solution to the problem proposed by Grimm and Strauss was to create a heroic aura around the classic authors. The contemporary public was made to swear allegiance to an author removed in time. Goethe now became an Olympian. Thus Herman Grimm announces in his final lecture on Goethe's life in Weimar that "Weimar . . . had become a real place of retirement for Goethe, where he worked quietly in his own residence, next to that of Carl August. For someone of his nature, this undisturbed yet eventful existence was a real gift of providence. He reigned there in a natural way, unbothered by the envy of others, and with regal goodwill was pleased to receive anyone who knocked at his door."[57] In his theater criticism Theodor Fontane proposed a different solution: viewers would be lifted out of their everyday existence, and the language and ideas of the classic authors brought to life for them, by staging the familiar dramas of Schiller and Goethe. "There is a growing desire," we read in his review of a production of Schiller's *Piccolomini* in November 1871, "to escape from wretched insipidity."[58]

The third, and probably the most interesting, solution to the problem of constructing a literary tradition is found in the writings of Nietzsche. He argued that the problem of tradition should be viewed from a different perspective. It had been taken as established fact since Gervinus, Hettner, and Schmidt that the evolution of German literature had culminated in Weimar classicism, that the German spirit had come into its own in the course of this development, and above all that it represented a release from the hegemony of French literature. Nietzsche turned that judgment upside down: he regarded this process as the ruin

---

[56]Grimm, *Goethe*, 1:8.
[57]Ibid., 2:300–301.
[58]Quoted in Oellers, *Schiller—Zeitgenosse aller Epochen*, pt. 2, p. 58.

of European classicism in Germany. Goethe and Schiller could never quite compensate for Lessing's destructive work. If there was anything that distinguished German tradition, it was its lack of tradition, of classicality. Nietzsche's early criticism of the bourgeois concept of classicism (of the cultural philistines) is intensified in 1878 in *Menschliches, Allzumenschliches* (Human, All Too Human) to a fundamental criticism of German tradition and the historical concept supporting it. Lessing no longer appears as the great precursor of German classicism but rather as the destroyer of French classicism, which could still claim Greek antiquity as its authority: "One only has to read Voltaire's *Mahomet* from time to time to bring clearly before one's soul what European culture has lost once and for all through this breach with tradition. Voltaire was the last great dramatist to subdue through Greek moderation a soul many-formed and equal to the mightiest thunderstorms of tragedy—he was able to do what no German has yet been able to do because the nature of the Frenchman is much more closely related to the Greek than is the nature of the German."[59] From this perspective, the classicistic Goethe could at most be acknowledged as an author who tried to recapture Greek tradition—the belated, exceptional case in German literature. The structure so painstakingly erected by liberal historiographers has been torn down. Except for Goethe, the German classicists fail to pass Nietzsche's test.

The radicalism of this polemic, however, does not lie so much in its attacks on individual authors—Schiller, for example—as in its intention of undermining the entrenched concept of tradition as such. This intention was already announced in Nietzsche's first *Unzeitgemässe Betrachtung*, in which he deplored the German victory over France as a danger to German culture. For the majority of critics it was an accepted fact that the way for this victory had been paved by German literature and that the outcome represented the fulfillment of the German tradition. Nietzsche hit upon the model from which this concept of tradition drew its strength by making a sharp distinction between the political and cultural spheres. His judgments of Goethe and of Schiller—whom he increasingly separated from Goethe and classified with the rest of German writers—can only be understood against the background of this general problematization of the German tradition. Could a connection with the literature of the past still be taken for granted? Were the classic canonical writers really as alive as critics and historians assumed? Academic literary history, the discipline entrusted with the task of constructing and guarding tradition, overlooked this question, be-

[59]Friedrich Nietzsche, *Human, All Too Human*, trans. R. J. Hollingdale (London, 1985), p. 103.

cause it relied unthinkingly on the category of historical development. Even though in the discussion of classicism after 1850 an increasing number of voices emphasized the historical distance between their time and the closing years of the eighteenth century, this historicization remained within the framework of a historical model that relied largely on the efficacy of the literary heritage. Historicization in the hands of such writers as Haym and Dilthey was not a renunciation of this heritage but rather a strategy for ending controversy over the relationship between classicism and romanticism. What did not enter into discussion of the literary heritage was the striking changes that occurred in the institution of literature, such as the rise of a new reading public and the growing capitalization of the literary marketplace.

· 7 ·

The Institutionalization
of Literary History

The Function of the History of Literature

A critical history of *Germanistik* and literary criticism still exists only in fragments, in divergent approaches that show all too clearly the difficulties connected with this task.[1] What would be the object of such a history? On what should the historian train his or her eye? On the educational content of the discipline of literary studies? On the theories and methods of the field, or on its organization? To simply write a history of the field would not permit one to describe some important processes, for the discipline as we know it was not yet established in the mid-nineteenth century. At that time German studies, together with philology, still included folklore and jurisprudence, but literary history (recent literature) and literary studies (text analysis) were not necessarily part of them. Before 1860 literary history was mainly in the hands of men who occupied chairs in other fields or were active as free-lance writers. Gervinus's field was history, and even after the completion of his history of literature (1835–42) he maintained close ties with the field of European history. Haym's field was philosophy, and Prutz came to the history of literature from classical philology. Dilthey, to cite a representative of the younger generation, began his studies in theology and never restricted himself to German literature.

Although literary history became an academic discipline with its own academic chairs after 1850, the subject and its methodology had al-

[1]See Klaus Weimar, "Zur Geschichte der Literaturwissenschaft. Forschungsbericht," in *Deutsche Vierteljahrsschrift für Literaturwissenschaft und Geistesgeschichte* 50 (1976):298–364; and Ursula Burkhardt, *Germanistik in Südwestdeutschland* (Tübingen, 1976).

ready been developed in the forties, largely under the guidance of Gervinus. There is good reason to distinguish in literary history between the institution and its organization. Discussion of theory and method preceded the organization of the discipline. The establishing of chairs in literary history in conjunction with the field of German studies and not, as earlier, with general history or aesthetics is an indication that the controversial discipline of literary history had become acceptable in the seventies. At the same time, the transition from a loosely organized institution to an established field of university studies—with academic chairs, regular courses, and final examinations—reflected a shift from open discussion to an attitude of affirmation. To understand this shift, one has to remember that such early historians of literature as Gervinus, Hettner, Schmidt, Prutz, and, indeed, even Gottschall were not writing for universities but for the *general public*. Gervinus specifically stated that his works were not meant for university and secondary school students but for the *nation*. Thus the development of the history of literature, which was closely connected with that of political history, was not only a question of theory and method but also of presentation. As late as 1859 Haym defended Schiller against attacks by professional historians, insisting that though he may have contributed little to scholarship, he contributed all the more to the form of historical presentation: "From the standpoint of historiography, they were by no means so worthless, and even less were they ineffectual. The neglect of form in the field of scholarship, the prevalence of learned pedantry, of laborious rigidity, and at the same time of sloppy crudeness is a basic German fault that to some extent we . . . have to acknowledge with shame even today."[2] Learned pedantry limits the efficacy of a work to a circle of specialists and makes it impossible to reach the general public. Characteristically, Gervinus, whose aim was to reach this very public, almost totally avoided scholarly apparatus and citations in his history of literature to make it more readable. As long as literary history was addressed to the general literary public sphere—that is, until about 1870—style was no less a part of the field of history than theory and methodology. It is significant that as late as 1873 Karl Hillebrand disparaged Gervinus's achievement by attacking his style. The alleged clumsiness of Gervinus's writing was for Hillebrand a sign that his history of literature was obsolete. By disputing the general intelligibility of Gervinus's famous history of literature, he hoped to dislodge it from the public consciousness. The question of presentation, to which we will return, proved a political issue.

The change from a public discipline with general cognitive interests

---

[2]Rudolf Haym, *Gesammelte Aufsätze*, ed. Wilhelm Schrader (Berlin, 1903), p. 83.

to a specialized field of scholarship was evident after 1848 in the discussion of methodology; on the organizational level, it was not complete until after the founding of the Reich. The relationship in chronology is anything but accidental. This change was not simply a process within the scholarly study of history which could be characterized as positivism. It was, rather, the reverse: the earlier positivism, exemplified by Wilhelm Scherer, reflected the change in institutional structure. Because literary history fulfilled a public function in the Vormärz, and even after 1850, it was bound—as was literary criticism—to the destiny of the public sphere. Until it began to conflict with the new ideology of the Reich in about 1870, its public task as politically reasoned literary history was substantiated through its theory and methodology. Hillebrand's polemic against Gervinus, published in 1873 in the *Preussischen Jahrbücher*, is a good source of information for the attack on earlier literary history. Its opening sentence makes no secret of the critic's destructive intentions: "It must seem an almost unsolvable mystery to the upcoming generation how a writer without style, a scholar without method, a thinker without depth, a politician without foresight, and a person ultimately without magic or strong personality could have gained an importance in German history, in the intellectual, moral, and political history of Germany, which only a very few men could boast of over the centuries."[3] Even though in a footnote the editors of the journal—Heinrich von Treitschke and Wilhelm Wehrenpfennig— dissociated themselves to some extent from the author's views, this hardly changes the fact that one of the most important liberal journals was criticizing the historian to whom liberal reasoned historiography owed some of its crucial impulses. What characterized this scathing review was that it did not stop with a discussion of theory and methodology, as earlier criticism had—for example, Danzel's—but was directed equally against Gervinus the writer and politician. Hillebrand's ultimate goal was to call into question the character and function of literary history as it had been introduced and practiced by Gervinus. What annoyed him was Gervinus's immense influence, which was attested to by Schmidt, the most prominent Nachmärz historian of literature, in his obituary for Gervinus. "I belong to the generation most strongly affected by his work," Schmidt acknowledges, "a generation of youths still engaged in study when it appeared."[4] In his article, which includes some critical remarks, he concludes that Gervinus's history of literature is one of the classic writings of the German nation. Schmidt

---

[3]Karl Hillebrand, "G. G. Gervinus," *Preussische Jahrbücher* 32 (1873):379.
[4]Julian Schmidt, *Neue Bilder aus dem geistigen Leben unserer Zeit*, vol. 3 (Leipzig, 1873), p. 344.

saw its value less in the information it contained, which seemed to him outdated, or its methodology, which had changed, than in the thought process Gervinus manifested in it. In this sense, he regarded his own works as a continuation of Gervinus's history of literature or, conversely, Gervinus as the precursor of national-liberal literary history. Accordingly, he avoided criticizing Gervinus' political position, which after 1850 increasingly contradicted the consensus of the profession. Because Gervinus, an erstwhile supporter of the constitution, did not join in the pro-Prussian turn of the Gotha group and later spoke out against the founding of the Reich under Bismarck, he was almost totally isolated among his colleagues in 1870. Hillebrand's polemic must be viewed against this background. It was directed against the now undesirable political implication of liberal reasoned historiography. In so doing, Hillebrand sharpened Gervinus' moderate position by putting it in a broader context. He linked it with the radical tradition of the Enlightenment and represented Gervinus, against Gervinus's express intent, as an ally of Börne. Thus he was able to denounce the historian, who belonged to the center right in 1848, as a disguised Jacobin: "At heart, both [Gervinus and Börne] proceeded from completely French points of view . . . ; except that the one stopped with 1791, and the other with 1793."[5]

Gervinus would not have recognized himself in this characterization, which contradicted his true nationalist sentiments. Still, it contained a grain of truth. Both the critic Börne and the historian Gervinus saw it as their task to exert political influence on public opinion through literary discussion. Accordingly, Hillebrand's criticism of Gervinus's style and method was but a prelude to his real accusations, in which his political difference from Gervinus was spelled out. When Hillebrand criticized the clumsiness of Gervinus's presentation and found fault with his subjective method, and when he singled out Gervinus's historical concept of south German liberalism as a failure, his real aim was to criticize the connection in Gervinus's work between scholarship and politics. Characteristically, Hillebrand pronounces Gervinus's reasoning concerning the goal of history unfruitful and plays Hettner's *Geistesgeschichte* off against Gervinus's teleological concept of history. It is "unfruitful, because they [Gervinus's reasons] do not convey the impression of an independent, significant personality; they do not illustrate aesthetic laws; they do not explain the causes of the success or failure of historical or literary achievements; they merely state what relationship those achievements had to the partisan interests and partisan emotions of Herr Gervinus in 1840 (or 1853)." Quite apart from the questionable

[5]Hillebrand, "G.G. Gervinus," p. 424.

aspect of this characterization, which hardly fits Gervinus, Hillebrand's polemic has an unmistakable purpose. It aims to relate the development of a critical position to "partisan emotions," that is, to an attitude that is irrelevant from a scholarly point of view. And conversely, it suggests that an objective, neutral position is appropriate in scholarship: "On the other hand, Gervinus's disputatious nature struggled against aesthetic contemplation and the historical neutrality that would have been necessary to do justice to the various manifestations of the national spirit in works of literature. . . . The historian—if he is not, of course, of Schlosser's school (like Gervinus)—takes the world as it is and tries to understand it, as a botanist does his flora; the systematizer tries to dictate to the world what it can and cannot do." Hillebrand recognizes and at the same time misrepresents Gervinus's intentions. Since Gervinus, following the earlier idealistic tradition (represented by Humboldt and Hegel), proceeds from a substantive concept of history, neutrality is a methodological impossibility. But this does not mean that Gervinus saw himself as a systematizer. On the contrary, his historical method can be defined as a criticism of idealistic systematology. The accusation of system building, popular since Haym's criticism of Hegel, is basically aimed at the critical claim put forth in Gervinus's theory of history: that it distinguishes strictly between the facts of history and historical truth. Hillebrand, in contrast, demands that the historian conform to the facts, that he recognize the true processes. Thus he cannot forgive Gervinus for failing to acknowledge, as did most of his profession, that the Prussian victory over Austria was the "greatest revolution since Luther," instead regarding it as a civil war wanted by the government, not by the *Volk*. He denies Gervinus's late historical criticism any scholarly value. Yet in the end, Hillebrand is honest enough to admit openly that his polemic has a political basis. It is only superficially a discussion of scholarship and questions of theory and method. The real point of contention is a metatheoretical one—the function of literary history. Gervinus's expectation that literary history would politicize the literary public sphere provoked vehement protest in 1873, because the once hoped for political consequences were no longer acceptable. "It is a real question," Hillebrand writes, "whether it is desirable for every citizen to take an active part in state affairs, whether there are not more immediate and higher duties than civic ones, whether such participation might not even be dangerous for an unqualified person; Gervinus's notion of the modern state as a necessarily democratic one is highly debatable."[6] The classification of citizens as qualified or unqualified, a specific aspect of late liberalism not altogeth-

[6]Ibid., pp. 392, 401, 411, 425.

er lacking in Gervinus, had a target that was not openly stated: the proletarian masses. Characteristically, Hillebrand considered absurd Gervinus's thesis that contemporary history was carried by the masses, and to stifle such ideas he referred to the shaping force of historical personalities. So self-evident was it to him in 1873 that history is made above all by people that he did not bother to substantiate his point of view.

As the obituaries for Gervinus state, his concepts of history and the history of literature left so clear a mark on the next generation that it could not avoid coming to terms with his great example. Even more than Leopold von Ranke, whose method became the great model to follow after 1870, Gervinus exerted a strong influence on the young, because in the striking formulations of his history of literature and his *Historik* (1837), he assigned literary history an important task within history as a whole. It was this theoretical and methodological achievement, imperfect though it was when measured against the demands of the following generation (represented by Danzel and Hettner among others), which first made it possible to define the public function of literary history. By conceiving the historical process as a uniform evolution that could express itself equally in different spheres and media, Gervinus saw an inner, rather than a merely mechanical, relationship between literary and political developments. Gervinus defined the political function of literary historiography as the clarification of this relationship. He first presented his interpretation in the introduction to his history of literature (1835) and later, with greater theoretical reflection, in his small *Historik* (1837).

Reasoned Literary History

Gervinus's argument for the history of literature begins with a criticism of scholarly studies and documentary investigations that lack not only a talent for presentation but a true historical point of view linking the past to the present. For Gervinus, only the cognitive interests of the present are able to raise the investigation of sources to the level of history. The choice of German literary history as a subject is justified in his view by its special position within German history. It alone possesses a certain measure of completeness that can make it a guiding principle for the present: "It has reached a goal, if there is any truth at all to be learned from history, from which one can successfully glimpse a whole, from which one can receive a calming, indeed an uplifting, impression and derive the greatest instruction." Gervinus justifies his choice of subject by arguing that German literary history, in contrast to political history, represents a meaningful whole that can be narrated:

"The highest goal of any complete series of events in world history can be reached only when the idea striving for expression in them has really been accepted and an essential improvement of society or humanity has thereby been achieved."[7]

Let us once again clarify the nature of this relationship between literary history and contemporary interests, the precise character of which would have to be determined: the present can learn from the past only when the latter brings forth an idea that the present can follow. The historical point of view, which legitimizes a link with the past, is based on the idea that shapes the material and holds it together. To this extent, the aesthetic point of view has to mediate between the present and the past; only when an event can be understood and depicted as a work of art can any meaning be drawn from it. Historical truth, which makes the depiction of history worthwhile, does not exist on the level of fact; rather, it becomes visible through the presentation of the idea, which absorbs the material. Even though Gervinus occasionally falls back on a pragmatic, didactic interpretation of history, his concept of literary history is inconceivable without a substantive concept of history. This point of view is made clear in his *Historik*, and especially in his reference to Humboldt's essay "Über die Aufgabe des Geschichtsschreibers" (On the Historian's Task) (1820–21). For Gervinus, the historian's work falls between the poet's and the philosopher's. Like them, he must separate the inessential from the necessary: "For by his ability to recognize what is necessary in a given series of facts, the historian places himself in the domain of the philosophers; and there is no danger at all in this, if only he will retain his basic feeling for the factual and not try to become a historical philosopher, or even a philosophizing historian, but simply a thinking historian." There is no need here to consider to what extent this statement is directed against Hegel and all attempts to create a historical construction, since we are concerned less with the contrast between Gervinus's approach and the philosophy of history than with their similarity with respect to the empirical interpretation of history. What Gervinus says in his *Historik* about the difference between a chronicle and a historical presentation applies, of course, to the history of literature as well: facts are the point of departure, but only a view of what is essential can afford insight into historical connections, which in turn make possible a unified presentation. Gervinus is convinced that these ideas are not constructions of the historian, but rather are inherent in the material itself. Thus the circular argument that ideas can only be derived from facts whereas facts can only be given order

[7]Georg Gottfried Gervinus, *Geschichte der deutschen Dichtung*, vol. 1, 4th ed. (Leipzig, 1853), p. 9.

with the help of ideas is for him not a significant circularity. In examining the material, he thinks, the ideas become accessible: "As soon as the historiographer makes the growth and development of such ideas the main thread of his historical work, he is granted the finest insight. He does not impose the idea on his material; rather, by losing himself freely in the nature of his object of study, by considering it with a purely historical understanding, the idea emerges from the subject itself and is transferred to his reflecting intellect."[8]

How can this contemplative attitude, reminiscent of Ranke, be joined to the engagement, the political activism, that Gervinus calls for elsewhere in his *Historik*? There he describes the historian as a partisan of destiny, a natural champion of progress. He can "not easily avoid the suspicion of sympathizing with the business of freedom, because freedom, after all, is equivalent to a feeling of power, and because it contains the element that he breathes and in which he lives."[9] In his own advertisement of 1835 for his history of literature, Gervinus spoke with the same decisiveness about the serious problem of the objective style that was becoming widespread in historical scholarship. Here, as in questions of methodology, Gervinus's logical inconsistency cannot be overlooked. He did not succeed in developing a formally consistent position. On the one hand, he emphasized his confidence in the objectivity of historical ideas, which the historian merely has to follow as an observer; on the other, he emphasized the subjectivity of the scholar, whose judgments are clearly injected into the material. This formal contradiction was not apparent to Gervinus, because in his view the subjective element of the historian emerges inevitably from the subject matter. Inasmuch as historical events are themselves a directed process—that is, a progression toward humanity—a reconstruction of the past offers the historian guidance for the future. The observer is part of this process, transmitting essential historical ideas whose past effectiveness he has reconstructed. For this reason, he is a partisan of destiny, someone who has allied himself with the objective process of history because it accords with the historian's subjective endeavors.

In Gervinus, resistance to objectivism, and thus protest against Ranke and his school, is not a plea for individual caprice, much less for historical impressionism. When Gervinus emphasizes his subjectivity, he sees himself, in full agreement with the liberal concept of the public sphere, as a participant in a public discourse that makes headway precisely because different points of view are competing. Truth—aesthetic no

---

[8]Georg Gottfried Gervinus, *Grundzüge der Historik* (Leipzig, 1837), pp. 33, 70.
[9]Ibid., p. 94.

less than political truth—is revealed through public *Räsonnement*. Thus even in his own advertisement of his history of literature, Gervinus emphasizes the function of his subjective opinion as a challenge to the public: "I have to make it absolutely clear to the reader what mine [his point of view] is; then he will recognize his own more easily, will not unjustly criticize me and my opinion, and will instead allow it to stand beside his own."[10]

What the succeeding generation of literary historians often called in Gervinus dogmatism and moralizing, Gervinus himself saw as necessary reasoning. The historian had a twofold obligation with respect to literature: to reconstruct leading ideas and to take a public stand as the only means of bringing the past into contemporary discussion. The similarity to Börne and the Young Germans, which Gervinus would have emphatically denied, is obvious. Just as Börne made literary criticism a medium of political reasoning, Gervinus made literary history a participant in political discussion. Like the Young Germans, he assumed a close relationship between literature and life: only a strong political life could result in a period of aesthetic flowering. Thus he writes at the end of his history of literature (1842): "Civic life is the only thing that still hinders free development; and until it is reformed, we will wait in vain for a great period of any kind."[11] Gervinus does not regard this attitude as voluntarism, but rather as the inevitable result of the historical process itself, which points beyond literature to political obligations. The mechanistic and undialectic character of this position is, indeed, evident in his criticism of Young German literature. His criticism goes wrong because it keeps to the artistic concept of Goethe's period; in other words, because it fails to reflect in its form those changes that Gervinus himself wanted.

Because Gervinus held to his principles even after 1848 and refused to consider the unsuccessful revolution an important turning point, he became a problem for the younger generation of historians. He exposed himself most of all in the introduction to his *Geschichte des neunzehnten Jahrhunderts* (History of the Nineteenth Century), because he radicalized and democratized his liberal concept of freedom rather than restricted it. He characterized the new epoch as a period of transition from the supremacy of the nobility to the rule of the many, and he emphasized in his treatment of the Napoleonic period that "princely reforms from above cannot be built upon, and for the people only *that*

---

[10]Georg Gottfried Gervinus, "Selbstanzeige der Geschichte," in Gervinus, *Gesammelte kleine historische Schriften* (Karlsruhe, 1838), p. 576.
[11]Gervinus, *Geschichte der deutschen Dichtung*, 5:666.

freedom is a reliable possession for whose acquisition and affirmation they themselves have worked."[12] The defeat of the bourgeoisie in 1849 was for him obviously not the basis for a theoretical and methodological revision. On the other hand, although they were indebted to the liberal tradition and by no means denied Gervinus's importance, younger historians such as Schmidt and Haym (who remained in contact with Gervinus and tried to recruit him for the *Preussischen Jahrbücher*) modified their concept of history.

Postrevolutionary Literary History

Until recently, postrevolutionary literary history has received less attention than the achievements of the Vormärz. The reasons are obvious. In attempting to revive the progressive tradition of literary scholarship, the West German left and the Marxist German studies of the German Democratic Republic have made Nachmärz historiography seem primarily a decline and fall: to the extent that postrevolutionary liberalism turned its back on its radical tradition and conformed, literary history became increasingly more conservative and at the same time poorer. Thus Bernd Hüppauf, citing Hettner, Schmidt, Gottschall, and Haym as examples, traced a descending line, a process of theoretical and methodological decline, which essentially came to an end with the founding of the Reich.[13] His presentation makes a direct connection between the development of German liberalism (seen as the ideology of the bourgeoisie) and the evolution of historical scholarship. There is no disputing that crucial changes occurred after 1850. But if they are construed within the framework of a model of decline, the result is a one-dimensional view in which the contradictions disappear from the dialectic process. The ideological and critical approach that seeks to demonstrate the superficiality of postrevolutionary literary history is in danger of underestimating the methodological and theoretical problems inherent in scholarship. The change in the function of literary history needs to be investigated from within as well as from without.

No postrevolutionary historian or critic understood this change in function more clearly than Prutz, who made structural changes the subject of analysis in *Die deutsche Literatur der Gegenwart* (1858). In contrast to Danzel and Hettner, he did not limit himself to a discussion of method and theory but instead subjected the Vormärz concept of literary history to a critical-historical investigation, which concentrated

---

[12]Georg Gottfried Gervinus, *Einleitung in die Geschichte des neunzehnten Jahrhunderts* (Leipzig, 1853), pp. 150–51.
[13]Bernd Hüppauf, in his *Literaturgeschichte zwischen Revolution und Reaktion* (Frankfurt a. M., 1972), pp. 3–55.

on function and from that perspective was able to explain the change historically. He characterized the literary history of the 1830s as follows: "The important thing was to shake the nation out of the one-sided literary culture, the abstract aesthetic interests, in which it had hitherto moved and to lead it toward the praxis of public life; the important thing was to strip literature of the absolute power it had hitherto exercised among us and to bring theory and praxis, literature and life, poetry and reality, art and the state into a proper, natural relationship with each other." Prutz rightly brings two aspects of this literary history to the fore: its negative-critical character and its political character: "Literary history became a criticism of our national life in general; books were held responsible for actions." From the perspective of 1858, this reasoned (*räsonierende*) literary history seemed the (unsuccessful) literary preparation for the Revolution of 1848.

Prutz's early historical works were unmistakably indebted to this concept of literary history; his criticism of moral-political methodology is a self-criticism. This self-criticism is the result, among other things, of his historicization of the history of literature. By contrasting the critical phase of the thirties and forties with the affirmative literary history of the twenties, Prutz was able to emphasize the linkage of a prevailing concept with a given historical situation and thereby to underscore its limitation. This reconstructive stock taking led to his criticism of the history of literature; as he did in the case of belles-lettres, he denied it a political function. Prutz concluded that the political defeat of 1849 did not fulfill its obligation to bring about political emancipation and national unity. He now rejected the emphatic idealism of the liberal model: "We really have other and more pressing things to do now than to read books and listen to verses. We have to study history and national economics in order to prepare ourselves for the practical issues that will be presented to us in the long or short run by destiny."[14] In this reordering of the relationship between theory and praxis, literary history was deprived of its political function; for if practice had to be left to its own resources, if—as Prutz assumed in 1858—solutions to practical political problems no longer resulted from literary theory and history but from practical activity, there was no longer any compelling need to force literary discussion. The relationship between literature and the sociopolitical sphere was now reversed: only a healthy social and economic life would give rise to a healthy literature. Significantly, Prutz no longer distinguished between literary history and literary criticism, because the public task of critics and historians was essentially identical.

[14]Robert Prutz, *Die deutsche Literatur der Gegenwart 1848–1858*, vol. 1 (Leipzig, 1859), pp. 4, 8, 17.

According to Gervinus, contemporary Germany needed to effect a transition from an aesthetic to a political culture. Prutz repeated this argument, but with an essentially different purpose:

> For our classical writers have given us a valuable clue to how these difficulties can be overcome, how these seemingly irreconcilable contradictions can be resolved. What they accomplished in the aesthetic realm is precisely what the nation must now do in the realms of history and political praxis. This is the real character of our classic epoch, this is why it bears that name, and this is above all the unforgettable, priceless inheritance it has bequeathed to us: that it imbued the foreign Hellenic form with the German spirit and thereby created a new, third entity, which is just as German as it is Greek, and in which the noblest and most amiable qualities of modern and ancient times are mingled and reconciled.[15]

A similar task is assigned to German politics. No longer should a totally new entity be created; instead, traditional forms should be filled with the German spirit. Goethe's time is no longer considered the flower from which political fruit must develop, as it is by Gervinus. By analogy it becomes the model for political theory and praxis. Classicism is now the lasting heritage to which the political liberalism of the Nachmärz can refer, ostensibly by doing what classicism had done in the fields of literature and art. The critical adoption of classicism has surreptitiously turned into an affirmative theory of inheritance.

The change in function described by Prutz in his *Literatur der Gegenwart* can be characterized as the dissolution of the service rendered by literary history to the political public sphere. In the fifties neither Prutz, Schmidt, nor Haym thought it sensible to make direct use of literature or literary criticism in order to achieve political and cultural ends. Culture and politics were once again conceived of as separate spheres, and it was gradually accepted that the cultural public sphere should be regarded as an epiphenomenon of the social structure. It would be precipitate, of course, to assume that this reorientation of liberal historiography necessarily led to the acceptance of Ranke's concept of history. Schmidt felt indebted above all to Gervinus, and despite his great admiration for Ranke's literary achievement, he regarded him with skepticism. When Schmidt compares Ranke and Gervinus, he takes Gervinus's part and declares himself for the tradition of reasoned historiography. "From the moment German historiography entered the field of general literature," Schmidt argues in the third book of his history of literature, "it was predominantly Protestant, enlightened, Prussian, bourgeois, and liberal." This tradition of reasoned history was em-

[15]Ibid., p. 21.

phatically embodied by Christoph Schlosser and his student Gervinus. Characteristically, Schmidt stresses Schlosser's moral integrity: "What Börne tried to do on a small scale, instinctively and without preparation, Schlosser carried out on a large scale, with thorough knowledge and mature understanding. His moral criticism, which was initially directed against the German nature, he then applied equally to all fields of history." In Schmidt's view, Gervinus's literary history belongs in the same category: "But the 'History of Literature' is more than a work of art; it is an act, a necessary and important step toward the liberation of our spirit."[16]

Schmidt's opinion of Gervinus is not entirely positive. He finds fault, for instance, with his lack of historical empathy, a certain rigidity resulting from the moral-critical *ductus* of his presentation. Essentially, however, he agrees with Gervinus: the latter's representation of German literature combined the art of synthesis with a critical rigor that was not lost in empathy with the material, as it was in Ranke's case. Schmidt shows a clear awareness that the historical school, which was later opposed to the historico-philosophical constructivism of Hegel and his students, had two very different branches: one enlightened and moral, to which Schlosser and Gervinus belonged, and the other cognitive and descriptive, represented by Ranke. His judgment of Ranke leaves no doubt that Schmidt includes himself in the tradition of moral historiography. Thus he objects that "we miss something in him: let us not call it ethical integrity but rather manly earnestness that neither through aesthetic satisfaction nor through personal, perhaps very justified sympathy allows itself to be deterred from being pitiless where it matters. In his criticism of the facts, he shows no leniency; in his ethical judgment, however, he tries with a certain timidity not to allow personality to intrude upon things." In contrast to a historical awareness that loses itself empathically in its subject and creates historical unity and completeness by means of a mimetic presentation, Schmidt posits a concept in which the personality and ethical judgment of the historian determine choice and order in history. On the occasion of a review of Joseph Maria von Radowitz, he called this point of view the superior one: "Without passion, without the anger of intense conviction, no firm will is possible, but also no secure knowledge." This subjectivism is not to be confused with impressionism. The subject who makes the judgment is moral and as such is above all a spokesperson for basic human principles. The reasoning historian believes him or herself to be in the service of universal enlightenment carried out by and in history. The

---

[16]Julian Schmidt, *Geschichte der deutschen Literatur im neunzehnten Jahrhundert*, 2d ed. (Leipzig, 1855), 3:450, 497, 503.

danger of this approach is not so much vagueness as a doctrinaire rigidity that misses the mark when people and tendencies are judged. This is the very weakness Schmidt criticizes in Gervinus, who occasionally lacks not firmness of will but discretion and maturity in his reflections.[17]

Schmidt's presentation of historiography had already been reduced to individual portraits, and it merely hints at the historical connection that Prutz developed dialectically. For Prutz, the concept of historiography was itself profoundly rooted in history and was accordingly subject to change under postrevolutionary conditions. In Schmidt, however, the history of historiography is broken down into competing traditions and schools, with which he deals in a selective and judgmental manner. Schmidt saw himself as continuing a reasoned moral historiography; this is clearly where his methodological sympathies lay, yet he was not blind to the dangers of this method. Since it did not reflect on its own assumptions, it could easily become doctrinaire. The solution for which Schmidt searched, without expressly saying so, was a synthesis of reasoning and empathy, a combination of Gervinus and Ranke. This combination, however, proved a compromise in which the components were neutralized rather than mutually supported. The correction of moral judgment through empathetic description weakened reasoning without sharpening reflection.

For Gervinus, classic German literature was the humanistic prelude to the political development and liberation of the German nation. Gervinus's appreciation of German classicism included criticism of its apolitical stance, especially Goethe's. This approach was taken up by Schmidt. His literary history, too, is critical of classicism and romanticism. The aesthetic perfection reached in Weimar was paid for, in Schmidt's view, by the separation of art and life, a separation that necessarily led to resignation. He reproached Goethe in particular for having failed in his life's task. His move to Weimar, flight to Italy, and ministerial service were concessions that deflected him from his real project. According to Schmidt, this was also true of Goethe's position on contemporary political issues. Goethe was incapable of supporting the French Revolution and the Wars of Liberation: "Nature gave him the strength and disposition to accomplish great and noble things, but in his small though glittering cage he was drained of his courage. No matter how beautiful the songs he sang in that cage, his life and writings awaken in us the feeling that our art will be truly uplifted only when our life is uplifted." Schmidt's objection to Goethe was a moral one; Goethe's alleged aestheticism made him regard literature "as a playful

[17]Ibid., 3:453, 462, 506.

sideline . . . , which had nothing to do with real life." Goethe's life and work are measured by Schmidt against the public tasks of his epoch: "Public affairs are the touchstone of a man's worth: perpetual self-reflection leads to untruth. As long as we are ruled by the superficial ideals of living beautifully and of coming to terms with tragic conditions through, at best, resignation, Germany as a whole will remain an unproductive nation incapable of flexibility or any historical up-swing."[18]

The linking of historical and political criticism in this statement is significant. Schmidt's point of departure is the public function of literature. To the extent that Goethe and his works shunned or opposed this task, they deserved the reproach, for the very reason that Goethe's fame made him a national model. For Schmidt, the historian's task is a descriptive and judicial one; judgment of the past is grounded in the historian's personal experience. This attitude should not simply be denounced as bourgeois and private.[19] Schmidt links the past to the present through the perspective of public morality, which attacks precisely such a private attitude. Thus Schmidt wrote in 1862: "In literature as well as in public life, in the realm of thought as well as in the narrow world of ethics, the chief enemies of freedom and progress are bourgeois pettiness and vague idealism."[20] Bernd Peschken has rightly pointed out that Schmidt's criticism of classicism has a political core.[21] Whether this criticism goes beyond Marx and Engels, as Peschken maintains, may reasonably be doubted, because in socialist theory the perfection of bourgeois society is no longer the critical standard it was for Schmidt. Yet Peschken has grounds for emphasizing that Schmidt's literary-historical works are in the liberal tradition, which links them to Gervinus and Schlosser. This is evident not least in his critical treatment of classicism. His early works show this reserve more than his later ones; but even in the second edition of his history of literature (1855), Schmidt considers *Wilhelm Meister* a realistic novel depicting German society in the eighteenth century, and he accordingly regrets the absence in this picture of the bourgeoisie: "But among the classes he describes, we miss most of all the greatest factor in the life of the German people, the bourgeoisie. Its representative, Werner, is a pitiful caricature."[22] Schmidt notes critically that in *Wilhelm Meister* only the nobility is

---

[18]Ibid., 1:285, 286.

[19]Thus Hüppauf, *Literaturgeschichte zwischen Revolution und Reaktion*, p. 50.

[20]Julian Schmidt, *Geschichte des geistigen Lebens in Deutschland* (Leipzig, 1862), p. viii.

[21]Bernd Peschken, *Versuch einer germanistischen Ideologiekritik* (Stuttgart, 1972), p. 83.

[22]Schmidt, *Geschichte der deutschen Literatur im neunzehnten Jahrhundert*, 1:231.

allowed to develop freely, whereas the bourgeoisie strives to rise above its station and in so doing loses its inner security. He thus criticizes the cultural ideal at the heart of the novel as being exclusively aristocratic and not the product of the daily reality of the bourgeoisie. Schmidt wants freedom of activity for the individual in the liberal sense, in which economic production and a moral praxis of life are combined.

Wherever the political and social criticism of classicism was retracted we can also expect to find a shift in the formulation of literary history. This occurred in the work of Schmidt in 1866 in connection with Prussian victory over the Austrian army.[23] Schmidt henceforth regarded the polemic against German classicism in his earlier editions outdated. The prospect of a *kleindeutsch* unification put the early history of literature in a more positive light. Moral criticism was transformed into historical affirmation. The nature of this change, however, must be examined more closely. It was not the moral, reasoned approach that changed but its conceptual content. Both Schmidt's joy over Prussian victory and his silence over the defeat of the liberals in the constitutional conflict indicate that, like the majority of liberals, he had changed his perspective from that of an emancipatory patriot to that of a Prussian nationalist. The model on which Gervinus had based his progressive history of literature was thus equally valid for legitimation of the status quo. In 1866 Schmidt took the existing situation, of which he approved, to be the inevitable result of the literary and political past. In his work, German literature finally became a national mission, but in a sense that was foreign to Gervinus.

This framework remained in effect even where the goal connected with it had long faded. Thus in 1872 Gottschall wrote in the introduction to the third edition of his history of literature that "the literary history of the present is only half *objective scholarship*. The other half tends to have a *practical and reformative effect* and seeks to play a significant role in the development of literature itself; it is like the Attic goddess of wisdom, who appears armed not only with a helmet and spear but also with the aegis that calls forth storms." Notwithstanding the warlike metaphor, it is clear that this is a diminution in comparison to Gervinus's approach, indeed even to Schmidt's: the political mission has turned into a cultural one: "It is the banner of modern culture, which cannot abandon the real poetry of the present if it is to become a poetry of the future."[24] Gottschall wanted to rescue postromantic liter-

---

[23]See Julian Schmidt's preface to the fifth edition of the second volume of his *Geschichte der deutschen Literatur seit Lessings Tod*, written September 7, 1866; on this see also Peschken, *Versuch einer germanistischen Ideologiekritik*, pp. 88–104.

[24]Rudolph Gottschall, *Die deutsche Nationalliteratur des neunzehnten Jahrhunderts*, quoted in 6th ed. (Leipzig, 1891), pp. xxiv, xxv.

ature from Schmidt's politically motivated devaluation and to introduce it into the present as a legitimate heritage. This led him to criticize the moralistic method and to return to romantic criticism, without, however, making the consequences clear. But even in Gottschall, the category of progress that had guided liberal historiography retains a certain significance. This can be said as well of such a moderate national liberal as Haym.[25]

Method and Ideology

Owing to the comparatively late development of literary history as a scholarly discipline and its not having become established as a university subject until 1848, the discussion of method was still largely in flux at the outbreak of the bourgeois revolution. The dominant model was the reasoned literary history represented by Gervinus, who most clearly expressed the political claims of the liberals. The disillusionment that followed the failure of the revolution was reflected in scholarly discussion as criticism of idealistic historicism—both in its liberal and in its Hegelian form. Danzel's epoch-making essay "Über die Behandlung der Geschichte der neueren deutschen Literatur" (On the Treatment of the History of Recent German Literature) (1849) and Haym's *Hegel und seine Zeit* (1857) exemplify the new problems and objections that were raised. Both works are evidence of the incipient positivism that for scholarly and objective reasons held that the political criticism of the Vormärz had to be negated. This change must be regarded not only as the expression of a growing conservatism among literary historians but as a confrontation with the unsolved problems of prerevolutionary historical scholarship which could no longer be postponed. The battle was fought on several fronts: between the moralistic camp and the aesthetic camp; between Schmidt and Gottschall; between a teleological and a genetic concept, both eventually leading—albeit along different paths—to positivism, which after 1870 was prepared to give theoretical and methodological legitimacy to German literary history.

The Criticism of Reasoned Literary History

For Danzel, earlier literary history suffered from not yet having gone beyond the stage of dilettantism. Its unscholarly nature was demonstrated by the failure of historians to make a clear, methodical distinc-

[25]On this, see Wolfgang Harich in the introduction to Haym's book on Johann Gottfried Herder (Berlin, 1954).

tion between the object under investigation and the subject as re-searched. When historians submerge themselves in the literature of the past, which serves them as material, and appropriate its aesthetic and poetical points of view, they inadmissibly blend their position with the object: "There can be no greater defect in a work of literary history than for it to be based on the opinions and points of view from which the critical writings of the Swiss, Lessing's epistolary essays, Goethe's life, and Schiller's critical essay on naive and sentimental poetry pro-ceed." The passion for objectivity demands a complete separation of past and present: on one side, the literature of the past together with its aesthetic norms; on the other, the historian who records and describes. "The writer of history," Danzel postulates, "must never incorporate into his subjectivity the very thing that he ought to be making objec-tive."[26] In support of this methodological principle, Danzel characteris-tically no longer relies on the philosophy of history but on psychology, in which precise questions of causality can be formulated.

We are not, however, fundamentally concerned with the establish-ment of causal relationships, but rather with the relationship of aesthet-ic and historical points of view. Gervinus had systematically excluded aesthetic considerations from the history of literature in order to main-tain a consistent historical position; for him, the aesthetic perspective was identical with a metahistorical approach that subjected all works of art to the same norms. Danzel's criticism follows Gervinus in method: it aims to put the historian on a higher plane, from which aesthetics, no less than works of art, is seen as a part of history. Gervinus's methodical juxtaposition of history and aesthetics was the result of his inability to recognize the historicity of aesthetic theories. Hence he wished to expel them from literary history. Danzel takes the opposite path, adding aes-thetics to literary history. The theories of Lessing, Schiller, and Goethe in turn become the objects of historical interpretation. The historian as subject is just as disengaged from these theories as from the artworks of the past. His or her subjectivity is formalized—which has its conse-quences.

This tendency is clearly evident in Danzel's attempt to meth-odologically separate the history of literature from that of philosophy. The succession of philosophical systems, which formerly was simply recounted as fact, was so construed by the idealistic philosophy of history as the history of the mind that it logically flowed into contempo-rary philosophy. The history of philosophy thereby became a means of

[26]Theodor Wilhelm Danzel, *Über die Behandlung der Geschichte der neueren Liter-atur*, quoted in Hans Mayer, ed., *Deutsche Literaturkritik im 19. Jahrhundert* (Frankfurt a. M., 1976), p. 318.

intellectual self-reflection. Danzel rightly observes that recent literary history has taken over this methodological principle from the idealistic philosophy of history: "The history of modern German literature has intentionally been treated with the understanding that its development casts light on the task of our time; indeed, that it is necessary for it to do so." Danzel continues with a description of reasoned historiography which begins with contemporary interests and looks back at history in order to obtain answers for the future: "Others, who are entirely caught up in the political aspirations of our day, believe that the development of the last century demonstrates that literary endeavors must be followed by endeavors directed toward the restructuring of the state; that a time of *literature* is a time of *action*." Although his name is not mentioned, this is undoubtedly a reference to Gervinus. Danzel accuses Gervinus of politicizing the history of literature, of tendentiously manipulating his material by projecting the interests of the present back into the past. The historian—to borrow Danzel's comparison—is like a preacher who uses the Bible for edification: "For a time, works of literary history, as Goethe said of Byron's poems, were suppressed speeches to Parliament."[27]

This objection, however, is only noteworthy because of its methodological reasoning, which strikes at progressive bourgeois literary history's weakest point. The complaint that it lacks an empirical foundation, which anticipates the position of later positivism, is not in itself particularly relevant. But it becomes crucial through the theoretical argument supporting it. The aim of creating a synthesis, which distinguishes reasoned literary history from earlier annalistic works, depends on a problematic concept of history, especially with respect to the relationship between history in general and literary history. Danzel summarizes Gervinus' interpretation as follows: "In the treatment of German literature of recent times, the perspective of national development has become dominant. Generally speaking, there is nothing wrong with this. If history is to be more than a superficial stringing together of isolated facts, something has to be there *that* develops, a substance of which individual phenomena are only modifications; and what should this substance be but the *Geist*, the mental attitude of a people, either in general or with particular respect to poetic production."[28] As Danzel rightly emphasizes, Gervinus had two prerequisites for the creation of a historical synthesis: the idealistic premise that there existed a developing collective spirit, and the assumption that this spirit could be given concrete form as a national spirit. If, with Gervinus, one assumes that

[27]Ibid., pp. 319, 320, 321.
[28]Ibid., p. 323.

the historical process involves a developing substance, then it is possible, indeed necessary, to join literature and politics, because both are merely modifications of a single spirit.

Danzel directs his justifiable criticism primarily against a nationally restricted literary history, for he points out that the assumption of national developments leads to fictions, which fail to do justice to the history of recent times because German or French literature can only be understood as part of the broader European literature. His criticism of idealistic suppositions, on the other hand, falters midway. If the idealistic concept of history is problematized, the relationship between social history and literary history breaks down. Danzel's arguments lean in this direction when he speaks of the various tasks of the spirit, all of which have independent histories. It follows from this that the history of literature must also be viewed and presented in accordance with its own requirements, that is, in accordance with the connection between aesthetic conventions and literary relationships. Danzel's approach moves toward this conclusion when he begins to conceive of the history of literature as "a kind of art history" rather than as a part of political history: "Its task, without looking right or left, is to trace metamorphoses of poetic production purely from that production itself."[29] He scarcely touches on the question how this literary evolution is to take place. One possibility he considers is to explain the dynamics of literary production through comparison with contemporary aesthetics and criticism—as the mastering of tasks formulated by aesthetics and conversely as the formulation of new tasks arising from the reading of works of art.

This criticism of Gervinus has two logical results: the emptying and formalization of the investigating subject, whose current interests are to be excluded as illegitimate matters for historiography, and the separation of literary history from general history. The political task as Gervinus had defined it was rejected through a criticism of his method. As soon as the idealistic premises of reasoned history became problematic, historical scholarship withdrew from the public sphere in the name of scholarship and left reasoned history to popular presentations. Henceforth a hiatus was to exist between scholarly demands and political engagement; the latter became independent, so that it was no longer part of literary studies. These consequences, to be sure, were not thoroughly worked out by either Danzel, Hettner, or Haym. The methodological and theoretical criticism of idealism found full expression only in dogmatic positivism, where it took the form of an attack on a teleologically grounded political approach; for then the historian be-

[29]Ibid., p. 326.

came an exclusively observing subject, whose practical interests had to be excluded.

This is the position arrived at in Scherer's review of Hettner's history of eighteenth-century literature (1865). His review is based on a theory of history which Hettner is basically unable to satisfy because he perceives historical relationships not in causal terms but as belonging to the history of ideas. In the forceful argument for empirical research which he directs against Hettner, the youthful Scherer does not include an exposition of his concept of history, but we can conclude from his polemic that he no longer assumes a connection between ideas. History has become material in which facts are causally joined. It is for this reason that he objects to the history of ideas: "The basic category of history, it has rightly been said, is causality. . . . Hettner's main fault is a lack of motivation."[30] By motivation Scherer means the disclosure of "the governing influences" on individual works, so that the whole becomes clear from the inductive reconstruction of causal relationships. He excludes teleologically grounded generalizations such as those found in Hettner and earlier liberal historiography. The standard of the new generation is no longer philosophy but natural science. Although this new orientation cannot be taken very seriously as a method, it had an important function for the self-understanding of positivist literary scholars: it allowed them to hold on to the concept of progress.[31]

The Aporias of Idealism: Rudolf Haym

The transitional character of late-bourgeois idealism, which though no longer in a secure position did not wish to abandon the idealistic tradition altogether, can best be studied in the works of Rudolf Haym. Haym's lectures on *Hegel und seine Zeit* (1857) contributed significantly to making the philosopher a "dead dog," whose system had become obsolete. This popular influence must be distinguished, however, from the aim and content of his lectures. Haym was by no means prepared to dissociate himself radically from the idealistic interpretation of history. His mild criticism of the Hegelian philosophy of history—which, as we might expect, he accuses of being overly constructivist—adheres consistently to a substantive concept of history. Thus his seventeenth lecture closes with the following statement: "It is

---

[30]Wilhelm Scherer, "H. Hettners Literaturgeschichte des 18. Jahrhunderts," in Viktor Žmegač, ed., *Methoden der deutschen Literaturwissenschaft* (Frankfurt a. M., 1971), p. 13.

[31]On this, see Klaus Laermann, "Was ist literaturwissenschaftlicher Positivismus?" in Viktor Žmegač and Zdenko Škreb, eds., *Zur Kritik literaturwissenschaftlicher Methodologie* (Frankfurt a. M., 1973), pp. 51–74.

obviously a step forward if our most recent historiography has again striven to be more factual, critical, and pragmatic, if it has tried to avoid constructing from generalized, transcendent points of view. That it has nevertheless adhered to belief in an ideal development, that it has acknowledged a reason for things and a dialectic for that reason, is, on the other hand, due not least to Hegel and the Hegelian philosophy of history."[32]

Haym's analysis of Hegel's philosophy will be discussed here only insofar as it pertains to methodological questions in historiography. His position is contradictory from the start. On the one hand, he shares the general opinion that the time for philosophical systems is past and tries in his lectures to offer historical criticism; on the other, he cannot and will not dissociate himself from the more general assumptions of Hegel and his contemporaries. In other words, his misgivings are directed not only against the dogmatism of the Hegelian system but also—even if less distinctly—against the metaphysical claims of philosophy, whose legitimacy has itself been made problematic by the course of history. Haym speaks of a "collapse of dogma, a disintegration of concepts that seemed to cling to the firmament of philosophical belief, a dissolution of system, of a metaphysical eternity, in the ruins of human history and human thought—in other words, a temporalization and secularization of what was once considered eternal and not of this world." This criticism is indebted unmistakably to the left-Hegelian school. But it exhibits a characteristic postrevolutionary modification, in which the political radicalism of the *Hallische Jahrbücher* has been eliminated in favor of a more moderate position that moves increasingly to the right. Haym's adherence to idealism results from his defensiveness toward a mechanical materialism that traces back "all phenomena of intellectual life to physiological processes and in the last analysis to material properties." The ruthless reduction of history by mechanical materialism provoked a halfhearted defense of idealism as doing more justice to history. Idealism had once again been saved by an inability to formulate a differentiated materialistic theory of history; indeed, it retained the critical eighteenth-century form of the Kantian attack on dogmatic metaphysics. This return to Kant, however, which Haym mentioned in the introduction to his book on Hegel,[33] can be understood as a concrete historical criticism that appeals, anticipating Dilthey's approach, to the movement of the human spirit.

Haym, in his criticism of Hegel, sees himself as progressive. In the name of human and political progress, he argues against a philosophical

---

[32]Rudolf Haym, *Hegel und seine Zeit* (Berlin, 1857), p. 453.
[33]Ibid., pp. 10, 12, 14.

system that ostensibly served to legitimize conservative power in Prussia. In particular, he directs his criticism against Hegel's legal philosophy. Haym extracts specific elements of Hegelian philosophy and turns them in historical form against Hegel's system building. They include the idea of progress, the substantive interpretation of history, the concept of a unity of historical phases, and the idea of a universal historical function of peoples. These elements are necessary for the history of literature and ideas; in Haym's view, this history cannot be left to materialistic presentations. To the extent that Hegelian philosophy had served as a justification of the restorative Prussian state, it had become a rigid ideology that had to be critically loosened. Hegel's reconciliation of reason and reality made his philosophy of the state suspect, because it transfigured Prussian reality and abandoned the principle of human and political progress. As a liberal, Haym insists on the value of *Räsonnement* and defends the position of such writers as Humboldt, Dahlmann, and Gervinus against the Hegelian criticism of subjective reason. He thus criticizes the Hegelian philosophy of history—to which he was otherwise more favorably disposed than he was to Hegel's legal philosophy—for subjecting individual human freedom to the commands of a *Weltgeist*. Haym finds the Hegelian concepts of freedom and progress unacceptable because they lead to a comprehensive construction of world history in which knowledge devalues life. His criticism of Hegel's legal philosophy leads to a criticism of the absolute *Geist* that makes a construction of universal history possible. In Hegel's system "the free self-determination of men does not insure progress and the realization of human interests; rather, the absolute idea exploits human endeavor purely for its own satisfaction."[34] Yet this reference to human praxis, which brings Haym close to the left-Hegelian school, does not lead to Feuerbach but back to Kant and Humboldt.

The clearest correspondence of systematic thinking and political self-understanding in Haym is found in his analysis of the Hegelian philosophy of history—specifically, in his call for a historiography that will do justice to humankind's free self-determination. His basis is Humboldt's theory of history, which in contrast to Hegel's allows for the possibility of this emancipation: "This enticing background, this fragrant distance, which made Herder's, Kant's, and Fichte's philosophy of history a practical science and at the same time an ethical admonition to individuals, has—and this is an essential part of it—totally disappeared from the Hegelian picture of history." Haym defends reasoned historiography against what he considers the excessive theorizing and scholarliness of Hegel's philosophy. When one therefore speaks, and rightly so, of

[34]Ibid., p. 447.

Haym's drawing nearer to positivism, one must also bear in mind that he did so not in order to evade the question of value but, on the contrary, to rescue historiography as a practical discipline. This very aim once again legitimizes to a certain extent the idealism of Hegelian philosophy. Despite all his criticism, in 1857 Haym still held that Hegel, in whom he found "all aspects of world history dominated and ruled by ideas,"[35] had continued Herder's and Humboldt's thinking and had thereby helped to overcome a purely pragmatic historiography—not by his constructive approach, which Haym found distasteful, but by his insistence on the public function of history and literary history. This function consisted in formulating a national mission. The introduction to *Die romantische Schule* (1870) characteristically speaks of the Vor-märz as a dream from which Germany has luckily awakened and offers this description of current interests: "A much more serious and practical struggle has begun, the confident, happy work of making progress on the ground of a national independence, proud of its power, which has been won as if by a miracle."[36] National unification under Bismarck, to which Haym manifestly declared himself reconciled, demanded a stock taking of literature. It became a duty to study romanticism so that the idealistic tradition, which had been neglected in the politically radical Vormärz, could be revived.

Haym approached the newly founded Reich with the conviction that literary-historical work can bring about the progress whose general outlines had been set by the idealistic philosophy of history. There is no hint in his work, however, that national unification is not commensurate with the concepts of human self-liberation he had previously called for. His methodical program for resolving this dilemma deserves closer attention. History for him is neither the history of ideas in the strict sense nor the history of works, because "in them, the double movement of the general and the individual *Geist* only seems to find definite expression." The dynamics of history is shifted instead to the activity of the individual, who as producer and recipient creates a field of forces in which ideas and works become fluid: "The real task of historical scholarship is to make these works flow backward and forward, toward their origins and toward their effects. If it is not simply to record facts and depict actions, it must dissolve what has taken place in the how of the event." For all its emphasis on empiricism, this program sets itself off from a positivism that breaks down literary history into facts. Haym is aware that historical processes cannot be revealed simply by collecting data and calculating factors, but he distrusts pure intellectual history, in

---

[35]Ibid., pp. 448, 452.
[36]Rudolf Haym, *Die romantische Schule* (Berlin, 1870), p. 4.

which people are merely the carriers of ideas. This position results in a synchronistic outlook: Haym wants to reconstruct the romantic movement from its biographical, psychological, and historical causes, which have to be recorded with "understanding and sympathy."[37]

Hermeneutic understanding is not yet a central issue for Haym. That people and works of art are comprehensible seems to him self-evident. His emphasis on understanding is directed against the system building of Hegelian philosophy. On the whole, for Haym the historical relationship between past and present is still secure. As a historian, he is interested in human progress—in this respect he still belongs to the tradition of reasoned historiography—and he derives his method from this cognitive interest. The misgivings we encountered in Danzel about the scholarliness of this procedure are not found in Haym. It is striking that his approach could be adapted to the changed political situation of 1870. The function of both his concept of history and his method proved alterable. From the perspective of the *Reichsgründung* (founding of the Reich), Haym's history of German literature, no less than Schmidt's, reads like a prehistory of Bismarck's empire.

Positivism and Nationalism: Wilhelm Scherer

If only Scherer's history of literature were known to us, we would have to describe him as a follower of Haym. His principles of presentation in it as well as his basic methodological concept are relatively close to Haym's approach. In accordance with his aim of reaching a broader public, Scherer writes fluently and avoids discussion of troublesome issues in scholarship. Scholarly discourse is consequently relegated to the appendix. The subsequent fame of this history of literature as a leading example of positivism can undoubtedly be attributed more to the reputation of its author than to its structure, in which positivist principles are only partially developed. Its success rests instead on its avoidance of methodical purism and its eclectic integration of that which seems useful for the presentation. Political points of view alternate with biographical ones; problems of social history are joined to those of the history of works. One searches unsuccessfully for a methodological concept, and Scherer has characteristically abstained from writing an introduction expounding his theoretical and methodological premises. The scholarly rigor insisted on by Scherer in his review of Hettner's literary history is not evident in his own work. Thus a decline is the first impression conveyed by comparing Hettner's history of literature with Scherer's. We must not forget, however, that the two works

[37]Ibid., p. 9.

have different purposes. Scherer intended to write a popular history of literature that would replace the successful studies of Vilmar and Gottschall. He attained this goal.

Still, the lack of methodological clarity, the syncretism of Scherer's literary history, is symptomatic of the connection between theory and ideology in Bismarck's Reich. A purely scholarly view of the history of criticism cannot grasp the function of earlier positivism, for this approach sees in nineteenth-century positivism only an inconsistent form of scientific principles, which seem obsolete when measured against the theoretical claims of neopositivism. Since it is generally accepted that positivism was supplanted by Dilthey's hermeneutics, theoretical and scholarly interest in history has usually been restricted to demonstrating its deficiencies, without inquiring why earlier positivism should have been so successful despite its evident theoretical weaknesses. To answer this question one has to keep in mind the historical constellation that shaped the dialectic of methodology and ideology.

Liberal historiography postulated a connection between the development of literature and that of national politics. In Gervinus in particular, German national self-determination appears as the ultimate metaliterary goal of literature. The theory of history that substantiates this connection is idealistic. The collapse of idealism as a compelling Weltanschauung robbed the liberal model of its methodological base and forced literary history to strengthen its insecure foundations. German studies called on positivism for help in supporting and justifying a concept grounded in idealism. It was not that the new method led to a changed concept of national literature but rather the contrary: the familiar concept was to be safeguarded by philosophical positivism. In literary history, this purpose was served by the positivist concept of scholarship, which was oriented toward the natural sciences, and a concept of progress concerned no longer with human self-development but with the development of productive forces in the form of technological improvements. Scherer's celebration of the natural sciences was an admission that the arts, literary history among them, had lost their autonomy: "The same power that brought railroads and the telegraph into being, the same power that gave rise to an unprecedented flowering of industry, increased the comfort of living, and shortened wars—in a word, that carried man's domination of nature an enormous step forward—that same power also rules our intellectual life; it does away with dogmas, it transforms the sciences, it makes its mark on poetry. Like a conquerer, *Natural Science* advances victoriously on the triumphal car to which we are all chained." The ambivalence in this statement is highly characteristic: on the one hand, it praises instrumental reason, the equation of progress with dominance over nature; on the other, it shows an awareness that the historical disciplines have become methodologically dependent on the theory of the natural sciences. When Scherer writes that his generation—that is, the generation that began writing in the 1860s—*"is not building any systems"*[38] but is only making use of the facts, the skepticism of Haym and his generation, which took Hegel and the Hegelian school as its point of departure, suddenly turns into a new faith. Scherer heralds a new outlook, which is ostensibly supported by epistomological positivism. He does not made sufficiently clear that a methodologically strict positivism must eventually lead to a fundamental critique of historicism, that is, that positivism is not concerned with historical forces. In particular, he is far from separating facts from values, which is characteristic of all critical positivism.

In the introduction to his history of the German language, Scherer proposes a program aimed at grounding the history of literature positivistically. Referring to Henry Buckle, he expressly rejects the concept of understanding as the central category of hermeneutics. Since Scherer is referring explicitly to a deterministic interpretation of history, one assumes that his presentation will be strictly descriptive and, in contrast to reasoned literary history, completely devoid of teleological argument. But this is not the case. In the same introduction, Scherer calls for a national economic and moral policy, "with which the Fatherland, in flesh and blood as it were, would confront its people with stern demands as well as loving generosity."[39] Epistemological interests, previously suppressed, are again in evidence here. The purpose of literary history, as Scherer emphasizes, goes beyond explanation of causal relationships. As in liberal historiography, he assumes that there is a national objective, which becomes the point of departure for a reconstruction of the history of literature. It is from this national literary tradition that Scherer seeks to derive a system of national ethical values which can serve to orient the future. For Scherer, this view is more important than the deterministic concept of history. First and foremost, literature "functions as a medium for a national *telos.*"[40] He does not by any means break with earlier historiography in this respect, as is generally assumed by academic historians, but adheres to a teleological concept, even though he has significantly redefined the national task. He now

---

[38]Wilhelm Scherer, "Die neue Generation," in Žmegač, *Methoden der deutschen Literaturwissenschaft*, p. 23.

[39]Wilhelm Scherer, "Zur Geschichte der deutschen Sprache," in Zmegač, *Methoden der deutschen Literaturwissenschaft*, p. 18.

[40]Laermann, "Was ist literaturwissenschaftlicher Positivismus?" p. 59.

declares that national unity, as achieved under Bismarck, is the goal of German literature.[41] His content is crucially affected by this modification, because the liberal humanism of reasoned literary history has been rejected or else has simply been turned into citations for festive occasions.

It would be wrong, however, to confine this change to Scherer. Restriction to a national literature had already begun in Gervinus, and Schmidt's and Haym's works of literary history are markers on the road to the affirmative concept of history of Bismarck's time. Characteristically, Scherer only partially continues Danzel's objections to reasoned literary history. He echoes Danzel's polemic against the essentialist thinking of earlier historicism, but he does not take up Danzel's criticism of national tradition. The question of scholarly objectivity raised by Danzel is decided in positivism in favor of the object, which is understood as a mass of discovered facts. Yet in Scherer this objectivism is anything but consistent. Because for him interest in history is determined by the ideology of nationalism, the investigating subject is guided not by form, as Danzel proposed, but by content. It can be said that "positivism . . . was a faithful mirror image of the attitudes of the established German middle class of the second half of the century, which had given up the political idealism of 1848 and was contenting itself with its comfortable economic position."[42] Yet this formulation overlooks the active character literary history acquires through the manner in which it organizes, processes, and evaluates its "material." Since literary history always appropriates the past, whether the historian is aware of it or not, and never merely copies it, methodology becomes the instrument of this process.

Positivism is characteristically blind to this relationship. The catalogue of themes presented by Erich Schmidt in his essay "Wege und Ziele der deutschen Literaturgeschichte" (The Methods and Aims of German Literary History) (1886) restricts the field of objects but not the investigating subject's position with respect to the object.[43] The rejection of metaphysics, taken over by Scherer and his school from Auguste Comte, leads to the exclusion of certain questions still crucial in earlier historicism and to a demand for stricter methodology which is not, however, redeemed in practice. At the same time it blocks theoreti-

---

[41]A good example of this search for a national tradition is the lecture "Über den Ursprung der deutschen Nationalität" (1873), in Wilhelm Scherer, *Vorträge und Aufsätze zur Geschichte des geistigen Lebens in Deutschland und Oesterreich* (Berlin, 1874), pp. 1–20.

[42]Jost Hermand and Evelyn Torton Beck, *Interpretive Synthesis. The Task of Literary Scholarship* (New York, 1975), pp. 15–16.

[43]Erich Schmidt, "Wege und Ziele der deutschen Litteraturgeschichte," in Schmidt, *Charakteristiken* (Berlin, 1886), pp. 491–98.

cal reflection on the requirements of historical insight and especially on the subject's contribution to it. Scherer's practice departs here from his theoretical principles. When he is confronted with authors and works, he does what it would be impossible for him to do as a methodical positivist: he makes aesthetic value judgments.

Gervinus's dictum that literary history is concerned with history, not with aesthetics, points to a theoretical problem that was to plague historians of the next generation. The distinction made by Gervinus is obviously inadequate, for aesthetic judgments are certainly part of history and not outside it. Gervinus's formulation of the problem is misleading; it results in the impression that treatment of the literature of the past does not give rise to aesthetic questions. His reservations against aesthetics can be understood, especially given the political orientation of his literary history, as a mediatization of art for the benefit of politics. Danzel's criticism hit the mark when he insisted that a history of literature cannot be written without taking into account the literary norms and conventions that set the standard for production at any given time. Danzel returned aesthetics to literary history by historicizing it. But the relationship between history and aesthetics remained tense in postrevolutionary literary history. Gottschall's polemic against Julian Schmidt only exaggerated the existing contrast by pitting aesthetic claims against moral ones. In 1860, in the introduction to the second edition of his history of literature, he remarked that "the standards *Julian Schmidt* applies in his judgment of writers are seldom of an 'aesthetic' kind but are taken mainly from the arsenal of moral convictions. As surely as aesthetic criticism should not conceal moral halfheartedness and lack of principle, the unhealthy aspects of literature—especially when they have a deeper relationship to contemporary cultural trends—just as surely is it unable to measure poetic greatness by this standard alone; above all, it must have a sense of the importance of artistic *talent*."[44] This not unjustified objection to Schmidt's dogmatism, to be sure, takes the issue of morality out of its context in reasoned literary history; for in Gervinus and Schmidt, the moral judgment of literature is not private but a matter for public *Räsonnement*. Gottschall's polemic touches the critical heart of reasoned literary history, which, to put it paradoxically, does not want to be evenhanded, since it has to judge. Gottschall wants to achieve an understanding criticism based on a refined "empathy" (*Anempfinden*), a delicacy of feeling. This change is not explained entirely by Gottschall's aversion to moralistic judgment. Behind it lies his intention to dismantle the whole liber-

[44]Rudolph Gottschall, *Die deutsche Nationalliteratur*, 2d ed., vol. 1 (Breslau, 1861), p. xviii–xix.

al, reasoned model and to replace it with individualized appreciation. Once again opposing Schmidt, Gottschall asserts that liberal historiography sees mainly the broad outlines and seldom takes the individuality of an author into account. By emphasizing the individual, Gottschall calls in question the constructing of historical relationships, crucial for liberal historiography. As contradictory as his introduction is, because on the one hand it argues against the presentation of general tendencies and on the other it supports a tendency—namely, idealistic (instead of realistic) literature—it still exemplifies the theoretical and methodological aporias of postrevolutionary literary history, which led in one direction to positivism and in the other to Dilthey's reflection on historical insight.

Scherer's posthumously published poetics was an attempt to bring together again what had come apart in Gottschall's work. In 1871, when a new edition of his history of literature appeared, Gottschall spoke of the two halves of literary history: one objective and scholarly; the other practical and reformatory, which seeks to intervene in the development of literature. Under the auspices of a "new impetus in national life,"[45] according to Gottschall, literature assumed the task of creating milestones for the nation's *via triumphalis*. Scherer, too, emphasized the national task, but rather than contrasting it to the scholarly task, he viewed it as a part of scholarship. In his poetics Scherer grabbed the problem of aesthetics by the horns and tried to find a scientific resolution to the question of evaluation in positivist terms. It can hardly be said that his attempt was successful. Scherer's early death put an end to his work before he could bring to fruition the ideas he developed in his lectures. The posthumous edition of his work is fragmentary, presenting hardly more than the framework of an approach. Still, it shows the direction of his thinking. Scherer's polemic against Aristotle characterizes his goal: "Yes, for me—apart from the expansion of our mental horizon, which alone has made us richer than he was—Aristotle is not enough of a natural scientist. He does not sufficiently treat the writing in hand with the cool observation, analysis, and classification of a scientist. He is, for me, too much of a lawgiver."[46] The same objection could have been made against Lessing or any neo-Aristotelian theory.

There are two aspects to Scherer's misgivings which for analytical reasons need to be distinguished: first, the question of the conditions under which value judgments can be made and, second, the question of the scientific grounding for a theory of poetry. Put differently, how can

[45]Gottschall, *Die deutsche Nationalliteratur*, 3d ed. (Leipzig, 1871), quoted in the 6th ed., p. xxvi.
[46]Wilhelm Scherer, *Poetik* (Berlin, 1888), p. 43.

the intrusion of personal prejudices into aesthetic judgments be avoided, and how can a universal poetics not derived from specific, historically determined dogmas be substantiated given the quantity of historical material and the diversity of history? Scherer has the same ready answer for both. A theory of poetry should be erected on a base of empirical observations, which are then generalized through induction. By this means he hopes to avoid an a priori construction of the basic categories. Historiographical justice does not result from immersion in an individual object, which thereby becomes unique and incomparable, but from turning something individual into an instance in an inductive series. The same process of methodical induction should justify value judgments in scholarship. The scholarly observer learns to distinguish between personal taste, which is irrelevant for a universal poetics, and empirical investigation of the formation of value judgments. Subjective prejudice is thus transformed by Scherer into a scientific judgment by being objectified, that is, turned into an object of empirical investigation.

To be sure, there is considerable difference in Scherer's poetics between this theoretical approach and its implementation, a difference explainable in part by the work's sketchy execution. Nowhere does Scherer do justice to the demands of strict empirical induction; in most cases he merely offers stimulating hypotheses. One has to ask, however, whether Scherer had a strict program in mind at all. His descriptive poetics is more traditional than he imagined, for its central categories are developed from abstract definitions that are only subsequently applied to his material. The result is an abstract schematization that contradicts positivist principles. In another respect, however, Scherer's poetics represents a break with tradition: if he had consistently pursued it, it would have done away with an individualizing historical approach, for in his poetics objects ultimately become material to be fit into systematic categories.

Scherer's poetics suggests the break between historicism and positivism which is reflected in Dilthey's theories. Dilthey holds a special position among the literary historians of this epoch because he no longer takes for granted that historical insight and investigation into literary history are possible, as did, despite their many differences, Schmidt, Hettner, Haym, and Gottschall. The question, then, is whether critical analysis of the aporias of historicism leads to a breakdown of ideology.

The Crisis in Methodology: Wilhelm Dilthey

Compared to Danzel's more stringent, methodical criticism, Dilthey's first attempts to scrutinize existing literary history are somewhat vague.

They do not really qualify as criticism, since they are calculated rather to show approval of Gervinus's, Hettner's, and Schmidt's achievements. In his essay "Literaturhistorische Arbeiten über das klassische Zeitalter" (The Historiography of the Literature of the Classical Period) (1866), Dilthey meant to pave the way for his own work by surveying what had already been accomplished. (His essay on Novalis had already been published, and his essay on Lessing was to appear shortly afterward.) But the moment Dilthey poses the questions which tasks literary history should assume and how it can do them scholarly justice, his survey presents methodological difficulties.

Dilthey views literary history as part of cultural development. Presentation of the literature of the past becomes crucial when contemporary readers no longer have the leisure to read the works themselves. Dilthey's main focus, consequently, is on factual information, for the reader must be able to depend on the historian. The historian's task is to bring out in his or her material what is of *lasting value*: "The literary historian has to decide what among the countless piles of written debris is worth saving and presenting in a thorough manner to the man who appreciates only what has proven effective for other people or proves to have an effect on him." Dilthey's main emphasis is clearly *positive*, namely, on the acquisition of a lasting tradition and not on its criticism. This attitude leads to a criticism—albeit a very cautious one—of the reasoned literary history of Gervinus and his students; for reasoned historiography sees its role as that of judge. It subjects the past to a moralistic political judgment that measures authors and works according to the goal of the historical process. *Räsonnement*, therefore, cannot protect the classic German authors if their works produce an effect inimical to the process of enlightenment. Characteristically, Dilthey regards this very process as subjective. He accuses Gervinus of having abandoned the task of writing pure history by going beyond concern for historical effect in order to make direct value judgments: "Only when he abandoned the point of view of historical effect and its great document, Goethe's autobiography, did Gervinus go badly astray; when he advanced his own judgments of *the* value of people, one extending beyond their own time." Dilthey rejects as morally abstract an evaluation oriented toward the present and favors instead judgment developed, as it were, from the object itself by adherence to the effect it produces in later times. Without explicitly calling attention to it, Dilthey here reverses the perspective, turning it against reasoned literary history: the point of departure for historical work is tradition and the agreed upon canon of significant authors, not the interests of the present.

During this time, Dilthey came close to positivist methodology, as for

example when he demands of objective literary history strict explanations of relationships: "We want to review the chain of cause and effect
in which intellectual events run their course in uninterrupted order, as
do those of political history. In this case, too, we call for disclosure of
the causal linkage of events."[47] Dilthey never expressly states that this
demand could not be satisfied by earlier idealistic historiography. Yet it
is noteworthy that, in 1866, among contemporary works of literary
history, he prefers Schmidt's to Hettner's. For all his recognition of the
breadth of Hettner's knowledge and the power of his presentation, he
faults him—as did Scherer—for a lack of causal deduction. Hettner's
treatment is merely descriptive, whereas Schmidt, in Dilthey's view,
offers a dramatic presentation that considers causal relationships more
thoroughly and more adequately. At this time, Dilthey found in
Schmidt what he himself hoped to realize: an empirically founded history of eighteenth-century ideas freed from the theoretical and methodological principles of liberal historiography. Dilthey was certainly
aware that Schmidt's approach to the history of literature was still
strongly indebted to the liberalism of the Vormärz, from which he
wanted to distance himself. His approval was possible only because
Schmidt had revised his work several times, and in the edition Dilthey
read there was no longer much evidence of the liberal engagement of the
first edition. Dilthey expressly approved these changes as a gain in
objectivity.[48]

There is the same cautious distance from reasoned historiography in
Dilthey's detailed essay on the historian Friedrich Christoph Schlosser,
which was published in 1865 in the *Preussischen Jahrbücher*. Dilthey's
critique once again takes the form of a historical appreciation. Using
Schlosser's development as an example, he traces the evolution of historical thinking in Germany and is able in this way to show the limitations of the liberal approach. Dilthey remarks approvingly that
Schlosser opposed Hegel's teleological philosophy of history and sought
to establish a unity of universal history only to the extent that he could
trace back "the multifarious historical phenomena to their causes or
laws and these, in turn, to man's nature." Nevertheless, the "development of history as a whole" remains a problem both for Schlosser and
for Dilthey, who interprets him. For Schlosser, the goal of history is the
perfection of humankind; thus he follows Kant in insisting on humanity's moral and political progress. But according to Dilthey, this very tie
to the Enlightenment is Schlosser's limitation. He shows himself to be a

[47]Wilhelm Dilthey, *Gesammelte Schriften*, vol. 11 (Leipzig, 1936), pp. 196, 197, 198.
[48]See also Dilthey's review of Schmidt's *Geschichte der deutschen Literatur seit Lessings Tod*, in *Gesammelte Schriften*, vol. 16 (Göttingen, 1972), pp. 257–60.

"child of the eighteenth century, whose ideal state has 'human rights' as its highest goal." The reasoned historiography of a Schlosser breaks down when faced with the diversity of the spirit. Schlosser "relates literature firmly to his basic idea, moral culture; that is, moral culture as he understands it, in which everything is governed by its direct relationship to active and civic life, in which, as a result, the world of the imagination recedes completely behind the will and sober understanding produced by such a life."[49]

Dilthey's interpretation establishes a relationship between Schlosser's progressive historical model and his instrumental examination of literature. The principal focus of the liberal historian is effect. In contrast, Dilthey aims to do justice to all phenomena of intellectual life. Unlike Schlosser, who is primarily interested in origins and effects, he insists on comprehending and describing phenomena. This is why he sees Ranke in part as a model for the younger generation. Dilthey admires the power and animation of Ranke's presentation, yet he disputes his constructive and analytical ability: "Ranke often seems to skate on the surface of things: he seems not to further causal understanding, but he is the great teacher just because he does not rely on explanation; his point of departure, rather, is the great world events themselves as seen in their universal relationship." It is never quite clear whether Dilthey considers Ranke's lack of causal analysis an advantage or a disadvantage. He uses the concept of relationship and argues against the concept of causality as a means of clarifying Ranke's method: "The abstract term cause, causality, does not cover what is here called relationship."[50] Thus when Dilthey refers to earlier idealistic historicism, he means the descriptive objectivism of a Ranke rather than the tradition of Schlosser and Gervinus.

In the sixties the young Dilthey vacillated between a causal-genetic method and a descriptive one. Positivism, as represented by his friend Scherer, had considerable attraction for him, because allegedly it had broken with the speculative philosophy of history and the idealistic concept of progress. The positivists were no less critical of reasoned literary history than was Dilthey. But the latter eventually decided against positivism and for an independent theory of intellectual scholarship. The reasons for this decision are examined in the following pages.

The crucial impetus for Dilthey's development of an independent scholarly methodology came from his early study of Schleiermacher and the problem of hermeneutics. In his prize-winning 1860 essay on Schleiermacher's hermeneutic system, the young Dilthey set himself the

[49]Dilthey, 11:154, 157, 161.
[50]Ibid., pp. 217, 218.

task of incorporating the heritage of romantic literary criticism and expository doctrine into the definition of literary history.[51] Dilthey bypassed Hegel and the Hegelian school, which was still strong in postrevolutionary literary history, and shifted the locus of the problem. Instead of asking whether it is possible to construct a *historical totality*, he asks whether it is possible to arrive at an *objective textual interpretation*. These metahistorical viewpoints are not discussed in the essay itself, which adheres strictly to the ideal of scholarly objectivity; that is, it deals exclusively with the presentation of Schleiermacher's hermeneutics and its historical context.

More information on the young Dilthey's methodological reflection is to be found in his contemporaneous diary entries, for they reveal clearly the extent to which the question of hermeneutics was for him linked to the question how one understands history. A detailed entry of March 26, 1859—from the time when he was working on his Schleiermacher essay—is noteworthy not least because of the way he links the important theoretical and methodological problems of his generation. By doing so, he is able to clarify for himself the significance of historical thinking (he makes no distinction in the process between history and literary history). This entry shows far more clearly than his later public utterances that Dilthey was well aware of the theoretical and methodological aporias and understood the inner relationship between a methodical approach and the result of a presentation. It was clear to Dilthey that history is the result of a *reconstruction*: "Insofar as it deals with the course of intellectual life, history is very dependent on the methodology of its historians. This concern for methodology has provoked a furious debate. To consider a work as the expression of an idea drawn from the general dialectic; to atomize the work into multiple motives and starts; to reproduce works, in daguerreotype fashion, within the tiniest space: how varied the historical pictures are that are designed according to such varied principles and with such varied techniques!" Here Dilthey compares the various schools of historiography: the philosophy of history of Hegel and his school, the new positivism, the epiclike historicism of a Ranke. In 1859 Dilthey departs most clearly from the philosophy of history, possibly under the influence of Haym's book on Hegel. He regards as an illusion the conception of a linear historical development that unfolds according to a "dialectic proceeding in a triad of elements. . . . This rational formation of the world proved to be an illusion in nature and in history. The irregularity of the world knows no other reason than the law." To be sure, his

---

[51]The work on Schleiermacher is finally available in print in volume 14 of *Gesammelte Schriften*.

criticism of absolute reason adheres to both the concept of progress and the concept of historical laws in order to have a framework for recording and presenting its material. Dilthey expresses the same basic idea in various formulations: the human intellect advances according to mechanical laws. The historical process is furthered by circumstances, not ideas: "History is concerned with *progressive* culture. Viewed mechanically, intellectual progress takes the form of a complication of ideas and relationships produced by the reciprocal effect of nations and their historical connection."[52] Elsewhere Dilthey speaks of the possibility of explaining the movement of history as a purely mechanical regularity. This reversal in polarity allows him tentatively to renounce earlier idealistic premises without abandoning the concepts of progress and universal history.

But other methodological problems remain unsolved: how can such laws be shown to exist in the history of the spirit, and how, finally, can progress be identified in the ordered flow of history? As Dilthey recognizes, the course of history must be given a direction. Thus he insists that the historical process moves not as a circular but as a linear process. Yet his only support for this assumption is that a *differentiation* of ideas can be established phenomenally from the historical material. At this point Dilthey brings in hermeneutics and appeals to Schleiermacher. After discussing the various competing methodologies, he adds: "Here, then, is the opinion it will be one of the main tasks of this investigation to substantiate, that the basic principles of Schleiermacher's hermeneutics describe masterfully, for the first time, the one essential side of historical methodology." Although Dilthey initially raises the problem of historiography in more general terms, he discusses it primarily with respect to cultural history and the history of ideas, for which mechanistic positivism is least suited. Before historical laws can be constructed in these areas we have to be certain that we understand the range of ideas encountered in texts. For Dilthey, consequently, hermeneutics is the first, unavoidable step for the historian. Dilthey always viewed the methodical understanding of ideas and systems of ideas as more than a mere review of judgments, for he was concerned with the "first, original impulses" that give rise to thought systems.[53]

Dilthey characteristically carries the positivist approach to the point where it contradicts its own basic premises. He expressly argues against the exposition of intellectual processes "by an atomistic mechanism of

[52]Clara Misch, ed., *Der junge Dilthey. Ein Lebensbild in Briefen und Tagebüchern, 1852–1870* (Leipzig, 1933), pp. 92, 82, 83.
[53]Ibid., pp. 92, 93.

motivations" and calls instead for understanding derived "from man's nature."[54] But if a text is regarded as a manifestation of human activity and a connection is established—in the sense of Schleiermacher's hermeneutics—between the individuality of the author and the structure of the text, the question arises how, in view of this individualizing approach, a universal historical context and the regularity of history can be maintained.

Dilthey recognizes the difficulties to which a hermeneutic grounding of the humanities would lead, and he therefore proposes a combination of hermeneutic and positivist methods. On the one hand, he requires historical methodology to prove that a work, a thought system, is part of a larger historical process—that is, he requires the particular to be subordinated to universal law. On the other, he expects historical methodology to enable us to penetrate the meaning of intellectual statements. Thus Dilthey remains critical of Schleiermacher, whose philological method is too sharply focused on the individual text and its author. In reference to Schleiermacher's interpretation of the New Testament, he notes in his diary: "Schleiermacher's method isolates everything into individualities, conceived as self-contained wholes with their own particular composition, their own particular inner form. To the extent that it pertains to art, this method is justified. . . . But the inner law of history demands that continuity should be pursued with absolute seriousness." It should be noted that Dilthey is speaking at this point of the inner, not the mechanical, law of history and is thus at least implicitly admitting that the desired combination of hermeneutics and positivism is not unproblematic. Idealism was not as easily overcome as Dilthey, under the influence of positivist trends, at first assumed. A diary entry of April 1861 shows that in order to conceptualize the historical process, Dilthey adhered to idealistic premises: "In general terms, *the historical process* means that the inner traits of our ethical and intellectual existence, since they are common to many, constitute forms of this commonality; that like all forms, however, they are not sufficient for the creative spirit, which progresses infinitely, and from various impulses they rebel against it as opposing parties and schools." This statement is undoubtedly closer to Hegel than to Comte; yet it does not lead back to pure spirit but rather to national history and comparative anthropology, from which the basic moral and intellectual traits are to be derived. The form in which this occurs is already clearly distinguishable from the positivist approach. Dilthey differentiates philological and hermeneutical from historical understanding more clearly

[54]Ibid., p. 93.

in 1861 than in 1859: hermeneutics is concerned with the individual text and its context; historical reconstruction, in contrast, is guided by the position that the work or philosophical system is a branch "of the history of ideas."[55] Dilthey tries to unify the two processes so that they supplement each other. Construction of the history of ideas (nothing is said about political history) depends on preparatory philological work, which aims at deciphering the meaning of texts.

We now see more clearly what Dilthey's objection to the lack of objectivity in reasoned historiography means: he leads us to hermeneutics as the method by which works are reconstructed in such a way as to show clearly that they are a unity. The content he draws from them through interpretation he then, as a second step, incorporates into the history of ideas. In this process, the question of truth shifts for Dilthey. He is disturbed by the unexpected moral and political attack of liberal historiography on the content of works; they are measured in terms of the telos of history. Dilthey, in contrast, is at once more and less critical. He is more critical insofar as he recognizes the failure of the moral approach to mediate between its judgment and the work of art; he is less critical insofar as he regards the truth of historical perception as already assured by an understanding of texts and a reconstruction of ideas. But this means that historical tradition has been removed from critical discussion. Dilthey's turn to political conservatism, which followed the Prussian victory over Austria in 1866,[56] is anticipated on a theoretical level in his studies of Schleiermacher and his early remarks on hermeneutics. Thus he writes in his diary in 1865: "The essence of history is historical movement itself, and if one wishes to call this essence a purpose, then it is the only purpose history has."[57] In other words, Dilthey shifts the goal of history to history itself—movement becomes the goal—and the historical process thereby becomes truth, of which works and persons are merely the signs.

Although Dilthey's early theoretical expositions concern history in general, his essays on Novalis, Lessing, and Goethe, which were to appear in revised form four decades later in *Das Erlebnis und die Dichtung*, apply his observations first and foremost to literary history. Both his choice of authors and his approach to them reflect his intense preoccupation with the basic problems of historical methodology. Dilthey chose a biographical approach, though it was not his intention to write biographies. But at the same time he conceived these essays as a first attempt at composing a literary history of Goethe's time. This is espe-

---

[55]Ibid., pp. 95, 147, 151.
[56]See Peschken, *Versuch einer germanistischen Ideologiekritik*, pp. 57–72; and Christofer Zöckler, *Dilthey und die Hermeneutik* (Stuttgart, 1975), pp. 227–39.
[57]*Der junge Dilthey*, p. 190.

cially clear from his introductory reflections on methodology in his essay on Novalis, which were largely repeated in his 1867 inaugural address in Basel. In the address Dilthey sums up his observations up to that point by applying them to a specific subject, the history of German literature between 1770 and 1830.

In contrast to earlier liberal historiography, he treats this time span as a closed, homogeneous period: "From a number of stable historical conditions there arose in Germany in the last third of the previous century an intellectual movement that ran a closed, continuous course—that formed a unified whole—from Lessing to the death of Schleiermacher and Hegel." This concept, a familiar one today, is linked in Dilthey's lecture to the basic methodological question of the prerequisites for historical cognition. What were the reasons for the homogeneity of the epoch between 1770 and 1830? For Dilthey, its alleged unity was manifest not so much in its opinions and works as in its successive efforts to attain a new view of the world. Dilthey ascribes a specifically *German* character to this new view. His explanation for a special German status is noteworthy; he takes over an important argument from liberal historiography but uses it in such a way as to change its meaning completely. For Gervinus and Schmidt, Weimar classicism was distinguished by its aloofness from the political problems of the German nation, by its unworldliness, to somewhat overstate the case. Dilthey agreed with this assessment and emphasized Germany's special situation by comparing it to the development of England and Spain. In those countries, literature came to flower against the background of a strong national state. The great English and Spanish writers approached their material "from the standpoint of an existing national spirit." Germany, in contrast, lacked national unity; it had neither a political nor a cultural center. The German bourgeoisie saw itself excluded from political participation. Under these conditions, according to Dilthey, cultural life took a very different form: "Thus their urge for life, all their energy in the years when they were at the height of their vigor, was *turned inward*: personal cultivation and intellectual distinction became their *ideals*."[58] Literature, Dilthey concluded, took the place of a political public sphere.

Gervinus had criticized this very tendency in his history of literature and had called for the politicization of intellectual life. With Dilthey, instead, the "German movement," spanning three generations, assumes the character of a positive national tradition. He speaks of a world view "in which the German spirit can find its satisfaction." Enlightenment, classicism, and romanticism are presented as three phases of a continu-

[58]Dilthey, *Gesammelte Schriften*, 5:13, 14, 15.

ous, unbroken development. Dilthey's choice of representative authors is striking. In his discussion of the Enlightenment he relies almost exclusively on Lessing, ignoring such writers as Wieland and Klopstock because their work is allegedly not typical of the character of the German Enlightenment. It is still more astonishing that even Kant's fundamental importance for the conceptual exploration and critique of the rationalist program is ignored. What sets Lessing above Kant, in Dilthey's view, is his poetic quality; that is, his intuitive perception as opposed to the conceptual discourse of philosophers. Lessing belongs to the better tradition, as it were, of Spinoza and Leibniz: "Lessing's reading of Leibniz gives life to historical consciousness. From Leibniz's teleological or ideal ground, historical phenomena appeared as the necessary steps of a development whose ultimate goal was enlightenment and perfection."[59]

From this perspective, the Enlightenment can no longer be seen as a preliminary stage for Goethe's time, when what was essential—namely, the pantheistic concept of nature—developed through the work of Goethe. The literature of the Enlightenment—and this is what it comes down to in Dilthey—was depoliticized through selection and emphasis. Dilthey similarly minimizes the politically motivated criticism of liberal, reasoned historiography toward German classicism and romanticism; for he ascribes necessity and legitimacy to the development that began with the Sturm und Drang and ended with romanticism. The ideological implications of this have already been pointed out by Peschken in his observation that the unity of the individual and nature in Goethe, which Dilthey emphasized, shows "the congruence of authoritarian monarchic policy with German interests,"[60] so that the political work of Parliament becomes of secondary importance. The Prussian victory over Austria sealed the fate of the Prussian liberal reform movement to which Dilthey belonged.[61] The success of his foreign policy allowed Bismarck to ignore the opposition of Parliament and to push through his conservative political concept as the prerequisite for German unification. The majority of German liberals, Dilthey included, were prepared to follow him in 1866.

There is a connection between Dilthey's political decision and his methodological and theoretical reflections (a relationship, incidentally, that cannot have been completely clear to him). His hermeneutical

---

[59]Ibid., pp. 13, 19.

[60]Peschken, *Versuch einer germanistischen Ideologiekritik*, p. 71.

[61]On the constitutional conflict, see Rainer Wahl, "Der preussische Verfassungskonflikt und das konstitutionelle System des Kaiserreichs," in Ernst-Wolfgang Böckenförde, ed., *Moderne deutsche Verfassungsgeschichte (1815–1918)* (Cologne, 1972), pp. 171–94.

approach to the history of ideas, which departs critically from the reasoned literary history of the liberals, anticipates the conservative *Reichsgründung*. Not only has the concept of German literary history changed significantly but also the *theory and methodology* of this discipline, which was just beginning to become accepted at German universities. As different as Dilthey's approach is from the positivism of the Scherer school, it arrives at the same result: literary history is put at the service of the new Reich. In the final analysis it is made a discipline with the task of legitimation. This is carried out, however, not directly but indirectly, as criticism of liberal literary history, which openly declared its political cognitive interests. In the name of *objectivity*, the comprehensive constructions of Vormärz historiography are rejected for the hermeneutic approach, which upholds tradition.

This inclusion of romantic hermeneutics in the theory of history, the bolstering of the general construction of history by an adequate understanding of individual works, has already been brought out in principle by Gadamer in the chapter on Dilthey in his *Wahrheit und Methode*, even though he relies chiefly on Dilthey's late and fragmentary writings. For Gadamer, Dilthey's project represents an attempt to substantiate the epic historicism of a Ranke by means of cognitive theory: "What his epistemological thinking tried to justify was fundamentally nothing other than the epic self-forgetfulness of Ranke."[62] The problems left unresolved in early historicism, Gadamer says, were taken up by Dilthey and made into a theme. Thus he considers Dilthey a critical follower of objectivistic historicism, but still a follower, who was not critical enough and who became entangled in objectivism owing to the way he posed his questions.

Gadamer's approach, however, overlooks the fact that Dilthey was not merely interested in a general understanding of the past but probably also had a very good idea of what should be transmitted from the past. Gadamer's own traditionalism blinds him to Dilthey's way of establishing history and literary history through selection and emphasis. Thus he fails to see that this "understanding" benefited certain real interests of society. The appropriation of tradition which mattered to Dilthey was more than understanding; it was an act of selective construction through which power could be indirectly confirmed. This side of Dilthey, which becomes apparent as soon as his concept is compared to the literary history of the Vormärz, is ignored in *Wahrheit und Methode*. Gadamer presents Dilthey's historical awareness as purely contemplative, not taking into account that his reflection on tradition—

---

[62]Hans-Georg Gadamer, *Truth and Method* (New York, 1975), p. 204. Translation of *Wahrheit und Methode*, 2d ed. (Tübingen, 1965).

no longer a matter of course—is accompanied by the question *how* it should be appropriated. In both method and content, Dilthey decided against reception of the literary tradition he found in the historiography of the Vormärz. In his view, the latter lacked scholarly objectivity. After 1848, however, the concept of objectivity, which Gadamer perceives only on the level of theory and method, was given meaning with respect to content, even though this was not explicitly made clear. The power of postrevolutionary rhetoric lay in its ability to let contemporary substantive interests disappear behind the apparatus of cognitive theory.

The Institutionalization of Literary History

Today, in studying literary history as an institution, one must proceed from the understanding that it is a scholarly discipline taught in universities.[63] The task of contemporary German studies, apart from the training of a new scholarly generation, is primarily to train teachers of German who will transmit the linguistic and literary tradition in various types of schools. As a discipline, literary history is no longer involved in contemporary literary life. The occasional scholar may participate in topical discussions of literature, but the discipline itself is not expected to contribute to the present literary scene. Because of the form of its organization (academic) and institionalization (scholarship and the training of teachers), the discourses of literary history and literary aesthetics have become separate. Literary history belongs to the *academic* public sphere, not to the literary public sphere. Symptomatic of this separation is the distrust that exists between Germanists and critics. The separation between academic literary studies and criticism was probably in effect by 1900: on the one side, a positivist scholarly activity that is legitimized through publication and the study of sources, neither any longer of interest to the general public; on the other, impressionistic journalistic criticism that deliberately spurns scholarly gestures and, with forced reliance on romanticism, equates the work of the critic with that of the artist—in other words, that seeks to rescue the critical element by opposing the subjectivity of critics and artists to the reification of scholarly activity. The revolutionizing of literary history owing to Dilthey's increasing influence after 1900 has done little or nothing to affect this separation, since the history of ideas, with the "objectivity" imposed on it by Dilthey, aims to be part of the academic, not the

[63]On the organization of philology and literary history as a subject, see Rudolf Lehmann in W. Lexis, ed., *Das Unterrichtswesen im deutschen Reich*, vol. 1 (Berlin, 1904), pp. 179–84.

literary, public sphere. Only when *Geistesgeschichte* has come in contact with the George circle—as in the works of Friedrich Gundolf—has a renewed effort been made to address the reading public. Through its style and composition, Gundolf's presentation deliberately provoked the scholarly discourse of positivism.

In the early twentieth century the field of literary history departed markedly from the aims of its first important representatives. Scherer's history of literature and literary essays, despite their methodological claims, are not yet directed exclusively at a scholarly public. His history of literature (1883) in particular is addressed to a broader literary public sphere. Its popular tone is immediately evident in the first chapter, the beginning sentence of which is more reminiscent of a historical novel than a scholarly investigation: "About the time when Alexander the Great was opening new fields to Greek science by his invasion of India, a learned Greek, Pytheas of Massilia, started from his native town, sailed through the straits of Gibraltar, along the western coast of Spain and France, and, passing Great Britain, discovered at the mouth of the Rhine a new people—the Teutons."[64] This almost has to be described as a forced popularization, which through its epiclike presentation plays down the methodological difficulties of a history of literature—of which Scherer was well aware—and relegates problems of research to an appendix. Although Scherer puts himself at a considerable methodological and theoretical distance from earlier literary history, he is still tied to its traditional form of presentation. His claim to scientific objectivity does not disguise the fact that he sees himself not exclusively as a scholar and specialist restricted to the university, but as one engaged in the public task of holding a dialogue with a broader public. Scherer—like Schmidt and Prutz before him, or his contemporary Gottschall—is at the same time a historian and a critic, who takes a stand on contemporary issues and involves himself in matters of literary policy. He has no quarrel with the feuilleton.

The unity of literary history and literary criticism was an aspect of the model of reasoned literary history developed in the liberal tradition. An inner relationship existed between the interests of historians and those of critics: literary history was part of criticism, manifesting itself as political criticism. This was true even for conservative authors such as August Friedrich Vilmar, who emphatically opposed the political tendency of liberal historians, and who thereby succeeded only in confirming the political character of literary history: "For him [Gervinus], scholarship was a medium for politicization. The task of the scholar

[64]Wilhelm Scherer, *A History of German Literature*, trans. F. C. Conybeare (New York, 1901), 1:1.

was to put politics on a scholarly basis."[65] By the time of romanticism, literary history was not exclusively, indeed not even primarily, aimed at the academic public sphere but rather at a broader educated public. There was a striking discrepancy between the modest audiences at lectures on the history of literature and the number of literary histories published. These works were regarded as part of the topical literature by which the literary public sphere oriented itself. The institutionalization of literary history was by no means dependent on the discipline of German studies, which in any case in its early period was not defined exclusively as literary.

This difference is shown by the organization of the discipline. It is difficult to establish who held the first academic chair in literary history. Hans Joachim Kreutzer's reference to Prutz,[66] who became professor extraordinarius of literary history at Halle in 1849—a position, incidentally, from which he resigned after a few years—overlooks the fact that Gervinus's appointment included literary history and that Vischer had become a *Privatdozent* for aesthetics and German literature in 1835. Nevertheless, there is no denying that in the Vormärz the connection between the academic discipline and literary history continued to be loose. The most important works were written by men from other fields. By and large, the organization of German philology and medieval studies was completed earlier than that of more recent literary history, which because of its political orientation must have appeared suspect to the regional authorities. Even after 1848 the authors of two influential histories of literature, Schmidt and Gottschall, did not belong to university circles but as journalists were instead at the center of the literary public sphere.

Did this institutionalization of literary history, which took place between 1830 and 1848 under the influence of a political mandate (agreement among the literary public on the relationship between literary and political problems), change after the failure of the revolution? So says Karl-Heinz Götze, who has suggested that literary history lost its public importance soon after 1848. After describing Danzel's criticism of the literary history of the Vormärz, Götze observes: "The road that Danzel proposed for taking it out of the public sphere led to noncommitment and the isolation of the ivory tower, which offers an exit only to the right."[67] Without any doubt, German literary historiography even-

---

[65]Karl-Heinz Götze, "Die Entstehung der deutschen Literaturwissenschaft als Literaturgeschichte," in J. J. Müller, ed., *Germanistik und deutsche Nation, 1806–1848* (Stuttgart, 1974), p. 215.

[66]See Hans Joachim Kreuzer's postscript to Robert Eduard Prutz, *Geschichte des deutschen Journalismus* (1845; rpt. Göttingen, 1971), p. 430.

[67]Götze, "Die Entstehung," pp. 185–88, esp. 186.

tually shifted to the right; yet there can be no question of its public status having diminished between 1850 and 1870. Danzel's methodical criticism, which in fact led to a modification of the model, initially had no impact on the level of institutionalization. The literary history of the Nachmärz was closely connected with the literary public sphere. This situation was characterized by the relationship between literary history and the important literary journals. Schmidt edited the *Grenzboten* together with Freytag, Prutz was in charge of the *Deutsches Museum*, and Gottschall directed the *Blätter für literarische Unterhaltung*. Both Prutz and Schmidt used the opportunity to publish parts of their histories of literature in their journals. Indeed, one may go so far as to say that their histories were composed of collected journal articles. Prutz and Schmidt, who were active as critics by the 1840s, continued the tradition of journalistic literary history, although, as we have seen, they made significant changes in its content and methodology. Haym and the young Dilthey likewise remained in the public sphere. As the editor of the *Preussischen Jahrbücher*, Haym was much involved in the political battles of his time, taking strong positions on political issues. In his early writings even Dilthey, whose later works are more appropriately described as products of the ivory tower, worked in the journalistic tradition. He was a collaborator on the *Preussischen Jahrbücher* and on the popular periodical *Westermanns Monatsheften*. In 1867 he published in them, among other things, the first version of his essay on Hölderlin and an essay on Heine.[68]

In some respects, however, the position of the younger generation differed considerably from that of the older generation. The establishment of academic chairs in German literary history changed the prospects of young professionals. Scherer and Dilthey could as a result count on more accelerated academic careers. Scherer's rapid rise is paradigmatic. This Germanist, who was born in 1841 and initially encountered difficulties as a student of Karl Müllenhoff in Austria, became a *Privatdozent* in Vienna in 1866. By 1868, when he was twenty-seven, he was already a professor of German language and literature in Vienna. Not much later, in 1871, he accepted a call to the newly founded Reichsuniversität in Strassburg, where he taught until 1877. When he was thirty-six he was appointed to a prestigious chair in Berlin established expressly for him. Dilthey's professional career was equally dramatic. After receiving his degree in Berlin, he was called to Basel in 1867, but because of his pro-Prussian leanings he did not feel at home there. After only three semesters he left Switzerland and accepted

---

[68]Originally published under the pseudonyms Wilhelm Hoffner and Karl Elkan; reprinted in *Gesammelte Schriften*, 15:102–16, 205–44.

an appointment in Kiel. He taught there until he was called to Breslau in 1871. Finally, in 1882, he became Rudolf Lotze's successor in Berlin. If his career is compared with that of Haym (b. 1821), it becomes abundantly clear that the year 1848 was a watershed. Haym, who earned his doctoral degree in 1843 with a dissertation on Aeschylus, was at first unable to find an academic position. He was forced to earn his living as a collaborator and editor for Ersch and Gruber's encyclopedia. In 1851, after actively participating in the revolution as a right-center member of the Frankfurt National Assembly, he became a *Privatdozent* in Halle. Because he was regarded as a democrat, his conservative colleagues put obstacles in his path. He was not made professor extraordinarius until 1860 and was appointed ordinarius only in 1868. Thus the reactionary measures of the government were directed primarily against the older generation, which had been involved in politics in the 1840s. Gervinus's life after the revolution is typical. In 1853, following the publication of the introduction to his *Geschichte des neunzehnten Jahrhunderts* (History of the Nineteenth Century), he was accused of high treason by the government of Baden and, among other things, punished by withdrawal of the *venia legendi*. Only with great effort was he able to avoid prison.[69] Prutz had similar problems. In 1857, after a speech on Schiller which he gave in Leipzig, disciplinary action was brought against him at the University of Halle, and he was given a leave of absence.

These setbacks, as might be expected, occurred primarily between 1850 and 1858, whereas the rapid rise of the younger generation coincided, significantly, with the new era and the revival of liberalism. As we have shown, literary history still played a crucial ideological role in the preparation of the founding of the Reich. The institutional establishment of literary history at the universities, which may be regarded as secure with Scherer's appointment at Berlin in 1877, led successively— if not yet for Scherer himself—to a divorce from the literary public sphere and to a methodological and institutional separation from topical criticism (the feuilleton). Fontane's critical remarks on the literary value of German studies are characteristic; he maintained that they had no feeling for, or competence to judge, aesthetic and literary questions.[70] As a critic, he rejected all scholarly discourse on literature.

In contrast, Dilthey attained the position of leading theoretician in the arts. His work represents a genuine retreat from the general literary public sphere. The publication of his *Einleitung in die Geisteswissenschaft* (Introduction to the History of Ideas) in 1883 was certainly a

[69]On the trial, see Walter Boehlich, ed., *Der Hochverratsprozess gegen Gervinus* (Frankfurt a. M., 1967).
[70]In a review of Otto Brahm's work on Gottfried Keller (1883), in Theodor Fontane, *Aufsätze zur Literatur*, ed. Kurt Schreinert (Munich, 1963), pp. 262–71.

scholarly event of the first order, but just as certainly not a literary event, as had been the publication of Gervinus's and Schmidt's histories of literature. A common model held literary history and criticism together in the years between 1830 and 1870. For all their individual differences, critical and historical writings shared a language. Forms that later diverged into scholarship and the feuilleton were still presented by such writers as Gervinus, Prutz, Schmidt, Hettner, Gottschall, and Scherer as a unified discourse.

. 8 .

Education, Schools,
and Social Structure

The study of the institution of literature cannot be restricted to the analysis of literary production and reception. The broader field of investigation must include the relationship of literature to other institutions, especially those with which it interacts. In the nineteenth century, the institution of education, including elementary schools as well as secondary schools and universities, was obviously of crucial importance for the transmission of literature; first, because it regulated the reading material of students; second, because it determined the general educational goals and content that helped shape the concept of literature. The institution of education created underlying conditions that would have a lasting effect on a society with a differentiated system of education serving the majority of the population. Thus one cannot speak of the nature of literary relationships in Germany in the nineteenth century without thoroughly considering what the schools contributed to the appropriation and discussion of literature. Empirical studies of student reading habits, such as those carried out in research on reception, have, however, only limited value for historical investigations. There are two reasons for this: empirical-statistical procedures are not applicable to the past, and, probably more important, it is assumed in empirical investigations of contemporary situations that the basic framework— that is, the organization of the educational system and the general concept of the meaning of education—is commonly accepted. Yet this is precisely where historical investigation has to begin. It is not enough to determine which authors and works were included in the course of instruction in various types of schools. Nor is a study of the didactics of German instruction meaningful unless we have a clear understanding of the status of language and literary instruction in the school system—in other words, the concept of *Bildung* used by the institution of the school in the treatment of literature.

In the mid-nineteenth century great significance was placed on the word *education* (*Bildung*). Everyone claimed to know what the concept meant. The very currency of the expression, its popularity in public discussion, and above all the way it was introduced into social conflicts made it imprecise. The public talked of a theory of education exemplified by Humboldt, Schleiermacher, Johann Pestalozzi, and Adolf Diesterweg without realizing that this idealistic tradition had become problematic. Matters were treated one way on the level of theoretical discourse and a very different way in practice. Prussian law, for example, declared, as before, that the principles of individual education served as the standard for school regulation, whereas the administrative policy of the 1850s followed by Ferdinand Stiehl and Ludwig Wiese took a completely different view. The Prussian Ministry of Education and Culture (*Kultusministerium*) made decisive efforts to control the tendencies toward social change inherent in the idealistic theory of education so that they could be integrated with the conservative principles of the postrevolutionary Prussian state. Ministers of education Raumer and Heinrich von Mühler were helped in these attempts by the fact that state supervision of schools and universities had been so securely established as a result of early nineteenth-century educational reform that by means of legislation or administration, educational goals and content as well as the education of teachers could be controlled. Because of this tradition, the language of the Humboldt-Süvern reform ordinances could be appealed to without honoring the intentions of the reform. After 1848 the efforts of the bureaucracy to exert the greatest possible control over the educational system and to put it at the service of the state were successful in Prussia and other states. The state defined itself as nothing less than a *Kulturstaat*, which assumed the care of its subjects' intellectual and spiritual needs and at the same time satisfied its own need for qualified officials who had undergone prescribed courses of instruction. This in itself was a departure from the ideas of Humboldt and Schleiermacher, who had both acknowledged the responsibility of the state for the education of its citizens yet had not envisioned the goal of education as a training ground for qualified civil servants or, more generally, for specific careers. That these distinctions were not recognized even by well-intentioned observers indicates that the concept of education held in Prussia in the period of reform was no longer understood after 1850. Promoted by the Prussian administration—even before 1848—the concept of education had changed so much as to be diametrically opposed to the intentions of the reformers. Nietzsche was among the few who recognized this misunderstanding and raised objections to uncritical praise of the German educational system.

Nietzsche's Criticism of the Educational System

Nietzsche's criticism of education, as it was formulated in his lectures "Über die Zukunft unserer Bildungsanstalten" (On the Future of Our Educational Institutions) (1872), offers us a good opportunity to study the problems of postrevolutionary educational policy. Even Nietzsche in his criticism was unable to reconstruct adequately the intentions and content of Prussian educational reform from existing circumstances and to recover it as a guiding principle. The shift in emphasis is evident in Nietzsche's lectures, in the very way he makes the *Gymnasium* the center of the school system. The reformers—specifically, Humboldt— also wanted to reorganize the Prussian *Gymnasium*, but they had no intention of giving it special status. Rather, it was to be open to everyone, offering a national education, not one for a special class, as Eduard Spranger pointed out in 1910.[1] Admittedly, this concept remained a utopian plan and never became reality.[2] The success of the reforms depended on a compromise with the older tradition, which viewed the *Gymnasium* primarily as a place for the training of future scholars and higher government officials. The system of formal qualifications adopted from state administration by educational institutions undermined the idea of a general, noncareer-oriented education. As Karl-Ernst Jeismann in particular has shown, this check on the radical concept existed in the later years of the reform period and was not, therefore, the product of a postrevolutionary educational policy.[3] Most important, the idea that education was a unified process, that different types of schools should not be independent but rather interrelated, failed to find acceptance.[4] The need for career-preparatory institutions led to an increased recognition of modern secondary schools (*Realschulen*) no longer committed to the concept of classical education.

Nietzsche's attempt to rescue the concept of true education by returning to the idea of the humanistic *Gymnasium* was made under condi-

[1]Eduard Spranger, *Wilhelm von Humboldt und die Reform des Bildungswesens*, 3d ed. (Tübingen, 1965), pp. 133–45.

[2]On this, see Peter Uwe Hohendahl, "Reform als Utopie: Die preussische Bildungspolitik, 1809–1817," in Wilhelm Vosskamp, ed., *Utopieforschung* (Stuttgart, 1982), 3:250–72.

[3]Karl-Ernst Jeismann, *Das preussische Gymnasium in Staat und Gesellschaft* (Stuttgart, 1974), pp. 361–72 and 395–98.

[4]See Helmut Sienknecht, *Der Einheitsschulgedanke* (Weinheim, 1968), esp. pp. 41–78.

tions that had already departed considerably from the concept of the reformers. This is clear from his explicit separation of the concept of pure education from the interests of the state and society; indeed, he sees an irrevocable dichotomy between education and the state. According to Nietzsche, education had been fundamentally weakened by placing the *Gymnasium* at the service of the state, as both its expansion and its diminution in quality showed: "In keeping with the first tendency, education was to be disseminated in ever wider circles; in accordance with the second, education was expected to abandon its loftiest claims and to subordinate them to a different form of life, namely, that of the state."[5] To restore the idea of education, Nietzsche called for self-sufficiency, for detaching education from the needs of the state and the wishes of society. It was to be confined exclusively to what, in Nietzsche's view, was the core of *Gymnasium* education—humanistic studies connected with language instruction.

In his lectures, Nietzsche outlined a continuous contrast between the debased education of the present and the true education of a relatively undefined earlier epoch. According to this schema, German schools had forgotten the idea of true education they once represented. Only a revival of this idea could save the German educational system from ultimate corruption. Since Nietzsche's polemic against the abuses of the present is the focal point of his lectures, they are treated in greater detail than the idea against which they are measured. But the emphasis in Nietzsche's criticism can be understood only if we reconstruct his basic concepts. His polemic is directed against mixing the realms of state and culture, in which he includes pedagogy; in the final analysis, it is directed against the politicization of education through state interference. Nietzsche regarded the widespread belief that a successful state policy is beneficial to culture as a fundamental error. State organization of the educational system had led instead to barbarism, because the spirit had been offered up to material interests: "Men are allowed only the precise amount of culture which is compatible with the interests of gain; but that amount, at least, is expected from them. In short: mankind has a necessary right to happiness on earth—that is why culture is necessary—but on that account alone."[6] A state that follows this principle of useful preparation for a living—that is, for a profession—and accordingly provides a differentiated education, promotes barbarism: "The most general form of culture is simply barbarism."[7] Nietzsche's

[5]Friedrich Nietzsche, *Gesammelte Werke*, ed. Richard Oehler, Max Oehler, and Friedrich Chr. Würzback, (Munich, 1921), 4:7.
[6]*The Complete Works of Friedrich Nietzsche*, ed. Oscar Levy (New York, 1964), vol. 3: *The Future of Our Educational Institutions*, trans. J. M. Kennedy, p. 37.
[7]Ibid., p. 38.

opposition to the democratization of education derives from this objection to pragmatic, usable training. True education, he maintains in opposition to the alleged policy of the state, can only be for the few, for those who have enough time to concentrate on what is essential for the spiritual development of the individual. Thus the *Gymnasium* in fact assumes a special position for Nietzsche: it is entrusted with universal cultivation, which does not provide for a specific career.

Nietzsche's criticism went far beyond contemporary complaints that the *Gymnasien* were overcrowded and that attendence in them should be restricted to those requiring a scholarly education for future careers. Nietzsche was opposed to viewing the *Gymnasium* as a school for scholars, because a learned person trained as a doctor, historian, theologian, or mathematician was no closer to true education than one who had to earn a living as a laborer or shopkeeper. To rescue the concept of education, Nietzsche once again differentiated between scholarship and education, in which the former was assigned the task of transmitting specialized knowledge and the latter that of providing insight into the whole. Thus, as soon as the *Gymnasium* curriculum took the needs of future scholars and learned people into account, it necessarily departed from the methods and content that made for education in the emphatic sense. Nietzsche demonstrates this not least by the changes that had occurred in Greek and Latin instruction. The rapprochement with antiquity, which the German idealists had regarded as the attainment of true humanity, had degenerated into routine language instruction that no longer made reading of the classical authors useful. Philologists and historians who made instruction scholarly by carrying the methods of the university into the schools, Nietzsche argued, reduced the process of education to the transmission of information.

In his lectures Nietzsche sought to go beyond discussion of the contemporary curriculum. State-approved educational goals, syllabi, didactic methods, and the training given to teachers were all merely symptoms of a fundamental failure of the modern educational system, which, under the control of the state, was oriented toward material and professional needs. Education had become a function of the state and society. But Nietzsche denied this function; he wished to free the concept of education by returning to the idealistic tradition and to nullify the influence of the state. But his lectures do not make clear how this can be realized in organizational terms, because he offers no alternative to state schools. His irritation with existing conditions nevertheless prompted him to develop a concept of education based on the neo-humanism of Goethe's time. True education could be achieved only when human needs and existential cares were no longer a concern. In Nietzsche's view, interests and education were mutually exclusive: "I will thus ask you, my friend, not to confound this culture, this sensitive, fastidious, ethereal goddess, with that useful maid-of-all-work which is also called 'culture,' but which is only the intellectual servant and counsellor of one's practical necessities, wants, and means of livelihood." The locus of true education, in contrast, is contemplation. By this Nietzsche did not only mean withdrawal from the daily routine based on division of labor in modern industrial societies. His defense of an intellectual aristocracy certainly includes this component—his hatred of democratization in education because it delivers the *Geist* into the hands of the masses—but there is more to his wish for a purely contemplative attitude; he believed in the possibility of a changed attitude toward nature, a response no longer characterized by alienation. To contemplate meant to be at one with nature in a way that prevailing reason could no longer be: "What is lost by this new point of view is not only a poetical phantasmagoria, but the instinctive, true, and unique point of view, instead of which we have shrewd and clever calculations, and, so to speak, overreachings of nature." The rapprochement with antiquity—transmitted, to be sure, through German classicism—served to provide access to the aesthetic realm, which remained aloof from social praxis. Nietzsche completely accepted the formalism of the neo-humanistic concept of education, for he saw strict linguistic exercises as a purification and preparation for the aesthetic realm. It must be said, however, that he misunderstood this formalism, because he no longer saw, or wished to acknowledge, its relationship to social praxis. For Nietzsche, social praxis had been taken over to ill effect by a state educational policy aimed at the dissemination of useful knowledge. Although he rightly criticized the emptiness of the neohumanism in the schools of the Nachmärz and recognized the "'universal development of free personality upon a firm social, national, and human basis'" as an ideology behind which solid social interests were concealed, he did not develop the alternative plan, which was supposed to restore the old humanistic ideal of education, in equally concrete terms. The cultural community that Nietzsche envisioned without defining its organization in detail was restricted to the small circle of those who were prepared to wait for the birth of "men of genius . . . and the creation of the works of genius."[8]

When Nietzsche uses a historical example—specifically, the student associations of the Wars of Independence—to describe what he understands as true education and its effect, it becomes clear that he ultimately means more by the restoration of education than aesthetic receptivity, namely, the inner renewal and stimulation of "the purest moral

[8]Ibid., pp. 94–95, 96, 112, 113.

faculties."[9] Yet even in his evocation of the period of reform in Prussia, his distance from the neohumanist idea of education cannot be overlooked, for the characteristic he prizes most in the members of student organizations is their submissiveness and obedience. For Nietzsche, development of the full powers of the individual is nothing more than an ideology, a concept corrupted by the state. This is why he tends to connect true education with an intellectual aristocracy. Such ideas should not, however, be misunderstood as support for existing conditions, for his criticism of the contemporary concept of education includes the *Gymnasium*. Only a future institution can be expected to save education. Thus this comment from the notes for his lectures: "*Equal instruction* for all until age fifteen. Because predestination for the *Gymnasium* by parents etc. is an injustice."[10] In the same context Nietzsche speaks in favor of a comprehensive school on which technical colleges can then build. This idea transcends the organization of various types of schools according to class, which was widely defended in state educational policy of the nineteenth century; an educational utopia emerges, one based on neohumanism but with no chance of being put into practice.

Nietzsche continued his criticism in his *Unzeitgemässe Betrachtungen*, most notably in his essay against David Friedrich Strauss, who represented a moderate educational liberalism. In it he described what disturbed him about his own time: the pseudoculture of shallow journalism, which conceived of culture as the "possession" of intellectual goods. Strauss's recommendation in the appendix to his book *Der alte und der neue Glaube* (1872) that readers should rely on the German classicists as their guides and counselors—substitutes for the lost Christian religion—was regarded by Nietzsche simply as a misuse of tradition by a cultural philistine. In fact, the establishment of a literary tradition in the fifties and sixties reinforced the notion of a sharply defined national culture that could be drawn upon at any future time: "We have our culture, say our sons; for have we not our 'classics'? Not only is the foundation there, but the building already stands upon it— we ourselves constitute that building."[11] The choice of authors prescribed in secondary school curricula corroborates Nietzsche's critical judgment. The core of German instruction was the "classicists," from whom students were to gain understanding of their cultural heritage. For Nietzsche, instead, studying the literary heritage did not mean ac-

---

[9]Ibid., p. 139.
[10]Nietzsche, *Gesammelte Werke*, 4:122.
[11]*The Complete Works of Friedrich Nietzsche*, 4: *Thoughts Out of Season*, pt. 1, trans. Anthony M. Ludovici, p. 14.

cepting it passively but continuing the work begun by the great German authors.

Neohumanistic Educational Reform

Nietzsche's discussion of the contemporary concept of education brings us back to the period between 1809 and 1817, when educational institutions took on the form they were to retain until the twentieth century. Proponents of the Nachmärz theory of education were, of course, not unaware of the relationship between the two. Generally speaking, they legitimized their own efforts by referring to the earlier reforms. The distinctiveness and direction of educational policy between 1850 and the founding of the Reich resulted from both the tension between the educational theory of the reform period and the conservative interpretation of it by the postrevolutionary government.[12] The policy of the fifties and sixties, especially with respect to the *Gymnasium*, was understood as a continuation of the great tradition, which, however, was now restricted to the schools alone. That this educational reform had once been regarded as an aspect of social reform, that educational reform, to be more precise, had been intended to change the corporate society of Prussia into a modern state, was no longer apparent in postrevolutionary discourse. The utopian element in this educational reform must be emphasized in order to clarify the extent to which the restorative educational policy and theory diminished the original aim.

In the early liberal theory of education—this is true especially for that of the young Humboldt—participation of the state in the educational process was by no means assured. On the contrary, in Humboldt's "Ideen zu einem Versuch, die Gränzen der Wirksamkeit des Staats zu bestimmen" (Ideas for an Attempt to Establish the Boundaries of the State's Effectiveness), the state was not assigned an essential role in the educational system; its responsibility was limited to providing conditions for individual self-fulfillment. Where the ultimate purpose of the individual was concerned—that is, the "integral development of his powers into a whole"[13]—the state had no place. State education, Humboldt argued, results in one-sidedness; it limits instruction to specific,

[12]On this, see Sienknecht, *Der Einheitsschulgedanke*, pp. 123–47; Andreas Flitner, *Die politische Erziehung in Deutschland* (Tübingen, 1957), pp. 165–79; and Hartmut Titze, *Die Politisierung der Erziehung* (Frankfurt a. M., 1973), pp. 197–218.

[13]Wilhelm Freiherr von Humboldt, *Werke*, ed. Andreas Flitner and Klaus Giel, vol. 1 (Darmstadt, 1960), p. 64.

definite points of view and neglects the diversity of human possibility. In his early works Humboldt assigned education primarily to the private sphere; it alone could further individual development, for the state was chiefly concerned with promoting the qualifications necessary for civic duty.

We know that Humboldt changed his mind after the Prussian defeat and supported the reform of state education; occasionally he even brought the power of the state to bear against corporate forces in order to carry out his reforms.[14] Nevertheless, his concept of education remained fundamentally unchanged. As head of the Department of Culture and Public Education, he sought to put his idea of a "human education" into practice by means of a plan of state-supported reorganization. According to him, a person should not be regarded as a static combination of particular capabilities and skills but should be understood as a dynamic force expressing itself and developing through free activity. This conviction assumes importance in Humboldt's work because it shifts emphasis from specific, given content and norms to the educational process, which allows the individual to develop versatility. Humboldt speaks of the "energy that is the source, as it were, of all active virtue and the necessary prerequisite for a higher and more versatile development."[15] In Humboldt's view, the state has no interest in this energy; instead, it imposes certain ideas and laws on the individual, creating uniformity but not developing the inner form.

The basis of Humboldt's reform was a comprehensive curriculum that would serve all citizens. Schools were to offer a general, formal education not restricted to the transmission of specialized knowledge and skills. The organizational problem Humboldt faced concerned the existing intermediate schools (*Mittelschulen*) and higher elementary schools for the middle class (*Bürgerschulen*), which did not prepare students for the university. In his Königsberg plan, Humboldt flatly opposed the intermediate schools: "Separation of the middle from the learned classes in two different institutions plainly disturbs the necessary unity of instruction which, in the choice of educational subjects, methods, and treatment of students, must have such uninterrupted continuity, from the moment a child grasps the basic rudiments until the time school instruction ends, that students will be prepared for class after class and semester after semester." In the philosophical view to which Humboldt appeals, there are only three stages of instruction: primary, secondary, and university instruction. Every child must pass

---

[14]See Eduard Spranger, *Wilhelm von Humboldt und die Reform des Bildungswesens,* pp. 69–132; Ursula Krautkrämer, *Staat und Erziehung* (Munich, 1979), pp. 29–54.
[15]Humboldt, *Werke,* 1:61–62.

through these logical stages of education, ideally without concern for the particular social tasks each will later have to undertake. Humboldt was clearly striving for a comprehensive school, but not one according to our definition of the term, that is, a school where different educational curricula are offered side by side. Education was to be "comprehensive," in the sense that schools would be organized in such a way as to hold the logical areas of education organically together. For the same reason, Humboldt wanted educational content to be so defined that students' powers would be challenged in every type of school. Thus he demanded that "all knowledge that advances them only slightly or too one-sidedly should be excluded from school instruction no matter how essential it might be, and specialization should be reserved for life."[16]

Humboldt was certainly aware of the political implications of his reform plans. By interfering with the class structure of the school system, he touched a sensitive nerve. He did not want elementary schools (*Volksschulen*) open only to the lower classes and those with low income. Educational quality would no longer depend on parents' social position: "Let everyone, even the poorest, receive a complete human education; let everyone without exception receive a complete education, limited only in the respect that it could lead to still further development; let every kind of intellectual individuality find its rightful place; let no one be forced to reach a decision earlier than his gradual development requires."[17] The Lithuanian school plan also reemphasized the principle of a general education that would be separate from the career preparation offered, for example, by the *Realschulen* in Bavaria. Humboldt even went so far as to recommend instruction in Greek for future carpenters. In other words, his support for instruction in the classical languages was not intended to benefit the professional interests of the intelligentsia but was based on the general educational value of language instruction; and Greek was again singled out as having particular merit.

Prussian educational reform should not be tied exclusively to Humboldt, however, as has occasionally been done since Eduard Spranger's investigations. In his work in the ministry Humboldt expanded on existing trends and earlier accomplishments. Moreover, he made use of existing pedagogical plans. The reform movement proved considerably more widespread than conventional description of it suggests. Besides Humboldt, Fichte, Schleiermacher, Franz Passow, Reinhold Jachmann, Wilhelm Süvern, and Schulze come to mind, even though their plans and concepts were very different. What they shared was their opposi-

[16]Ibid., 4:168, 172.
[17]Ibid., 4:175.

tion to adapting the school system to existing society. Because it was abstract, the idea of a general human education formed the start of a radical reorganization, not only of the educational system but of the structure of society. The goal of the various plans for reorganizing the school system was a general education for the *Volk* as a whole which would allow pupils to become citizens who would participate in the organization of society. Reform, therefore, cannot be related solely to the *Gymnasium* or university; the reorganization of the higher schools was only part of a comprehensive reform of the educational system.

Even before Humboldt entered the Ministry of Education and Culture, Fichte had responded to the emergency in Prussia, in his *Reden an die deutsche Nation*, by provocatively emphasizing the political function of education.[18] For Fichte, the renewal of Prussia was not so much a matter of diplomacy and military strength as one of inner renewal, of exposing and overcoming moral weakness. The new nation envisioned by Fichte would no longer be created by the power of a monarch uniting the people under a bond of subservience but as the result of a general education that would be available to all elements of the population. This inevitably led Fichte to demand that traditional boundaries between the *Volksschule* and the *Gymnasium* be dissolved, indeed to his rejecting the very idea of usefulness as an educational goal. Nationality, in Jeismann's apt formulation, is "merely another word for political and social equality."[19] To this extent, the manner in which Fichte puts the state at the service of education is comparable to Humboldt's early position; for Fichte, too, was not interested in turning over control to an absolutist state. His objective in his *Reden* was to create a new state through national education, in which political responsibility would be assured. Not much later, in the *Archiv deutscher Nationalbildung*, Jachmann introduced Fichte's idea into educational theory in a more radical form.[20] Following Kant, Jachmann made schools the locus of a pure human education that would later exert an ennobling influence on the state. Once again, the state was not the *point of departure* but rather the *goal* of these deliberations—a goal that could be attained only through reform of the educational system. The material interests of the state and the emancipatory interests of human beings had to be reconciled, but in such a way that the state would adjust to the new ideal of education. Significantly, Jachmann did not

---

[18] On Fichte, see Krautkrämer, *Staat und Erziehung*, pp. 120–81; and Jeismann, *Das preussische Gymnasium in Staat und Gesellschaft*, pp. 224–30.

[19] Jeismann, *Das preussische Gymnasium*, p. 227.

[20] On Jachmann, see Heinz-Joachim Heydorn's instructive introduction to the reprint of Reinhold Bernh. Jachmann and Franz Passow, eds., *Archiv deutscher Nationalbildung* (Frankfurt a. M., 1969).

equate the idea of national education with the needs of Prussia; rather, for him Germany is the comprehensive whole into which the various territorial states have to be dissolved.

The new concept of education conflicted with a school organization oriented toward the interests of a corporate society. It was directed against a system in which each class and group received a separate education preparing its members for their legitimate place in society. This moral and political incentive should be kept in mind when examining the reform of education; it was not a matter of intraschool organization. Modernization of the educational system, which promised to make schools and universities more effective, was in the interest of broader political and social goals. As Hartmut Titze has aptly put it, it was the "self-overcoming of absolutism by legal means."[21] Its revolutionary character was recognized even by such opponents as Metternich. Thus the dismantling of the reform movement after 1817 was closely connected with the conservative turn of Prussian and German politics.

The reform movement was accepted only in part. With the restructuring of the Prussian educational system between 1809 and 1818, Humboldt's and Süvern's goals tended to be realized more often on the university and *Gymnasium* level than in elementary education. The new curricula for *Gymnasien* came closest to Humboldt's idea of a formal education that does not take professional praxis into account. After Humboldt's resignation from the ministry, Süvern continued his work as head of the department.[22] In the classical humanistic *Gymnasium* priority was given to Latin and Greek as an intensive introduction to the structure of language and, to a lesser degree, to the ancient monuments of literature. For Humboldt, language instruction held out the hope that art and literature would become more accessible to students: "The whole field of ideas, everything that concerns the human being first and foremost, the very thing on which beauty and art depend, enters the mind solely through the study of language, the source of all thought and feeling."[23]

The Prussian bureaucracy did not implement the reform plans in their entirety. This was mainly because after 1817 the reform movement began to stagnate. From the start, however, those in power around Karl August von Hardenberg kept away from the neohumanistic programs. Humboldt's successor had already carried out reform more in the spirit

[21] Titze, *Die Politisierung der Erziehung*, p. 99.
[22] Süvern's plan, which could no longer be implemented, is reprinted in Gerhardt Giese, *Quellen zur deutschen Schulgeschichte seit 1800* (Göttingen, 1961), pp. 93–109.
[23] Letter to Caroline von Humboldt, in Anna von Sydow, ed., *Wilhelm und Caroline von Humboldt in ihren Briefen* (Berlin, 1909), 3:260.

of technical administrative continuity than from any philosophical conviction. Even the establishment of an independent Ministry of Education and Culture, headed in 1817 by Karl Altenstein, did not guarantee continuation of reform.[24] The decision to put elementary, middle-class (*Bürgerschulen*), and academic schools under separate authorities was particularly disadvantageous, for it reaffirmed the difference between basic schools and schools of higher learning which the reformers had tried to eliminate. This administrative decision worked precisely to the advantage of those interests favoring a clear separation by class between basic and advanced education. As soon as the *Gymnasium* could be differentiated from other schools—for instance, by employing teachers who were better paid because of their academic training—a hierarchy developed among teachers as well as students.

In contrast, one of the permanent results of reform was the right of the state to supervise the educational system as a whole. A significant tool for this purpose was the *Abituredikt* of 1812 establishing final school examinations, by which the state regulated access to the university. Unquestionably, such measures had a leveling effect on society. Their thrust was at first directed primarily against the private education received by the nobility. Subsequently, the leveling effect was confined to the educated bourgeoisie, which in this way was more strictly regulated and disciplined. For higher officials the edict was a good means of regulating the self-replenishment of the system. Thus the results in no sense agreed with the ideas of the neohumanists, whose aim was to destroy the rigidity of the old social system through education. The edict worked more to the advantage of the state than to that of its citizens, because it fostered the development of a group oriented toward and dependent on the state. The *Gymnasium* was in the process of becoming a school for a social elite whose qualifications were secured through education. The reformers supported the edict, however, because they hoped that stricter state supervision would result in greater control over the schools. The acceptance of the new distribution of departments and new educational content hinged, in their view, on the possibility of undertaking and securing the changes. Belief that progress in the educational system would be guaranteed by state measures presupposed that the state would have to identify with the neohumanist program—an illusion of the reformers.

It could be argued that the utopian excess of the educational reform, its ideal of a cultivated and responsible nation, was precisely what contributed in the following decades to widening rather than narrowing the separation between the educated and the *Volk*. The neohumanists'

[24]For details, see Jeismann, *Das preussische Gymnasium*, pp. 346–48.

concept of education, which was aimed at the development of the individual, and the organization of schools, which embodied the interests of the state, moved increasingly apart. This gap necessarily affected the concept of education. Even though the *topoi* of neohumanism were continued, their function had already changed by the twenties. These immanent, structural changes were reinforced by the growing conservatism of the Prussian government. Hardenberg and Altenstein saw the politicization of students after the Wars of Liberation as a threat to reform and sought to rescue what they could by disciplining the universities.[25] On the other side of the political spectrum, the conservative powers exploited student unrest in order to discredit the reformers and their ideas.

Conservative policy in the twenties and thirties, which was bent on checking all political movement, sought to eliminate the social implications of the reform movement wherever possible.[26] Only those aspects of reform which strengthened the overall position of the state were supported: general state supervision of the educational system and regulation of the qualifications that had made school education the formal prerequisite for civil service.[27] It should be emphasized, nevertheless, that even during the years of reaction, the progressive impetus of educational reform could not be entirely suppressed. It survived in pedagogical theory and didactic methodology. This was especially apparent in 1848, when the spirit of reform was revived among teachers.

Postrevolutionary Educational Policy

The Stiehl directives of 1854 demonstrate the extent to which the Prussian state felt threatened by teachers' demands and wishes. The Ministry of Education and Culture reacted to this threat with decrees restricting the educational goals of the *Volksschulen* in order to prevent any adverse influence on political life. Wilhelm IV had already made it clear in 1849, in an address to teachers of education, that he held the concept of education favored by the liberal teachers' colleges of the Vormärz largely responsible for the revolution: "The misery that has descended on Prussia in the past year is your fault, yours alone, the fault of the pseudoeducation, the irreligious human wisdom that you dis-

---

[25]See Titze, *Die Politizierung der Erziehung*, pp. 106–8.

[26]The edict of June 28, 1826, on religious education was significant for the spirit of restoration. See Giese, *Quellen zur deutschen Schulgeschichte*, pp. 115–16.

[27]E.g., establishment of the curriculum by the *Circular-Rescript* of October 24, 1837, and the regulations of June 4, 1834, for the *Abitur* examination. See Giese, *Quellen zur deutschen Schulgeschichte*, pp. 117–27.

seminate as true wisdom, with which you have destroyed the faith and loyalty in the minds of my subjects and turned their hearts against me." Ferdinand Stiehl (formerly director of the *Lehrerseminar* in Neuwied), who had entered the Ministry of Education and Culture in 1844 under Johann Eichhorn, was appointed by Raumer in 1850 as consultant for *Volksschulen* and colleges of education. In this capacity he put the new educational and school policy of Prussia firmly into place by means of three directives. They are more than instructions for reorganizing elementary schools and teachers' education. Their core is a polemic against the neohumanistic idea of education, which is rejected as pointless, even harmful: "Experience has shown that the idea of a general human education based on the formal development of intellectual capacity through abstract content is ineffectual or harmful." At the same time, his directives formulate a positive educational policy that must be understood as an answer to neohumanistic theory: "*The life of the Volk needs to be fundamentally reconstructed by developing its originally given, eternal realities on a foundation of Christianity*, which in its ecclesiastically authorized form will permeate, develop, and support family, profession, community, and state." If the neohumanist reformers intended to take even the elementary schools out of direct, pragmatic relation to society and to use them to develop human powers, the October directive did the opposite, appealing to the practical needs of contemporary society. The *Volksschule* was to serve society by preparing pupils for their individual roles. The directive explicitly criticized formal theories of education and called for a "firm restriction of instructional material" in order to promote a content-oriented education.[28] Curricula did not necessarily need to be restructured, but the weight given different subjects and the time allotted them had to be changed so that the Christian concept of education could be fostered. Instruction in the *Volksschule* would now be limited to four basic areas: religion; reading, writing, and the German language; arithmetic; and singing. This deliberate restriction of education, which had the unmistakable aim of confining pupils to a conservative way of thinking, applied not only to elementary schools but to the education of teachers, whom the conservative forces accused of having acted against the interests of the state. The same principle applied to students in education as to pupils in lower grades: no formal education—that is, no encouragement of thinking but rather a confinement to that material the teachers would later present to their pupils. The first directive thus eliminated

---

[28]Quoted in Berthold Michael and Heinz-Hermann Schepp, eds., *Politik und Schule von der Französischen Revolution bis zur Gegenwart*, vol. 1 (Frankfurt a. M., 1973), pp. 313, 315–16.

the subjects of pedagogy, anthropology, methodology, and psychology, as well as didactics and catechetics.[29] These were replaced by a general, content-oriented study of education centered on the Bible. The injunction to instill Christian humility also contains the basic principle of the new pedagogy: to establish a connection between learning and obedience, both in the relationship between pupils and teachers and in that between teachers and the authorities. The restriction of teachers' training to essentials—mainly to knowledge of the Bible—would assure a mechanical transmission of knowledge posing no danger for the political status quo. A curious consequence of this school policy was that students in education were kept away from classic German literature. Even private reading of Lessing, Schiller, and Goethe was forbidden.[30] These massive attacks on the freedom of future teachers show that not only the pedagogical component of the liberal concept of education was called into question but the very concept itself. If the liberals were convinced that the classic authors had paved the way for political emancipation—even if inadequately—the suppression of those authors was unmistakable evidence that the Ministry of Education and Culture wanted to suppress this relationship between classic literature and politics. The desired process of disciplining the masses was begun, logically, in the one place the state, supported by the church, could intervene most directly: in the *Volksschulen*, which everyone had to attend. State supervision of schools, which had been pushed through by reformers two generations earlier, now worked to the advantage of the conservative forces in the Prussian Ministry of Education and Culture.

In the long run, however, the position of the ministry proved contradictory. To begin with, the Industrial Revolution made it impossible to sustain the restriction of education to elementary knowledge for very long; commerce and industry required specific qualifications.[31] Moreover, the bureaucracy still had to take into account the liberal Prussian tradition of education, which left its mark even on the imposed and revised constitution. Articles 21 to 26 created a framework for the educational system to which the special legislation anticipated in article 26 would have to be adapted. Prevailing interpretation in the field of national law was that the ordinances of the Ministry of Education and Culture had to conform to the articles of the constitution, even though, as we have seen, this was not always the actual case.

In accordance with paragraph 152 of the 1849 constitution of the

[29]See Giese, *Quellen zur deutschen Schulgeschichte*, p. 147.
[30]See Titze, *Die Politizierung der Erziehung*, p. 195.
[31]For instance, by Friedrich Harkort in his speeches in the Prussian Parliament. See Harkort, *Schriften und Reden zur Volksschule und Volksbildung*, ed. Karl-Ernst Jeismann (Paderborn, 1969), pp. 110–21.

Reich, article 20 explicitly affirmed the freedom of scholarship and its teaching. Interference with teaching on the university level was permitted only if definite abuse of this freedom could be established. It was typical of the postrevolutionary situation, however, that even during discussion of the article there was loud opposition to its adoption or insistence that certain specified restrictions be clarified in a codicil. It became evident during these discussions that the state was by no means willing to surrender or restrict its right of supervision. Thus it argued: "In this statement the government meant only to say, and could only say: it desires scholarship to be free insofar as that is compatible with the state's objectives."[32] But the school system was expressly excepted from this basic principle; article 20 was suspended until a law could be passed governing instruction. In other words, it was virtually left up to the bureaucracy to regulate practices by ordinances. Because no law governing instruction had been passed by the end of Bismarck's Reich, the conditions prevailing before the constitution went into effect remained basically unchanged throughout the century.[33] On the whole, articles 21 to 25 consolidated the general position of the state in the educational system, and divergent views were fundamentally excluded. It was not the liberal model, as it was formulated, say, in the Belgian constitution, which was adopted but a structure based on Prussian tradition, in which the state assumed management and direction of the entire educational system. Schools were thus basically incorporated into the domain of the state, and the liberal demand for separation of school and state, occasionally voiced in revolutionary teachers' associations, was expressly rejected.[34] This was the case not only in article 21, which established state responsibility for the public education of the young, but above all in article 23, which subjected even private schools to state supervision.

We thus see a state that may be characterized, beyond its police and legal duties (security, for instance), as a creator and supporter of culture, one that satisfies the needs of society—quite to its own advantage as well, because as Minister of Education Ladenberg remarked, through state supervision this instruction educates the nation in such a way as to protect and support the state: "If you take away the state's influence over instruction, it will soon cease to exist altogether."[35] Articles 21 and 23 complement each other: the one defines the state's responsibility

[32]See Gerhard Anschütz, *Die Verfassungs-Urkunde für den preussischen Staat* (Berlin, 1912), pp. 370, 369.
[33]On the plans, see Helga Romberg, *Staat und höhere Schule* (Weinheim, 1979), pp. 75–89.
[34]But even in the Prussian teachers' associations there was a tendency in 1848 to assign responsibility for education to the state. See Giese, *Quellen zur deutschen Schulgeschichte*, p. 133.
[35]Quoted in Romberg, *Staat und Höhere Schule*, p. 74.

for providing enough public schools, the other establishes the state's superintendence of the educational institutions it provides. A private educational system could not satisfy the needs of society as a whole, it was assumed, because it catered to special interests and hence took only special needs into account.

Ladenberg's school bill of 1850 pursued this idea by emphasizing equality of opportunity in education. To achieve a balance between the educated elite and the propertied classes, it established scholarships for needy students at higher schools of learning. In this regard, Bethmann Hollweg's 1862 bill went a step farther: from paragraph 1 of article 21 he derived a general state responsibility for education, for both lower and higher schools. This responsibility would not be subject to enforcement. Nevertheless, within limits his proposal was in the liberal tradition of school policy. It was limited to the extent that the *Gymnasien* were no longer to be organized and maintained for the purpose of instilling a general human culture; rather, they were to ensure development of the administrative elite needed by the state. This is evident in the commentary on paragraph 122: "The aim of the *Gymnasien* is based on the idea of a spiritual education capable of contributing to the fulfillment of the highest duties of state and church."[36] The bill thus gave the state the right to control the educational goals as well as the "pedagogical efficacy" of the higher schools. Education was acknowledged to have an important influence on public life, and for this very reason state supervision was considered mandatory: "The interests of the state and of public life play a major part in the basic ethical, religious, political, and patriotic perceptions and trends pursued in institutions that educate the nation's elite."[37] The unmistakable intention once again was to check the ability of education to effect change by having the state set educational goals. In any case, state and social interests were not to be separated. In the view of the Ministry of Education and Culture, harmony between them was best achieved in a school system hierarchically organized. Postrevolutionary liberal theory did not depart very far from this point of view.

The State and Education

The relationship between the state and education in postrevolutionary theory needs to be examined more closely. In this theory the state—

---

[36]A. W. Friedrich Stiehl, ed., *Die Gesetzgebung auf dem Gebiete des Unterrichtswesens in Preussen vom Jahre 1817 bis 1868* (Berlin, 1869), p. 257.

[37]On the reasons for the bill, see ibid., p. 226.

which now no longer meant Prussia alone—was held to be a *Kulturstaat*, one that took into account and promoted the cultural aspirations of its citizens. In its formulation of this task, Nachmärz theory followed the basic precepts of early liberalism. In the narrower sense, a *Kulturstaat* was one that supported scholarship, art, and religion, establishing a special bureaucratic organization for this purpose. Liberal theory saw interference by churches and other private organizations as a possible threat to these functions, but as a rule it did not formulate specific safeguards against the dangers of state intervention. The autonomy of culture and education demanded by the young Nietzsche was foreign to the liberal theory of the Nachmärz; first, because it endorsed existing conditions, but also because it expected state government to represent general interests more fairly than did corporations and individuals.[38]

This relationship is exemplified in Hermann von Schulze-Gaevernitz's *Das preussische Staatsrecht*. His definition of culture is unmistakably in the tradition of Humboldt and Schleiermacher: "The highest goal of mankind is the perfection of *all* the powers of the spirit. The highest task of a moral-religious education should be to unite the intellectual development of our mental faculties with the aesthetic development of taste. The total yield from an individual's work for these goals is what we call *Bildung* in the highest sense of the word." Although achievement of *Bildung* is the result of individual actions, the process of education, as Schulze-Gaevernitz, a constitutional lawyer, emphasizes, is carried out in the community. The state, as the representative of the community, assumed a "mission in world history" when it took over the entire educational system of Prussia. In Schulze-Gaevernitz's view, this decision presented the *Kulturstaat* with three tasks to undertake in "the administration of intellectual life": "*First*, it [the government] provides, through laws, institutions, and arrangements of all kinds, for the instruction and education of youth; *second*, it seeks to educate the *entire* population, to raise and ennoble even adults; and *third*, it tries to protect the people from threats to public morality presented by outbreaks of vice, brutality, and unrestrained sensuality." Schulze-Gaevernitz does not, however, interpret the responsibility for education and culture as an appeal for equality of educational opportunity; rather, he expects the state, in deciding what it will impart through its institutions, to adjust to the development and structure of society. The standard of education to be imparted will be determined by

---

[38]This attitude was already evident during the Revolution of 1848. The resolutions of teachers' conferences include numerous demands that the schools should be state institutions. See Giese, *Quellen zur deutschen Schulgeschichte*, pp. 131–33.

future professional tasks. Thus according to Schulze-Gaevernitz "the majority of the people must be content with this modest degree of knowledge, and in their simple circumstances they can make do with it," whereas higher education, apart from its general function of fostering scholarship, is directed primarily toward the needs of future high officials, "because the modern state cannot do without scientifically trained civil servents."[39] At this point, the author clearly departs from the neohumanistic concept of education and declares himself in favor of a career-oriented educational system designed to satisfy the needs of society. Thus he recommends *Realschulen* that will provide suitable training for the higher economic and professional classes.

Schulze-Gaevernitz represents the liberal position on the question of private instruction and denominational schools. On the issue of denomination, for example, he expressly follows the ideas of Heinrich Rudolf Gneist.[40] This does not, however, prevent him from declaring himself for the Christian *Volksschule* and against a separation of secular and religious education. He sees a need for an ethical Christian foundation, especially in the *Volksschule.* By this means, the moral goal of education will be set from the start and will no longer be a matter of discussion in the schools. Such an orientation will have to be reflected as well in the transmission of literature—in the selection of texts (the question of primers) and the form of their presentation.

In discussing the *Gymnasium*, Schulze-Gaevernitz typically does not do much more than review existing conditions; that is, he summarizes the results of Prussian educational reform. Interestingly, his review puts less emphasis on reform than on the increase in state supervision of scholarly qualifications. Thus he regards 1834, the year in which compulsory final examinations (the *Abitur*) were finally introduced, as the crucial date rather than 1809, because the *Abitur* afforded the state an instrument for regulating entrance to the university. In contrast, he banishes the idea of a humanistic education, which dominated theory at the beginning of the century and inspired reform, from school education; in constitutional law it is henceforth relegated to the paragraph on the state's responsibility for the general cultivation of the people. There it is explicitly stated—though without legal obligation—that as a *Kulturstaat* and "the bearer of the broadest human education," the modern state should embrace "the ideas of the true, the good, and the beautiful."[41]

The liberal educational theory of the Nachmärz was, typically, adapt-

[39]Hermann von Schulze-Gaevernitz, *Das preussische Staatsrecht*, 2d ed. (Leipzig, 1890), pp. 336–37, 339, 340, 341.
[40]Rudolf Gneist, *Die confessionelle Schule* (Berlin, 1869).
[41]Schulze-Gaevernitz, *Das preussische Staatsrecht*, p. 364.

ed to existing social conditions; in any case, the educational system was not expected to change. It was to be organized in such a way that the pupils' school background would correspond to their future status in life.[42] This correlation gave rise to the concept that a specific course of education and specific types of schools were appropriate for specific classes.[43]

The rejection in Nachmärz theory of the idea of a unified, comprehensive education encompassing all types of schools, its differentiation of the concept of education according to class and career, is blatantly evident in the control exercised over the *Volksschule*. The Stiehl directives, in force until 1872, reduced the educational goal of those attending *Volksschulen* to the point where they made intellectual and emotional growth impossible. Individuals were made to fit a particular mold and were not prepared for future, as yet unspecified, tasks and possibilities.[44] Stiehl's pedagogical arguments scarcely disguised the political aim of the directives. The institution of the school, firmly in the hands of the state, was to be a restorative means of deflecting the increasingly pressing social question of the political claims of the fourth estate. Existing inequality between classes was to be reaffirmed by differentiating the institutions of learning. A farsighted liberal educational theorist and pedagogue such as Adolf Diesterweg could readily see the hidden problem in these directives, and in his *Rheinische Blätter* he took Stiehl firmly to task.[45]

Education in the higher schools, meanwhile, was not unaffected by the curtailed concept of education in the *Volksschule*; there, too, a stronger class consciousness became apparent. It had never been decided whether the *Gymnasium* should provide only a general education or also prepare students for future careers. The gradual collapse of reform policy after 1820 strengthened the attitude that *Gymnasium* education was primarily a necessary qualification for higher civil service. The policy of the Ministry of Education and Culture as conducted by Ludwig Wiese after 1850 reinforced this belief.[46] Wiese tried to reestablish Christian humanism in the *Gymnasium*, regarding it as the core of higher education. The following comment on a potential reform of the curriculum is typical: "He [Raumer] would have preferred, as

[42]See Romberg, *Staat und höhere Schule*, p. 113.
[43]On this, see also Johann Caspar Bluntschli, *Allgemeines Staatsrecht*, 5th ed. (Stuttgart, 1876), p. 470–71, and Medicus in his article "Kulturpolizei," in J. C. Bluntschli and Karl Brater, eds., *Deutsches Staats-Wörterbuch* (Stuttgart, 1861), 6:149–62.
[44]See Karl-Ernst Jeismann, "Die 'Stiehlschen Regulative,'" in Rudolf Vierhaus and Manfred Botzenhart, eds., *Dauer und Wandel der Geschichte. Festgabe für Kurt von Raumer* (Münster, 1966), p. 439.
[45]Adolf Diesterweg, *Schriften und Reden*, ed. Heinrich Deiters (Berlin, 1950), 1:277–384.
[46]See Ludwig Wiese, *Lebenserinnerungen und Amtserfahrungen*, 2 vols. (Berlin, 1886).

would I, to return to the simple old curriculum limited to religious instruction, ancient languages, and mathematics, leaving further education, on this foundation, primarily to individual study; but who would have dared do this when the modern concept of culture, which centers on the diversity of our intellectual life, has long made it necessary for schools to have an encyclopedic character?"[47] His criticism of the modern concept of education shows that Wiese was an opponent of the practical education (*Realbildung*) arising from the needs of an industrial society but not necessarily a proponent of the neohumanistic tradition. It is no accident that he gives first place to religious instruction. His basic aim, had the minister of education been on his side, would have been to abolish the distinction between religious education in the *Volkschule* and that in the *Gymnasium*. As he made clear to Bethmann Hollweg, the minister of education, in 1861, he wanted to see a clearer relationship to the church even in the *Gymnasium*—that is, a renewed cooperation between church and state in the supervision of schools.

Christian humanism, as promoted by Ministers Raumer, Bethmann Hollweg, and Mühler, can be understood as an attempt to preserve the special status of the *Gymnasium* and thus to underscore its character as a school for the elite. At the same time, the emancipatory element in Humboldt's concept was to be neutralized by tying the goal of education firmly to religion. This shift was not even attempted in the *Realschule*; according to Wiese, its task was restricted to satisfying the needs of industry and trade. By and large, differentiation of the educational system—for instance, by making a distinction between first and second-class *Realschulen*—served to meet the need for specialization among professional groups; the classical *Gymnasium*, in contrast, retained its special status. This aim is unmistakably reflected in the reformed curriculum plans of 1856. They confirmed the priority of ancient languages in the *Gymnasium*, whereas in 1859 instruction in German and in the natural sciences was strengthened in the first-class *Realschulen*. German instruction was given even greater priority in the *Bürgerschulen*, where it played a central role together with the natural sciences.[48] The idea of qualification unquestionably reinforced the concept, typical of the late nineteenth century, that culture was an intellectual possession. Emphasis had shifted from the form and process of education to a specific content fixed by the school curriculum, familiarity with which showed a person to be "cultivated" and therefore also a member of a particular social group. Certain kinds of knowledge became an indication of whether one belonged among the "intellectuals."

Differentiation among classes in the concept of education can be

---

[47]Ibid., 1:184.
[48]See Ludwig Wiese, *Das höhere Schulwesen in Preussen* (Berlin, 1864), 1:27, 29.

traced even in contemporary didactics. In Raumer's *Geschichte der Pädagogik*, his treatment of German instruction frankly presupposes a class structure. About the *Volksschule* Raumer writes: "These are the schools in which peasants and craftsmen are educated; that is, those classes [*Stände*] which earn their livelihood chiefly by physical labor."[49]

The *Gymnasium*, on the other hand, was said "to provide the rudiments of a general higher education for our future clergymen, judges, and doctors." That this definition had little in common with the model of the reformers was brushed aside with the remark that this was the "true situation," which not even the neohumanists could change. Raumer drew the conclusion from this general distinction that German language and literature had to be approached in very different ways. Characteristically, and in complete conformity with the Stiehl directives, he limited German instruction in the *Volksschule* to reading and writing, not even mentioning the transmission of literature: "*Reading and writing*, the old elements of the *Volksschule*, are still its basis today, and any instruction in the German language not directed toward them is injurious to the *Volksschule*." Grammar was included in language instruction, because it aided correct speech and writing, but not the exercise in thinking in connection with language which Humboldt had in mind. Raumer made scarcely any attempt to disguise his class-conscious orientation: "We, on the other hand, are of the opinion that the good of these classes is best served if one spares them such stale scraps from the tables of the rich and tries earnestly to bring them to the point where they can read the High-German books intended for them and put down on paper reasonably well the things life requires of them." This "realistic attitude," which warned against excessive education, implied a particular concept of the *Volk* without explicitly defining it. Raumer referred to conditions in the eighteenth and early nineteenth century, to a preindustrial order with a hierarchical structure. The *Volk* was seen as naive; hence, any educational content that might disturb this naivete was rejected. A reflective appropriation of literature thus had to be rejected as well. Raumer's few remarks about the purpose of textbooks show that although he wanted texts that disseminated basic knowledge, he would also have liked to include writings that "would awaken and preserve a poetic sense in the *Volk*."[50] His object seems to have been not literature but—like biblical texts and verses in hymnals—a means of *edification*.

[49]Karl von Raumer, *Geschichte der Pädagogik*, pt. 3, 6th ed. (Gütersloh, 1897), p. 187.
[50]Ibid., pp. 208, 189, 188–89, 191.

· 9 ·

Culture for the People

"The purity of bourgeois art," Horkheimer and Adorno argue in *Dialectic of Enlightenment*, "which hypostatized itself as a world of freedom in contrast to what was happening in the material world, was from the beginning bought with the exclusion of the lower classes—with whose cause, the real universality, art keeps faith precisely by its freedom from the ends of the false universality."[1] This statement is a concise formulation of the dichotomy between the culture industry—which gave the masses the feeling that they were participating in authentic culture while at the same time it sought to control them—and the culture of a bourgeois elite legitimized through an autonomous art. Adorno and Horkheimer agreed that this contrast existed from the start—that is, since the end of the eighteenth century—and that it was necessary and therefore could not be reversed. Critical Theory is not intent on justifying the dominant middle class through the concept of autonomous art. It is rather the reverse: the concept of autonomy, which sets art apart from social praxis, and the logic of the aesthetic evolution leading up to the avant-garde make this dichotomy unresolvable. The "culture industry" of the twentieth century is thus the historical result of a cultural process of differentiation which began in the eighteenth century and whose logic unfolded at the expense of the oppressed class.

This perspective, however, fails to do justice to historical development in the nineteenth century. In *Dialectic of Enlightenment*, it assumes an inevitability that in reality was not so unequivocal. Even if one

---

[1]Max Horkheimer and Theodor W. Adorno, *Dialectic of Enlightenment*, trans. John Cumming (New York, 1972), p. 135.

agreed with Adorno and Horkheimer that the democratization of social and especially political institutions had failed, and with it the participation of the lower classes in traditional culture, one would have to investigate the historical reasons for this failure more carefully than could Adorno and Horkheimer. For there was no lack of effort on the part of either the bourgeoisie or the proletariat to overcome this cultural dichotomy. There were, of course, always strategic arguments contesting the possibility of a general culture for all classes and insisting that culture could only be grounded in a specific, definite stratum or class. For a premodern society this argument was self-evident, because it lacked the very concept of universality that Adorno's theory presupposes. But the argument had already acquired a different status in the conservative apologia of the nineteenth century. It was precisely the notion of a concrete social foundation from which both the specific and the authentic aspects of this culture were derived that rejected the political claim to emancipation arising from the demand for general education and cultural participation. The question whether the plebeian masses could or should be included in an existing literary culture was never purely cultural; it was social and political as well. For literarization was viewed by conservatives as the first step toward illegitimate social demands and by the liberals as preparation for a civic society capable of including all the people. As soon as the social problem in Germany was recognized as such and no longer regarded merely as a natural consequence of traditional social hierarchy—a change that occurred in the thirties and forties as a result of the pauperization of large segments of the population—it became clear that education, and with it culture, were related problems. At the beginning of the century, idealistic educational reform could still proceed abstractly from the concept of humankind and the individual, but a generation later such men as Friedrich Harkort and Adolf Diesterweg were already alluding to the economic and social problems of their time and ascribing sociopolitical significance to their proposals for reform of the educational system. Their programs, which were clearly in the liberal tradition, were responses to a historical situation in which the economic condition of the pauperized masses made it impossible for them to participate culturally and thus to develop their full human potential.

It might be argued that these attempts continued the tendencies of the earlier book clubs, which in the late eighteenth century had sought to bring literary culture to the *Volk* by organizing reading material for broader levels of society; the cultural associations of craftspeople may be recalled in this connection. Still, it should not be overlooked that by the second third of the nineteenth century the problem of education had assumed a new form. The breakdown of class structure sharpened the contrasts between affected social groups. The problem, as Harkort and Diesterweg saw it, was no longer that of bringing culture to the petit-bourgeois members of guilds but of incorporating a group that remained completely outside society in the thirties and forties—the proletariat. Reinhart Koselleck has shown the connection between Prussian reform and the emergence of this group: "In the forties there thus existed a new stratum that must be described as a product of liberal Prussian economic policy: a mass of landless country dwellers that had not existed under the former system of estates and that became increasingly more proletarian and, with short-term labor contracts and in search of better work, now found itself on the move, even though a still relatively undeveloped industry was unable to absorb it."[2] The result was a situation with which neither the earlier *Ständestaat* (corporate state) nor the new liberal social order was prepared to deal. Liberal economic policy, which was supposed to free individual powers, did not provide for the impoverished rural and urban masses. Thus in the industrial sector—in the textile industry, for example—the Prussian government proceeded from the assumption that the state could encourage the establishment of a free market but that it could not intervene in the social problems caused by it.[3] In the first phase of the reform movement responsibility for the uprooted masses was still regarded to an extent as a matter for the state; later, however, it became the accepted view that social problems, whose existence no one denied, should be left to the marketplace. The hope was that a developing industry would eventually be able to give work to the proletarian masses. In view of the notorious weakness of German industry, this hope proved illusory, and the state eventually had to intervene again with sociopolitical measures—for example, with the poor law of 1842, which once more gave greater responsibility to local communities.

Comparable conditions in France revealed the danger of a potentially revolutionary situation. In particular, the insurrection of Lyon, which dealt primarily with social rather than political conflict, gave rise to an image of *classes dangereuses* which disturbed the sensitive liberal concept of a free civic society. The disintegration of society into classes no longer having common interests was an extreme provocation for early liberalism, for its concept of society did not allow for such a separation. Because liberal theory had banished economic problems from the realm of the political public sphere, it could deal with these social issues only indirectly, through the cultural sphere. As soon as individuals attain a

[2]Reinhart Koselleck, "Staat und Gesellschaft in Preussen 1815–1848," in Hans-Ulrich Wehler, ed., *Moderne deutsche Sozialgeschichte*, 3d ed. (Cologne, 1970), p. 71.
[3]See also Reinhart Koselleck, *Preussen zwischen Reform und Revolution* (Stuttgart, 1967), pp. 560–640.

political voice, the argument ran, they can help themselves. This was where social and cultural issues touched; according to early liberal theoreticians, the dangerous masses should be reintegrated into society through the acquisition of culture. For as cultivated, responsible citizens they would be able to solve their own social problems.

In the literary public sphere, this problem gave rise to the question how the dichotomy between authentic literature and light fiction could be overcome. For bourgeois theoreticians, the problem of culture was the contradiction between the higher aesthetic claims of the classic literary tradition and the limited receptivity of the broader masses, who were neither economically nor intellectually able to adapt adequately to this tradition. Thus the question arose whether and by what means a broader base could be created for literary culture. The concept of popular literature (*Volksliteratur*) played a central role in these deliberations as they were expressed by, among others, Robert Prutz and Berthold Auerbach.

Robert Prutz

Prutz's essay "Über Unterhaltungsliteratur, insbesondere der Deutschen" (On Light Literature, Especially by the Germans) (1847) is significant in this context because, on the one hand, it unmistakably continued the Young German tendency to democratize literature—in fact it radicalized it—and on the other, it held to the concept of authenticity in literature, so that the notion of light reading, which Prutz introduced with all good intentions, assumed pejorative overtones. His aesthetic and pragmatic historical reflections contradicted each other, and he was unable to reconcile the contradiction. In order to throw light on the problem, he emphasized the contrast: on the one side a small cultured elite acquainted with the literary tradition; on the other the untrained masses, who, given their poverty, could hardly be receptive to art: "In their shabby abodes, in their lowly huts, amid their looms and machines, which are happier than they are because they are not starving— how could the idea of, the desire for, beauty dawn on them? How could eyes used to being cast on the ground in the narrow confines of daily toiling, seeing nothing around them but dirt and misery and tatters, be receptive to the brilliance of art? How could they learn to turn away from the vulgar, not to be blinded by pretty lies, and to cling with devotion only to the image of the Graces?!" Prutz compares this situation to the small world of the cultivated, the home of classic literature: "Real cultivation, like real possessions, real wealth, is limited to the very few; in a world where everything is privileged, taste and a feeling for beauty have also become a privilege. In this intellectual area, too, the others, the majority, have to be satisfied with a mere semblance of culture, just as they have to be satisfied in practice with the mere semblance of justice, the illusion of possession." This comparison is intended to show that measured by the ideal of Greek culture, both sides were at bottom deficient. Neither the cultured elite nor the impoverished masses had a true cultural praxis, in which the assimilation of literature could be reflected even in daily life. Prutz, too, remains unmistakably tied to neohumanistic ideals when he sees the fulfillment of *Bildung* exemplified by the Greeks: "The Greeks were the only really human, the only really artistic people; none can compare with them in the harmony of their cultivation. And only the harmony of cultivation *is* cultivation. . . . What we moderns have to abstract with effort from books and systems—understanding for artistic form, taste, and cultivation—was for the Greeks far more a spontaneous, innate tact; the Graces, whose faces we see only after we have laboriously worked our way through a thousand veils, stood smiling by the cradle of the Greeks."[4]

As unoriginal as the import of these sentences may be, the conclusions Prutz draws from them transcend the discourse of neohumanism. He uses the argument familiar to us from romantic literary theory to criticize society—that a harmonious *Bildung* was no longer available in modern (that is, postantique) history, that spirit and life have been sundered. The majority of the population, excluded from authentic art, is conceded to have an aesthetic claim; the cultural dichotomy no longer seems the natural, and hence legitimate, expression of class structure but is instead the sign of a correctable defect. In this Prutz shows himself to be a Hegelian, not a dogmatic humanist. He presents the culture of antiquity not as an unattainable standard but as a stage that has been surmounted, and he expects historical development to reach a new level equal to, in fact surpassing, that of the Greeks. Prutz's goal is a popular literature in which aesthetic and entertainment values merge and finally become identical. The concept of *Volksliteratur* used by Prutz must be clearly distinguished from what he calls light reading (*Unterhaltungsliteratur*). By the *Volk* he means the whole nation, not a specific group or class. Just as Homer and Sophocles represented the literature of the people for the Greeks, Prutz anticipates a new literature in the Vormärz which will finally overcome the existing cultural dichotomy and in which instructional and entertainment values will no longer be divided.

[4]Robert Prutz, *Schriften zur Literatur und Politik*, ed. Bernd Hüppauf (Tübingen, 1973), pp. 11–12, 19, 14–15.

What significance did this have for literary production? At about the same time as Auerbach, Prutz formulated for the first time the synthetic model that was to become so important for aesthetics after 1848. Serious literature (*Hochliteratur*), aimed at the literati, had to reach a broader public by freeing itself of reflection and returning to entertaining material. Prutz proposes writers such as Dickens and Fenimore Cooper as possible models for German literature in its efforts to regain the vitality it had lost through endless reflection. The rejection of Young German literature that typified the Nachmärz was already in evidence, even if it was not Heine's name but Goethe's and those of his romantic critics which were mentioned. Characteristically, Prutz draws a distinction between Schiller, who was close to his audience and the people, and "Goethe, the solitary sun." He cites with approval what Schiller wrote in the announcement for his *Rheinische Thalia*: "All my ties have been cut. The public is now my all, my studies, my sovereign, my confidant. I now belong to it alone. Before this and no other tribunal will I stand. Only it will I fear and honor." Prutz wished for a German literature that, like English or French literature, showed a belief in the general public, a literature that would accommodate the public's interests and preferences rather than sticking to an exclusively theoretical concept of art. Alexis, Immermann, and Gotthelf represented this new literature for Prutz. But its true paradigms were unquestionably Auerbach's stories of country life (*Dorfgeschichten*), "those loveliest of pearls, which the current of the last years has tossed up on the unfruitful shore of our light fiction."[5] Prutz expressly distinguishes the work of these authors from the fashionable light literature of a Sternberg or the Countess Hahn, which was intended for the salon.

This differentiation also shows how Prutz intended the concept of *Volksliteratur* to be understood. The literature of the people is aimed at the general public, not at specific groups. It is intended exclusively neither for the literary salons and intellectuals nor for the lower classes. On precisely this point Prutz's program revealed itself as utopian. When he included the proletarian masses within the general public, he formulated a concept that had no meaning in the 1840s. The proletarian masses could not possibly read Gotthelf or Auerbach, as educators and publishers well knew. On close examination, the cultural dichotomy lamented by Prutz remains a problem confined to the middle class. His theory of *Volksliteratur* was already moving toward the bourgeois realism of the Nachmärz, not only in its attempt to develop a positive concept of nonreflective literature, using Auerbach and Gotthelf as ex-

[5]Ibid., pp. 27, 26, 31.

amples, but in its aim to identify the literary public of Prutz's time with the people. Thus the boundary of the contemporary literary public sphere also became the boundary of the *Volksliteratur* of the future.

Prutz's limitations were shared by other theoreticians as well. The debate concerning country-life stories, in which Auerbach played a leading role, reveals a similar dilemma: the attempt to break from the prevailing concept of literature by introducing new themes and forms of presentation even though the genre remained bound to the same group of authors and the same circle of readers. Uwe Baur has pointed out that the controversy in the forties over the term *Dorfgeschichte* shows us "how strong competition was among the literati of the forties, how dependent their creations were on the market."[6] Those authors who intended to discover new literary territory with their *Dorfgeschichten* were unmistakably part of the prevailing literary system. The first stories of country life were accordingly printed in such liberal journals as Gutzkow's *Telegraph für Deutschland, Europa*, and the *Zeitung für die elegante Welt*—that is, in what were unmistakably the organs of a salon culture. In other words, these stories were directed at a reasoning public, that same public Prutz sought to address in his essay on light literature. The new genre of country-life stories was not as much literature for the people, as Prutz too hastily assumed, as literature about the people (at least its rustic element). Its motives, themes, figures, and writing style—in short, its discourse—reveal that the liberal intelligentsia had become aware of a problem. They wished to break out of the narrow confines of a familiar literary culture by including the people as a new subject of literature. This is why the conclusion that country-life stories and novels about peasants were politically conservative proved to be problematic. In the Vormärz their authors were, rather, preponderantly engaged liberals, who with the help of the new genre sought to change the consciousness of their readers. Their discovery of provincial life was not based on a naive desire to paint pictures; it was connected, rather, with their sociocritical goals. Thus Auerbach was well aware of his distance from the milieu he was describing in his *Dorfgeschichten*. Although he was acquainted with the world of the peasant from firsthand experience (from his past), he had distanced himself from it. And it was only from afar, by having entered the world of the educated, that he could depict this milieu. To this extent, reflection—contrary to what Prutz's program recommended—could not be eliminated.

[6]Uwe Baur, *Dorfgeschichte. Zur Entstehung und gesellschaftlichen Funktion einer literarischen Gattung im Vormärz* (Munich, 1978), p. 29.

Berthold Auerbach

Any study of Auerbach's *Schrift und Volk* (1846) must begin by putting aside the odium of a conservative traditionalism to which the later development of country literature gave rise. Auerbach did not want a return of earlier historical conditions such as those existing in village life. In opposition to the old order, which relied on the authority of church and state, he proposed a new idea: "Free education is the guiding principle of the new life of the world and of people; the individual must find his center of gravity within, not merely rely on something outside himself; independent parts must therefore come together into a living whole."[7] What is significant in this interpretation is the intent to abandon the contrast between individual and community in favor of the concept of a living whole—in other words, the idea of an organically structured society. Here we see Auerbach's limitation and with it that of early German liberalism: as much as he wanted change, as much as he opposed the bureaucratic institutional state, which recognized citizens only as subjects, his concept of society had no room for industrialization. Auberbach worked from the assumption that the continual basis of society has always been the *Volk*, over which the other groups have elevated themselves (this is why he turned to a rural milieu). On the other hand, he did not recognize that the impoverishment of the rural and urban masses had made the sociologically undefined concept of *Volk* problematic.

To be sure, Auerbach—unlike Prutz, for example—sought to differentiate between the concepts of *Volk* and *Volksliteratur* historically, geographically, and to a certain extent sociologically. Although his ultimate aim was a concept of the responsible citizen, his initial definition of the *Volk* amounted to a description of a mentality: "By it [the *Volk*] we mean that large number of people whose view of life and the world is derived predominantly from independent experience and the immediate present." The scholarly, rational discourse of the state and universities, which is systematic and deductive, stood in opposition to this way of thinking. But in describing the *Volk* mentality as intuitive and prescientific, Auerbach was characterizing, intentionally or not, an earlier form of thinking still completely at one with things: "A calm naivete reposing within itself has not yet mastered its own world; it does not dominate it. It remains within itself like a pure product of nature." This concept of the *Volk* obviously precluded the concept of a reasoning public. Auerbach's program for a popular culture thus presented a basic difficulty. He favored the extension of political responsibility to all

[7]Berthold Auerbach, *Gesammelte Schriften* (Stuttgart, 1864), 18:222.

citizens, but his concept of the *Volk* was incompatible with the critical deliberations of an enlightened public sphere. To this extent, only someone who, like Johann Hebel or Auerbach, came from the people yet had distanced himself from the cultural milieu of his home could mediate between a naive *Volk* culture and modern education. It became his task to build a bridge between these realms, which were separated by a gulf. But he did not do so in the sense of the Enlightenment, which measured progress by its own standards and gradually tried to raise the people to this level. For Auerbach, "the vital prerequisite for all parts of a national body" lies in the *Volk*, and *Volksliteratur* was accordingly "the original point of departure" for all literature.[8] The rapprochement with the tradition of the *Volk* was thus not a step backward but rather a return to the beginning and basis of society.

Yet Auerbach did not agree at all with the romantics, who saw fairy tales as authentic *Volk* literature and sought to revive them. Auerbach's historical and philosophical consciousness prevented him from returning to the fairy-tale form, because it was no longer suited to the modern intellect. In this connection he included even the *Volk* among the moderns: "The human intellect has risen to perception and recognition of the universal; it is pointless to try to force it to return to an outdated view." But his historico-philosophical model had to be valid for popular writing as a whole. Contrary to what Auerbach says in his introduction about his concept of the *Volk*, he discovered in the course of his investigation that the people are not exempt from historical evolution and that their mentality is thus also subject to historical change. Using Hebel as an example, Auerbach shows how modern popular poets avoid the marvelous without altogether giving way to the prosaic. Auerbach's program is, to be sure, best represented not by the didactic poetry of the Enlightenment but by Schiller's aesthetics. He cites Schiller's theory to demonstrate that art is free of extra-aesthetic points of view. Moreover, following Schiller's aesthetics, he stresses the necessity of an idealistic presentation—significantly adding, however, that Schiller made the reconciliation of idealism and realism the prerequisite for a vital poetry. In keeping with the idealistic tradition, artistic truth is related to reality, without becoming identical to it: "The poet can and should bring life and states of mind to an ordered perfection, which they have perhaps not reached, nor can reach, in bare reality."[9]

By removing the work of art from direct social praxis in accordance with the aesthetics of idealism, Auerbach confronts the problem of the

---

[8]Ibid., 18:9, 11, 10, 11.
[9]Ibid., 18:62–63, 72, 26–27.

social context of *Volksliteratur* in a far more radical way than does Prutz, who makes the idealistic tradition itself responsible for the unpopular character of German literature. This is true in a double sense: according to Auerbach, neither the pragmatic context of didactic poetry nor the tendencies of political writing can do justice to German literature. The change Auerbach hopes poetry will bring about is a "deeper consideration of life," which will lead to humanity. The depiction of life with all its concrete causes and effects, not pragmatic suggestions for improvement, is what makes literature effective. In the process, as Auerbach points out, the emphasis in popular poetry shifts from the hero to the chorus, from the great individual to the average person: "Popular poetry lifts individuals out of those circles that have usually been comprehended only as a whole. It shows the more or less complete isolation of the individual life, its obstacles and encouragements, loneliness and abandonment on one side and forcible bonds to society on the other." It remains for poetry, in its own way, to present models by which reality can orient itself more or less closely. Auerbach speaks of the obligation of popular writing to "prepare for the free unification of people so that they can help one another and advance their common interests, to stimulate minds to use what is available, and to point out and open paths to the new." The mediating concept between literature and reality for Auerbach—here he shows himself to be a typical liberal—is the humanization of people through aesthetically won moral freedom: "Thus it is poetry that strives to make people moral and free, that brings them into harmony with themselves and with universal reason, not by the external means of ordinances but by inner clarification."[10]

Auerbach insists, however, that the humanity of poetry cannot remain uncommitted: "Active humanity demands that people be committed to one another—new ways of life have to be created which will lift up and support a liberated existence." The special character of the social function of literature—compared to other discourses—is carefully brought out by Auerbach. He tries to distinguish between poetry and direct proposals for reform by setting the former apart from the servile petitioning of those in power, on the one hand, and from its instrumentalization in the social struggle, on the other: "Both can result from it, but only indirectly, from the whole of life, with all its consequences."[11] This indirect procedure depends on the freedom of the writer when confronting reality, which he can change in his work of art so as to arrive at an obvious conclusion not yet exhibited by the existing social

[10]Ibid., 18:104, 105–6, 251, 239.
[11]Ibid., 18:100, 101.

reality. For Auerbach, the superiority of art over other discourses consists precisely in its understanding and representation of the essence of reality rather than its factual data. Hence poetry points to the future, and Auerbach attributes a prophetic awareness to poets.

The poetic transfiguration of reality is thus anything but a form of aesthetic affirmation. Its truth for Auerbach lies in its capacity to transcend prosaic reality, to contribute a utopian element that simple depiction of reality could not reveal. Consequently, Auerbach urges writers to step out of the poets' corner: "Works of art can no longer find their fulfillment in themselves; art, too, must be sacrificed to the liberation of human existence." To this extent, art no less than philosophy is included in the dialectic movement of history and serves human emancipation, even if not directly. Thus poetry assumes the task of "showing the free individual once again in his relationship to the life of the world and of man."[12]

The stress Auerbach puts on the free individual is also reflected in his social theory, at the heart of which is the responsible individual: "The ultimate aim of political communal life is the free individual, who should and must be preserved in the organic union of individuals." Characteristically, however, this concession to civic society, which promotes free competition on every side, is at once qualified by the demand for an organic union of individuals. Auerbach fears an atomistic disintegration of society, because after the dissolution of the old corporate order, to which the individual was tied, everyone would be free to pursue their own selfish interests. Within the framework of Auerbach's social theory, the ensuing material inequality, the impoverishment of the masses of which he was naturally not unaware, could be prevented only by a "moral principle": "Egoism must be overcome by the spirit, by training and education, not simply by external advantage and calculation, although these can certainly have a powerful effect."[13] In any case, according to Auerbach the state did not have the right to intervene directly.

It is noteworthy that Auerbach, who initially conceived the idea of the *Volk* entirely from the mental side, increasingly includes the social aspect in the course of his presentation and feels pressed to pose questions at cross-purposes to his original approach. He cannot overlook the fact that the liberation of the individual from earlier social conditions, which he welcomes in principle as necessary and progressive, leads also to increased material inequality. But this would intensify

12Ibid., 18:102, 106.
13Ibid., 18:249, 246.

rather than narrow the cultural dichotomy he is intent on overcoming. Auerbach concedes this to his socialistic opponents. He recognizes that the humanistic solution, which seeks to prepare the way for a better society by training and educating individuals, does not come to grips with the problem; but at the same time he rejects the socialist approach as equally one-sided, since it takes only external conditions into account and is not interested in the elevation and self-conquest of humanity. As in his theory of aesthetics, Auerbach is looking for a mediation between idealism and materialism, although he definitely prefers the former. He clings to a social theory supporting the rise of the middle classes. The *Volk* will have to adapt to this process; at any rate, they have no history of their own apart from that of the bourgeoisie. Auerbach expressly avoids mention of the fourth estate (the working classes). This synthesis should be fostered by popular literature and will eventually give rise to *one* cultivated nation of free citizens. "We must write and think incessantly about providing the people, who struggle with life's burdens, with the possibility not only of quenching their thirst at the rich well of life but also of drinking its pleasures," he concludes in *Schrift und Volk*.[14] Despite Auerbach's repeated warnings against utopian planning, this faith in the humanization of life through literature contains a utopian element—if only because he never raises the question how the impoverished masses are to gain access to literature. When he does address this problem he obviously has in mind the well-ordered rural communities depicted in his country-life stories. His demand for political education presupposes that the people concerned are able to read and write. Auerbach refers to the customs and traditions of existing peasant culture without asking himself whether these very traditions, which he values, would not be lost through the liberalization and atomization of society. His description of traditional popular culture and his liberal historical and social theories contradict each other.

By concerning himself with social issues, Auerbach, unlike Prutz, abandons the realm of bourgeois culture. His analysis, however, has scarcely any effect on his concept of literature. In the forties, Auerbach, as he later expressed it, had faith in the future, as did others "who feel deeply about the sheer beauty of life and art, about the freedom of mankind and the fatherland."[15] He hoped for the incorporation of the proletariat into the community of free citizens. Because his concept of art and literature was grounded in German idealism, Auerbach, too, in the final analysis remained a captive of the traditional literary system.

[14]Ibid., 18:249, 253.
[15]Ibid., 18:255.

Friedrich Harkort

Educators and social thinkers of the 1830s and 1840s proved more radical in the sense that they were less burdened by the aesthetic theory of classicism and were directly concerned with the solution of social problems. Most of them were unaware that they were "instrumentalizing" literature and thereby doing precisely what Auerbach sought to avoid. To an extent this was due to their adherence to older rationalistic traditions. The functional thinking of Enlightenment pedagogics reappears especially in the writings of the socially committed, liberal industrialist Friedrich Harkort, whose theories concentrated less on the individual than on the collective needs of society and the state. For him the purpose of education lay outside education itself; it was the means of creating a society in which each of its members could achieve the greatest contentment and prosperity. It was in this spirit that Peter Villaume, in his essay "Ob und inwieweit bei der Erziehung die Vollkommenheit des einzelnen Menschen seiner Brauchbarkeit aufzuopfern sei" (Whether and to What Extent in Education the Perfection of Individuals Should Be Sacrificed to Their Usefulness), had laid down the principle a generation earlier that the state is justified in asking the individual to forgo his or her ultimate development for the sake of society as a whole: "Society has an unchallenged, sacred right even to man's greatest sacrifice, the sacrifice of part of his refinement and perfection."[16] The philanthropinists had argued that education must always consider the social function of the individual being educated. That did not mean, as one might assume, that mass education could be dispensed with, but rather that it had to be adjusted to the functions and particular needs of the lower classes. A key question posed by the Erfurt Academy in 1793 is characteristic of this school of thought. It asked among other things, "What is civic freedom, and in how many different ways can a correct concept of it be disseminated among the ranks of society, especially the lower classes?"[17] As is clear from the context, this question presupposed that the governed were living under a wise and benevolent regime and thus had no cause in principle for dissatisfaction. Under such conditions the main thing was to instill in the *Volk* an appropriate concept of civic freedom. Enlightenment of the *Volk* was desirable, but only for the advancement of society as a whole. The philanthropinists divided society into classes and occupational groups that were to be educated

---

[16]Quoted in Andreas Flitner, *Die politische Erziehung in Deutschland* (Tübingen, 1957), p. 30.
[17]According to Flitner in ibid., p. 52.

according to their duties and functions—that is, as farmers, artisans, officials, men and women of learning, and the like. Thus Joachim Heinrich Campe pointed out that in the past education had not taken one's future occupation sufficiently into account and had therefore failed to do justice to the tasks of the craftsperson and artist. Without vocational training, he feared, young craftspersons and artists might "totally lack the opportunity and guidance to repeat what they have learned, to reinforce and put into practice the ethical and religious principles they have acquired in school, and to prepare themselves for finding later employment as journeymen."[18] Campe advocated the improvement of economic conditions within the existing political and social structure—through a more careful training of artisans, for example. The proposals of Heinrich Stephanis for the establishment of trade schools were of a similar bent. Inasmuch as all people were expected as active members of society to be guided by reason, this can be called a democratization of education. Yet one must bear in mind that the concept has more than one meaning. Philanthropinism was concerned with instrumental action, not really with individual emancipation, which was, for instance, at the center of Humboldt's theory.

As a theoretician and politician, Harkort unmistakably followed the tendencies of the Enlightenment. Like Lessing or Condorcet, he took for granted the advancement of humanity, and from the 1840s on he supported popular education in the Prussian Parliament. As Harkort in particular never tired of emphasizing, social and economic conditions had changed since the eighteenth century. Plans for mass education in the nineteenth century had to take into account a society in the process of industrialization, one in which the *Volk* had sunk to the level of a common herd, even if it had not yet become a proletariat. Unlike professional educational theorists, Harkort as an industrialist had firsthand knowledge of the social condition of workers. In his *Bemerkungen über die preussische Volksschule und ihre Lehrer* (Remarks on the Prussian Volksschule and Its Teachers) (1843) and a little later in his general study *Bemerkungen über die Hindernisse der Civilisation und Emancipation der unteren Klassen* (Remarks on the Obstacles to Civilization and the Emancipation of the Lower Classes) (1844), he concerned himself with the possibility of democratizing education. In the introduction to the latter, Harkort openly acknowledged his debt to the Enlightenment and looked to the spread of education to abolish intellectual bondage: "Even the poor will inherit their share of culture and pros-

---

[18]Quoted in Frolinde Balser, *Die Anfänge der Erwachsenenbildung in Deutschland in der ersten Hälfte des 19. Jahrhunderts* (Stuttgart, 1959), p. 44.

perity."[19] His point of view, however, differed from that of the great educational reformers of about 1810 in that it took into account the economic development of Prussia—that is, the consequences of freeing the peasants and of early industrialization—and recognized it as the real problem. The humanistic argument that "good schools are the principal lever of humanity" assumed a new dimension in his work.[20] Only the increase and improvement of primary schools could guarantee that Prussian society would undergo a progressive but nonrevolutionary development. Hence Harkort made the school into an instrument of political control—a position we will encounter again in Diesterweg; for the liberal entrepreneur saw the uncultivated, impoverished masses as a threat to the proper evolution of society. Harkort believed that the Enlightenment could be furthered only if the common people (the plebeians) participated in the enlightenment of the middle class.

With Harkort and Diesterweg the politicizing of the issue of education had clearly entered a new phase. Harkort made an explicit connection between education and the material conditions of life: "The pauper is prevented from acquiring property; he thus thinks of distributing it by physical force. We pass laws against dividing up property, we favor primogeniture—look at the results in Ireland." In this he is in agreement with the early French socialists, and indeed, he referred explicitly to Blanqui when he described the goal of social development. He did not, however, accept the conclusions drawn by the socialists; rather he postulated, in accordance with liberal theory, equal educational opportunities for all. Inasmuch as the state allows everyone to hold possessions and even protects the "sanctity of property," educational opportunities should be available to all so that everyone will be in a position to acquire property and thereby enter the middle class. The society of free citizens Harkort desired would be ensured by counteracting the accidental differences of birth through education. By maintaining the right to education he was saying that the existing state of material inequality, with which he was closely acquainted, was a temporary and secondary phenomenon. Thus, "the position in the state which the individual inherits by birth is purely accidental; however modest that birth may be, everyone has an equal claim in the realm of the spirit."[21]

It would be a distortion to say that Harkort's reference to the disciplinary power of education was the primary justification for his concept of education, but his ideas tend in that direction. He advocated the

[19]Friedrich Harkort, *Schriften und Reden zu Volksschule und Volksbildung*, ed. Karl-Ernst Jeismann (Paderborn, 1969), p. 64.
[20]Ibid., p. 11.
[21]Ibid., pp. 68, 69.

political education of the masses in order to avoid a violent revolution. The critical situation in the 1840s induced him to issue a warning: "Do not forget that a great crisis is at hand! It is not confined to morality and religion alone; no, the solution of political problems has likewise stirred every class of society. Accordingly, the *Volk* must also be given their share of political education." Socialist and communist agitation was to be neutralized through enlightenment. Behind Harkort's ideas there still lay, of course, the hope that the competing interests of society could eventually be harmonized. Workers and managers, he remarked in an 1849 letter to the German workers, can share in the public wealth that capitalism has created.[22] This was why in 1844 Harkort already supported worker participation in profits; such a policy would attract hardworking and motivated workers to industry.

Harkort expected the state to avoid potential social problems by instituting politically appropriate measures conducive to the advancement of education, such as prohibiting child labor and establishing and improving trade and elementary schools. This would result in the elimination of poverty without the restructuring of society: "A thorough education will ensure for all people the free development of their potential and remove obstacles to their acquiring property through work."[23] A proletarian who shares in the wealth is no longer a proletarian and thus no longer a threat to the advance of culture.

Although Harkort's proposals were prompted by the contemporary lack of equal education for all classes, he did not accept the situation as a matter of course. Under the influence of the increasingly pressing social problems of the forties, this issue, which was just beginning to come to the fore in the age of the Enlightment, became for him a class issue. Cultural differences became the mark of privilege or deprivation: "Such a relationship [a friendly intercourse between the classes] cannot exist when the *Volk* is split into two great factions, one the cultivated world of the rich with its refined pleasures, the other the coarse, ignorant, and needy masses. The result is a gulf that both sides cross only rarely; a repugnant element is created."[24] The contrast Harkort describes is no longer one between the culture of the *Volk* and the culture of the educated, such as characterized the earlier modern period. It is, rather, the result of class conflict arising from economic liberalism.

He considered the civilizing of the masses from the same point of view. Elementary schools and institutions of higher learning would build the foundations of a universal culture. Aesthetic demands were far

[22]Ibid., pp. 77, 101–4.
[23]Ibid., p. 86.
[24]Ibid., p. 90.

from Harkort's mind. His estimation of popular literature was motivated, rather, by pragmatic considerations. He expected such literature to be accessible to common people and to teach them something that would be of use in life. What the popular writer had to provide was intelligible information in the fields of the natural sciences, economics, and politics. England, where such an informative literature already existed, was his model. He had England in mind as well when he countered the prejudiced notion that education could not be popularized. Yet he failed to take the activity of the masses into account; they appear in his work only as the object of education. The culture to which the masses were to be introduced was for him quite simply bourgeois culture. It never occurred to him that the proletariat could develop its own culture and its own literature. His goal, like Auerbach's, remained the integration of the proletariat into bourgeois society.

Adolf Diesterweg

The educator Adolf Diesterweg, who directed a *Seminar* (teacher-training school) in Moers and later in Berlin, had a different point of view; but the results of his deliberations on the cultural condition of the lower classes do not differ essentially from Harkort's views. He shared the latter's opinion that existing social problems could be solved only by a comprehensive reform of the elementary school system. No less than the liberal entrepreneur Harkort, he openly politicized pedagogical theory. His frank speech and untiring political activity were so little appreciated by the Prussian government that in 1847 he was given an early retirement. This decision afforded him the opportunity to participate more intensively in politics. As a member of the Prussian Landtag in the Nachmärz, he was one of the energetic opponents of Stiehl's school policy.

Diesterweg's pedagogical thinking was strongly influenced by the Enlightenment, especially by philanthropinism, but—and this sets him apart, for example, from Harkort—he also studied the ideas of Pestalozzi, thereby moving closer to neohumanism. At the same time, the young Diesterweg gave equal weight to the political controversies of the period between 1813 and 1818. The liberal and national programs had a sustained influence on his political thinking.[25] These political experiences later caused him not to isolate pedagogical issues but to link them to contemporary political and social issues. Under the influence of

[25]See Eberhard Gross, *Erziehung und Gesellschaft im Werk Adolph Diesterwegs* (Weinheim, 1966), p. 19.

his friend Johann Friedrich Wilberg, Diesterweg focused his interest on questions of the further education of teachers in relation to the social problems resulting from industrialization. In 1837 he summed up his ideas in the *Beiträgen zur Lösung der Lebensfragen der Civilisation* (Contributions to the Solution of the Vital Questions of Civilization).

Diesterweg systematically related the sociopolitical to the pedagogical realm by means of the fundamental idea that pedagogy and the schools have a significant contribution to make to the solution of social problems. He believed that only with the help of a comprehensive educational program extending to all levels of society, one that would prepare individuals for their future political and social tasks, could contemporary society be transformed into a community of free citizens. For this reason he declared himself a representative of pedagogical realism and a strong opponent of Thiersch, who defended neohumanism in its narrowest form. Education, he argued, should not align itself with classical antiquity, because this would hinder its orientation toward contemporary society. Instead, he called for the use of materials that would facilitate the pupil's integration into contemporary society. Political instruction should be given, so that future citizens would have an idea of their rights and duties. This program expressly included the poor, who only by such instruction could be integrated into the community of citizens. Agreeing with the fundamental principles of political liberalism, Diesterweg began with the basic assumption that humanity is composed of individuals who forge "the history of mankind under conditions created by the Lord God." This history presents itself as the collective progress of humankind from its simple beginnings toward ever greater perfection. But the anticipated general progress—at this point Diesterweg's own thought begins—is foiled and called into question by the unequal distribution of material goods: on one side a few wealthy individuals; on the other the masses, who do not know (here he follows Chateaubriand) "how to cover their nakedness and still their hunger." Such a contrast of interests was a fundamental provocation for Diesterweg, since in line with early liberal theory he was convinced that in the name of humanity a balance could be achieved. He favored the principle of proportionality, according to which the amount of personal freedom (even in the acquisition of material goods) is restricted by the concern for social *fairness*. According to Diesterweg, however, social inequality can never be abolished, since people are different; one should insist, however, on the creation of a base that will prevent pauperization. He talked of the "minimum [required] for human life."[26]

[26]Adolph Diesterweg, *Schriften und Reden*, ed. Heinrich Deiters (Leipzig, 1950), pp. 111, 109, 117.

Characteristically, Diesterweg, who sought to abolish the disadvantage of being poor, once again turned to the idea of the perfect state:

We expect from a civic society aiming to satisfy even a modicum of the needs of a time that has reached a certain level of social culture not simply that it should value the rights of each individual but that it should give positive and direct encouragement to all the legal and moral desires of human beings and to all those desires that will encourage their free development; that it should increase and stimulate the limited and feeble strength of the individual by cooperation, consultation, and action; and, as far as possible, that it should make the affairs of the individual, to the full extent that he could wish, the focal point of the community and of society.

The regulative idea of a perfect communal polity became the main premise of a pedagogical theory having as its goal the elimination of material and cultural inequality. Diesterweg envisioned a state acting in accordance with this basic principle; but he did not rely exclusively on a utopian concept. To show that the poor had to be educated, he appealed to the interests of an existing, by no means ideal, society: "You quarrel over dogmas and bring pygmies into the world, while the facts, like giants, are too much for you. Just wait a bit, fifty or a hundred years, and you will live to see the results! But *even tomorrow* they might grab you by the hair."[27]

The moment the impoverished masses became aware of their condition and grew in strength, society would be in danger. Diesterweg vividly described the revolutionary mob that would destroy the structure of society and civilization: "That is the terrible power of the mob when it presses together in great masses. What it is capable of, once it has broken through the dam of the law, we have seen in Paris and Lyon."[28] In this connection, Diesterweg the educator transformed idealism into pragmatism: in order to prevent an imminent revolution, he recommended education for the proletariat. Fear of the unleashed mob would force the dominant social groups to change conditions. Diesterweg even carried this argument beyond Harkort by reversing the relationship between education and material conditions. Whereas Harkort sought to equalize material inequality by educating the poor, Diesterweg argued that only an improvement in material conditions would create the basis for a better general education. Thus the argument has been shifted: the task of the state begins in the social realm; it must make general education possible for the masses, Diesterweg insists, by providing a level of subsistence.

For Diesterweg, the political goal of education was to train responsi-

[27]Ibid., pp. 123, 133–34.
[28]Ibid., p. 134.

ble citizens capable of participating in the political discussion of the public sphere. Elementary schools (*Volksschulen*) could contribute only in small part to this end. To reduce the educational deficiency of the poor, educational institutions had to be established for adults. Sufficient enlightenment, Diesterweg hoped, would decrease class conflict: "Thus, every future citizen must be given the necessary instruction in the political constitution; in the whole organization of the state, from municipal ordinances to the supreme, inviolable ruler; in its legislative process and administration; and in the laws themselves—instruction in the general theory of civic rights and obligations."[29] This attempt to change the threatening social situation by giving adults a political education goes back to a model of thought centering on the notion of the best conceivable state. Because Diesterweg is not content, as a practical educator, to criticize the prevailing theory of education but is looking for a solution, his project is entangled in contradiction—practical suggestions on the one hand, abstract plans on the other. In either case, however, the lower class once again enters into consideration only as the object of educational plans. That it could take an active part in the restructuring of educational institutions never enters Diesterweg's mind.

Even though Diesterweg, as a pedagogue and teacher, was superior to the literati in that he did not confine to literature his analysis and proposed solutions to the problem of democratization, he too remained tacitly bound to a concept of culture derived from bourgeois tradition. Even when demanding independence for the *Volk*, he did not call for a new and different culture but for the tradition of the bourgeois Enlightenment. Diesterweg's main concern was the spread of this culture and its literature. In the final analysis, he still believes it is possible to constitute a public sphere for all. To be sure, the political aspect of that public sphere already clearly outweighs its literary side, for the heart of Diesterweg's deliberations is not literary but political education. When Diesterweg was dismissed from office in 1847 for allegedly spreading socialist-communist ideas and supporting a subversive demagogy, his intentions were misunderstood. Although he had familiarized himself with socialist ideas—with Saint-Simonianism, for instance—his thinking was grounded in liberal theory, which, in view of the inescapable social problems of the present, he tried to develop and adapt. He saw himself confronted by an issue that had not yet been an urgent problem for the preceding generation: the right of the masses to have their interests considered in the public sphere. Diesterweg's answer was that the classic public sphere would be reconstituted by a general educational system that included the proletariat.

[29]Ibid., p. 154.

The limits of liberal theory now became evident: the concept of humanity and the category of historical progress permitted, at least in the abstract, the inclusion of all people in the process of education and cultivation, even at the proletarian levels of society; but the bourgeois concept of education and culture remained the standard for these endeavors. The difficulty in realizing the liberal programs lay not only in the obstacle presented by early capitalist conditions but to an equal degree in the concept itself, in which the masses were mere objects. Still, it cannot be overlooked that these liberal endeavors were an important stimulus, not least for the artisans' educational and cultural associations (*Bildungsvereine*).

The Workers' Associations

The educational and cultural associations of artisans that began to form in the thirties, often under the guidance of bourgeois notables, combined cultural and political objectives in various ways.[30] The claim to cultural equality was reinforced by the radical political ideas commonly found in these associations. This was particularly true in the associations founded in Switzerland and France, which were less closely supervised by the state.[31] Artisans and workers took the same road the bourgeois Enlightenment had taken in the eighteenth century. They aimed to follow the "road of truth, moral education, and enlightenment,"[32] demanding entry to and a voice in the literary and political public sphere hitherto reserved for the middle class. As Wilhelm Weitling succinctly put it in 1842, "We, too [the workers], want a voice, because this is the nineteenth century, and we have never had one. We, too, want a voice in public opinion so that we can become known, for up to now we have really always been misunderstood. We, too, want a voice so that our constricted hearts can have space to breathe and our just complaints can reach the ears of the powerful."[33] The suspicion with which the German authorities reacted to the journeymen's associations, and their readiness to impose prohibitions and regulations, cannot be traced exclusively to a fear of political unrest. The very claim that they intended to change their social position by organizing themselves, a claim that went beyond all demands for freedom and equality, was disturbing. Their will to become autonomous subjects in the cultural as well as the political sphere was objectionable to the government.

---

[30]See Balser, *Die Anfänge der Erwachsenenbildung*, pp. 53–54, 86–99.

[31]See Wolfgang Schieder, *Anfänge der deutschen Arbeiterbewegung* (Stuttgart, 1963).

[32]According to Balser, *Die Anfänge der Erwachsenenbildung*, p. 88, n. 74.

[33]Quoted in Georg Adler, *Die Geschichte der ersten sozialpolitischen Arbeiterbewegung in Deutschland* (Breslau, 1885), p. 30.

Before 1848 the bourgeoisie was on the whole inclined to favor this development, because one expected cultivated and enlightened artisans and workers to support bourgeois society. This is exemplified by the founding of the workers' cultural association in Hamburg in 1846. A bourgeois association going back to the eighteenth century, the Patriotische Gesellschaft gave legitimacy to the new form of workers' association (*Arbeiterbildungsverein*), and thus could be understood as a continuation of the bourgeois Enlightenment. The consensus was that in the long run a general cultural improvement would do away with social inequality. For, as stated in an address delivered in 1848 at the celebration of the founding of the association, "Cultivation is the greatest enemy of disparities, of all injustice, stagnation, and prejudice."[34]

Even though workers and artisans began to define themselves in their associations as independent political agents, before 1848 their concept of culture remained, on the whole, indebted to the bourgeois tradition. The predominant view in their proclamations and programs was that the first order of business was to eliminate the existing cultural deficit. The statutes of the Mannheim Arbeiterbildungsverein refer to the "higher things of life, for them [the workers] hitherto almost unattainable.[35] A general bourgeois education was considered a prerequisite for participation in public life; hence the need for instruction in world and natural history, for learning about useful inventions, and above all for studying notable writers. The main focus of these educational programs was on the practical needs of artisans and workers, who wanted to capture the bourgeois public sphere for themselves. The separation from liberal theory that developed in the Bund der Gerechten and later in the Bund der Kommunisten seems to have been less pronounced in the cultural sphere. The educational associations were supposed to further the spread of culture, yet they did not fundamentally attack the bourgeois concept of culture. This may have been related to the fact that the development of the associations led from cultural to political work. Their politicization did not necessarily make the cultural sector problematic.[36] It was assumed, rather, that the workers would overcome the existing cultural dichotomy. Until 1849 this hope was justified. After the revolution, when the workers' movement made a cleaner political break with the liberal bourgeoisie, cultural differentiation again became an issue. A model equating the bourgeois concept of culture and literature with culture and literature per se must have appeared problematic. At the historical moment when the workers' move-

---

[34]Quoted in Heinrich Laufenberg, *Geschichte der Arbeiterbewegung in Hamburg, Altona und Umgebung* (Hamburg, 1911), 1:97.
[35]Quoted in Balser, *Die Anfänge der Erwachsenenbildung*, p. 93.
[36]See Schieder, *Anfänge der deutschen Arbeiterbewegung*, pp. 174–300.

ment left the bourgeois public sphere—as with Lassalle's founding of the Allgemeiner Deutscher Arbeiterverein—the kind of cultural work that had characterized the educational associations of the Vormärz lost its legitimacy. The pressing question became whether bourgeois literature could still be binding on the proletariat. How great an influence, meanwhile, was still exerted by the model of cultural integration is clear from the position taken by Wilhelm Liebknecht, who overtly criticized the bourgeois public sphere and attacked reactionary Prussian school policy yet did not dispute the concept of a homogeneous culture encompassing all classes.[37]

The early workers' movement had no cultural theory of its own. By establishing associations that for the first time unmistakably made artisans and workers the subjects of cultural affairs, it moved decisively beyond the position of liberalism. The question is whether and to what extent socialist theory had outlined a cultural program before 1848 which addressed the problems left unsolved by such liberal theorists as Harkort and Diesterweg. In the workers' cooperative founded in 1848 by Stephan Born, this was obviously not the case. Born supported such radical democratic proposals as free elementary school instruction and free public libraries, but he held to the position that the status of workers would be safeguarded by the acquisition of culture.[38] Fundamentally, Born's concept of *Bildung* remained idealistic. His image of society was a harmonious one in which nonantagonistic qualities predominated. The significance of education was stressed in the cooperative precisely because it was hoped that intensive work in the field of education would overcome class differences. Efforts undertaken at the workers' congresses to develop an educational system aimed essentially at making the working class an equal partner. Thus the statutes of the Allgemeiner Arbeiter-Verbrüderung in southern Germany declared that "the purpose of the workers' cooperatives is: to strive for a general and moral education for workers, to use every legal means to bring them the full enjoyment of all civic rights, to train them commercially and politically to be true citizens, and in general to represent and further their material and spiritual interests."[39] When the workers reorganized in the sixties, this model, which was still influenced by liberal theory, had lost some of its plausibility. First, the educational policy of the state had made it clear that the ruling classes wanted to exclude the lower classes from any extensive knowledge; and second, relationship between the working class and the liberal bourgeoisie had changed decisively. The

[37]See Brigitte Emig, *Die Veredelung des Arbeiters* (Frankfurt a. M., New York, 1980), pp. 128–53.
[38]See Balser, *Die Anfänge der Erwachsenenbildung*, pp. 194–207.
[39]Quoted in ibid., p. 206.

previously sought after integration must henceforth have seemed to the workers' movement an instrument of control and domination. The attempts of the liberals in the Progressive party to use the institutions of the workers for their own purposes was bound to fail the moment the divergence of political and social interests (as in the issue of voting rights) became obvious.

The Socialist Concept

The claim advanced by the Allgemeiner Deutscher Arbeiterverein under the guidance of Lassalle went considerably beyond the earlier concept of integration: the working class was no longer the fourth estate, which had to be integrated, but represented all of oppressed humanity: "Its [the workers' class] interest is in truth the interest of the *whole of humanity*, its freedom is the freedom of humanity itself, and its domination is the domination of *all.*" Although Lassalle emphatically opposed the strategy of the liberals in the Progressive party and in particular strongly rejected the restriction of the workers' movement to the economic realm, his view of the state as a neutral agent of which the working class could make use strongly prejudiced his theory of culture. For Lassalle believed that the state's purpose was to bring "man to *positive expansion,* and *progressive development,* in other words, to bring the destiny of man—that is the culture of which the human race *is capable*—into *actual existence*; it is the *training and development* of the human race to freedom." This superelevation of the state, which is once again entrusted, beyond all class conflict, with the cultural education of humankind, allowed him to adopt the traditional concept of culture and to put it at the service of the proletariat. In the workers' program of 1862 Lassalle suggested that when the workers were in control the moral duty of the state would be unequivocally carried out—in contrast to a bourgeois state, which, as the instrument of the dominant bourgeoisie, can only take a one-sided interest in the needs of its own class: "It is the moral earnestness of this thought which must never leave you, but must be present to your heart in your workshops during the hours of labor, in your leisure hours, during your walks, at your meetings, and even when you stretch your limbs to rest upon your hard couches, it is *this* thought which must fill and occupy your minds till they lose themselves in dreams." The idealistic extravagance of this statement cannot be overlooked. Lassalle hoped—indeed, he counted on it—that the workers would be able to join a cultural tradition protected from private interests. The working class would then show itself to be the legitimate heir to the idealist concept of culture (as proposed by Fichte and Hegel) and would achieve "an efflorescence of morality, culture, and science,"[40] by overcoming private interest through solidarity. Before this new flowering could occur, however, the liberal concept of education as propounded in exemplary fashion (thought Lassalle) in the writings of Julian Schmidt would have to be confronted. This criticism anticipates some of what the young Nietzsche was to attack a few years later in his *Unzeitgemässe Betrachtungen*: the self-satisfaction of the liberal idea of education, which watered down the idealistic heritage, and the decline of the literary public sphere, which had become an appendage of commercial interests. Lassalle expected the workers to concur in this criticism of the liberal concept of culture; but at the same time he counted on their adopting and continuing its idealism. Although Lassalle emphatically rejected the liberal theory of proletarian integration into bourgeois society, he never asked whether the existing cultural heritage met the interests of the new class. His cultural concept was an imposition on proletarian democracy, without any grounding in a popular tradition.

If we want to understand Lassalle, it must be added that his plan anticipated a situation in which the working class controlled the state. The heritage of idealism transformed itself into an educational utopia. But from the perspective of the daily business of parties and educational associations, carried out under conditions imposed by an authoritarian government, the task looked quite different. The cultural policy of the state—to the extent that such a policy existed before 1870—did not support the work of the educational associations; on the contrary, it did everything in its power to prevent it. Faced with the terrible state of education in the Nachmärz, workers reorganized their associations in the early sixties. Old goals were in part revived. The statutes of the *Arbeiterverein* in Esslingen state that "the purpose of the association is to strive, through a mutual exchange of opinions on commercial and scientific events in the industrial area, and through informative scientific lectures, song, instruction, and appropriate reading material, for ever-greater intellectual improvement and thereby to help spread an ever-greater degree of education and humanity."[41] Characteristically, no political stands were taken. The united workers and artisans of the associations sought by defining their own cultural interests to overcome the disadvantages imposed by the state educational system. They were,

[40]Ferdinand Lassalle, *The Workingman's Programme*, trans. Edward Peters (London, 1884), pp. 46, 57, 59–60, 54.
[41]Quoted in Wolfgang Schmierer, *Von der Arbeiterbildung zur Arbeiterpolitik* (Hanover, 1970), p. 58, n. 66.

in fact, still partly counting on the support of the progressive bourgeois camp.[42]

The slogan "Education will make you free," spoken on the workers' day in Rödelheim in 1863, is linked to the tradition of the Enlightenment. Working for education, it was believed, would bring about social change, even if a political revolution did not take place. Although Lassalle still supported this tendency, despite his strong attacks on the bourgeoisie, Liebknecht took a clear stand against it. His lecture of 1872, "Wissen ist Macht—Macht ist Wissen" (Knowledge Is Power—Power Is Knowledge), expressly cited the slogan of the educational associations, but no longer in the hope of achieving a cultural synthesis. His intention instead was to investigate the relationship between class dominance and cultural hegemony. Liebknecht characterized the class-bound character of culture as a law of history: "There has never been a dominant caste, a dominant station, a dominant class, which has used its knowledge and power for the enlightenment, education, and training of those it dominated; which did not, on the contrary, systematically deprive them of true education, the education that makes you free." This assertion fundamentally called into question the bourgeois claim to represent the general cultural interests of humankind, which Lassalle, caught as he was in the trap of German idealism, still accepted. If bourgeois culture was the instrument of bourgeois domination, the obvious conclusion was that it had to be replaced by a new one; the possibility of a proletarian counterculture was worth exploring. Yet Liebknecht did not draw this conclusion. He held to the concept of general education and thus also to the notion of a universal culture removed from power structures: "Those who dominate want to make themselves strong and those they dominate weak. Whoever thus favors universal education must fight against all domination."[43] Since power and the human perfection expressed in the concept of culture were mutually exclusive, Liebknecht favored the ideal of general education over class struggle. Hartmut Titze has rightly pointed out that in taking this stand Liebknecht remained indebted to the intentions of the bourgeois Enlightenment, although he radically reversed its political strategy.[44] This strategy was directed against those obstructing factors—that is, the educational institutions of the state—which fostered and perpetuated cultural dichotomy: "The present-day state and society against which we are struggling are the enemies of education; so long as

[42]Thus the Württemberg associations opposed Lassalle and supported Schulze-Delitzsch's program. See ibid., pp. 61–65.

[43]Wilhelm Liebknecht, *Kleine politische Schriften*, ed. Wolfgang Schröder (Leipzig, 1976), p. 134.

[44]Hartmut Titze, *Die Politisierung der Erziehung* (Frankfurt a. M., 1973), p. 224.

they exist they will prevent knowledge from becoming common property. Whoever wants knowledge to be shared equally by all will thus have to work toward a restructuring of state and society."[45] No further support for education could be expected from Bismarck's government because, as Liebknecht explained, he had made educational matters the instrument of a politics based on class. To this extent, the proletarian educational policy was no substitute for political struggle. Its goal of a general human education could be achieved only through political struggle. The intensified politicization of the educational system during the years of reaction, which not even the liberalization that occurred in 1872 under Falk's ministry could reverse, brought the issue of power to the fore. The cultural dichotomy that Liebknecht, in agreement with Buckle, regarded as unique to Germany would be overcome only when the educational system—indeed all cultural institutions—were in the hands of a free people.

As Titze has shown, Liebknecht recognized that emancipatory educational programs were an illusion: "Only to the extent that the proletariat gains power through force can it acquire liberating knowledge for itself."[46] But Titze's conclusion does not take into account that even when Liebknecht criticized the culture of his time he did not touch its traditional content. His polemic against the superficiality of German culture and the great gulf that separated the *Volk* from the educated tacitly assumed that under different social circumstances human cultivation would be possible. Liebknecht insisted that "uniformity in education is a cultural requirement. Equality in education is the cultural ideal." He meant by this a culture embracing all classes. At the end of his talk he returned to idealism, advocating a free *Kulturstaat* in which different interests lived in harmony: "harmony of the individual through the development of all capabilities and the elimination of the contradiction between the ideal and the real, theory and praxis, morals and action."[47] In this, Liebknecht comes close to Humboldt. Surprisingly, he has resurrected the cultivated utopian society, even though he no longer expects to achieve it without a struggle. But this political strategy obstructed his understanding of the idealistic character of his concept of *Volksbildung*. He took its content for granted; at least he did not consider it a problem. In this respect he continued the tradition of Lassalle. Only when the state was in the hands of the people would education spread to the general population and a cultivated society result: "Educating the people is the highest task of the state. Only the

---

[45]Liebknecht, *Kleine politische Schriften*, p. 171.
[46]Titze, *Die Politisierung der Erziehung*, p. 226.
[47]Liebknecht, *Kleine politische Schriften*, pp. 142, 172–73.

state can carry out this task; and if the state proves incapable of doing so, it has no right to exist."[48] This point of view undoubtedly had a lasting effect on the cultural policy of social democracy in the succeeding decades; on one side was the claim voiced by Lassalle and Liebknecht that the working class represented true human culture, on the other was the adherence to idealistic cultural theories based on the concept of humanity.

The cultural concept of the German social democracy, and not merely that of Lassalle's followers, was backward compared to that of Marx and Engels. Marx's criticism of the Gotha group's program made this clear even within the party. When Marx directed his main attack against the idea that the state is an independent entity, he also struck at Lassalle's cultural program, which gave the state a decisive role in overcoming the pseudoculture of the bourgeoisie. By treating the state as a dependent body whose function hinges on the structure of society, Marx excluded the possibility that the existing state could be made responsible for disseminating *Volksbildung*. In his criticism of the Gotha program, he pointed out that only a new state emerging from the dictatorship of the proletariat could assume the task of constituting a new culture. Only after the revolution, as the *Communist Manifesto* maintained, would free development be possible.

Marx and Engels's criticism of bourgeois culture went a crucial step beyond even Liebknecht. Whereas Liebknecht demonstrated how much the educational system of the bourgeois state hindered the spread of culture, Marx and Engels were intent on showing, even as early as *Deutsche Ideologie*, that the idea of a culture transcending class is impossible. This was succinctly underscored in the *Communist Manifesto*, where bourgeois *Bildung* is defined as a product of the bourgeois distribution of property.[49] Since the educational system was part of the social system and functioned within it, Marx and Engels expected that only a new society could shape a different system of education. Only then—and this is the point Liebknecht lost sight of—would the new goals and content become apparent. It is not so much the corruption of bourgeois education stressed by Liebknecht as the fundamental limits of cultural systems grounded in social structures which are the focus of Marx and Engels's criticism. This is why cultural and educational policies play only a subordinate role in the *Manifesto*. It calls for a link between education and material production, but it is unclear if this means a variation on the industrial school. More important is the idea that the educational process cannot be separated from material produc-

---

[48]Wilhelm Liebknecht, *Wissen ist Macht—Macht ist Wissen*, 2d ed. (Leipzig, 1875), p. 40.
[49]Karl Marx and Friedrich Engels, *Werke* (Berlin, 1958–68), 4:477.

tion. Marx later discusses the possibility of redefining the function of the schools, which were adapted to the needs of capitalism, so that they would prepare the way for the abolition of the old division of labor: "While the factory legislation, in a meager concession wrested from capital, has linked only elementary education to mass production, there is no doubt that the inevitable conquest of political power by the working class will also win a proper place for technological instruction, both theoretical and practical, in the workers' schools."[50] The distinction between being and consciousness, which Marx had strictly maintained since the publication of *Deutsche Ideologie*—that is, as a historical consequence of the division of labor in society—has canceled the independence of the cultural realm. Culture as spiritual production, in contrast to material production, is an attempt to legitimize the dominance of one's own class. Whether and in what way literary tradition can be made independent of social history need not be discussed in this context, since we are not concerned with the problem of a reductive interpretation but with that of a critique. The concept of culture and education, which is not subject to analysis in idealism, is understood by Marx as a function of society. Culture (cultural assets), which is objective with respect to the individual and which the individual must appropriate in order to be able to participate in the cultural sphere, is the result of specialized work. Marx's criticism of cultural production fundamentally proceeds, by way of the concept of alienation, from the notion of specialized work. The limits of culture are apparent not only in its ties to class but also in its specialization. Thus culture would not only have a different purpose and content after the proletarian revolution but be different in essence.

In view of its radicalism, Marx's criticism presented insoluble problems for the Social Democratic party: because the practical work of the party had to be carried out under capitalist conditions, its demands, as the Gotha program shows, were concerned with the present. The proposed general, equal education for the *Volk* made demands on the existing state, not on the future people's state. Thus political strategy, no matter how sharply critical of existing conditions, tended simply to end in reform.

The Religious Criticism of Liberalism

The integration model was indispensable for liberal theory, including its radical democratic variations, even after 1848. This was true for

---

[50]Marx, quoted in Berthold Michael and Heinz-Hermann Schepp, eds., *Politik und Schule von der Französischen Revolution bis zur Gegenwart* (Frankfurt a. M., 1973), 1:451.

Hermann Hettner and Gottfried Keller no less than for Julian Schmidt and Gustav Freytag. Keller insisted as much on the didactic responsibility of art to educate the *Volk* as did the conservative Gotthelf.[51] Only the question of its aesthetic transmission was in dispute, as Keller remarked in his diary as early as 1843: "Propaganda is mistaken if it believes that the art of poetry was created only for action and for political or reformatory purposes. The poet should raise his voice for the *Volk* when it is oppressed and in need; but afterward his art should once again be the flower garden and holiday retreat of life."[52] In any case, the audience for Keller is the *Volk*. This is why he insists on the autonomy of poetry; for poetic transfiguration emphasizes the moral and human element as opposed to prosaic reality, and this is what the popular poet must be concerned with: "Literature must be popular poetry, a product of the needs of the *Volk*. In the *Volk*, production and reception are combined."[53] But Keller never makes it clear who the people are. He stands by the concept without troubling himself much about its content. His polemic against subjective caprice (for example, romanticism and Young Germany), which was typical of the early realists, resorted to the concepts of *Volk* and popularity (*Volkstümlichkeit*) at the very moment when they were losing their significance as a social reality owing to the widening gulf between the bourgeoisie and the proletariat. But even though Keller came increasingly to the conclusion in the sixties and seventies that his concept of popular literature was utopian and that it could not gain acceptance in view of the direction society had taken, he was unwilling to abandon it, because there was no available alternative. For him the bourgeois public sphere remained the area where literature had to unfold and come under discussion. Just as he could only conceive of the public sphere as homogeneous and open to all citizens, so he could only develop the concept of culture against the background of that public sphere.

The demand in *Grenzboten* that common sense determine how social reality is depicted poetically is in keeping with Keller's program. Only an experience shared by all rational judges can be defined as a true experience. What distinguishes the editors of the *Grenzboten* from Keller is their belief, typical of the moderate liberalism of the Nachmärz, that the third estate was essentially identical with the *Volk* as a whole. The bourgeoisie was once again assigned the task of guiding society in the cultural sphere. Freytag and Schmidt regarded these endeavors not only as a continuation of earlier liberalism but as a criticism of its

---

[51]See Hermann Kinder, *Poesie als Synthese* (Frankfurt a. M., 1973), pp. 218–31.
[52]Gottfried Keller, *Sämtliche Werke*, ed. J. Fränkel and C. Helbling (Erlenbach-Zürich, 1926–49), 21:54.
[53]Kinder, *Poesie als Synthese*, p. 234.

inconsistency with practice. The structure of culture could be erected only on a foundation of bourgeois work.

The weakness of this position lay in its hasty generalization of the bourgeois concept of literature and culture. The social conditions of literary reception and cultural participation were not taken into account. In this respect, attempts by the church to overcome an entrenched cultural aloofness, on the part of both Catholics and Protestants, proved more successful and also more realistic. Adolf Kolping, the founder of the Catholic journeymen's associations, recognized from his own experience as a journeyman that traditional artisan culture was breaking down and that as a result itinerant journeymen lacked ties to society. There was no longer a unifying bond, he decided, between the educated and the masses. In "Der Gesellenverein, eine Volksakademie" (The Journeyman's Association, a People's Academy) (1848) he wrote: *"The young worker lacks* a *place of refuge,* other than the hostel and the public house, where he can find proper rest and nourishment for his soul, which is intended for him and suits his purposes. Furthermore, he *lacks* the *opportunity to prepare himself for his trade, for his future,* apart from the technical skill he is supposed to receive from the workshop of his master. Even more, *he lacks suitable conversation and amusement that will truly strengthen and uplift his spirit and mind,* such as he gets neither at home, nor at public houses, nor at public places of amusement."* The journeymen associations established after 1846, which quickly spread throughout Germany and Austria, were Kolping's answer to this need. We can conclude from their success, even among non-Catholics, that his program did justice to the situation. He and his co-workers deliberately avoided emphasizing the confessional character of these associations and hostels. Kolping envisioned a religiously grounded academy of the people, a place where the traditional culture of the *Volk* could continue to exist. His program differed from the liberals' concept of integration precisely in its distance from the secularized liberal idea of culture. For Kolping, modern education was an *alienated* education, as his example of metropolitan society made clear. The academically educated and their wives were no longer versed in church doctrine; the kitchen maid showed her superiority by being able to recite the seven *Stücke* (precepts) by heart. This examination of the liberal concept of education was continued in 1854 in Kolping's essay "Was ist Bildung?" where we read, among other things, that "the 'cultivated' world with all its pure knowledge is on the wrong track."[54]

Kolping's criticism was directed against a concept of education

[54]Adolf Kolping, *Ausgewählte pädagogische Schriften,* ed. Hubert Göbels (Paderborn, 1954), pp. 5, 26, 83.

focused on externalities: "In the popular sense, one is said to be educated when one has assimilated that *knowledge* that is disseminated, as I see it, by our public institutions of learning—schools, *Gymnasia*, boarding schools, universities, etc.—and the richer this 'knowledge' becomes, or is, the 'more educated' a person is said to be."[55] A knowlege of languages, familiarity with literature, and the ability to talk about it in a circle of experts—for Kolping, all of this smacked of pseudoeducation. Viewed historically even in this negative verdict, the features of the Enlightenment are still recognizable: culture as a sociable discourse on art and literature from which a humanizing influence emanated. Because Kolping saw this education as a reduction to mere knowledge, it could not be genuine. The very heart of the enlightened concept of culture, humankind's claim to self-determination in the public sphere, had been rejected. Kolping was aware that this interpretation was out of step with the times and that it would be unacceptable, above all to the educated. He therefore forestalled possible objections by making them seem ridiculous. He contrasted the underclasses, to whom his appeal was directed, with the educated; their traditional culture was superior to the "fashionable" education of the bourgeoisie. The educated bourgeoisie had distanced itself from the Christian origins of education and had thus lost the moral praxis by which the value of culture must be daily reconfirmed. Modern education, Kolping objected, results in acquiring culture without acknowledging responsibility.

In listing symptoms, Kolping, as a Catholic, fully agreed with radical socialist critics: the mid-nineteenth century no longer had a homogeneous culture. There were now two camps: the culture of the "educated" produced by the Enlightenment and popular culture grounded in Christianity. It was clear to Kolping, however, that this foundation of popular culture was no longer secure, as his efforts on behalf of journeymen demonstrate. Yet he still wanted to contrast to the dominant liberal concept of culture a Christian concept capable of supporting the *Volk*. Based on human beings' godlike qualities, education was the process that brought them closer to their Creator: "The image and reflection of God in man, which so properly constitutes his being and shows it to be significant, *should be taken further by education to the point of likeness with God, should be more sharply, more definitely shaped*, indeed, should be raised to the highest perfection that this image can attain with respect to the original." Thus, as Kolping repeatedly emphasized, education was foremost a religious upbringing, instruction in the Christian way of life, reliance on the example of the

[55]Ibid., p. 81.

Redeemer, in whom truth, love, and strength were to be found. This Christian education was acquired not through the mind but through the heart; herein lay its superiority to a worldly, liberal education. Its worth was proved by practice—by the exercise of Christian love: "A simple man often seems less good and is all the better; goodness, however, is the surest sign of a true education, which cannot be attained without a strong, active Christianity."[56]

As an editor, Kolping was more aware than his liberal colleagues that the bulk of the population—peasants, artisans, workers—was excluded from the culture of the educated. But popularized education was not his solution to the problem of integrating those who were excluded. Instead, he sought an alternative by which to halt what, in the Catholic view, was the corrupting process of enlightenment. His program was based on the existing needs of the masses. Besides establishing journeymen associations and hostels, he made use of the organs of publicity: journals and almanacs. He regarded almanacs as an especially suitable instrument for popular pedagogy, for they permitted the author to come in contact with a part of the population excluded by the literary system of the educated. The wide circulation of his publications shows that Kolping had hit the right note.[57] Their didactic narratives—stories about country life, criminals, and fantastic adventures—were mostly written by Kolping himself to illustrate his moral doctrine. They tended to be religious and politically conservative.[58]

Kolping and his co-workers did not expect this alternative popular culture to be independent. They hoped by their educational work to lead the *Volk* back to the church. "Without the church," the *Rheinische Volksblätter* stated, "a religious life would plainly be impossible for the people."[59] Their taking responsibility was thus fundamentally out of the question. Kolping typically mistrusted and rejected public opinion as an institution capable of regulating. It seemed to him malleable and lacking in character. Hence he counted the liberal press among his opponents and seized every opportunity to criticize it, seeing enlightened and revolutionary tendencies everywhere. His social conscience was offended by what he regarded as a lack of concern on the part of the bourgeoisie about the fate of ordinary people. As an alternative he advocated a Christian family community in which traditional moral and religious values could be preserved. When this idea was taken up by the press, however, it took the decidedly liberal direction

[56]Ibid., pp. 71, 86–87.
[57]First, the *Katholische Volkskalender* (1851–53) with an edition of ten thousand; later, the *Kalender für das katholische Volk* (1854–65) with fourteen thousand.
[58]See Michael Schmolke, *Adolph Kolping als Publizist* (Münster, 1966), p. 151.
[59]Quoted in ibid., p. 165.

pursued by Ernst Keil in *Gartenlaube*. Keil, too, wanted to break out of the ghetto of the educated public and address readers whom the old journalism had ignored.

Johann Hinrich Wichern's plan in the area of social work to go beyond the Protestant, and especially the Lutheran, church parallels Kolping's work in several ways. Wichern proceeded from the assumption that in the towns, and to a degree in the country, the established regional Lutheran churches had lost contact with the poor. The proletariat—a term Wichern uses frequently—had increasingly departed from the Christian faith because the church showed no interest in its fate. The church was thus faced with a new task: it had to do missionary work at home. In 1849—that is, a year after the revolution, which played a significant role in his thinking—Wichern summarized his program in a memorandum titled *Die Innere Mission*: "Our Inner Mission does not concern this or that *individual* work but the *total* work of love born from belief in Christ. It seeks the inward and outward restoration *to Christendom of those masses* that have fallen victim to the power and dominance of the manifold outer and inner corruption arising directly or indirectly from sin, without having been reached by the prevailing organized Christian ministries as would be necessary for their Christian renewal."[60]

As Wichern defined it, the Inner Mission was the part of the Protestant church that took in the poor, the excluded, and the lost, who were no longer being reached by the state church. The organizations of the Inner Mission gave spiritual and material help to these people in order to lead them back to a Christian way of life. Wichern's motivation in this work was no doubt primarily theological: concern for the spiritual well-being of the atheistic masses. Practical work, however, brought the members of the Inner Mission to a social engagement that seemed alien, if not alarming, to many representatives of the established Lutheran church. Wichern sought to restore what he perceived as a degenerate society, so that everyone could find a suitable place in it and lead a Christian life within the bonds of family and state. Among the moral tasks defined by Wichern was the overcoming of the widespread desire among the people for reading:

> Its corrupting nature is too well known to require detailed discussion here or a detailed demonstration in this respect of the Inner Mission's task. Some good has already been accomplished by associations and by individuals who have distributed popular writings and news sheets or founded good lending libraries; but not nearly enough—in innumerable places

[60]Johann Hinrich Wichern, *Sämtliche Werke*, ed. Peter Meinhold (Berlin, 1962), 1:180.

nothing has been done to suppress bad literature and to give better literature the space and influence it needs to have. Let us say only that what is
meant is not devotional and ecclesiastical literature in the narrow sense but
a popular, wholesome, instructive, pleasing, and entertaining language that
already satisfies the purpose of the Inner Mission if it does not go against
the Gospels.

The Inner Mission was concerned above all with the moral ruin of the
family, yet Wichern was aware that this symptom of decline was closely
linked with socioeconomic conditions. Thus the Christian socialism of
someone like Wichern proved, in a more precise sense than did
Kolping's, to be a reaction to early socialism—specifically, to French
socialism, which he included in the concept of communism. As early as
1848, under the immediate influence of the revolution, Wichern explained this relationship in two essays published under the title "Kom-
munismus und die Hilfe gegen ihn" (Communism and How to Counter
It). For Wichern, communism was the result of the pauperization of the
masses and their seduction by socialist agitators. The consequence was
the destruction of the basic order of society and the dissolution of moral
norms grounded in Christianity. The final result would be chaos. The
required countermeasures would reestablish a national Christian way
of life: "The church has entered the phase in its history when it will be
most called upon to cooperate fully but indirectly in solving those political and social problems that, if solved badly, could lead to the decline
of Germanic education and morality. It must raise the banner of
Christ's redeeming love in word and in *deed* with confident faith, firm
trust, a clear eye, and a heart filled with love for the people." Blame for
the disintegration of traditional society was laid not on liberalism but
on communism, which was inclined to be atheistic and antireligious.
Thus Wichern argued:

> Various ways have hitherto been tried to make the minds of the aforemen-
> tioned working class receptive to communist ideas. Emissaries have been
> sent in all directions for this purpose; institutes founded especially for this
> purpose have emerged, often with the innocent-sounding name of *educa-
> tional associations*; other existing associations, musical associations, and
> reading associations have been transformed into the organs of this propa-
> ganda, and the press, especially local papers, have opened ever-new chan-
> nels for transmitting this spirit to the "workers."

The Inner Mission considered itself a countermeasure. Its aim was to
provide help and support within the framework of the existing society,
which recognized state, church, and family. The workers' cooperatives
of 1848 were expressly declared false forms of self-help. In their place,

Wichern advocated Christian associations embracing all the different classes.[61] The result would be a Christian-social synthesis, which would then find expression in a homogeneous Christian culture. This program, like Kolping's, was bound to clash with the goals of the labor movement.

[61]Ibid., 1:251, 135, 139, 258, 275.

. IO .

Epilogue:
The Road to Industrial Culture

The Culture Industry

The expression "industrial culture" was coined more than a century ago by Friedrich Nietzsche. In *Die fröhliche Wissenschaft* (The Gay Science) he observed that "soldiers and leaders still have far better relationships with each other than workers and employers. So far at least, culture that rests on a military basis still towers above all so-called industrial culture: the latter in its present shape is altogether the most vulgar form of existence that has yet existed."[1] Nietzsche was not the first to establish a connection between the development of industrial capitalism and the change in culture; the Young German writers had repeatedly addressed the issue of literary commercialization. Heinrich Heine, in his Parisian writings, had underscored the influence of capitalism on the production and reception of art. The liberal public sphere of the first half of the nineteenth century was far from the ideal described by later historians when they compared conditions then to those under late capitalism. Nietzsche's observations and those of other contemporary critics went significantly beyond the criticism made by Vormärz writers. They suggested nothing less than the end of what the liberal elite had hitherto regarded as its culture. Nietzsche traced the demise of the classic national German culture to a number of factors. Among them, he cited the prosperity of the bourgeois cultural elite in Bismarck's Reich, the expansion of the state school and educational system, and the decline of illiteracy among the masses, who now sought

---

[1]Friedrich Nietzsche, *The Gay Science*, trans. Walter Kaufman (New York, 1974), p. 107.

to participate in culture. Yet Nietzsche's critical remarks did not develop into a sociohistorical theory. Horkheimer and Adorno were the first to formulate such a theory in their *Dialektik der Aufklärung* (Dialectic of Enlightenment) (1947). Although they may have been influenced by Nietzsche, they were clearly continuing Georg Lukács's analyses of reification (*Verdinglichung*) under advanced capitalism. The object of their criticism was the America of the 1830s and 1840s rather than imperial Germany. But like the early Nietzsche, they were pointing up a historical contrast; the contemporary American culture industry—which they equated in some respects with conditions in Germany under national socialism—was different from the European culture of the nineteenth century. This is especially clear when Horkheimer and Adorno refer to German history. It was precisely the backwardness of German society, they argue, that protected its culture from the encroachment of organized capital:

> In Germany the failure of democratic control to permeate life had led to a paradoxical situation. Many things were exempt from the market mechanism which had invaded the Western countries. The German educational system, universities, theaters with artistic standards, great orchestras, and museums enjoyed protection. The political powers, state and municipalities, which had inherited such institutions from absolutism, had left them with a measure of the freedom from the forces of power which dominates the market, just as princes and feudal lords had done up to the nineteenth century.[2]

Whether this description is valid or only a nostalgic transformation of the past will be considered later. More important in Horkheimer and Adorno's theory is the assumption that the formation of culture as a whole was determined by the developing mechanism of the capitalistic marketplace. This is why the nations of Western Europe and the United States, as classic examples of capitalist society, offered a better field for Horkheimer and Adorno's study of the culture industry than Germany, which entered upon this process later.

The stages of capitalist development also mark the stages of industrial culture. In late feudalism the cultural realm was protected against the marketplace because of its dependence on princely and state control; in contrast, liberal competition capitalism made art a commodity but did not substantially interfere with it. The autonomy of art and capitalistic distribution went hand in hand. The structure that Horkheimer and Adorno, following Nietzsche, characterize as the culture

[2]Max Horkheimer and Theodor W. Adorno, *Dialectic of Enlightenment*, trans. John Cumming (New York, 1972), pp. 132–33.

industry—namely, the wholesale marketing of cultural assets, including formerly autonomous works of art—developed under monopoly capitalism, whose origins are shifted by Horkheimer and Adorno to the twentieth century (World War I seems to have been the dividing line). Production, distribution, and consumption were equally commercialized. Horkheimer and Adorno are really concerned with the psychology of consumption. They analyze the passivity of consumers, who were manipulated into believing that they had to be content with their hopeless circumstances.

Critical Theory defines the culture industry as a mass culture conditioned by monopoly capitalism. It consists of an apparatus by which the production of cultural assets is systematically managed as a business: "Movies and radio need no longer pretend to be art. The truth that they are just business is made into an ideology in order to justify the rubbish they deliberately produce."[3] It is unnecessary to reiterate Horkheimer and Adorno's theory in detail, but two aspects should be noted. In the area of production they emphasize the development of a major apparatus unknown in the period of liberalism. Cultural products are thus subject to the same laws as material products: they are produced in large quantities for a large public. The result is that products and recipients have adapted to each other; both have long since lost their individuality and autonomy. In the area of consumption Horkheimer and Adorno emphasize the manipulation of recipients, who are kept unwittingly passive by the apparatus of the culture industry. The function of this apparatus, which in turn is dependent on big industry, is to entertain a large public. Because the working masses have apparently been freed from the pressure of work for society, they have become all the more involved in this work; leisure-time entertainment, Horkheimer and Adorno theorize, is nothing but an extension of work, not its negation, as the leaders of the culture industry claim.

Notwithstanding its brilliantly formulated insights, the theory of the culture industry presents a number of unresolved problems, connected in part with the cultural outlook of its authors, in part with its theoretical premises. Their statements concerning European culture of the nineteenth century are unmistakably tinged with nostalgia. They can hardly be considered adequate descriptions of the situation in imperial Germany. State protection of the educational system—of schools as well as universities—and control over theaters and opera houses prove on closer inspection to have been a highly problematic defense against capitalism—quite apart from the fact that in Germany and Austria the stage was already run largely with commercial ends in view. At any

[3]Ibid., p. 121.

rate, it is not difficult to show that improvement of the theatrical reper-
tory in Wilhelmine Germany was the result not of state protection but
of such private ventures as the Freie Bühne, which strongly resisted state
control.[4] The book trade, not mentioned in *Dialectic of Enlightenment*,
developed after 1867 into a highly capitalistic industry, which dealt
with literary concerns only if they had economic value. The assumption
of surviving feudal structures within the political public sphere would
lead back in the cultural realm to a problematic assertion of backwardness from which art presumably profited. If Adorno and Horkheimer
had held to the core of their theory—the close connection between the
culture industry and advanced capitalism—they would have seen that
organized capitalism in imperial Germany (cartels and trusts) definitely
provided opportunities for industrial culture. Their emphasis on Germany's special situation brought an element to the fore which had no
place in their economically grounded theory but which, in my opinion,
was important for the genesis of the culture industry: the role of the
state. In marked contrast to France and England, the structure of the
political system crucially affected the cultural realm. Yet this influence
could hardly be said to have had a protective effect in Horkheimer and
Adorno's sense. It must rather be described as a bureaucratic organization of culture which fostered the development of an industrial culture.
State influence and capitalism must therefore be seen not as antagonists
but as complements. The important question, then, is: What cultural
formation will result from a situation in which an authoritarian political system with a strong central executive power is faced with an economic system that in one generation has completed the transition from
an agrarian to an industrial structure?

The theory of the culture industry was not intended as an evolutionary analysis; its focus is on the epochs following World War I, and the
genesis of the culture industry is only a secondary concern. Nevertheless, mention is made of some of the historical factors contributing to
the rise of that industry. For Adorno and Horkheimer the sociohistorical prerequisite for the culture industry was the development of big
industries with a corresponding bureaucratic apparatus at their disposal. Organizations necessary for large-scale production emerged
along with a large public whose desires could be made to conform.
Significantly, Horkheimer and Adorno refer throughout their book to
the masses. The culture industry is neither bourgeois nor proletarian
but a formation in which all social groups and levels take part. Whereas

[4]See on this Manfred Brauneck, *Literatur und Öffentlichkeit im ausgehenden 19. Jahrhundert* (Stuttgart, 1974), pp. 50–86; Michael Hays, *The Public and Performance: Essays in the History of French and German Theatre, 1871–1900* (Ann Arbor, Mich.,
1981), pp. 67–77.

in the nineteenth century only the nobility and the middle class for the most part had the leisure to share in culture, the reduction in working hours which began in the twentieth century permitted even the wage-dependent mass of the population to participate. Adorno and Horkheimer thus see a close historical connection between the increase in leisure time and the development of the culture industry: "Amusement under late capitalism is the prolongation of work. . . . What happens at work, in the factory, or in the office can only be escaped from by approximation to it in one's leisure time."[5] In other words, in late capitalism organized culture serves to make the working masses toe the line, to satisfy their desires enough to keep them tractable. To this extent, it is always, directly or indirectly, an apology for existing conditions.

The relationship of the culture industry to the state is almost lost sight of in this analysis. Since *Dialectic of Enlightenment* is primarily concerned with mass culture in the United States, the description stresses the manipulation of the masses by the privately owned film and radio industries. This model would obviously not have applied to Germany under national socialism. To understand the origins of mass culture in Germany, one must examine more closely the importance of the state. This connection was clear to observers of the time. Critics placed no small part of the blame for the corruption and degeneration of culture in imperial Germany on the state. This may have been so partly because interference by the apparatus of the state was more evident than the cultural consequences of economic change, for which no theory had yet been developed. Yet objections to educational policy or state guardianship over theaters and the press were by no means insignificant. Vague and sweeping though the arguments of critics often were, their vehemence nonetheless shows that the traditional liberal concept of culture was inadequate to explain the profusion of troublesome manifestations in the cultural sphere. Contemporary observers not infrequently linked the changes with the founding of the Reich, declaring them to be the result of Germany's new political power. Unfamiliar phenomena were described as symptoms of decline—not only by Nietzsche but by Paul de Lagarde as well. The new German Reich no longer seemed a place where classic German culture could develop, even though its official representatives constantly appealed to that tradition. The more it became apparent that the longed-for national unification had served primarily to consolidate Prussian power, and the less capable the official new Germany was of realizing the hope for cultural renewal, the more such criticism was directed against the Reich and

---

[5]Horkheimer and Adorno, *Dialectic of Enlightenment*, p. 137.

solutions were sought by which the German spirit could overcome the materialism of the times. Thus Nietzsche hoped in the early 1870s that a counter-public sphere would find its place in Wagner's Bayreuth, until he was forced to acknowledge that as soon as Wagner's festival performances became reality, they bore little relationship to his idea. They exhibited precisely those commercialized traits Nietzsche rigorously opposed.

Bourgeois Criticism of Culture

The cultural criticism of the seventies, which found the new Reich shallow, relied primarily on the concept that had dominated liberal discourse in the early nineteenth century: legitimacy is derived from education. There was an ever-widening gulf, the argument ran, between the aesthetic educational program of the classic period and educational institutions of the present. Criticism was aimed above all at the educational policy of the state, which for various reasons was at the center of discussion in the early seventies. The issue of education went far beyond legal and technical details, for these could be regulated by laws and ordinances. It became, especially for Nietzsche and Lagarde, the central problem of modern culture. Because the state educational system allegedly was a failure, or supported the wrong tendencies, Nietzsche and Lagarde awaited the decline of German culture.[6] Whereas specialists in the history of education are familiar today with the debate over Falk's school reform, the discussion of cultural criticism, which was closely tied to that debate, has been detached from the special historical conditions under which it arose. It is important, however, to reestablish the connection so that its motives and arguments will be understood.

Both in the controversial laws of March 11, 1872, dealing with school supervision, and in the "general regulations concerning the elementary school, preparatory, and teachers-training system," which were issued in October of the same year, the intent was to revoke the counterrevolutionary school policy of the fifties, succinctly defined in the Stiehl directives, and prepare for an appropriate education for industrial society.[7] Public reaction to Falk's reform program, which called for no drastic changes but sought instead to protect schools by adapting them to the changed social conditions, showed how important the edu-

[6]On Lagarde, see Fritz Stern, *The Politics of Cultural Despair* (Berkeley, Calif., 1961).
[7]On the following, see Christa Berg, *Die Okkupation der Schule. Eine Studie zur Aufhellung gegenwärtiger Schulprobleme an der Volksschule Preussens (1872–1900)* (Heidelberg, 1973); and Folkert Meyer, *Schule der Untertanen. Lehrer und Politik in Preussen, 1848–1900* (Hamburg, 1976).

cational issue was considered. The intention of the state to remove the church, as embodied in its priests and ministers, from its traditional office of supervision over elementary schools, was regarded by the parties and institutions concerned as the sign of a new era in school policy. If the reactionary school policy of the Nachmärz had been pursued against a background of cooperation between state, church, and family, the Falk measures seemed an attempt to establish a permanent educational state monopoly. To the extent that these laws and ordinances were directed against the Catholic church, they were part of the cultural struggle of the Prussian government under Bismarck aimed at destroying the influence of the church in the public sphere.

But this was not the only significance of the reforms. In the final analysis, the desired changes went beyond reconstruction of the elementary school system to a redefinition of the cultural public sphere. The changes for which Bismarck had fought ultimately could only strengthen the position of the state. That his intentions were motivated by power politics became clear in the course of discussion in the *Staatsministerium* (Ministry of State); for him the law was above all a tool for restraining and regulating certain elements presumed to be politically unreliable (for example, Catholics and Poles).[8] It was not the government's intention to broach the fundamental question of a cultural state monopoly. Yet even though Falk explained to the upper chamber that the issue was not the separation of school and church "but a more precise delimitation of the rights of the state and the church with respect to schools—nothing more, especially not a resolution to the relationship between church and school,"[9] opponents had reason to fear that this was merely the first step on the road to school secularization. As was to be expected, the Catholic church argued against the law, saying it would weaken its historic and constitutional rights. State monopoly of education would be contrary to the interests of both the church and parents and in the last analysis was bound to lead to a secular society no longer compatible with Christian values. These arguments were made even by conservative Catholic intellectuals such as Konstantin Frantz.[10] More important for us, however, are those who distanced themselves from the immediate situation and concerned themselves instead with cultural-political implications: Nietzsche, in Basel, who cited the danger to culture posed by state-controlled education, and Lagarde, a few years later, who raised objections to Prussian school policy. Nietzsche and Lagarde agreed that Prussian school policy

---

[8]Berg, *Die Okkupation der Schule*, p. 26.
[9]Quoted in ibid., p. 35.
[10]Konstantin Frantz, *Die Religion des Nationalliberalismus* (Leipzig, 1872), esp. pp. 88–125.

had misapplied the concept of education by changing higher schools into career-preparatory institutions. These schools had been turned into licensing agencies having scarcely anything to do with the idea of education. Although the *Gymnasium* was the primary object of their attacks, elementary schools indirectly also came under criticism. In contrast to *Gymnasien*, elementary schools were to be open to the masses and to educate them to perform useful work for society.

Both Nietzsche and Lagarde criticized the spread of education to broader segments of the population. To them this step, which the Prussian state had pursued since the fifties by establishing middle-class elementary schools (*Bürgerschulen*) and modern secondary schools (*Realschulen*), seemed to dilute the real educational objectives of the *Gymnasium*. Nietzsche's lectures in Basel left no doubt that he thought it was not the responsibility of the state to educate the masses. The improvement of elementary schools was not in the interest of a cultivated society:

> The education of the masses cannot, therefore be our aim; but rather the education of a few picked men for great and lasting works. We well know that a just posterity judges the collective intellectual state of a time only by those few great and lonely figures of the period, and gives its decision in accordance with the manner in which they are recognized, encouraged, and honoured, or, on the other hand, in which they are snubbed, elbowed aside, and kept down. What is called the "education of the masses" cannot be accomplished except with difficulty; and even if a system of universal compulsory education be applied, they can only be reached outwardly.

Even if Nietzsche intended otherwise, this interpretation was more in line with Stiehl's concept of popular education than with Falk's reform program. When Nietzsche proposed that true education be reserved for a small elite, he was not, of course, referring to the process of selection which had been followed by Prussian school policy. On the contrary, his Basel lectures were directed against the state's authority to set qualifications—against the instrumentalization of higher schools for the purpose of preserving fine gradations of social and economic privilege. Professional careers, Nietzsche complained, were predetermined by the number of classes a student had taken. He rightly pointed out that this system had nothing to do with the classic ideal of education but rather corresponded to the needs of the state, which had to provide qualified functionaries for its apparatus. Hence Nietzsche's criticism was directed not so much against the new *Realschulen* as against the *Gymnasien*, which were being used for purposes other than those originally intended. "To say the least, the secondary schools cannot be reproached with this; for they have up to the present propitiously and honourably followed up tendencies of a lower order, but one neverthe-less highly necessary. In the public schools, however, there is very much less honesty and very much less ability too; for in them we find an instinctive feeling of shame, the unconscious perception of the fact that the whole institution has been ignominiously degraded, and that the sonorous words of wise and apathetic teachers are contradictory to the dreary, barbaric, and sterile reality."[11]

Lagarde passed similar judgment on the *Gymnasium* of his time; he, too, was convinced that higher schools and universities were transmit-ting not education but a merely superficial knowledge. Like Nietzsche, he held the state's authority to set qualifications responsible for the wretchedness of the higher schools; the competition for social advan-tages had filled the *Gymnasium* with pupils unfit for higher education: "Since, besides, . . . institutions for instruction are very overcrowded, despite their large number, even born teachers are unable to reach the masses, or can do so only as long as their strength holds out. All individualization of instruction ceases, and with it, real instruction; in every aquarium and zoo there is individualization, but not in a Prussian school, which is interested only in handing out diplomas." Lagarde's analysis, however, led him to different conclusions from Nietzsche's. Whereas Nietzsche wanted to restore a pure concept of education, Lagarde proposed abandoning general education and introducing a purely technical school system: "I see only one way to save the situa-tion. For all the reasons just mentioned, the state and the nation must emphatically and with full awareness stop chasing after the phantom of universal education, the phantom, in fact, of an education belonging to a bygone era; they must have the courage to base public instruction— insofar as it is not simply elementary instruction based on personal love—on the only principle on which all public life rests, the principle of duty."[12]

However different their suggestions for a solution might be, they were in agreement on one point: on contesting the state's monopoly over education. Nietzsche above all emphasized the incompatibility of public education and true cultivation:

> With the real German spirit and the education derived therefrom, such as I have slowly outlined for you, this purpose of the State is at war, hiddenly or openly: *the* spirit of education, which is welcomed and encouraged with such interest by the State, and owing to which the schools of this country are so much admired abroad, must accordingly originate in a sphere that

[11]*The Complete Works of Friedrich Nietzsche*, ed. Oscar Levy (New York, 1964), vol. 3: *The Future of Our Educational Institutions*, trans. J. M. Kennedy, pp. 75, 97–98.
[12]Paul de Lagarde, *Deutsche Schriften*, 4th ed. (Göttingen, 1903), p. 164.

never comes into contact with this true German spirit: with that spirit which speaks to us so wondrously from the inner heart of the German Reformation, German music, and German philosophy, and which, like a noble exile, is regarded with such indifference and scorn by the luxurious education afforded by the State.

In Nietzsche, criticism of the educational system was joined with a criticism of pseudoculture; the false desires awakened by the schools gave rise to decadent *Bildung*:

Such a degenerate man of culture is a serious matter, and it is a horrifying spectacle for us to see that all our scholarly and journalistic publicity bears the stigma of this degeneracy upon it. How else can we do justice to our learned men, who pay untiring attention to, and even co-operate in the journalistic corruption of the people, how else than by the acknowledgment that their learning must fill a want of their own similar to that filled by novel-writing in the case of others: *i.e.* a flight from one's self, an ascetic extirpation of their cultural impulses, a desperate attempt to annihilate their own individuality.[13]

Humanistic education, Nietzsche proposed, could only be saved if it was completely separated from the interests of the state. Yet his Basel lectures offered scarcely more than a hint of how this renewal could be brought about. In his conclusion he evoked the spirit of the German students' associations—their unconditional idealism—in order to give an idea of the energy required to overcome the pseudoculture of his time.

The literary intelligentsia's greater interest in the educational system reflected concern for the cultural development of Bismarck's Reich, on which the national liberals had pinned their hopes. The liberal intelligentsia, who called for national unification as the prerequisite for emancipation and were therefore prepared to align themselves with Bismarck after 1866, had counted on the founding of the Reich finally to give German national culture the political form it needed. Thus David Friedrich Strauss expressed the hope in his *Der alte und der neue Glaube* (The Old and the New Faith) (1872) that the liberal concept of culture could be introduced into the new Reich. Nietzsche's vehement protest against this cultural concept in his first *Unzeitgemässe Betrachtung* should be read as symptomatic, not merely as the criticism of a stylistic formation but as the denunciation of a solution no longer historically productive. For Strauss and the moderate liberals, the Reich

---

[13]*The Complete Works of Friedrich Nietzsche*, 3:88–89, 135.

at first represented the fulfillment of their hopes. They overlooked the fact, however, that unification did not simply consolidate existing forces but produced structural changes not confined to the political and economic sphere. It suddenly became apparent that society had changed, although this change could not be conceptualized. As a rule, discontent was confined to complaints about the crass materialism of the *Gründerjahre* (the years of rapid industrial expansion in Germany after 1871).[14] The unexpected changes were still best described by the metaphors of decline and degeneration. For Nietzsche the literature of Young Germany (such as that of Gutzkow) was the first step toward the perverted journalism of his time.

We should not underestimate the fear of the traditional intelligentsia—which included Nietzsche and Lagarde—of the effects of social change on their own position in society. The educational system was of central importance to their status. The intelligentsia received their legitimacy from the state institutions of education. No matter how dissatisfied they may have been with their situation, because they had no share in political power they were not threatened from below, as long as the state employed schools and universities to stabilize existing conditions. The education they acquired was proof of their elevated social position, even if they were not always assured of economic privileges. As long as only a small percentage of the population attended higher schools, the privileged position of the academically educated was obvious. The expansion of the educational system—by increasing the number of *Realschulen* and improving the *Volksschulen*—tended to level status. Whereas elementary school teachers educated in teachers colleges supported this tendency because it furthered their social aspirations, *Gymnasium* teachers were hostile even to the prospect of being on an equal level with teachers in the *Realschulen*.[15] The claim of teachers in the *Volksschulen* to be counted among the cultivated was largely rejected by the humanistic intelligentsia. This was just one of many reasons school legislation was so controversial in the seventies. Lagarde, for instance, equated extension of the school system with loss of prestige for the teaching profession. More schools would have to be established, his argument ran, because of the spreading system of qualification. This would create a greater demand for teachers. Because there were not enough trained teachers available, unqualified candidates would be

---

[14]For more detail on this, see Richard Hamann and Jost Hermand, *Deutsche Kunst und Kultur von der Gründerzeit bis zum Expressionismus*, vol. 1: *Gründerzeit* (Berlin, 1965).

[15]Berg, *Die Okkupation der Schule*, pp. 48–49; Meyer, *Schule der Untertanen*, pp. 117–51; Detlev K. Müller, *Sozialstruktur und Schulsystem* (Göttingen, 1977), pp. 154–78.

hired. The result would be a lowering of the prestige of the teaching profession as a whole.[16] Lagarde saw the German Reich headed for an educational catastrophe that could only be ruinous for the intelligentsia.

Nietzsche's criticism of the German system of education also betrays a fear of leveling. The state aim of giving a larger segment of the population better preparation for future professions by establishing more secondary schools and improving elementary schools was denounced by Nietzsche as the introduction of pseudoeducation, although he did not contest the practical value of those efforts. Above all he fought against the claim of the masses to take part in classical education. In Nietzsche's third *Unzeitgemässe Betrachtung* he called the masses herd people, who were too dull to think and act for themselves and therefore had to rely on public opinion. If it was the goal of culture to produce genius,[17] then the masses, according to Nietzsche, had no part in this task. In the writings of the eighties, sentiment against the claims of the masses was extended to equal rights. Not only was the most basic education barbarism, as Nietzsche put it in 1871, but in *Die fröhliche Wissenschaft* he compared feudal and bourgeois-capitalist culture and gave the earlier formation the decided edge, because it kept the masses under better control. Nietzsche feared that the new rulers did not have as much authority as the aristocracy: "If the nobility of birth showed in (the manufacturers' and entrepreneurs') eyes and gestures, there might not be any socialism of the masses. For at bottom the masses are willing to submit to slavery of any kind, if only the higher-ups constantly legitimize themselves as higher, as *born* to command— by having noble manners."[18] This criticism of capitalism did not favor the masses; on the contrary, they were viewed as a serious threat which could be countered only by a strong hand: "An age of the greatest stupidity, brutality, and wretchedness among the *masses*, and of the *greatest individuals*," is the characteristic remark in Nietzsche's posthumous notes of the eighties.[19]

The crisis in the Bismarckian Reich was a matter of record in the cultural sphere even before the socialist legislation of 1878 brought it to the surface in the political system. In this crisis, political and economic causes were so closely interwoven that for contemporary observers they were all but inseparable. In any case, the means for overcoming them seemed to lie beyond the socioeconomic sphere—in cultural renewal. A

[16]Lagarde, *Deutsche Schriften*, p. 163.
[17]*The Complete Works of Friedrich Nietzsche*, vol. 5: *Thoughts Out of Season*, pt. 2, p. 127.
[18]Nietzsche, *The Gay Science*, pp. 107–8.
[19]Friedrich Nietzsche, *Werke*, ed. Karl Schlechta (Munich, 1954–56), 3:911.

regeneration of the German spirit was demanded, as in Nietzsche's early writings, but above all in the works of Lagarde and Julius Langbehn and in the publications of the Bayreuth circle around Hans von Wolzogen.[20] Dissatisfaction with the results of industrialization—especially its second phase, which was marked by economic depression—was expressed in the desire to escape the logic of economic concentration and urbanization by "overcoming" it. The problem of industrialization was temporarily put aside by attributing it to outside difficulties, which could be resolved by looking back to one's own national spirit. In contrast, apologists for the liberal concept of culture saw themselves faced with a difficult task, for their available theoretical models were obviously no longer capable of giving an adequate formulation of the changed situation.

In the 1860s, the idea of political emancipation had in large part already been sacrificed to the authoritarian bureaucratic state; now, with the economic crisis of the seventies, the theory of free trade lost its power to convince. The liberal theory of the public sphere no longer proved compatible with political and social realities after the founding of the Reich. Thus in the last third of the nineteenth century the concepts of the public sphere and public opinion changed. They largely lost their normative content and were introduced descriptively by such theorists as Franz von Holtzendorff, Albert Schäffle, and Gustav Schmoller as a way of explaining the effects of ideas and ideologies on the public. Schäffle viewed the public sphere as a sociopsychological necessity of nature not based on legislative whim, and he thereby eliminated the content of liberal theory.[21] The public sphere was no longer the area where a responsible public could come together for deliberation but rather one where the masses were guided by a higher authority. The sociopsychological approach advocated in the early twentieth century by Wilhelm Bauer and Ferdinand Tönnies proceeded from the premise that the public sphere fundamentally could be manipulated. German industrialization revealed the weakness in the liberal theory of the public sphere: despite its apparent openness, the theory made the cultivated bourgeoisie the representative of universal interests. No room was left for the masses. It was thus not by chance that this theory lost its validity in the face of the Industrial Revolution. Neither the development of the press nor the new form of theater or literature could be understood with the classic arsenal of ideas. Under the circumstances, the only alterna-

[20]On Langbehn, see Stern, *The Politics of Cultural Despair*, chaps. 8–10; on the Bayreuth circle, see Winfried Schüler, *Der Bayreuther Kreis von seiner Entstehung bis zum Ausgang der Wilhelminischen Ära* (Münster, 1971).
[21]Albert Schäffle, *Bau und Leben des socialen Körpers* (Tübingen, 1875), 1:448.

tive was to adapt theory to the changed conditions, as Holtzendorff and Schäffle did, or to lament the decline of the public sphere.

The Rise of Industrial Culture

The concept of mass culture introduced into the Anglo-American cultural realm suggests a timeless contrast between the majority of the population on one side and a privileged elite on the other. It thus depends on the standpoint of the observer whether mass culture is welcomed as a democratization of culture or rejected as a leveling of authentic culture. The disadvantage in this conceptual formation is its historical imprecision. It allows for no distinction between the early and the late nineteenth-century constellations. In this respect the concept of the culture industry introduced by Horkheimer and Adorno is more precise. It ties the genesis of the new cultural formation to the transition from liberal competition capitalism to monopoly capitalism. In *Dialectic of Enlightenment*, to be sure, the beginning of this transition is placed too late. The economic development after 1873 can no longer be regarded as competition capitalism, even in a backward Germany. Economic depression gave rise to a movement toward concentration which in the course of a generation fundamentally changed the structure of heavy industry.[22] During this phase of organized capitalism, the urbanization of Germany, the key to the reorganization of the cultural public sphere, was accelerated.[23] This reorganization may be traced in a number of examples.

The theater is not mentioned by Horkheimer and Adorno as a medium of the culture industry. The reason is obvious: compared to films, theater in the twentieth century has long since lost its leading role as a mass medium. This preindustrial medium could be adapted only to a limited degree to the conditions of mass reception. Nonetheless, it would be wrong to draw a sharp distinction between theater and cinema. In the second half of the nineteenth century, industrialization had a lasting effect on the theater as well—on its buildings, on the organization of its apparatus, on the form of plays, and on the relationship between actor and public. To begin with, there were notable changes in the ground plans and interior decoration of theaters built

[22]See Hans-Ulrich Wehler, "Der Aufstieg des Organisierten Kapitalismus und Interventionsstaates in Deutschland," in Heinrich August Winkler, ed., *Organisierter Kapitalismus* (Göttingen, 1974), pp. 36–57.

[23]See the statistical evidence in Gerd Hohorst, Jürgen Kocka, and Gerhard A. Ritter, *Sozialgeschichtliches Arbeitsbuch. Materialien zur Statistik des Kaiserreichs, 1870–1914* (Munich, 1975), p. 45.

after 1885.[24] Although the exteriors of these theaters—the Deutsche Theater in Prague (1885) and the Deutsche Schauspielhaus in Hamburg (1900) are good examples—were little altered, their interiors were adapted to new needs. Their auditoriums, foyers, and corridors were given new forms. The space in which the public circulated before and after performances was considerably reduced. Auditoriums, in contrast, were enlarged in capacity by reducing the number of loges (sometimes by removing the central loges altogether) and replacing them with tiers. The two changes were complementary, with the space intended for audiences being used more economically. By sacrificing loges and large lobbies, the chief areas in which the aristocracy and the haute bourgeoisie had displayed themselves, more viewers were given the opportunity to attend the play, albeit at the cost of public space. It is fair to assume that the new tiers of seats were intended for the petite bourgeoisie, who had not attended court theaters and only rarely bourgeois theaters. The new seating arrangements prevalent after 1885 suggest that the composition of the audience had changed. Previously the nobility had predominated in the loges and the bourgeoisie in the parterre; now the nobility were displaced by the petite bourgeoisie, while the haute bourgeoisie retained their traditional places.

This democratization of the theater, however, led not to a radical petit-bourgeois theatrical public sphere but to an arrangement in which the public increasingly lost its distinguishing characteristics and became subordinate to the theater. It renounced its self-presentation. Indeed, comparison may be drawn with Wagner's new theater in Bayreuth (1876). There, too, we find (with a few exceptions) that loges were abandoned and seats arranged so that the audience concentrated not on itself but on the stage. This orientation of the audience toward the stage did not mean, however, that it was brought into closer contact with the play. The opposite occurred. Lighting and the arrangement of the orchestra pit created the illusion of another world on stage. The same effect was achieved in the new theaters by enlarging the proscenium. The darkening of the auditorium, introduced by Wagner in Bayreuth in order to prevent the audience from being distracted, intensified the direct effect of the stage action on the spectators, who lost their own reality, as it were, in the darkness and focused on the world of the stage. Democratization of the theater resulted, in other words, in a passive audience whose participation in theater was restricted to looking. Wagner had already insisted in Bayreuth that performances should not be interrupted by applause for individual scenes; he also forbade the repetition of successful scenes. These measures were intended to elimi-

[24]On the following, see Hays, *The Public and Performance*, pp. 67–72.

nate the mundane aspects of a visit to the theater so that the special atmosphere of a festival production could predominate.

Yet Nietzsche had already observed that the sacralization of the Wagnerian *Gesamtkunstwerk* did not necessarily heighten its aesthetic effect but rather manipulated the audience. Wagner's theater, Nietzsche objected in *Der Fall Wagner*, was intended to move the masses, to overwhelm them by a combination of theater and music. What in Bayreuth was the result of careful planning was only gradually accepted—and by no means without opposition—in municipal and court theaters. But when we trace the development of the German theater from Heinrich Laube to Max Reinhardt—that is, from the middle of the nineteenth century to the beginning of the twentieth—the structural changes stand out clearly. Whereas the form given to the Burgtheater by Laube's theatrical practices precisely fulfilled the expectations of a bourgeois audience, Max Reinhardt's productions—his *Ödipus Rex* in the Zirkus Schumann (1910), for example—were not dependent on a reasoning bourgeois public sphere. They were intended for a huge audience no longer differentiated according to class. The disappearance of the bourgeois theater—bourgeois in the sense of a liberal public sphere—was a process extending over more than two generations, and it would be problematic to describe it merely as an increasing manipulation of the masses. Certain aspects of this manipulation, however, should not be overlooked. They can be characterized as (1) a tendency to subordinate dramatic texts to visual effects, (2) disbandment of actors' ensembles, and (3) domination by the director.

The first sign of change in the use of the stage became noticeable in the Burgtheater under the direction of Dingelstedt.[25] Franz von Dingelstedt was in no sense a revolutionary when he made his debut at the Burgtheater; his work tended to repeat his earlier successes on the Munich and Weimar stages. Whether his adaptations of Shakespeare's plays, which subordinated the dramatic text to his dramaturgical conceptions, can be regarded as homogenized products of the culture industry is a matter of dispute.[26] But his staging, which hypnotized the audience through artful lighting effects, was certainly a step in the direction of total stage illusion. The same can be said for the theater in Meiningen under the direction of Georg II of Sachsen-Meiningen. The duke surely did not intend, through the use of historically accurate

[25]On this, see more recently Simon Williams, "The Director in the German Theatre: Harmony, Spectacle and Ensemble," *New German Critique*, no. 29 (Spring-Summer 1983):107–31.

[26]Michael Hays has raised objections to this interpretation, pointing out that the purpose of the adaptations was to bring Shakespeare's plays closer to the classical form. See Hays, "Theatre and Mass Culture: The Case of the Director," *New German Critique*, no. 29 (Spring-Summer 1983):133–46.

staging, to attract a new audience unaccustomed to culture, but rather to preserve a prebourgeois condition. Yet the effect of the Meiningen style did not necessarily correspond to this intention. Reviewing a performance of *Julius Caesar* by the Meiningen troupe, Otto Brahm remarked that the power of the production lay in its mass scenes, although the performances of individual actors were mediocre so that by the fourth and fifth acts tension was noticeably reduced.[27] However, neither the historical accuracy of the costumes nor the precise choreography of the crowd scenes, for which the Meiningen troupe was famous, resulted in a more accurate rendition of the dramatic work; rather, they exaggerated certain elements of the text. The intrusion of the director is evident in the imposition of his interpretation on the text and the ensemble of actors, which compelled the audience to accept his conception. It was certainly not Georg II's interest in archeology that made the Meiningen theater an influence on later directors; a greater source of inspiration was the calculated overall effect to which individual elements, including the actors, were subordinated. In Germany it was Max Reinhardt who learned most from the Meiningen troupe and made the new concept of directing a success. This new concept subordinated both the actors and the audience to the will of the director.

The rise of the director to the central figure of the theater and the decline of the ensemble went hand in hand during the nineteenth century.[28] The actors of the bourgeois theater formed companies bound by contract, in which every member had a specialty. As it functioned in Vienna under the direction of Heinrich Laube, this organization conformed to the ideas of liberal capitalism. The restrictions imposed on an actor's self-expression were not comparable to the alienated situation that prevailed around 1900. They were, rather, the limits imposed on bourgeois discourse to set it apart from aristocratic gesture. The individual, as Hays put it, is "not missing from the picture, s/he is redefined and integrated into the social whole, just as Laube's actors were integrated into the concept of the performance."[29] In the organization of the early bourgeois theater, the director played a subordinate role. According to Philipp Düringer and Barthel's 1841 dictionary of the theater, the director was primarily a technical manager; in any case, his function was not to interpret the dramatic text by means of his production. The relationship between the actors' ensemble and the theater director may already have been changing under Dingelstedt and the Duke of Sachsen-Meiningen, but the new arrangement did not gain general acceptance until the eighties. The turning point came with the

[27]Otto Brahm, *Kritiken und Essays*, ed. Fritz Martini (Zurich, 1964), pp. 91–94.
[28]On the following, see Hays, "Theatre and Mass Culture."
[29]Ibid., p. 139.

opening of the Deutsche Theater in Berlin in 1883. Although details of the historical relationship are still being debated, the structural change that occurred toward the end of the century is no longer in question. The concept of the director had taken on the meaning it has today. Henceforth the director would be the central figure in theatrical presentations, mediating between the dramatic text and the actors as well as between the production and the audience. When a director controls the form of a performance down to the smallest detail, there is room for neither an ensemble nor the active participation of the audience. The actor submits to control by direction, and in the darkened theater the audience remains in an essentially receptive role, which it may step out of only at a few predetermined points by applauding. The director has a monopoly over interpretation. Through his or her staging, which involves actors, decorations, lighting effects, and so forth, it is the director who primarily decides the interpretation of the text being performed. This shifts communication from the audience's engagement with the play to its reaction to an interpretation placed before it. With this change the audience has obviously ceded the role it had in the classic literary public sphere. It has become mute. This alienation indicates a transition to a new cultural formation.

The institution of the theater, except for the director, included the same elements in 1900 as in 1850, but they had a radically different relationship—quite apart from the question whether we are dealing with a traditional theater or an experimental stage, whether the masses were involved as a viewing public or not. The theater made itself independent, as it were, of the literary public sphere; it was no longer an expression of the latter but rather an apparatus by which that public sphere could be regulated and controlled. At best, viewers found themselves in the position of learners; at worst, they were indoctrinated.

The Press

In classic liberal theory the articulation of public opinion was the responsibility of the press. In 1873 the Leipzig historian Heinrich Wuttke defined the role of newspapers: "And it is the task of newspapers to mediate between those who in this spirit are called on to lead and the mass of the population, to give the latter the necessary enlightenment and understanding, which will allow them to form independent judgments, so that they will not be bewildered by the confusing whirlpool of events but will instead be motivated to take the upward path."[30]

[30]Heinrich Wuttke, *Die deutschen Zeitschriften und die Entstehung der öffentlichen*

We can disregard the question to what extent this circuitous formulation departs from the classic definition of the function of the press (as in distinguishing between leaders and followers). Wuttke stressed the goal of enlightenment not because he was convinced that the contemporary press was fulfilling this task but because he believed it could no longer do so. Toward the end of the century an ever greater number of voices were raised in criticism. The press had assumed a form, liberal observers concluded, which increasingly contradicted its function as an organ of public opinion.

The upheavals described by Wuttze in the early seventies were only a modest beginning, for the new type of paper—the popular, unaffiliated *Generalanzeiger*—did not gain general acceptance until the eighties.[31] Its massive circulation, which only a generation before had seemed unthinkable, was the result in part of rapid development in the printing process but above all of a new economic concept. Whereas earlier dailies had been financed primarily by the sale of subscriptions, *Generalanzeiger* relied mainly on advertisements. The commercial press presupposed a new kind of advertising organization, such as the one Rudolf Mosse and other farsighted entrepreneurs introduced in the sixties. In 1867 Mosse founded his Annoncen-Expedition in Berlin, which soon opened branches in other large cities. By offering himself as a mediator between the newspapers and the advertising public, he revolutionized the advertising business and indirectly also the press. The advertising section was now systematically used to sell papers. Newspapers were addressed not only to the reader but to the advertising business as well. By organizing the advertising market, Mosse brought about a reciprocal increase in production and consumption. Thus in 1883 August Scherl was able to publish his *Berliner Lokal-Anzeiger*—initially a weekly—with a beginning circulation of two hundred thousand, without having to rely on subscriptions, its costs being covered by advertisements. During its first year of publication Scherl charged his customers a small delivery fee of ten pfennigs. Only when the number of buyers leveled off at about 150,000 in 1885 did Scherl resort to subscriptions, at a monthly rate of one mark. The circulation of the *Berliner Lokal-Anzeiger* was considerably larger than that of other Berlin newspapers.[32] Scherl was more consistent than his competitors Mosse and Ullstein, because he organized his paper around the adver-

---

Meinung, 3d ed. (Leipzig, 1875), p. 192.

[31] See Kurt Koszyk, *Deutsche Presse im 19. Jahrhundert* (*Geschichte der deutschen Presse*, pt. 2) (Berlin, 1966), pp. 267–75.

[32] *Berliner Tageblatt*, seventy-four thousand (1871), *Berliner Zeitung*, twenty-five thousand (1878), according to Wilfried B. Lerg and Michael Schmolke, *Massenpresse und Volkszeitung* (Assen, 1968), pp. 17–18.

tisement and not the editorial section. Mosse's appointment of distinguished editors (Artur Levyson, Theodor Wolff) made the *Berliner Zeitung* into a notable liberal paper, but this approach held no interest for Scherl. The *Berliner General-Anzeiger* responded to the requirements of the commercial press: its editorial page followed the dictates of the advertising business.

The consequences of this orientation had been described ten years earlier by Wuttke. Newspapers became dependent on advertising and were thus unable to report objectively on matters involving their advertisers: "Businesses dependent on the exploitation of people usually submit articles intended for columns in the main body of the paper. The opinion of the paper is thus determined by the 'advertisement section.'"[33] Even when there was no direct influence, the editorial section of the commercial press, which was primarily profit-oriented, was under pressure to comply with the wishes of its clients. The editorial staff could no longer regard itself as the representative of the public sphere; it was rather an active organ of the management. Public opinion consisted of the combined wishes and interests of the paper's important clients. The abstract concept of a universal public sphere, illusion though it was, had given early liberal journalists moral support against the pressures of the marketplace. Readers were addressed as reasoning people, whether or not they qualified as such. In contrast, the consideration of the commercial press for its readers and their interests and expectations was motivated by a desire to increase circulation. It is no accident that Scherl began his career as a publisher of dime novels (*Kolportageromane*). As the journalist Maximilian Harden grimly observed, Scherl had an opinion only if it was marketable: "You are now at the crossroads. Local gazette, weekly: wonderful—innumerable gold pieces and a little spot in the history of culture, before Aschinger and behind Wertheim, close by Loeser and Wolff and Tietz. He was a man, it will be said, who had the bright idea of driving politics out of the paper and of stuffing customers with information and little pictures until they were full and, happily satiated, fell asleep."[34]

The new journalism was closely linked to an increase in circulation; it was not, however, created by mass production. The large market and new editorial policies were, rather, variables resulting from the system of the commercial press. Whether the presses bought up old papers or started new ones in the form of the *Generalanzeiger*, the change was essentially the same: the public sphere was dominated by private interests, which were disseminated as public opinion. The commercial press

[33]Wuttke, *Die deutschen Zeitschriften*, p. 20.
[34]*Die Zukunft* (February 16, 1901), pp. 281–82.

came on the scene not as the ideological opponent of the opinion press but as its illegitimate heir. Under the pretext of delivering information to the public sphere at a reasonable price, it presented the news as if it were a consumer product. The more extensive the news apparatus of the big papers became and the quicker it could report topical events, the less meaningful individual news items became for the reader, who was simply overwhelmed by the profusion of unconnected details. In this respect the procedures of the commercial press paralleled those of the new theater. They allowed—in fact, encouraged—the petit-bourgeois masses to participate, but they disguised the price required for that participation: the masses were pressured to behave as the apparatus intended them to. The fact that recipients regarded this pressure as their own inclination only gave added strength to their subjugation. Although readers felt that they were represented by the apparatus of the press, the press considered the readers' interests only as long as they remained willing consumers.

Toward the end of the nineteenth century this was nowhere more apparent than in the development of the illustrated magazine. Whereas the family journal, which to a certain extent can be considered the historical predecessor of the magazine, was still interested in summarizing and articulating the opinions of its readers—petit-bourgeois liberal nationalism, for instance, in *Gartenlaube*—the illustrated magazine was the first medium to create its own audience. In 1891 Ullstein Publishers put out the earliest example of this type of publication, the *Berliner Illustrirte Zeitung*, which was to be a major influence on the character of the press in the coming century. Although the magazine had few illustrations during its first years because the requisite technology was not yet available, its low price of ten pfennigs an issue soon gave it a circulation of forty thousand. The illustrated magazine borrowed from the family magazine such elements as the serialized novel and cultural and business news, but it presented them in topical form so that the paper could be sold on the street. In a 1927 history of Ullstein we read: "The object of the journal was to be so absorbing that no one would want to switch." The commitment of readers, however, was no longer secured by the usual subscriptions but rather by weekly competition on the streets. Therefore layout was extremely important: "When the B.I.Z. [*Berliner Illustrirte Zeitung*] began, and as long as no new methods of illustration were found, its text was almost more effective than its pictures, its main weekly attraction being the gossip in each issue." The journal did not attain its full effect until photographs were reproduced mechanically: "The autotype—i.e., a photomechanically transferred tonal etching—quickly completed its triumphal advance and displaced the woodcut not only because it was cheaper . . . but because it took less time to produce."[35] What distinguished the *Berliner Illustrirte* from dailies and cultural periodicals was its mixture of local information and cosmopolitan reportage, literary entertainment (novels by Max Kretzer, Rudolf Herzog, Ricarda Huch, Georg von Ompteda, Bernhard Kellermann, and Arthur Schnitzler, among others) and popular science. Political information and the formation of public opinion were, in contrast, secondary. The nonpolitical reader was the ideal consumer for periodicals no less than for popular newspapers. The feuilleton, and especially the feuilleton novel, was, as the social democratic press eventually discovered, of central importance for the early magazine form, which could not yet rely on extensive pictorial reportage with running commentary.

If the goal of the new press was to extend the literary public sphere, to make literature accessible to the masses, its result in that public sphere was a change the force of which contemporary observers had difficulty assessing. Complaints about the commercialization of literature and the dependence of literary production on an industrial apparatus give only a partial picture of this change, since they were directed primarily against the commodification of literature. The wholesale transformation of cultural assets into commodities, which Adorno and Horkheimer identified as the distinguishing characteristic of the culture industry, was merely the prerequisite for a new structure that changed general conditions of reception. Walter Benjamin had correctly cited this characteristic in arguing against traditional cultural criticism, although he restricted it too much to technological development.[36] Technical reproduction was merely the medium for a form of communication already anticipated by the apparatus of the press. The new journalism depended on readers looking for a quick source of information, for whom a large, varied quantity of news was more important than a coherent formation of public opinion. Literature had to adapt to these conditions of transmission. Reception was no longer motivated by a concern for personal cultivation but rather by curiosity: an interest in things foreign, sometimes bizarre, but in any case exciting, which the dime novel had introduced into literature in the seventies. Characteristically, the *Berliner Illustrirte* began its series of novels by printing the reminiscences of a Berlin police lieutenant. Popular papers such as the *Berliner Morgenpost*, as Arthur Bernstein was able to show, for the

[35]Kurt Korff, "Die 'Berliner Illustrirte,'" in *50 Jahre Ullstein. 1877–1927* (Berlin, 1927), pp. 280, 283, 286.
[36]Walter Benjamin, "The Work of Art in the Age of Mechanical Reproduction," in his *Illuminations* (New York, 1969), pp. 217–51.

most part became feuilletonistic: "A primary characteristic of the new type of newspaper, the morning post, was that its 'feuilleton' did not— as in other papers—lead a modest existence 'below the line' but instead infiltrated all parts of the paper. Local and crime news, even politics, were 'feuilletonistically' distributed."[37] In other words, the news was presented as a "story" in order to appeal directly to the emotions of the reader. In this process literary-aesthetic and historico-pragmatic discourses drew closer together. The hallmark of industrial culture was an ever-greater meshing of realms and discourses, primarily in the great newspapers but also in the large book publishing firms, which could rightly be called industries.

The Book Market and Mass Literature

Much can be learned about the change in the literary system in Germany from the development of the book market after 1870. The fifties and early sixties were marked by a long recession in the book trade, but the market recovered after 1867 and experienced an exceptional upswing in the seventies and eighties, even though general economic conditions in those decades were anything but encouraging. Between 1868 and 1877 the annual number of books published increased from 10,563 to 13,925.[38] Ten years later it exceeded 17,000. Between 1868 and 1888 production (in titles) rose 62 percent. Ronald Fullerton has rightly pointed out, however, that the number of titles does not give an exact picture of the increase. For this reason he also quotes figures for returns. They confirm a rapid increase. Returns rose from twenty-five to fifty-five million marks. There was a corresponding increase in numbers of bookstores. The 3,079 stores in Germany in 1865 more than doubled by 1885 to 6,304. This growth exceeded that of the population, so that the network of distribution was denser in the eighties than ever before.

A number of factors contributed to the expansion of the book trade, among them development of a national postal service, increase in the number of universities and schools, and urbanization of the population as a whole. Yet these factors alone could not have been decisive, since they did not have the same effect in other economic spheres. More important was the structural change in the book trade and in publishing: the transition from a type of enterprise still rooted in a handicraft-oriented past to one adapted to mass production. Even though the

---

[37]*50 Jahre Ullstein*, p. 160.
[38]Ronald A. Fullerton, "The Development of the German Book Markets, 1815–1888" (Ph.D. diss., University of Wisconsin-Madison, 1975; University Microfilms), p. 325.

important publishing firms were still largely conducted as family enterprises and did not take the form of corporations, their history clearly shows a new phase beginning in the seventies.[39] Traditional business habits were replaced by practices indistinguishable from those in other areas of capitalist endeavor. The special status of the book industry as a trade responsible for the transmission of culture proved an increasing liability and was rejected by the most active publishers. Somewhat later than the editors of periodicals—that is, about 1870—they discovered the reading masses. There were great numbers of readers with no common class background. The traditional liberal concept of education could be reconciled with the capitalist principle of increased turnover and profitability if the literary canon of the classic authors could be successfully offered to a large public for a reasonable price. This was precisely what happened with the series published by Brockhaus and by Gustav Hempel. Hempel was the first to make full use of modern marketing techniques to sell his "Nationalbibliothek." The series was announced with four million prospectuses and three hundred thousand letters, and free copies of its first installment were distributed in large numbers. Even before the series appeared on the market, forty thousand subscribers had been signed up.[40]

Although subscriptions proved an effective method for selling the classics, a new method proved even more successful. The issues of Reclam's Universalbibliothek, which began in 1867 with Goethe's *Faust*, were offered for sale individually—and for a price that remained substantially below that of the competition. Even though the press could depend on the appeal of the series once it had been introduced, each title had to be sold separately. The selection of works was thus crucial for the success of the series. Reclam was well aware of this and emphasized in its advertisements that readers could pick from the Reclam series what attracted them most and assemble an individual library. Reclam's Universalbibliothek in fact gained a reputation for making the German classics available to the masses. True though this is, it does not accurately characterize the nature of the series. The selection mixed cultivation and entertainment—canonical texts which one had to read to be considered cultivated, and some that were suited to summer reading and travel literature.[41] This marketing technique unmistakably homogenized literature as a whole. Standards were lowered and aesthetic pretensions were compromised for economic reasons. If the classic con-

---

[39]See Fullerton, *Development*; and Ilsedore Rarisch, *Industrialisierung und Literatur* (Berlin, 1976).
[40]See Fullerton, *Development*, pp. 332–34.
[41]The published authors included Goethe, Schiller, Lessing, Jean Paul, and E.T.A. Hoffmann, but also Kotzebue.

cept of education—as it was once again formulated, for example, by Adalbert Stifter in the fifties—had strictly distinguished the canon of literary classics from the quasi education of the metropolises, the new book industry persuaded its customers that this view was no longer valid. Though the classics were made as accessible after repeal of the perpetual copyright as contemporary light literature, this was in the final analysis detrimental to the idealistic concept of education, because the latter proceeded from the premise that a classic literary text owed its special quality to its reception, a quality also reflected in the purchase of the book. The editions published by Cotta respected this quality, which the new series and Reclam editions purposely disregarded.

I have no intention of lamenting the destruction of the classic concept of cultivation, which had become an ideology by the fifties (cultivation as social status); my concern is, rather, to define industrial reception. In the Reclam series a play by Schiller or Lessing acquired changed status: contemplation was replaced either by study or by consumption. Edification, which had always been an aspect of the bourgeois conception of culture in the nineteenth century, was eliminated. The new editions encouraged a more objective relationship to literary tradition. Objectification, however, by no means excluded the reification of tradition; on the contrary, the complete series of classics appearing on the bookshelves of the *Mittelstand* did not necessarily promote intimate knowledge of literary texts.

As long as the majority of the population was either completely or partially illiterate, mass literary culture (newspapers, periodicals, books) was impossible. This was undoubtedly the case in Germany in the first half of the nineteenth century. The masses were certainly not readers; even less were they buyers of books. They lacked both the necessary education and the economic means. The turning point came between 1850 and 1870. Although these decades were on the whole still characterized by a concept of literature that excluded the masses, conditions for the most part changed after the first phase of industrialization came to an end. Large urban industrial and commercial centers emerged, densely populated areas in which economic and social interaction presupposed a literate population. Indeed, this process now included the proletarian levels of society. By about 1880 illiteracy had all but disappeared in Prussia except in the eastern provinces.[42] This created conditions ripe for an enormous literary output. The popular book market, which had, of course, existed before, expanded after 1870. The process was a continuous one capable of exploiting the technical advances in the printing industry. The high-speed printing

[42]See Rolf Engelsing, *Analphabetentum und Lektüre* (Stuttgart, 1973), pp. 122–49.

press and the reduction in the cost of paper made possible the mass production of cheap editions. This benefited such traditional mass publications as almanacs, health books, and religious tracts, but also the new type of novel which in the seventies and eighties was the primary leisure reading of the proletarian masses. We know that dime novels, whose authors included such writers as Franz Pistorius, W. Frey, and Karl May, reached readers not through the regular book trade but through book peddlers, who sold buyers subscriptions and delivered installments on a weekly basis. Both production and distribution were strictly organized by the publishers. Authors were expected to follow existing schemes and formulas in their treatment of plots and characterization. To assure the optimum effect on readers, publishers reserved the right to make changes in the text.

The literary pattern for dime novels was set by the 1870s. The narratives of Sue and Dumas could be imitated, but in order to reach the audience, the effect had to be intensified. Whatever one might say about the practices of publishers such as Münchmeyer in Dresden, Grosse in Berlin, or Oeser in Neusalza,[43] they succeeded for the first time in breaking through the barriers of the traditional book market and selling to proletarian readers.[44] This was made possible by the new method of distribution in weekly installments, which were affordable at ten pfennigs even though the total price of a dime novel usually exceeded that of a comparable novel in a regular bookstore. Whereas family magazines continued to address bourgeois readers—though these already included the petite bourgeoisie—the dime novel was aimed primarily at proletarian readers, who had different wants and literary expectations. That these authors—most important among them Karl May—were able to satisfy the desires and interests of the proletariat, despite being guided and controlled by profit-oriented publishers, tells us that once again a relationship, albeit in an ominous form, had been created between a class and a literary genre. The problem is in assuming that these novels were essentially nothing more than a transformation of the earlier gothic or picaresque novel.[45] Though motifs and themes were undoubtedly taken over from older forms, the dime novel, with its social focus, is not simply equal to its predecessors, as the example of Karl May shows. For one thing, producers sought to make their novels topical by reference to recent historical events and figures; for another, the novels had a more pronounced tendency toward social criticism.

---

[43]See Fullerton, *Development*, p. 411.

[44]For details, see Herbert Meinke, "Produktion, Distribution und Rezeption des deutschen Lieferungsromans nach der Reichsgründung 1870/71" (Master's Thesis, Berlin, 1979).

[45]Thus Fullerton, *Development*, p. 419.

Dime novels exhibited the unmistakable marks of industrial culture: schematic production on a large scale, precisely calculated distribution, and a writing style that tried to reach readers by relying on literary formulas and conventions. Some of the traits of the American film industry, as described by Adorno and Horkheimer, seem to be anticipated here. These novels could in no way pretend to be autonomous works of art, as was obviously clear to contemporary observers. Nevertheless, they can only to a limited extent be considered forerunners of later illustrated novels or entertainment films. That this genre could never free itself of the odium of moral disreputability, that it was either ignored or morally condemned by bourgeois criticism (including social democratic criticism), is a sign that it could not escape the cultural ghetto. It remained bound to the proletarian milieu. By the nineties, the dime novel had already passed its peak and was replaced in the book market by newspapers and periodicals. But the new popular papers and magazines, which were aimed at a large audience, were scrupulously concerned with their reputations. We need only compare the novelists of the *Berliner Illustrirte Zeitung* with the authors of dime novels to see the difference. This development can be summed up as follows: only after the disappearance of the dime novels in about 1900 was the literary public sphere ready for homogenized offerings that could be directed successfully at heterogeneous social groups and classes. The mass audience of the commercial press differed from that of the dime novels; petit bourgeois at its core (artisans and salaried employees), it reached the bourgeoisie on one side and the workers on the other. The book market was headed for a similar future. Publishing houses needed to steer literary production in a direction that would make it independent of specific class wants and expectations. This could be accomplished, however, only when the presses had developed their apparatus to such a degree that they could extensively manipulate production and distribution. These conditions did not exist before World War I. Best-sellers were more likely to be the result of fortunate, but uncontrollable, circumstances than of systematic planning.

An Alternative Public Sphere and Counterculture

Industrialization in Germany unquestionably led—especially during its second phase, after 1870—to the development of a literary mass culture in which a majority of the population participated. But can this mass culture be regarded as a culture industry in the sense meant in critical theory? Was it, in other words, a culture in which broad capitalist concerns systematically exploited the cultural wishes of the masses?

Did reasoning readers, to put it in somewhat exaggerated terms, become consumers? The restructuring in the press, the book trade, and the theater conveys a contradictory picture of the developments. The development most easily subsumed under Adorno and Horkheimer's concept of a culture industry is that of the popular press. Here the establishment of large publishing houses, such as those of Mosse, Scherl, and Ullstein, to name only the most familiar, led to systematic control of the Berlin press, from high-quality organs of opinion to tabloids. The book industry, in contrast, remained divided into two unrelated markets serving different social classes. The economic scale of the book publishing houses, unlike that of the newspaper companies, remained essentially that of extended family enterprises, which were unable individually to dominate the market. Under these circumstances, leading publishers were more concerned with the literary reputation of their firms than with supplying a mass market.

A look at the development of culture as a whole in Wilhelmine Germany prompts one to ask whether the thesis that the conditions of organized capitalism inevitably led to the development of a culture industry is tenable. The erosion of the bourgeois concept of culture cannot be correlated linearly with the development of organized capitalism. In Germany, at least, one must consider additional factors that make the total picture decidedly more complex, for example, on one side the development of a state cultural policy going far beyond merely negative measures (censorship) and, on the other, efforts of the organized working class to create a cultural counter-public sphere. These two forces exerted an influence on the cultural formation of imperial Germany probably equal to that of capitalist industry. Although the state program and the socialists pursued contrary goals, their demands and the measures they took were sometimes in agreement—in the fight against dime-novel literature, for instance. Both sides sought to eliminate certain aspects of the capitalist book industry as hostile to culture. I believe that industrial mass culture was fundamentally influenced by the cultural policies of the state and the organizations closely connected with it. It was the interplay of capitalist organization and state intervention, with its rich potential for conflict, which gave rise to the formation that Adorno and Horkheimer were to characterize in the twentieth century as the culture industry. The importance of the state remained hidden in classic critical theory for two reasons: first, Adorno and Horkheimer were primarily concerned with the United States, where state influence historically played a minor role and where there was no bureaucratic apparatus for organizing culture; second, the cultural policy of the German Reich is not easily defined. Even among the states that made up the Reich there was no unified cultural policy. The Prussian Ministry of Education and Culture, for instance, dealt with religious matters and issues of public education but left supervision of theaters to the police.

Ever since the elimination of censorship and the liberalization of laws governing the press (such as abolition of securities and stamp duties), the restrictive influence of the state had considerably lessened. The book trade especially benefited from these measures. What replaced negative regulation? Although literary production was left largely to the free market, the state interfered continuously in cultural life by imposing political and organizational measures on the educational system. In comparison, positive state measures affecting the cultural public sphere were relatively modest. Whereas censorship of the theater remained largely confined to restrictive operations, Bismarck's press policy, which systematically shaped public opinion by building an apparatus and manipulating information, was essentially confined to the political sphere. It was not clear to him that the political public sphere could also be influenced by cultural events. Bismarck failed to recognize the possibilities of an aesthetic politics. Significantly, he flatly rejected Wagner's pleas for support of the Bayreuth festival.[46] This decision was undoubtedly influenced by Prussian government reluctance to appear as a competitor to the Bavarian king, who was known to be a patron of Wagner. At bottom, however, Bismarck had no understanding of Wagner's concept of national festivals. If he had recognized their political value, he would presumably have used them, as well as the Wagner-Verein and the Bayreuth circle, for his own purposes. Ludwig II's support also remained tied to the pattern of royal patronage, which owing to its personal character did not readily translate into political control.

The bourgeois intelligentsia and the new proletarian intelligentsia had a decidedly better understanding of this relationship. The shift of the social democrats to cultural organizations, after prohibitions had been placed on the party, should not be understood solely as a screen for political activity; it was also based on the recognition that mass policy required intervention in daily affairs. This was easier to accomplish through cultural than through political action. The most obvious example of the politicization of culture on the part of the bourgeoisie was the circle of Wagner's friends and admirers which assembled for the Bayreuth festival. As part of the national movement that was spreading rapidly in the eighties, this circle used the works of the master to support German cultural reform.[47] The translation of aesthetic opin-

---

[46]See Michael Karbaum, *Studien zur Geschichte der Bayreuther Festspiele (1876–1976)* (Regensburg, 1976), p. 20–21.

[47]See Winfried Schüler, *Der Bayreuther Kreis. Von seiner Entstehung bis zum Ausgang der Wilhelminischen Ära* (Münster, 1971).

ions into political ideology was already present in Wagner's writings—initially, about 1848, with a radical-democratic aim, later with a popular-nationalistic aim. The goal of the Bayreuth circle was to disseminate Wagner's message. As Carl Friedrich Glasenapp put it: "But now we should tell ourselves that it is our task, as true apostles and evangelists of a new covenant and as living witnesses, to pass on what we have seen."[48] It is not within the scope of this book to give even a brief sketch of the history of this circle and the development of its Weltanschauung. Only one point needs to be made: the Bayreuth circle formulated an aesthetic view of life aimed at exerting political influence. It set itself the task to regenerate German culture from the spirit of German art. The aesthetics of Bayreuth were emphatically opposed to the contemporary commercial theater and opera. With his formula "art as expression," Friedrich von Hausegger offered the Wagnerians a catchword in 1884 that would distance them from formalism. Art became the expression of the national folk character. Great artists were thus expected to transcend individualistic liberal culture and create a new heroic culture in which the German national character could find appropriate expression.

The core of the state's promotion of culture continued to be educational policy. Through its monopoly of school supervision, which the state had claimed for itself, at least in principle, since the early nineteenth century (though in practice it was shared with the church and local authorities), the state had direct access to the cultural sphere. For this reason, discussions of school policy give us a penetrating, if not always clear, picture of the problems created by industrialization. Both the strengthening of modern secondary schools (*Real-* and *Oberrealschulen*), which ultimately gave them equality with the *Gymnasien*, and the reform of primary schools were responses to social change. The traditional division between higher education for a small elite and basic education for the mass of the population was obviously no longer appropriate in the age of industrialization. On the other hand, the ministry bureaucracy could not overlook the fact that any change in the school structure could have an effect on social structure. If the aim was to stabilize the social status quo, changes had to be made with great caution. Hence educational policy in imperial Germany fluctuated between two tendencies: extending the modernization of society to the educational system and putting educational policy at the service of dominant social groups, which used the educational apparatus to freeze existing class conflicts.[49] The triumph of the restoration after 1849 had

[48]Letter of April 29, 1883, quoted in Schüler, *Der Bayreuther Kreis*, p. 53.
[49]See Frank Wenzel, "Sicherung von Massenloyalität und Qualifikation der Arbeitskraft als Aufgabe der Volksschule," in *Schule und Staat im 18. und 19. Jahrhundert* (Frankfurt a. M., 1974), pp. 323–86.

brought with it a fear of the extension of popular education. Prussia had reacted with the Stiehl directives, which restricted the education of primary school pupils to the basic functions of reading, writing, and arithmetic and to religious instruction. This unsatisfactory situation was finally brought to an end in 1872 by Falk's "general regulations." A new plan took into account "the current state of general education, the present development of industry and agriculture, and the situation in public life as a whole" and advocated a new type of school appropriate to the changed conditions.[50] Falk and his collaborators were justly convinced that the traditional one-class elementary school did not provide sufficient knowledge. The multiple-class elementary school became the new, though by no means universal, norm. The curricula for the middle and upper levels put emphasis on the *Realien*—that is, history, geography, nature description, and natural history. Expectations, however, were severely limited in the field of the natural sciences. Schools lacked the learning materials needed to introduce children to developments in technology. Moreover, the adjustment to changed economic and social conditions was in no sense intended to be revolutionary. Falk let it be known in an address to the Reichstag that he viewed school reform as a contribution to the struggle against social democracy.

The reforms undoubtedly strove to make the masses literate in order to qualify them for their future occupations. But this aim was thwarted by simultaneous efforts to secure their religious and political loyalty. Even Falk's ministry held to the view that moral-religious training was at the core of education. Stronger financial support of elementary schools and increases in teachers' salaries, which were perceived by the public sphere as a growing interest by the government in elementary schools, did little to change this basic attitude. Prussia's elementary school policy remained contradictory. The government was completely opposed to separation of church and state, favoring instead church support for the moral education of children. Robert von Puttkamer voiced this view in 1879 when he stated, after Falk's resignation: "An ethical and religious training and instruction of the young in schools is a matter in which the state, which bears legal responsibility for the direction and supervision of all aspects of education, and the church—the Evangelical no less than the Catholic—as the Christian place of healing, have an equal interest, an interest that should be reflected by the work they do together in the schools."[51] What German idealism meant for the *Gymnasium*, religion meant for the elementary school—the firm base on which the structure of knowledge would be erected. This re-

---

[50]Quoted in Berg, *Die Okkupation der Schule*, p. 69.
[51]Quoted in ibid., p. 92.

ligious concept of education, still based largely on prebourgeois conceptions, was intended, among other things, to be a restraint on social democracy.

The politicization of the schools became especially evident after 1889.[52] The order of Wilhelm II on May 1 of that year officially brought class conflict into the schools. The intensification of the political conflict shifted priority to measures that would foster "fear of God and love of the Fatherland," as Wilhelm II said. The modernization of the schools thus became an explicit political issue. On one side, overt indoctrination was demanded in order to show pupils the destructiveness of social democratic doctrine; on the other, the Social Democratic party (SPD) backed efforts to adapt elementary schools to the requirements of modern economic life (as stated in the election manifesto of 1884). The increasingly conservative educational policy of the Prussian state, the primary goal of which after 1890 was to repulse the socialists, returned to the image of the subservient citizen and subject. To expand education, which would have encouraged independent thinking, was no longer in the interest of the state. If the tendencies of Falkian reform could be regarded as support for the new industrial culture—which is why the conservatives attacked it—the growing political conflict between the various powers supporting the state and the socialists restricted the policy of reform, though without suspending it entirely, since it accorded with the needs of an industrial society. Pupils were to identify with existing conditions and at the same time to acquire as much practical knowledge as was necessary to qualify for a profession. Under the circumstances, the state viewed the literacy of the masses—even when unpolitical, as in the reading of entertainment literature—with suspicion. Legislation against the dime-novel trade, accused of immorality by its bourgeois critics, was evidence of this concern in the bureaucracy.[53]

The Wilhelmine state had an ambivalent relationship to industrial mass culture. It opposed mass culture when the latter cast doubt on existing conditions; it adapted to mass culture—indeed, fostered it— when it promised to support the status quo. This pragmatic approach remained strangely blind to the more profound changes in the cultural sphere. By so obviously politicizing education, the emperor and government obscured their view of the more far-reaching consequences of mass culture, which in the long run—even when it was politically neutral—did not support the authoritarian system of the empire. Few

[52]See Hartmut Titze, Die Politisierung der Erziehung (Frankfurt a. M., 1973), pp. 226–62. But by the seventies Moltke had already stressed the significance of the Volkschule for the defense against revolutionary forces. See Titze, p. 228.

[53]Meinke, Produktion, pp. 72–88.

attempts were made, beyond the scope of educational policy, to come to terms with the new cultural formation. Guidance was largely left to local authorities and to organizations not connected with the state, such as churches or associations that for one reason or another were concerned with the spread of culture, for example, the library movement. In public discussion the earlier *Volksbibliotheken* were condemned by most librarians as being poor in quality. After 1895, however, the *Bücherhallenbewegung* (library movement) gave rise to a new concept of the public library, which, based on the American model, was not restricted to a specific social class. The new public libraries were to be open to all citizens, the choice of books taking into account the wants of a broader public. Constantin Nörrenberg (1862–1937), one of the leading spokesmen of the movement, advocated merging existing public and municipal libraries into general educational libraries: "Reading rooms should be maintained on a regular basis by cities or local government units, perhaps with state support. It would be desirable to create central offices for advising communities or associations seeking to establish reading rooms."[54] Before World War I, however, local government financing for these new educational libraries was less than anticipated. In most cases, the establishment of new reading rooms depended on the initiative of individuals or associations, though up to a certain point preexisting organizations could count on municipal help. Institutions offering support included the Gesellschaft für ethische Kultur, founded in 1892; the Comenius-Gesellschaft; and the older Gesellschaft für die Verbreitung von Volksbildung. The task of these institutions was to prepare the ground for municipal public libraries. They also gave money to equip libraries when cities and communities were unable to assume the costs themselves. Thus in 1899 the Comenius-Gesellschaft urgently requested the magistrates of German cities with more than one hundred thousand inhabitants to establish public libraries, offering as one of their reasons that they would lower the costs of relief for the poor and of fighting crime. The ideologues of the *Bücherhallenbewegung* advocated public support for libraries as a means of giving a higher ethical tone to the population. The state and communities, the argument ran, should provide for libraries, as public institutions of learning, to the same degree that they provided for pupils, theaters, and museums.[55] It was suggested to municipal and state administrations that social problems—not least the bad influence exerted on the masses by trashy literature—could be resolved by fostering public libraries.

---

[54]Wolfgang Thauer and Peter Vodosek, *Geschichte der öffentlichen Bücherei in Deutschland* (Wiesbaden, 1978), p. 45.

[55]See Ernst Schultze, *Freie öffentliche Bibliotheken, Volksbibliotheken und Lesehallen* (Stettin, 1900).

Despite this propaganda, cities and communities held back. Even the Prussian state approached the new task with hesitation. Although the Ministry of Education and Culture supported the establishment of public libraries in an edict of 1899,[56] its yearly subsidy of fifty thousand marks shows that the state expected them to have no appreciable influence on the populace. Plainly, a comprehensive cultural policy had not yet been developed. The initiative was deliberately left to private associations and organizations, which were to pacify the masses by working for education. The company library established by the Krupp firm and headed since 1898 by a leader of the public library movement, Paul Ladewig, may have agreed to a certain extent with the intentions of the state (warding off social democracy), but the library founded in Hamburg in 1899 by the Patriotische Gesellschaft was closer to the spirit of enlightened concern for the general good. Cities and communities before World War I by and large played the role of well-intentioned observers. The planning of new libraries and the formulation of politically motivated cultural goals was the work of private associations and their spokespersons. The latter continued the tradition of the Enlightenment, which sought to bring literature gradually to the people. Yet the situation in about 1900 was fundamentally different from that of the early nineteenth century. The literate masses were now pressing for cultural participation. A decision had to be made about the form this participation would take. Although librarians were generally against politicization of public libraries,[57] they repeatedly found themselves between two fronts. In bourgeois circles it was often feared that public reading rooms would serve the forces of the political opposition. The socialists, on the other hand, were convinced that these libraries were intended as countermeasures to the workers' libraries of the party and trade unions.

The public library movement had proceeded by and large from a traditional concept of cultivation. Its goal was to bring good literature to the population. At first, the question whether this concept of education was still applicable did not arise. It became important only after the policy dispute of 1912 between Ladewig and Walter Hoffmann provoked vehement discussion among librarians. The cause of the dispute was Ladewig's *Die Politik der Bücherei* (The Politics of the Lending Library) (1912). Whereas Ladewig took up the idea of the American public library, defining it as a matter of public communication, Hoffmann, in his response, made its educational value paramount. He

---

[56]*Centralblatt für die gesamte Unterrichts-Verwaltung in Preussen* vol. 30 (Berlin, 1899), pp. 760–72.
[57]See Thauer and Vodosek, *Geschichte der öffentlichen Bücherei*, p. 63.

stressed the individual character of library work (guidance and teaching), vehemently opposing American methods, which were adapted for large numbers of people. Ladewig's point of view was in fact a departure from traditional concepts. In opposition to Hoffmann and his school's concept of education, Ladewig argued in 1914 that education was not the goal but the consequence of library work.[58] He called for libraries that would serve the public as did the post offices and the railroad. In short, he proceeded from the premise that culture was no longer the privilege of a social group but rather the concern of the masses. Whereas Ladewig regarded the reading masses as responsible, Hoffmann saw his readers as in need of guidance; the advice of librarians was thus of central importance. Such phrases as "decorative educational mechanisms," which were used to describe large libraries, demonstrate the spirit of the cultural criticism of the time.[59] Differing criteria for the selection of books reflected the opposing concepts. Whereas librarians in Hoffmann's camp aimed at imparting a literary-aesthetic education and accordingly sought to restrict both the potential circle of readers and the kinds of books in circulation, Ladewig's and Erwin Ackerknecht's supporters, who belonged to the so-called Stettiner Richtung, favored a new cultural concept. They took for granted that the Industrial Revolution had brought literacy to the masses, and they viewed literature as one among a number of forms of communication. In contrast to Hoffmann, Ladewig and Ackerknecht were prepared to recognize contemporary culture as an industrial mass culture.

Culture Industry or Counterculture?

This brings us to the central question: Was the development we have just described inevitable? Was industrial mass culture unavoidable? It is worth noting that the social democrats did not pose the question in this form.[60] They undoubtedly favored equal cultural participation for the proletarian masses from the start, yet they did not choose to characterize the spread of culture in Nietzsche's sense as industrial culture.[61] Rather, they assumed that correct guidance and education would help the proletariat adapt to bourgeois culture without changing the sub-

---

[58]Paul Ladewig, *Katechismus der Bücherei* (Leipzig, 1914).

[59]Cf. the positive evaluation of Hoffmann's work in Werner Picht, *Das Schicksal der Volksbildung in Deutschland* (Braunschweig, 1950), pp. 160–76.

[60]See Frank Trommler, *Sozialistische Literatur in Deutschland. Ein historischer Überblick* (Stuttgart, 1976).

[61]See Frank Trommler, "Die Kulturpolitik der DDR und die kulturelle Tradition des deutschen Sozialismus," in P. U. Hohendahl and P. Herminghouse, eds., *Literatur und Literaturtheorie in der DDR* (Frankfurt a. M., 1976), pp. 13–72.

stance of the cultural assets acquired. To this extent, social democrats shared the concern of the bourgeois intelligentsia that trashy literature (labeled bourgeois) could have a bad influence on the masses. The social democratic polemic against entertainment literature—that is, against dime novels—was not fundamentally different from bourgeois criticism.[62] In his famous lecture "Wissen ist Macht—Macht ist Wissen," Liebknecht informed members of the Leipzig Workers' Educational Association in 1872 that Bismarck's state was by no means the *Kulturstaat* it made itself out to be. Liebknecht criticized both the press and mass literature, concluding that "the cheapest kind of light entertainment literature, which is mainly bought by the *Volk*—including the so-called *Kolportageromane* or dime novels—are almost without exception (I think one can say without exception) in form miserable trash and in content opium for the mind and poison for morality."[63] It did not occur to socialist critics to take into account the potential sociocritical content of dime novels.[64] Their arguments against the new mass literature, from which the working class had to be protected, were comparable to the objections of bourgeois critics; emphasis was on aesthetic mediocrity and moral decadence. When Liebknecht made the claim for social democracy as the party of culture, he referred not to Marx or Engels but to Aristotle: "What is education? According to the classical definition of the Greeks it is the *kalon kagathon*, the beautiful and the good brought to expression in a personality—'the development of all the virtues,' which Aristotle defines as the purpose of education, the harmonious development of all the capabilities, both physical and mental, slumbering in an individual."[65] This classical definition was at the heart of Liebknecht's cultural policy, which demanded the development and restructuring of elementary schools and insisted that the class dominance of the bourgeoisie distorted education. Liebknecht undoubtedly wanted to eliminate educational privilege, to make knowledge the common property of all, but it never occurred to him that the concepts of culture and education might in themselves be ideological. In his justified criticism of a false training for literacy among the masses,

---

[62]See Meinke, *Produktion*, pp. 89–96; Kristina Zerges, *Sozialdemokratische Presse und Literatur. Empirische Untersuchungen zur Literaturvermittlung in der sozialdemokratischen Presse 1876 bis 1933* (Stuttgart, 1982).

[63]Wilhelm Liebknecht, *Kleine politische Schriften*, ed. Wolfgang Schöder (Leipzig, 1976), p. 149.

[64]On their sociocritical content, see Manuel Köppen and Rüdiger Steinlein, "Karl May: Der verlorene Sohn oder Der Fürst des Elends (1883–85). Soziale Phantasie zwischen Vertröstung und Rebellion," in H. Denkler, ed., *Romane und Erzählungen des bürgerlichen Realismus* (Stuttgart, 1980), pp. 274–92.

[65]Liebknecht, *Kleine politische Schriften*, p. 166.

which, as Liebknecht pointed out, was merely a preparation for military service, he held to the view that the authentic concept of education could be restored through political strategy. Triumph over class dominance, Liebknecht assured his audience at the end of his lecture, would restore harmonious education in a free society.[66]

Liebknecht's concept of culture found a parallel in Ferdinand Lassalle's and Franz Mehring's concept of literature,[67] which followed the idealistic tradition and made the new class heir to bourgeois literature. Lassalle emphasized the importance of Weimar classicism. Mehring, for political reasons, favored early bourgeois literature over contemporary naturalism, which as a movement saw itself to an extent as the literary counterpart of socialism.[68] He insisted that a socially critical literature had to take an optimistic approach transcending the present. "Only where naturalism has gone beyond capitalist thinking itself," he wrote, "and is capable of grasping the beginnings of a new world in its inner essence is its effect revolutionary, does it become a new form of artistic representation, which even now is not inferior in its singular greatness and power to any earlier one and which is destined one day to surpass all others in beauty and truth."[69] Although Mehring believed that this spirit was present in Hauptmann's *Die Weber*, he was later to be more skeptical about the modern age of literature, to which he attributed a deep pessimism incompatible with the future of the proletariat.[70] In 1896 he warned in general against overestimating the role of literature in the workers' struggle for emancipation, citing the political struggle in Parliament, in which the bourgeoisie of the eighteenth century could not have participated.

One should not, however, conclude from this assessment, which was shared by Liebknecht and Bernstein, that the ideological literary struggle was underestimated and ignored by the SPD at the end of the nineteenth century. The character and function of working-class literature was insufficiently discussed because the leading theorists of the party favored a traditional concept of culture and made the literary heritage the central issue. How should the party have reacted to this literature, which had been born in the milieu of the labor movement? What rela-

[66]See Brigitte Emig, *Die Veredelung des Arbeiters* (Frankfurt a. M., 1980), pp. 128–53.
[67]On Lassalle, see ibid., pp. 47–61.
[68]See Manfred Brauneck, *Literatur und Öffentlichkeit im ausgehenden 19. Jahrhundert*, pp. 99–116; and Dietger Pforte, "Die deutsche Sozialdemokratie und die Naturalisten," in H. Scheuer, ed., *Naturalismus* (Stuttgart, 1974), pp. 175–205.
[69]Franz Mehring, *Aufsätze zur deutschen Literaturgeschichte* (Leipzig, 1972), p. 319.
[70]See Mehring, *Kunst und Proletariat*, in his *Gesammelte Schriften*, ed. Thomas Höhle, Hans Koch, and Josef Schleifstein (Berlin, 1960–67), 11:135.

tionship did this proletarian writing have to the massive quantity of literature then being distributed? Should dime novels have been opposed, or should this new form have been accepted so that new readers could be found for the party's publications? Kristina Zerges has rightly pointed out that the functionaries of the SPD were well aware of the importance of these questions.[71] Literary strategy was debated not only at the party congress of 1896, as Zerges has shown, but over the course of several decades. After the socialist legislation was rescinded, social democracy was confronted by a different type of press—the mass commercial press, which because of its price policy was able to penetrate the workers' milieu. The party sought to counter the new strategy of the bourgeois press by fighting it with its own weapons. But this strategy presented problems insufficiently understood and thought through by the socialist editors. As long as the contrast between bourgeois and proletarian culture was substantially maintained—that is, as long as primary emphasis was on class differences—the changes brought about by industrialization were not readily perceived. No appropriate theories and methods for dealing with the new mass press yet existed.

The SPD reacted to the feuilletonistic press by founding *Neue Welt*, a weekly arts supplement to the regional party papers: "When organizing and structuring individual issues of *Neue Welt*, its editors copied the layout of bourgeois entertainment journals, especially *Gartenlaube*."[72] (The text comprised serialized novels and short prose essays, either on the literary life of the time or addressing questions in the natural sciences. It also included poems, and from 1892 on monotony was relieved by a puzzle corner and a letters to the editor section on the last page of the paper.) Its leading editors, first Curt Baake and later Edgar Steiger, were convinced that class-conscious workers needed to clearly distinguish themselves from bourgeois literary activity. Both Baake and Steiger allied themselves with naturalism and wished to see the political struggle for proletarian emancipation joined with the radical social criticism of the naturalists. On naturalistic literature, *Neue Welt* said: "We wish therefore to learn from it and to be inspired by it in our struggles. And perhaps the hour is no longer far away when alongside the despairing poetry of the bourgeoisie there will appear a hopeful new proletarian poetry that will be literature, that will truly be the spirit of our spirit."[73] This alliance with naturalism presented problems for *Neue Welt*. The newspaper was criticized at the party congress of 1892 because of party concern that the interests of its editors did not accord

[71]Zerges, *Sozialdemokratische Presse und Literatur*, esp. pp. 72–117.
[72]Ibid., p. 52.
[73]*Neue Welt* I (1892):6.

with the wishes of its readers. In particular, the novels printed in the paper appeared not to meet readers' expectations. Although this criticism was repeated in one form or another at every party congress, the issue was never fundamentally resolved because the attempt was being made to reconcile two mutually exclusive concepts. On one side, the delegates called for a popular entertainment journal able to compete with *Gartenlaube*; on the other, they sought to improve readers by offering good novels and exemplary biographies. Whatever the case, trashy literature was unwanted. They appealed either to the classic concept of culture or to the interests of readers, which were more in accord with family magazines than with the classics. Both concepts could be characterized as popular education, and it was not always clear from the discussion that they were very different in content.

After 1896 *Neue Welt* developed into an entertainment supplement that took into account the tastes of its potential readers. The concept was no longer that of a counterculture but rather of a parallel culture that placed the social democratic apparatus alongside the bourgeois apparatus as a means of preventing the proletariat from becoming bourgeois. The same can be said of the magazine *In Freien Stunden*, founded in 1897. Its aim was to keep workers away from the worthless novels offered by the popular presses and the publishers of *Kolportage*. A compromise was reached by allowing the voices of both bourgeois and socialist authors to be heard. Novels by, say, Hugo and Robert Schweichel were printed at the same time. During the first years of its publication, the magazine maintained a certain literary standard; in 1899, however, its editors attempted to meet capitalist competition by printing Xavier de Montepin's dime novel *Töchter des Südens* (Daughters of the South).[74]

The social democratic press wavered, as we have seen, between a countercultural and a subcultural conception. Whereas social democratic literary theory favored a concept of culture stressing its contrast to late-bourgeois literary activity, and thus either appealed to early-bourgeois literature (such as that of Mehring) or supported the naturalistic avant-garde, pragmatic journalism, not least because of the pressure of competition from the new mass press, moved closer to the concept of a subculture offering the same forms and works as the dominant culture. Comparisons were drawn to the culture of the bourgeois camp. Thus *In Freien Stunden*'s choice of novels, for instance, was not essentially different from that of a bourgeois fiction magazine. Bourgeois authors such as Alexis, Grillparzer, Schücking, Gotthelf, and

---

[74]There was no lack of criticism. Such a novel, it was said, could not educate morally and ethically. See Zerges, *Sozialdemokratische Presse und Literatur*, p. 87.

Gerstäcker, predominated. This selection was in part determined by economic factors; in order to reduce fees, the editors often selected authors whose works could be printed at no cost.[75] Yet the repertoire was obviously determined by a literary concept derived from the bourgeois camp. The link with an older bourgeois culture was regarded as important because it provided a common opponent: the mass literature denounced as trash. Social democrats suddenly joined bourgeois cultural critics without asking themselves whether the concepts of classic idealistic aesthetics were still applicable in socialist criticism. The socialists may have condemned capitalist mass literature, but they had no criteria of their own for distinguishing between worthwhile and worthless literature. This would have been possible only with the help of an ideological-critical method, which was not available to social democratic literary theory in this area. To this extent, the intention to create a separate literary public sphere—and such an intention unquestionably existed—inevitably resulted in the imitation of the bourgeois literary public sphere; that is, in the establishment of another camp, which, although opposed to the bourgeois camp, was yet structurally similar.[76]

The moralizing of literary critics, the fear of trashy literature, proved to be the Achilles' heel of social democratic cultural policy, for it prevented analysis both of the conditions of literary production under organized capitalism and of the receptivity of proletarian readers. Why did workers and their families read "bad" literature with the same enthusiasm as petit-bourgeois readers? Why was an author such as Eugenie Marlitt, whose petit-bourgeois origins were obvious, also popular among proletarian readers? Clearly, the literary education of the masses did not proceed as the SPD would have liked it to. When it established libraries for workers, the party hoped to reach beyond its members. But it never succeeded wholly, or even significantly, in influencing the literary consumption of the working class. This was due partly to the character of the workers' libraries, which were not always geared to the tastes of their readers; partly to competition from commercial lending libraries; and after 1900 increasingly to competition from public libraries. The working class made extensive use of public libraries because their collections clearly accommodated the interests of their readers. As late as the nineties, workers' libraries were still not uniformly organized. It took considerable effort to bring the numerous small, scattered libraries together, for local associations often resisted disbanding their collections and placing them in a central library. Such

---

[75]See ibid., p. 195.

[76]On the thinking in the various camps, see Oskar Negt and Alexander Kluge, *Öffentlichkeit und Erfahrung* (Frankfurt a. M., 1972), pp. 341–55.

concentration made progress only after 1900, so that "in the spring of 1914 . . . according to a statistical study undertaken by the central board of education of the SPD, there existed a total of 1,147 workers' libraries in 748 localities."[77] Of these, 51.5 percent were centralized, and 48.5 percent were under the jurisdiction of individual parties or trade union organizations. Most libraries were small and could offer workers only a limited choice of the literature they wanted.

As the librarian Ernst Koch defined them, workers' libraries were the educational institutions of the organized proletariat; they were intended to provide workers with the mental equipment for the class struggle. Librarians, however, had to grapple with the same problems confronting social democratic newspaper editors. Libraries had to help prepare for the socialist culture of the future and at the same time take into account the current needs of the proletariat. The expansion of libraries, which was a response to these needs, did not necessarily accord with the goals of the class struggle. Like the social democratic press, workers' libraries took the route of accommodation; more belletristic literature than the party preferred was purchased. Not even the reading recommendations of leading party functionaries—Otto Bauer, for instance—had a lasting effect on the reading habits of the workers. According to the calculations of Dieter Langewiesche and Klaus Schönhoven, during the period between 1908 and 1914, 63 percent of the works in circulation were belletristic whereas only 4.3 percent were related to the social sciences. The sources show clearly that literature dealing with the class struggle of workers accounted for only a fraction of the works borrowed; the largest proportion was bourgeois entertainment literature or canonical bourgeois literature. Although social democratic literary theorists—notably Mehring—put special emphasis on the classical period, there was little interest in the classic German authors. On the other hand, representatives of European realism—for example, Zola, Scott, and Dickens—were thoroughly appreciated. This is worth noting, because it disproves the notion that trashy literature was the workers' primary reading material. Among the ten most-read authors in the social democratic Ortsvereinbibliothek (community library) of Leipzig were Heyse and Rosegger, but also Zola, Raabe, and Anzengruber. Dumas was read, but so were Tolstoy, Bulwer-Lytton, and even Fontane. This information does not differ essentially from that imparted by the circulation figures of public libraries. In fact, the record of works borrowed from the library of the Krupp firm demonstrates that workers were more interested in the traditional canonical authors, such as

---

[77]Dieter Langewiesche and Klaus Schönhoven, "Arbeiterbibliotheken und Arbeiterlektüre im Wilhelminischen Deutschland," *Archiv für Sozialgeschichte* 16 (1976):135–204; quotation from p. 159.

Schiller, Lessing, Kleist, and Goethe, than were salaried employees.[78] Of course, such considerations have to account for the choices available. A library's collection determined circulation. Librarians sometimes ignored books by authors such as Marlitt or Nataly von Eschstruth, even though workers enjoyed reading them. Wherever light reading was made available, as in the Vienna workers' library, it shows up in the statistics. Marlitt, Heimburg, and Doyle were favorite authors. In contrast, the working-class poetry fostered by the party found only moderate response in Austria and Germany. Langewiesche offered the following succinct formulation of the situation in the twenties: "Literature by and for workers—we learn from circulation records—is not automatically what workers read, just as in general the origins of a piece of literature and the group for which it is intended do not necessarily tell us anything about the specific groups receptive to it."[79]

The reading habits of workers did not accord with the wishes of the socialist parties, which sought above all to further socialist literature. It never occurred even to class-conscious proletarian readers—which is what, we may assume, users of the workers' libraries were—to regard the reading of novels and plays as mere preparation for scholarly literature. Still, the party could consider it a positive result that those who used the workers' libraries were exposed more than other groups of readers to sociocritical literature. One can hardly conclude from this, however, that the workers' libraries created a socialist counterculture. This is precisely what they did not achieve. Yet neither do existing data indicate that they simply duplicated capitalist literary activity. The heaviest borrowing, despite overlapping, did not take place in public libraries. Class-conscious workers were more influenced in their reading by sociocritical engagement than such bourgeois groups as salaried employees.

This fact throws new light on the problem of industrial mass culture. Contrary to the assumption of Adorno and Horkheimer, who proceeded from the premise that specific cultural class formations no longer existed under monopoly capitalism, these structures were to a certain extent preserved. Culture did not become as homogeneous as was assumed in critical theory. Not only bourgeois cultural criticism but also social democratic literary criticism was opposed to leveling culture through mass production and distribution. This concern for spreading

---

[78]Ibid., pp. 167, 192–93, 186.
[79]See Dieter Langewiesche, *Zur Freizeit des Arbeiters. Bildungsbestrebungen und Freizeitgestaltung österreichischer Arbeiter im Kaiserreich und in der Ersten Republik* (Stuttgart, 1980), pp. 187, 203–4.

culture to the working masses, for raising and improving them, was in the final analysis a conservative attitude, even if it was understood as a means of helping the workers in their struggle for emancipation. The revisionist stance of the SPD, which in theory adhered to revolutionary goals but in practice fought for the improvement of social and political conditions among the working class, also affected cultural policy.[80] It became a policy of offering an alternative; but precisely in developing that alternative, the policy remained indebted to the basic structure of hegemonic culture. The creation of a separate cultural camp did not resolve the contradictions within the dominant culture but reproduced them. This was demonstrated on the social democratic side by helplessness in the face of literary mass production. Moral rather than political and ideocritical arguments were used. But in the end what was needed was a change in the function of mass literature, not of dime-novel literature.

Mass culture in imperial Germany, which must indeed be understood as a new cultural formation, was not simply a product of organized capitalism; in other words, there was no simple correlation between conditions of production and cultural formation. There were, instead, a number of factors affecting the genesis of industrial culture (we will avoid the concept of the culture industry). The most important of these, in my opinion, was the establishment of state and public bureaucracies. No matter how limited the general cultural policy at the disposal of the state, in specific areas—educational policy, for example—it had already developed an apparatus by which it could gain control over and influence parts of the cultural public sphere. Bismarck's press policy shows that the state claimed the right to control public opinion.[81] Even though comparable interference in the cultural public sphere was rare, there was a notable tendency to control culture on the level of associations and semipublic groups. These organizations owed their existence not least to the commercialization of culture, which became widespread after 1870. The public library movement, for example, was a response to the mass book market and to commercial lending libraries. The clearer it became that the capitalist book market no longer supported the traditional concept of culture but in the long run undermined it, the louder became the demand for reorganization of the literary public sphere on the part of the socialists no less than of the bourgeoisie. Yet this was precisely what brought the cultural sphere increasingly under

[80]On the SPD's political stance, see Dieter Groh, *Negative Integration und revolutionärer Attentismus* (Frankfurt a. M., 1973).

[81]See Irene Fischer-Frauendienst, *Bismarcks Pressepolitik* (Münster, 1963); Heinz Schulze, *Die Presse im Urteil Bismarcks* (Leipzig, 1931).

the influence of administrative apparatuses, whether state, local, or party organizations. The aim of the movement was to fight capitalist abuses. But in the long term, the cultural realm was restructured by institutions that developed without such intentions. The outcome of this reorganization was that cultural planning was carried out by a new type—the professional cultural functionary. The development of a public library system was symptomatic of this bureaucratizing of culture. Only since 1890 have systematic attempts been made to understand and describe readers. Librarians in reading rooms and workers' libraries began to study circulation, the number of registered readers, reading preferences, and similar data as a means of controlling the cultural process. The irony of the situation was that these attempts at control were undertaken in the name of supposedly autonomous culture.

Although more recent scholarship on German working-class culture, following English scholarship, has distinguished between the culture of the workers' party and that of the proletariat,[82] and has taken a deeper interest in the cultural formation of the working class,[83] we still have a far from adequate picture of the restructuring of culture. A survey of literary production and a knowledge of the numerous cultural organizations (theater societies, sports associations, musical associations) and of the library system reveal aspects of this restructuring, yet without allowing us a thematic grasp of the process as such. The social context that gave rise to the new cultural formation is also still largely hidden from view. By now, however, it must be clear that the theory of the culture industry developed by Horkheimer and Adorno does not adequately explain the change. Compared with its bureaucratic reorganization, the convergence of culture with the activity of industrial production must have been of secondary importance. The industrialization of Germany, insofar as it urbanized the German population over the course of two generations, served rather as a general driving force. This urbanization was accompanied by the dissolution of older precapitalist cultural formations. Industrialization, finally, was also closely linked with the change in the rhythm of life that E. P. Thompson, using England as an example, has described so impressively.[84] The separation of work and leisure cleared the way for what we have called industrial culture. In particular, the reduction in the length of the workday after

[82]Gerhard A. Ritter, ed., *Arbeiterkultur* (Königstein, 1979), esp. the introduction by the editor and the contributions of Ritter and Dieter Langewiesche.

[83]See, e.g., the important sixteenth volume of the *Archiv für Sozialgeschichte* (1976), with contributions by Klaus Tenfelde, Lutz Niethammer, Dieter Langewiesche, Klaus Schönhoven, Jürgen Reulecke, Alfons Labisch, and Eckehart Lorenz.

[84]E. P. Thompson, *The Poverty of Theory and Other Essays* (New York, 1978).

1900 created for wage earners ample free time that had to be filled. The new cultural formation was inseparable—and this does not apply only to the working class—from the amount of time available for relaxation, regeneration, and entertainment. In this respect, as Horkheimer and Adorno have emphasized, the culture market did indeed play an important part, because it provided the means for organizing leisure time. How those means, in the form of books, magazines, brochures, films, and pictures, determined the activity of the masses is still largely unknown. The thesis of constant manipulation, which underlies the theory of the culture industry, is certainly not tenable. And even Habermas's thesis that the classic literary public sphere broke down at the end of the nineteenth century provides only a negative explanation of the change.[85] A new concept of industrial culture can offer a starting point for investigating the cultural change that occurred after 1870. Such a concept would have to begin by avoiding all culture-critical prejudices and debate anew the problematic correlation between the conditions of production (organized capitalism), social formation, and political structure (state intervention).

[85] Jürgen Habermas, *Strukturwandel der Offentlichkeit*, 2d ed. (Neuwied a. Rh., 1965).

Index

Ackerknecht, Erwin, 341
Adorno, Theodor, 24, 35; *Dialectic of Enlightenment*, culture industry concept in, 42–43, 271–72, 308–11, 320, 328, 333, 334, 348, 350–51
aestheticism, 111, 113
aesthetics: art vs. life debate, 110–15, 300; classical, 139, 186; and concept of autonomy, 30–32, 114, 121–22, 126, 148, 171, 271; and class society, 29–30; and history, 229; and idea of institution, 32–33. *See also* reception theory
Alexis, Willibald, 276, 346–47; *Isegrimm*, review of, 135–37
Altenstein, Karl, 260, 261
Althusser, Louis: and literature, 22–24, 25, 34; and social institutions, 20–23, 28, 29, 33, 37, 39, 40; theory of the state, 18–20
Apel, Karl Otto, 27
Auerbach, Berthold, 186; ideas on popular literature, 278–82, 287; stories of country life, 276–78
autonomy, aesthetic, concept of, 30–32, 114, 121–22, 126, 148, 171, 271

Baake, Curt, 344
Balibar, Etienne, 22–24, 29, 40, 41
Balibar, Renée, 22, 41
Balzac, Honoré de, 114
Bassermann, Friedrich Daniel, 53
Bauer, Otto, 347
Bauer, Wilhelm, 319
Baumgarten, Hermann, 74, 75–77, 84, 108
Baur, Uwe, 277
Bayreuth circle, 319, 335–36
Benjamin, Walter, 29, 35–36, 328

Bennett, Tony, 40–43
Bernstein, Arthur, 328–29, 343
Bismarck, Otto von: conflict with Parliament, 55, 69–72; and culture, 342; link with workers, 95–96; national unity under, 187; politics of, 78, 86; as prime minister, 55, 57–58; system of, and public sphere, 76, 89–94, 335, 349. *See also* Prussia; state
Blanckenburg, Christian Friedrich, 136
Böhme, Helmut, 54–55, 56, 57
Bonapartism: description of, 86; German fear of, 66, 67; and labor, 95, 98, 103; Marx's interpretation of, 86–89, 98; and public sphere, 84, 91, 93, 94, 96
book trade, 310, 329–35; and concept of culture, 349–50
Born, Stephan, 100, 293
Börne, Ludwig, 105, 204; debate with Heine, 118–19, 126; and literary criticism, 119–20, 148, 150, 156, 209; as model, 120
bourgeoisie, bourgeois: criticism of culture, 312–20; as cultural leaders, 271, 300–301; importance of economic concerns for, 62, 63, 84, 85, 94, 112; intelligentsia, 57, 85, 274, 277; literature about, 215–16; literature for, 37, 239, 276–77, 346; petite, 85, 346; theater for, 321–23. *See also* middle class
Brahm, Otto, 323
Brecht, Bertolt, 29
Büchner, Georg, 121, 196
Bürger, Peter, norm theory of, 30–34, 35–36, 37
Burckhardt, Jacob, 181

Campe, Joachim Heinrich, 284
capitalism: and book industry, 334–35;
and culture, 29–30, 307, 308, 349;
danger to Bismarck's system, 89; and
middle-class weakness, 54, 56; and
public sphere, 45–48
Carriere, Moriz: on Schiller, 180–81;
review by, 131, 134–35
Chomsky, Noam, 14
church. *See* religion
class(es), social: and culture, 19, 32, 37,
271–74; and history, 56; and
literature, 37–38; political roles of,
64, 85; and production, 19–20;
struggle between, 19, 37–38. *See also*
education; lower class; middle class;
workers
classicism, German: aesthetics of, 139,
186; canonization of, 142–43, 144–
46, 148–51, 156, 158, 161, 162, 163,
166, 177, 179, 188, 198, 343; as
heritage, 212; linked to romanticism,
145, 159–61, 165, 166, 167;
literature of, for the masses, 330–31,
346, 347–48; as prelude to German
nation, 214–15; role in education,
193, 194, 263. *See also* Weimar
conservatism: criticism of liberalism,
80–83; newspapers of, 92. *See also
under* political groups and parties
critic(s): in the Nachmärz, 128–29; role
of the, 119, 120, 125, 137, 139, 187
Critical Theory, 271, 309, 335, 348–49
criticism, literary. *See* literary criticism
Culler, Jonathan, 30; and institution of
literature, 26–28; and reading, 15–
16; theory of semiotics, 13–16, 34–
35, 36–37
culture, German: bourgeois criticism of,
312–20; classical, demise of, 307–8;
idea of counterculture, 341–42;
industrial, 307, 320, 328, 329, 349;
literary mass, 271, 274, 275, 311,
320, 333–35, 338, 341–45;
politicization of, 335–41; renewal,
idea of, 319, 337; restructuring of,
349–52. *See also* book trade; culture
industry; press; state; theater(s)
culture, people's, 257, 269, 338;
bourgeois concept of, 300–301;
Christian concept, 300–306; as
educational goal, 266, 272, 286–87;
historical development concerning,
271–74; socialist concept, 294–99.
See also theater(s); *Volk*
culture industry, concept of, 42–43,
320, 334; description of, 271, 308–9,

328; limitations of theory, 271–72,
348, 350–51

Dahlmann, Friedrich, 52
Dahrendorf, Ralf, 17n, 56
Danzel, Theodor Wilhelm, 169, 206;
theory of literary history, 174, 186,
203, 217–21, 228, 229, 244–45
Dickens, Charles, 114, 276, 347
Diesterweg, Adolf, 249, 268, 272–73;
educational theories of, 249, 285–91,
293
Dilthey, Wilhelm, 3; Basel lecture of,
146, 167, 169, 239; and the German
poetic canon, 146–47, 167–73, 174;
methodology of, 226, 231–42;
professional career, 245–47; on
Prussian tradition, 190–91
Dingelstedt, Franz von, 323
Dorfgeschichten (country-life stories),
276–78
Düringer, Philipp, 324
Dumas, Alexandre, 332, 347

Eagleton, Terry, 19n
Echtermeyer, Theodor, 121
education: Christian thinking and, 194,
262–63, 267, 268–69, 301–4, 337;
class structure and, 253, 257, 260–63,
267, 269–70, 272, 278, 286, 290,
293, 314, 338; concept of *Bildung*,
249, 266, 275, 293, 298, 316, 342;
link to culture, 249, 266, 272; literary
canon in, 192–96, 249, 254, 263; in
Nachmärz, 261–65, 267–68, 313;
neohumanistic reform of, 256–61,
272; Nietzsche's criticism of, 250–55,
266, 295, 313–19; planners, 257–59;
politicization of, 249, 251, 253, 255–
56, 260, 261, 263–70, 284–99, 312–
14, 317–18, 336–39; teaching
methods, 192, 195; theories of, 250,
252–53, 255–59, 283–91
Engels, Friedrich, 24, 100, 101–2, 298–
99; *Communist Manifesto*, 290
England: as educational model, 287; as
historical model, 47–48, 50, 310;
industrialization in, 350–51; literary
criticism in, 125
Enlightenment: literary criticism, model
of, 27, 117–20; literature and writers,
240; pedagogics, 283, 284, 287, 302;
political model, 50, 61, 98, 107, 115–
16, 296; role of, in German literary
history, 166–71, 184, 191, 233–34,
240; and role of public sphere, 117–
19, 290, 341

Falk, Adalbert, educational reforms of, 312, 313, 337, 338
Fichte, Johann Gottlieb, 165, 257, 258
Fish, Stanley, 4, 5; and literature as institution, 11–13, 26–28, 30; and theory of reader, 9–11, 28
Fontane, Theodor, 198, 246, 347
France: dictatorship in, fear of, 66, 67; and education, 285; literature of, 197, 198, 199, 332; as political example, 62, 81, 273–74, 310. *See also* Bonapartism
Frankfurt Parliament (National Assembly), 246; different parties in, 60, 61, 63; 1848 election of, 52; and equal voting rights, 53, 67
Frantz, Konstantin, 313
Frederick II (the Great), 188, 189, 191
Freytag, Gustav, 113, 115, 127, 175, 300; review by, 129, 135–37; *Soll und Haben*, reviews of, 124–25
Fullerton, Ronald, 329

Gadamer, Hans-Georg, 3, 241–42
Gagern, Heinrich von, 53
Gall, Lothar, 49, 50, 89
Geist, German, 224; call for renewal of, 319, 337; education and, 193, 253; link to Enlightenment, 168, 170
Georg II of Sachsen-Meiningen, 322–23
German language: importance of, 257; teaching of, 192, 270
German Reich, new: and culture, 311, 316, 334–41; founding of, 86; literary canon for, 196–200, 330; literary heritage of, 196, 197–98; and literary history, 203, 224, 241, 246
Germany: constitutional conflict in 1860s, 69–71; differing political solutions in Nachmärz, 60–69; *kleindeutsch* solution for, 44, 57, 64, 189; liberal history of, 54–69; question of national unity, 55, 77–78, 159, 182, 187, 189, 196. *See also* German Reich; liberalism, German; Parliament, Prussian; Prussia; society, German; state
Gervinus, Georg Gottfried, 49; evaluation of, 164, 165, 202–6, 218–21; influence of, 148, 169, 206, 228; liberal views of, 76, 187; as literary critic and historian, 142, 149, 150, 151–59, 160, 174, 176, 183, 201, 202, 244; on Prussian literature, 188–89; and theory of literary history, 143–45, 161, 205, 206–10, 216, 229
Glasenapp, Carl Friedrich, 336

Gleim, Johann, 188, 189
Gneist, Heinrich Rudolf von, 70
Goethe, Johann Wolfgang von, 263; aesthetics of, 126, 139, 155; canonization of, 142–48, 159, 174, 193, 197, 199; criticism of, 148, 149, 214–15; link with Schiller, 144, 145, 148, 152, 182–83; as literary model, 174–76, 178, 212; reinterpretation of, in Nachmärz, 183–88; seen as detached, 184–85, 214–15, 276. *See also* Weimar
Goethe, Johann Wolfgang von, works: *Dichtung und Wahrheit*, 188, 191; *Hermann und Dorothea*, 184, 185; *Wilhelm Meister*, 134, 173, 176, 178, 186, 215–16
Gotthelf, Jeremias, 276, 300, 345–46
Gottshall, Rudolf, 115, 243, 244; as critic, 138–39; historiography of, 229–30; as literary historian, 111, 142–48, 161–63, 169, 177–78, 202, 216–17, 229, 245
Götze, Karl-Heinz, 244–45
Gramsci, Antonio, 18–19, 21
Grenzboten, 115, 123, 124–25, 127, 245; circle, theory of art, 111, 113, 114, 122, 300; and literary criticism, 115, 185–86; reviews in, 131, 135, 138
Grillparzer, Franz, 179
Grimm, Hermann, 186–87, 190, 197–98
Grimm, Jakob, 151, 181, 182
Groeben, Norbert, 3, 4
Gründerjahre, 129, 186, 317
Gugel, Michael, 56, 59, 72
Gundolf, Friedrich, 243
Günther, F. J., 194
Gutzkow, Karl, 118, 127; novels, reviews of, 129–35, 138
Gymnasien: criticism of, 314–15; curriculum of, 252, 259; educational programs in, 192, 195–96, 259, 267; role of, 250–52, 254, 260, 265, 268, 269, 270, 314

Habermas, Jürgen, theory of the public sphere, 24–26, 35, 45–48, 84, 351
Hamann, Johann, 165
Hamerow, Theodore S., 52
Harden, Maximilian, 326
Hardenberg, Friedrich von. *See* Novalis
Hardenberg, Karl August von, 259, 261
Harkort, Friedrich, 272–73; educational theories of, 283–87, 293

Hauptmann, Gerhart, 343
Hausegger, Friedrich von, 336
Haym, Rudolf: career of, 201, 245, 246;
  as historian, 53, 110, 164, 167, 173,
  202, 210; method of, 147, 221–25,
  227, 228; views of, 113, 172
Hays, Michael, 322n, 323
Hebel, Johann Peter, 279
Hegel, G. W. F., in literary tradition,
  142, 167, 170, 172, 227; philosophy
  of history, 107, 109, 110, 120–21,
  159, 221–24, 233. See also Hegelians,
  left
Hegelians, left, 110, 112, 123; concept
  of literature, 120, 121; literary
  criticism of, 113, 116, 118, 122, 129–
  30, 159, 222
hegemony, idea of, 19, 31
Hehn, Viktor, 183–85
Heine, Heinrich: debate with Börne,
  118–19, 126; in literary canon, 105,
  147, 194, 276; as literary historian,
  108, 111, 118, 142, 148–50, 156,
  157; as model, 120; theory of art,
  107, 111, 114, 307
Hempel, Gustav, 331
Herder, Johann Gottfried, in literary
  canon, 157, 194, 195; as literary
  forerunner, 165, 168, 174, 193; and
  theory of history, 141, 192, 224
hermeneutics: in historiography, 226,
  227, 234–38; and readers, 2, 4;
  reexamination of, 3
Herwegh, Georg, 118, 177
Hettner, Hermann, 147, 202, 206, 300;
  evaluation of, 233; link of classicism
  and romanticism, 145, 159–61, 165,
  166, 167; literary history of, 146,
  175n, 177, 178–79, 186, 206, 221;
  on Prussian history, 191–92
Hiecke, Robert, 192–94, 196
Hillebrand, Karl, 202–3, 204–6
historian(s): careers of, 244; role of the,
  207–9, 215, 218, 231, 232
history: concepts of, 161, 217; Hegelian
  philosophy of, 107, 109, 110, 120–
  21, 159, 221–24, 233; Marxist idea
  of, 54, 56; social classes and, 56;
  theories of, 49, 141, 192, 223, 224,
  225–31
history, literary. See literary history
Hoffmann, Walter, 340–41
Holland, Norman, 6
Hofmannsthal, Hugo von, 177
Holtei, Karl von, 175
Holtzendorff, Franz von, 319, 320
Horkheimer, Max, 24; Dialectic of
  Enlightenment, cultural industry

concept in, 42–43, 271–72, 308–11,
  320, 328, 333, 334, 348, 350–51
Huber, Ernst Rudolf, 71
Huber, Viktor Aimé, 100
Hülsmann, H., 194
Humboldt, Wilhelm von: and education,
  249, 255–57, 259, 266, 284, 297;
  theory of history, 49, 223, 224
Hüppauf, Bernd, 210
Husserl, Edmund, 3

idealism, 61; aesthetics of, 279–80; in
  educational theory, 289, 297, 337; in
  literary history, 221–25, 226
Industrial Revolution and culture for
  the masses, 45, 263, 319, 341; and
  classes, 56, 89; consequences of, 55,
  85, 89, 112
industrialization, effects of,
  dissatisfactions with, 319; and
  education, 288; and liberalism, 54–
  60; and structuring of culture, 54,
  350–51; and the theater, 320–24. See
  also Industrial Revolution
Ingarden, Roman, 3
institution, concept of, 11, 12, 17, 23;
  adequate theory of, elements of, 34–
  43; in critical theory, 24–26, 30;
  functional, 28–29, 31–34;
  interactionist, 17–18, 28, 34; and
  literature, 26–34; 105; materialist,
  18–24, 28–30
Iser, Wolfgang, 3, 5, 6; approach of, 27;
  and the text, 7–8, 10, 11

Jachmann, Reinhold, 257, 258–59
Jäger, Georg, 196
Jäger, Wolfgang, 47–48
Jameson, Fredric, viii
Jauss, Hans Robert, 3, 6,; and literary
  work, 8–9, 10, 13
Jeismann, Karl-Ernst, 250, 258
journals and newspapers: authors
  published in, 345–46; country-life
  stories in, 277; liberal and socialist,
  92, 344–45; links to literary history,
  245, 247; and literary debates, 119; in
  the Nachmärz, 115, 116, 127, 128,
  138, 185–86; new popular, 325–27,
  333; role in liberal theory, 324–25;
  for teaching, 303. See also press
journals and newspapers, noted:
  Allgemeine Zeitung, 90; Berliner
  Illustrirte Zeitung, 327–28, 333;
  Blätter für literarische Unhaltung,
  115, 124, 127, 245; Deutsches
  Museum, 108, 116, 127–28, 185,

journals and newspapers (*cont.*)
245; *In Freien Stunden*, 345–46;
Gartenlaube, Die, 116, 127, 304, 328,
344, 345; *Hallische Jahrbücher*, 109,
118, 121, 176, 222; *Neue Welt*, 344–
45; *Preussische Jahrbücher*, 75, 171,
203, 245. *See also* Grenzboten

Kant, Immanuel, 165, 166, 167, 191,
222, 240, 258
Keil, Ernst, 127, 304
Keller, Gottfried, 300–301
Kinder, Hermann, 111
kleindeutch (Little Germany) solution,
57, 189, 190; explanation of, 44; and
literary history, 216
Kleist, Ewald von, 193, 196, 347–48
Klopstock, Friedrich, 152; devaluation
of, 154–55, 174–75; as literary
forerunner, 146, 164, 168–69, 193
Koch, Ernest, 347
Kolping, Adolf, 301–3, 306
Koselleck, Reinhart, 117, 273

Laas, Ernst, 195–96
labor movement. *See* workers
Ladenberg, Adalbert von, 264, 265
Ladewig, Paul, 340–41
Lagarde, Paul de, 311, 312–19
Langbehn, Julius, 319
Langewiesche, Dieter, 347, 348
Lassalle, Ferdinand: criticism of
liberalism, 82–83, 94–97; and the
workers' movement, 68, 293, 294–98,
343
Laube, Heinrich, 118, 322, 323
Leibniz, Gottfried Wilhelm, 170, 240
Leppert-Fögen, Annette, 56, 57
Lessing, Gotthold, 263; as critic, 126,
170–71; as liberal model, 116, 135;
role in German literature, 149, 151–
53, 154, 164, 165–71, 190–91, 193,
194, 199; *Nathan der Weise*, 168,
171
Levin, Harry, 16–17, 141
liberalism, German: attacks from left,
82–83, 94–97; breakdown of, 46, 54,
68–69, 90, 216, 240; classic theory,
61, 63–64, 66–67, 68–69, 84, 290,
291; conflict with Bismarck, 69–72;
conservative criticism of, 80–82;
early, 49, 50–51, 53; economic
policy, 273, 286; and German social
structure, 49–54, 116, 255–56; and
industrialization, 54–60; of
Nachmärz, 49, 60–69, 127; Schiller's
dramas and, 181–82; self-assessment
of, 75–80

libraries, public, 339–41, 349, 350;
workers', 346–48
Liebknecht, Wilhelm, 293, 296–98,
342–43
Link, Hannelore, 4
literary canon, German: Dilthey and,
146–47, 167–74; in education, 192–
96, 249, 254, 263; and literary
tradition, 146–59, 165, 173; for new
German Reich, 196–200, 330;
rearrangement of, 146, 174–200;
romanticism included in, 146, 147,
163, 164–73. *See also* classicism,
German
literary criticism: changes in, 115–22,
126–27, 138, 139; definitions of, 118,
120, 129; function of, 1–2, 38; link
with literary history, 38, 243–47; and
literary polemics, 125–27, 138; in
Nachmärz, 122–39; new models in,
1–4, 127; restructuring of, 105; and
theory of culture, 24–26, 348–49; in
U.S., vii–viii, 11, 12–13; views on,
12–13, 27–28, 118, 119. *See also*
critic(s)
literary history: as academic discipline,
201–2, 242, 244; concept of
evolution, 145, 152, 167–70; concept
of progress, 158, 162; function of,
201–10; and general public, 202,
243; historical approach, 143–48,
198–200; idea of integration, 152,
165; and literary criticism, 242, 245–
47; methodology, 141, 217–42;
model of decline, 210–11; and
Revolution of 1848, 161, 217;
theories of, 205, 206–17, 300;
traditional task of, 140–41; views of,
111, 203. *See also* idealism; literary
studies; positivism
literary studies: background on, vii–viii;
and criticism, 38–40, 242; German,
201; interdisciplinary approach, ix; in
Nachmärz, 186; restructuring of, 105;
in U.S., vii–viii, 11, 12–13; in
Vormärz, 106–8. *See also* literary
history
literary tradition: classical epoch, 141–
46; concept of, 140–41; in education,
192–200; historical approach, 143–
48; and history of literature, 192; and
the German canon, 146–59, 165,
173; harmonious continuity in, 165–
68, 171, 239–40; integration of
romanticism, 164–73; and the new
German nation, 196–200; and
Prussian history, 188–92; and the
public, 179–88; rearrangement of the

literary tradition (*cont.*)
canon, 146, 174–200; treated in the
Nachmärz, 159–73
literature, German: authors in
educational programs, 193, 194;
epochal development, 152–53, 165;
evolutionary scheme, 168–70; linked
to political events, 187, 188, 190–91,
197–98; of Nachmärz, 44, 45; and
national literary order, 112, 143, 150,
153, 159–60, 192, 227–28; popular,
274–82, 287, 300, 303, 326, 328–33,
343, 346, 347–49; teaching of, 192–
96. *See also* classicism, German;
literary tradition; novel; poetry;
romanticism
literature, institution of: changes in,
105–6, 200; as concept, 2, 11, 12,
16–26; democratization of, 274; vs.
extraliterature, 1–2; and idea of
reading formation, 40–43; link to
politics, 105–10, 117, 126, 127, 134,
179–82, 187; Marxist theory of, 22–
24; norms and conventions, 38–40;
and production, 5–6, 8, 22–23, 40;
public function of, 25–26, 46, 215;
beyond reception theory, 4–16; search
for new model, 2–4, 5; views on role
of, 110–11. *See also* institution,
concept of; literary history; literature,
German
lower class: attempts to control, 318; vs.
bourgeoisie, 53–54, 68, 81, 83–86,
97, 101–2; education for, 253, 262–
63, 270, 272; integration into
bourgeois society, as goal, 287, 292;
literacy of, 342, 346, 347–49
Ludwig II, 335
Lukács, Georg, 40, 104, 105, 308

Macherey, Pierre, 22–24, 28, 29, 40, 41
Maistre, Joseph de, 157
Marcuse, Herbert, 24
Marggraff, Hermann, 111, 139; on the
critic, 124–25
Marlitt, Eugenie, 346
Marx, Karl, 100; class division idea,
98–102; early concept of art, 35; and
education, 298–99; interpretation of
Bonapartism, 86–89, 90, 98;
Communist Manifesto, 290
Marxist theory, 40; and concept of
institution, 18–24, 28–30; of history,
54, 56; and literature, 22–24, 42;
reexamination of, 3
masses. *See* lower class
May, Karl, 332

Mayer, Gustav, 95, 96
Mayer, Hans, 152
Medick, Hans, 49
Menzel, Wolfgang, 148, 150–51
Mehring, Franz, 40, 188; concept of
literature, 343, 345, 347
middle class (*Mittelstand*): alliance with
political elite, 54–55, 57–58, 85;
divisions in, 56; vs. lower class, 53–
54, 68, 81, 83–86, 97, 101–2; public
sphere, 46–48, 64–65, 79–80, 84,
116–17; theoretical apology for, 61–
64, 66; weakness of, 56, 64, 73–74,
94, 95. *See also* bourgeoisie
Mill, John Stuart, 47
Montepin, Xavier de, 345
Mosse, Rudolf, 325–26, 334
Mühler, Heinrich von, 249

Nachmärz (postrevolutionary period),
106, 147; critical debate during, 110–
15; educational theory and policy,
255, 261–65, 267–68; journals of,
115, 127; literary criticism of, 122–
39; literary feuds during, 124, 138;
literature of, 44, 45; political parties
in, 60–69; reviews, examples of, 129–
35; revision of literary canon, 146,
174–200; theory of literary history,
210–17, 300; treatment of, in literary
history, 159–73; weakening of middle
class, 73–74
Napoleon. *See* Bonapartism
New Criticism, 139; theories of, 6, 9, 10
Nietzsche, Friedrich: on education, 250–
55, 266, 295, 311, 313–19; on
German culture, 307–8, 311, 312; on
literary tradition, 197, 198–200; on
Wagner, 322
norms, theory of, 30–34
Nörrenberg, Constantin, 339
North German Confederation, 55, 78
Novalis (Friedrich von Hardenberg),
171–73
novel: criticism, 130–32, 134, 136, 178;
dime, 332–33, 334, 342, 345;
German, beginning of, 175n; in
magazines, 328, 345

pantheism, 149, 171
Parliament, Prussian (Landtag), 284;
Bismarck's conflict with, 55, 69–72;
role of, 50–51, 55, 83
Parsons, Talcott, 17–18, 21
Paul, Jean. *See* Richter, Johann Paul
Friedrich
Peschken, Bernd, 146, 188, 215, 240

Pestalozzi, Johann, 249, 287
Planck, Carl Christian, 177
Pletzer, F., 124–25
poetry: vs. criticism, 123; national, start
    of, 189; romantic, 157; in school
    programs, 193, 194–95; theories of,
    171, 231, 280
political groups and parties: in
    Nachmärz, 60–69; and Schiller
    celebration, 181–82
    Conservative, 63, 67, 68; and
        Schiller, 181–82
    Democratic, 61–62
    Progressive, 57, 58–59, 68, 84, 95,
        96, 294; vs. Bismarck, 69–72
    Social Democratic (SPD): cultural
        policy, 341–49; and education,
        338
    See also workers' associations
positivism, in literary history, 217, 220,
    225–31, 243; explanation of, 226–
    27; as method, 227–31, 232–33, 234,
    236–38
Preisendanz, Wolfgang, 114
press: attacks on, 96, 254, 342;
    Bismarck and, 91–94, 335, 349;
    freedom, fight over, 90–91; as
    instrument of public opinion, 91, 96–
    97, 324; new popular, 325–29; of the
    SPD, 344–46. *See also* journals and
    newspapers
progress, concept of, 110; in literary
    history, 158, 162
Prussia: constitutional conflict, 69–72,
    81, 82–83, 90; economic policy, 55,
    57–58; history linked to Germany,
    188–96; liberal support for, 54–55,
    57–58, 216; and literary tradition,
    188–92; Ministry of Education and
    Culture, 249, 258, 262, 263, 335,
    340; school policy, 313–14, 317–18,
    336–39; as victorious state, 72, 73,
    187, 189, 240. *See also* Germany;
    state
Prutz, Robert: career of, 201, 202;
    criticism of the Vormärz, 108–10,
    122, 127; and function of literary
    history, 210–12, 214; as journalist,
    127–28, 185; as literary critic, 106–8,
    113, 115, 116, 139, 243, 245, 246;
    and popular literature, 274–77, 282
public sphere: classic model, 51, 53, 94;
    changes in, 45–46, 84–86, 90, 93,
    97–98, 319; cultural, 212, 290, 313;
    definition of, 24–25; importance of
    suffrage, 51–54, 65, 67–69; and
    institution of literature, 25–26, 46,

215; and literary criticism, 116–17,
    138; middle-class, development of,
    46–48, 64–65; and politics, 76–83;
    and production, 30; question of public
    opinion, 64, 79–80, 91; role of
    industrialization, 54–60; workers'
    emerging place in, 94–103
Puttkamer, Robert von, 337

Ranke, Leopold von, 206, 208, 212
Räsonnement: definition of, 139;
    democratization of, 120; denial of, 80,
    93, 232; liberal faith in, 61, 77, 223;
    and public sphere, 51, 208–9, 229
Raumer, Karl von, 194, 249, 262, 268,
    270
Raumer, Rudolf von, 194–95
reader(s), 138: community of, 10–11,
    27, 34; historical, 42; ideal, 14–15;
    and literary heritage, 179; -response
    theory, 3–5, 9–11, 28; text and, 7–8;
    and traditional literary theory, 2, 4, 6
reading: concept of reading formation,
    40–43; and the institution, 27;
    programs in schools, 192–96, 337; by
    the workers, 347–48
realism, theory of, 123; and idealistic
    tradition, 279; link to idea of work,
    113; in Nachmärz, 111–15, 128; and
    Revolution of 1848, 106. *See also*
    aesthetics
reception theory, 3; assessment of, 5–9;
    and readers, 2, 4; and semiotics, 26–
    28
Rechberg, Johann B. von, 57
Reclam Universalbibliothek, 330–31
Reinhardt, Max, 322, 323
religion: and education, 194, 262–63,
    267, 268–69, 301–2, 313, 337–38;
    and the people, 303–6
Revolution of 1848–49: and concept of
    history, 161, 217; effect on literature,
    104–5, 106, 112, 179; middle-class
    defeat in, 54, 55, 60; outcome of, 44–
    45, 46. *See also* Nachmärz; Vormärz
Richter, Johann Paul Friedrich (Jean
    Paul): Börne on, 150, 156, 177; in
    German literature, 145, 193; Gervinus
    on, 152, 153, 156, 176–77; Heine on,
    148–49, 150, 156
Rochau, Ludwig August von, 60, 84; on
    the *Mittelstand*, 61–64, 74; public
    sphere and the state, 64–67, 77–80;
    on socialism, 62
Roggenbach, Franz von, 74
romanticism: accepted in canon, 146,
    147, 163, 164–73; critical polemics

romanticism (*cont.*)
concerning, 147, 150, 159; Gervinus
on, 142, 152, 157–58, 160; Hettner
on, 145, 159–61, 165, 166, 167;
linked with classicism, 145, 159–61,
165, 166, 167; rejection of, 111, 117,
176
Rosenkranz, Karl, 139; review by, 129–
31, 132, 134
Ruge, Arnold, 111

SPD. *See* Social Democratic *under*
political groups and parties
Sanders, Hans, 17n
Saussure, Ferdinand de, 14
Schäffle, Albert, 319, 320
Scheller, F. E., 53
Schelling, Friedrich Wilhelm, 149, 150,
170
Scherer, Wilhelm, 146, 203, 243; career
of, 245, 246; historiography of, 225–
31; review of Hettner, 221, 225
Scherl, August, 325, 326, 334
Schiller, Friedrich, 263; aesthetics of,
126, 139, 155, 279; canonization of,
144–45, 148, 150–51, 159, 174, 193,
276; celebration to honor, 179–83;
criticism of, 199; link with Goethe,
144, 145, 148, 152, 182–83; as
politically involved, 157, 181–82,
185. *See also* Weimar
Schlegel, A. W., 141, 142
Schlegel, Friedrich, 142, 149, 157, 167
Schleiermacher, Friedrich: Dilthey on,
167, 170, 172, 190, 234–35; on
education, 249, 266; method of, 236,
237
Schlesier, Gustav, 121
Schlosser, Friedrich Christoph, 233–34
Schmidt, Eric, 228
Schmidt, Julian, 75, 243, 244, 295,
300–301; evaluation of, 164–65, 229,
233; and Gervinus, 203–4, 210, 212–
14; historiography of, 212–15, 228;
literary criticism of, 75, 111, 113,
114–15, 123–24, 127, 138, 139;
literary history of, 145–46, 147, 161,
162–63, 174, 176–77, 178, 185,
187–88, 189–90, 245; review by,
131–34; revision of classicism, 189–
90
Schmoller, Gustav, 319
Schöll, Adolf, 188
Schönhoven, Klaus, 347
schools, 251, 257, 260, 286–87, 317,
336–38; laws concerning, 312;
Realschulen, 267, 314; trade, 284;

Volksschulen, 261, 262, 267, 268,
270, 338n. *See also Gymnasien*
Schulze-Delitzsch, Hermann, 100
Schulze-Gaevernitz, Hermann von, 266–
67
Schwenniger, Franz, 99
semiotics, theory of, 13–16; and
reception theory, 26–28 Shakespeare,
William, 149, 176, 180, 194, 195,
197, 322
Smith, Adam, 49
socialism, 348; Christian, 302–4;
criticism of liberalism, 82–83, 96; and
education, 285–86, 294–99, 338;
movement in German Reich, 98;
opposition to, 62, 69, 305. *See also*
Social Democratic *under* political
groups and parties
society, German: culture and capitalism,
308; and functional concept of
literature, 31; in liberal theory, 49–
54, 116, 255–56; state vs., 66–67,
86, 95
Spinoza, Baruch de, 149, 170, 240
Spranger, Eduard, 250, 257
Sprengel, Peter, 156
Staël, Madame de, 148
Stahl, Friedrich Julius, 80–81
state: classic liberal view of, 59–60; and
the culture industry, 309, 310, 336; as
Kulturstaat, 249, 251, 265–66, 295,
297, 337, 342; perfect, idea of, 289;
and the press, 96–97, 335; private
morality, 79–80; and society, 66–67,
86, 95; theory of, 18–20. *See also*
education
Steiger, Edgar, 344
Stephanis, Heinrich, 284
Stiehl, Ferdinand, school regulations of,
194, 249, 270; description of, 261–
63, 268, 337; opposition to, 287, 312
Strauss, David Friedrich, 197, 254, 316
Sturm und Drang, 146, 152, 157, 165,
166
Sue, Eugène, 332
suffrage, universal: importance of, 51–
54; opposition to, 65, 67–69, 96
Süvern, Wilhelm, 249, 257, 259

theater(s), changes in, 321–25;
commercial, 336
Thompson, E. P., 350–51
Titze, Harmut, 259, 296, 297
Tocqueville, Alexis de, 47
Tompkins, Jane P., 5
Tönnies, Ferdinand, 319
tradition, literary. *See* literary tradition

Treitschke, Heinrich von, 60, 75, 203
Twesten, Carl, 58, 59, 70, 72

Ullstein Publishers, 325, 327, 334
United States: Horkheimer and Adorno's
treatment of, 308, 311, 333, 334;
literary criticism and studies in, vii–
viii, 11, 12–13
Unruh, Hans Victor von, 71

Villaume, Peter, 283
Vilmar, August Friedrich, 189, 243, 244
Vischer, Friedrich, 177, 244; on Schiller,
180, 181
Volk (people): concepts of, 277, 278–
79; education for, 270, 283–91, 292,
296, 301–3, 314; libraries for, 339–
41; literature for, 274–82, 287, 300,
303, 326, 328–33, 342, 346, 347–49;
religion for, 303–6. *See also* culture,
German; culture, people's
Voltaire (François Arouet), 197, 199
Vormärz (prerevolutionary period):
criticism in, 106–8, 116, 129, 163,
174, 203; criticism of, 109, 122–23,
126; liberal tradition of, 111;
literature of, 105

Wagner, Richard: circle of, 319, 335–
36; and national festivals, 312, 335–
36; new theater at Bayreuth, 321–22
Weber, Max, 48
Wehler, Hans-Ulrich, 55, 56, 86, 89
Wehrenpfennig, Wilhelm, 203
Weimar: aesthetics, 112, 122, 128;
authors, 111, 123, 142, 239;
humanism as model, 160; and
Prussian history, 188–89; and the
public, 179. *See also* classicism,
German; Goethe, Johann Wolfgang
von; Schiller, Friedrich

Weitling, Wilhelm, 291
Welcker, Karl Theodor, 51, 53
Wichern, Johann Hinrich, 304–6
Wieland, C. M., 145, 152–54;
devaluation of, 155, 174–75; as
literary forerunner, 164, 168–69, 193
Wiese, Ludwig, 249, 268–69
Wilberg, Johann Friedrich, 288
Wilhelm II, 338; period of, 334
Williams, Raymond, 18–19, 21–22
Winkelmann, Johann Joachim, 152, 154,
155; as literary pioneer, 164, 174
Winkler, Heinrich August, 69
Wolff, Theodor, 92
Wolzogen, Hans von, 319
workers: counter-public sphere of, 334;
culture for, 294–99, 350; and
liberalism, 56; libraries for, 346–49;
and literary criticism, 39–40;
literature for, 343, 344, 347–48; and
middle class, 53–54, 67, 68, 73, 81,
83–86, 97, 98–99; place in public
sphere, 94–103; and right to vote, 51,
53. *See also* lower class; workers'
associations
workers' associations: cultural goals of,
291–94, 295, 342; religious elements,
301; social and political goals, 68, 69,
100–103
Wuttke, Heinrich, 324–25, 326

Young Germany, 126, 307; evaluation
of, 164; opposition to, 108, 111, 116,
118, 134, 175, 176, 317; program of,
120, 121, 122, 209, 274

Zerges, Kristina, 344
Zimmerman, Bernard, 36
Zola, Emile, 347

Library of Congress Cataloging-in-Publication Data

Hohendahl, Peter Uwe.
[Literarische Kultur im Zeitalter des Liberalismus 1830–1870. English]
Building a national literature, the case of Germany 1830–1870 / Peter Uwe
Hohendahl ; translated by Renate Baron Franciscono.
p.   cm.
Translation of: Literarische Kultur im Zeitalter des Liberalismus 1830–1870.
Includes index.
ISBN 0-8014-1862-3 (alk. paper)
ISBN 0-8014-9622-5 (pbk.: alk. paper)
1. German literature—19th century—History and criticism. 2. Literature and
society—Germany—History—19th century. 3. Criticism—Germany—History—19th
century. 4. Books and reading—Germany—History—19th century. 5. Liberalism—
Germany—History—19th century. I. Title.
PT391.H5813   1989   830'.9'007—dc19   89-899